Mount Sinai

◆

*"Convent of
St. Catherine,
with Mount Horeb."
David Roberts, 1839.*

Joseph J. Hobbs

◆

MOUNT
SINAI

UNIVERSITY OF TEXAS PRESS

Austin

The maps on pages 7, 98, and 262 are by the Department of Geography/Geographic Resources Center, University of Missouri–Columbia; Karen S. Westin, cartographer.

Requests for permission to reproduce material from this work should be sent to Permissions, University of Texas Press, Box 7819, Austin, TX 78713-7819.

♾ The paper used in this publication meets the minimum requirements of American National Standard for Information Sciences—Permanence of Paper for Printed Library Materials, ANSI Z39.48-1984.

Library of Congress Cataloging-in-Publication Data

Hobbs, Joseph J. (Joseph John), 1956–
Mount Sinai / Joseph J. Hobbs. — 1st ed.
p.   cm.
Includes bibliographic references and index.
ISBN 0-292-73091-8. — ISBN 0-292-73094-2 (pbk.)
1. Sinai, Mount (Egypt)
DS110.5.H63   1995
953'.1—dc20   94-31952

FOR MOM

Mount Horeb of Sinai is a most excellent and lofty mount; a mount inhabited by God and frequented by angels; a mount of light, fire, and burning; a mount of dreadful clouds and darkness; a mount of wisdom and learning; a mount of pity and promise, of righteousness and cursing; a mount of lightning and flashing fire; a mount of trumpets and noise; a mount of kindness and alliance; a mount of clemency and propitiation; a mount of sacrifice and prayer; a mount of fatness; and a mount of visions and contemplation.

— FELIX FABRI, 1483

CONTENTS

ACKNOWLEDGMENTS

I did the field work for this study from May to December 1989 with grants from the American Council of Learned Societies and the American Research Center in Egypt, and in August and September 1993 with grants from the University of Missouri–Columbia Graduate School and Department of Geography. The Egyptian Ministry of Higher Education provided institutional support. Kit Salter of the Department of Geography and Deans Larry Clark and Ted Tarkow of the College of Arts and Science at the University of Missouri–Columbia arranged leave to make the research possible. Steve Goodman of the Field Museum of Natural History in Chicago planted the seed for this research by asking me to be part of an expedition to Sinai that was never funded. Karen Westin of the Department of Geography/Geographic Resources Center at the University of Missouri–Columbia designed and drafted the maps. Heather Hathaway, an undergraduate geography major at the University of Missouri, uncovered many of the sources used in Chapter 2. The *Journal of Cultural Geography* granted permission for some material to be reprinted here from a 1992 article (Hobbs 1992).

Bedouin hospitality is legendary but not inviolable. I thank my constant companion Mahmuud Mansuur and all the people who welcomed me and put up with my incessant questions. Many other researchers have preceded me in Sinai, so the Jabaliya are not strangers to this manner of inquisition. They relate this anecdote: "There was once a botanist who kept asking his Jabaliya guide, 'what's this plant, what's that plant' all day long, for days. The botanist and his guide arrived at the Blue Hole, very tired after a long walk, and the scientist immediately pointed to the algae in the pool and asked 'what's that?' The fatigued guide snapped 'it's crap' (*khara*). The botanist later published 'crap' as the Arabic name for algae." My Jabaliya wayfellows never lost their patience. The monks of St. Katherine, whose hospitality is overtaxed, were also very generous. I thank especially Father Makarios for his hard work and sacrifice to defend his monastery.

As a male I was unable to communicate in depth with Jabaliya women, so my perspectives on Bedouin life are inevitably male. The translations from Arabic conversations are my own. Block quotations are drawn from my recordings on audio and video tapes.

Dr. Mohamed Kassas of the Cairo Herbarium provided indispensible practical and moral support and kindly introduced me to colleagues working on environmental problems in the Sinai. Among those who guided me to sources and identified my field collections are Dr. Nabil El-Hadidi, Dr. Iman El-Bastawisi, Dr. K. H. Batanouny, Mr. Mohamed Ibrahim, Mr. Ahmed Fahmy, Mr. S. El-Daggar, and Mr. H. Husni. As always I am grateful to Ibrahim Helmy for encouraging me to work in the field in Egypt. Mr. Dave Ferguson of the U.S. Fish and Wildlife Service International Affairs Office has worked hard to maintain linkages between all those interested in Egypt's natural environment, and with Dr. Essam al-Badry made it possible for me to do some follow-up field work in 1993. Mary and Theodore Cross and Susan Brind Morrow encouraged me to write this book. Colbert Held and an anonymous reviewer for the University of Texas Press helped me with revisions.

Thank you, Cindy, all of our family members, and Leo, for your love and support.

◆

CONVERSIONS
AND TRANSLITERATION

Monetary equivalents are based on the exchange rate between U.S. dollars and
Egyptian pounds in September 1989 (1 dollar = 2.6 Egyptian pounds). Figures
for wages and prices also date to 1989. Metric and British Standard equivalents
are: 1 centimeter, 0.3937 inches; 1 meter, 39.37 inches; 1 kilometer, 0.621 mile;
1 hectare, 2.471 acres; 1 kilogram, 2.2046 pounds.

The transliteration system is my own attempt at a phonetic rendition of Jabaliya
spoken Arabic. The consonant *'ayn* is represented by an apostrophe.

Where possible, common English names, Jabaliya Bedouin Arabic names, and
Latin scientific names of plants and animals appear in sequence.

Pronouns referring to God begin with upper-case letters, except where quoted
sources render them in lower case.

Mount Sinai

◆

◆

INTRODUCTION

On May 22, 1989, I sat beneath a cypress tree outside the walls of the Monastery of St. Katherine, speaking with one of the monks of that ancient institution at the foot of Christianity's traditional Mount Sinai. Father Makarios and I had just met, and becoming acquainted we talked about politics, weather, and wildlife. Did the fingers of cirrus cloud mean rain was coming? No, he said, and the monastery had not seen much rainfall this year, although a few miles away in at-Tarfa there had been more. Egypt was readmitted to the Arab League yesterday, I told him, thinking news probably came slowly to this remote place. Had he seen many snakes around the monastery? He had not. The monks do not pay much attention to animals, he said, adding that very few of the many tourists who visit the monastery take an interest in nature, either. The area's tourist developers never take the environment into account, he complained. The priest pointed at what he called "unsightly" telephone wires strung down Wadi ad-Dayr, the valley in which the monastery sits. He said that the sprawling hotel complex on the Plain of ar-Raaha, where the Wadi ad-Dayr empties, occupies the sacred place where the Israelites camped while Moses met with God on nearby Mount Sinai. The monks, who claim the plain as their own, had protested the hotel construction to Egyptian officials. The government responded by insisting that the monks owned no more than a 60-meter perimeter around their monastery. Father Makarios mused sarcastically, "Someday they will build a funicular up Mount Sinai."

On June 21 I met with an official of the Egyptian Environmental Affairs Agency at his office on the island of Gezira in Cairo. I had known him for many years and was surprised by his stern, businesslike manner that morning. Without the usual exchange of questions about health and family he asked my opinion about a project cost-benefit description that had just come across his desk. A funicular was to be built on Jebel Musa (Arabic, "Mount Moses")—the monks' Mount Sinai—and it required his agency's approval. This aerial cable car would run from the hotel on the Plain of ar-Raaha to the western end of the mountain, the proposal read, "to allow the old and infirm pilgrims to have access to the site, and to promote tourism." From the mountain terminus a paved pathway would lead walkers to the summit of Mount Sinai. When completed the project would attract 565,000 tourists yearly. My colleague objected. What would happen to the mountain's unique plant life? What would become of the waste all those visitors would create? Where would their water supply come from? What did I think?

On July 4 I greeted Father Makarios and we sat under our cypress tree. "I bring you bad tidings," I told him, relating what I had learned in Cairo. He reacted as if someone had struck him. Later I thought of something the Byzantine historian Procopius had written in the sixth century when the Monastery of St. Katherine was built: "A precipitous and terribly wild mountain, Sina by name, rears its height close to the Red Sea. On this Mount Sina live monks whose life is a kind of careful rehearsal of death, and they enjoy without fear the solitude which is very precious to them."[1] Already besieged by up to fifty thousand tourists each year, the monks would certainly lose whatever solitude they still enjoyed. "If they do this we are finished," Father Makarios said.

In the months which followed I traveled between the Sinai and Cairo speaking with a variety of people about this mountain and what might happen to it. There was a wide range of opinion. My environmentalist colleague defended Jebel Musa as vulnerable natural habitat. The director of his agency, who approved of the tramway project, insisted that Mount Sinai was just "a geological structure" which construction could not harm. The monks of St. Katherine saw the mountain as a sacred landscape on which such building would be sinful. The area's indigenous Jabaliya Bedouins, who also revere the mountain, objected to the project. Tourists and pilgrims I spoke to rejected the funicular with dismay and disdain.

No one spoke impassively of the mountain and its future. As word of the proposed development spread, the tramway on Mount Sinai became a contentious issue that involved the diplomatic community in Cairo, the international news media, and Egypt's president. The debate brought into sharp focus several difficult definitions and choices that people would have to make. Should there be some distinction between ordinary and sacred places? In a shrinking world what is to become of the wild and special places which are the common heritage of humanity? If unique places can generate tourist revenue how might tourism development avoid spoiling them? How many visitors should be allowed? Is there a difference between pilgrims and tourists, and should they be treated differently? What rights do traditional people have to decide how land should be used? As they read newspaper articles about the Mount Sinai cable car controversy, people around the world reflected on the question "Is nothing sacred?"

There is no universal human reaction of reverence to any spot on earth. Nevertheless sacred places do exist. Believers feel their power and nonbelievers who experience otherworldly sensations at them become believers. Just curious or driven by tourism's "must-see" compulsion, others visit holy places and feel nothing at all unusual; Jebel Musa is just a mountain.

In the setting of its neighboring peaks Jebel Musa is low and undistinguished. But for many people this is one of Earth's greatest mountains. Almost 2,000 years of human experience have enlarged and elevated it. Christian hermits on the trail of the Exodus discovered and protected the mountain's holy places. Byzantine monks and Bedouin shepherds landscaped this granite mass reverently, placing chapels and mosques on its holy sites and observing taboos against harming the mountain. Pilgrims came from as far away as Spain as early as the fourth century, arriving on bended knees and departing with joyous hearts. Travelers came, some of them scholars, others spies and thieves. They wrote about the mountain and its monastery. They brought the world's attention to this unique place but also stole its sense of isolation and some of its cultural treasures. Tourists came in their wake. They have been a mixed blessing. They have spread knowledge of Mount Sinai to the ends of the earth, further enlarging its reputation. They have also invited grand schemes that would change the appearance and the character of Jebel Musa forever.

"Above all else, sacred place is 'storied place,'" wrote theologian Beldon Lane.[2] This book is the story of Mount Sinai. Lane suggested that in our triumphs of history over nature, time over space, and technical mastery of the land over a gentle reverence for life, we have been left exhausted as masters of a world stripped of magic and mystery. Perhaps by telling the stories of the beliefs and experiences that have sanctified Mount Sinai this book will recover some of the ebbing spirit of the place and revitalize those who would care for it.

One

◆

"A TERRIBLE AND
WASTE-HOWLING
WILDERNESS"

The Sinai Peninsula appears from space as one of Earth's most distinctive landmarks. Many popular collections of photographs of the world from space include an image of the Sinai. This is due in part to convenience; the peninsula is cloud-free most of the year and is an easy target for photography. The three bodies of water that define the peninsula advertise it, their deep blue framing a triangle of bright desert light. The diversity of landforms within the peninsula may catch the astronaut's eye. In the yellowish northern two-thirds of the peninsula there are veinlike patterns created by drainages that coalesce and flow northward in great arteries. The southern third is very different, a dark brown bulge broken up by many more but much shorter valleys, telling the astronaut: "There are mountains here." Biblical associations may come to the space traveler: to the west is the land of the Pharaohs from which Moses fled; there is the sea Moses crossed; here is Sinai where his people wandered; to the northeast is a strip of green on the eastern Mediterranean shore, a land of milk and honey.

THE LAND

Egypt's Sinai Peninsula has an area of some 61,000 square kilometers, about the size of Ireland or the American state of West Virginia (Map 1). The base of the triangular peninsula is along the Mediterranean Sea at about 31 degrees, 10 minutes north latitude and its vertex, Ras Muhammad, juts into the Red Sea at 27 degrees, 44 minutes north latitude. The Suez Canal

*The Sinai from
space. Courtesy of
NASA (Shuttle
mission AS7-5-1623)
and Professor
Robert K. Holz.*

and Gulf of Suez border it on the west, and the Gulf of Aqaba and a 200-kilometer-long political boundary with Israel border it on the east. The peninsula is topographically and geologically complex, "a happy hunting-ground for geologists," as Augusta Dobson described it.[1] In the south the 1,300-square-kilometer mountain block of the upper Sinai massif, with elevations between 1,500 and 2,665 meters, is the peninsula's most diverse region.[2] It contains some of the world's oldest rocks, "basement complex" granitic and volcanic materials which formed as early as 600 million to 1 billion years ago in the Precambrian Era and were uplifted in the Miocene Epoch 25 to 10 million years ago. Covering about 80 percent of the area, the most characteristic rock is red "Ikna" granite that is about 580 million years old.[3] In some places this granite is overlaid with younger and darker diorite, syenite, rhyolite, and ignimbrite, rocks associated with volcanic activity at the end of the Miocene Epoch about 10 million years ago. Among the peaks created in this relatively recent activity are Sinai's highest, Jebel Katarina or Mount Katherine (2,665 meters) and nearby Jebel Musa (2,288 meters), the subject of this book.

Local Jabaliya Bedouins recognize that a ring of these dark volcanic

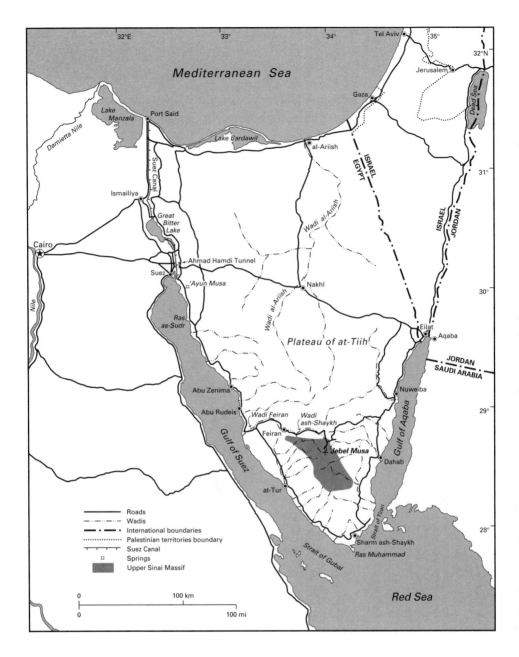

MAP I

*The Sinai and
adjacent regions,
with principal roads,
settlements and
drainages.*

rocks, the geologist's "circular dike," surrounds their high red granite homeland. They recite the principal mountains (jebels) of this circle: al-Huwayt, Abu Tarbuush, Madsuus, Mugassim, Jiraab ar-Riih, Abu Rumayl, Katarina, and Musa. They recognize that red and black rock types create different environments. In black areas plants germinate and complete their life cycles earlier than in nearby red areas. The black country is hotter and harsher and is filled with hazardous rockslides. Jebel Abu Tarbuush is merciless in summer, not even offering rockshade. The Bedouins say that Israeli climbers of that mountain have suffered heatstroke there, even throwing up water their guides offered them. The Jabaliya say the sounds of one's own footsteps in black districts is unpleasant: the disturbed rocks clink against each other like metal. Black rocks tip easily and throw the walker. Pilgrims have despised such landscapes for centuries. In 1384 a Tuscan visitor complained, "The mountains of the desert . . . are sterile in the manner said and have large immeasurable rocks, so great that sticking out of the ground they look like houses, so great are they. And from the parching heat they are black and roasted, as if they were in a furnace; and from the great heat they are split one in one way, another in another. And many huge rocks bursting from the terrible heat roll down the said mountains."[4] It is refreshing to reach the silent, stable, and easy ground of red granite.

WEATHER

Sinai is a desert. It has always seemed a difficult environment to those who compare it with the verdure of the Nile Valley or the "fine country" of Canaan, which God promised to the Israelites (Deuteronomy 8:7). Sinai is "this terrible and waste-howling wilderness, a land of fiery snakes, scorpions, thirst" (Deuteronomy 8:14–16).[5] The sun is the dominant natural feature. It inflicts the drought that is the norm here. Its heat raises the convective storms that bring relief from drought but also destruction. Its movement across the sky creates what the Jabaliya call the "four seasons of the day," from spring at dawn through the summer of midday, the autumn of dusk, and winter at night. As it moves the sun interacts with a spectrum of color in the granite to create impressive moods ranging from tranquility to hostility. "The sunlight of the afternoon mellowed and transfigured everything," Augusta Dobson wrote, "the low shrubs, half-withered in appearance, which dotted the plain, the smaller herbs dried up for lack of rain, all these caught the radiance and shone through a golden mist; the darkest and most rugged mountain on which the sunset glory was reflected seemed clothed with an adorning more beautiful than the softest velvet-green verdure."[6] Biblical narratives of Mount Sinai are filled with images of storm and light.

The clouds that add an extra dimension to the mountain scenery are absent from mid-May to mid-September. The air is very dry and summer days can be very warm, sometimes hot, but never insufferable as they often seem in mainland Egypt. The mean maximum temperature in July and August at 1,600 meters, where the Monastery of Saint Katherine stands, is 30 degrees Centigrade, with occasional extremes of 34 degrees Centigrade.[7] Atop Jebel Katarina where high altitude moderates the heat, mean and extreme maximum temperatures in midsummer are 24 and 33 degrees, respectively.[8] Bedouins take shelter in the early afternoon, reciting a rhyme "the rock shade is better than the tree shade" (*dhill al-hajar ahsan min dhill ash-shajar*). Their domestic livestock and wild ibex also retire during the hottest hours. In mid-September fingers of high cirrus portend a change of seasons. There are September days when the sky darkens and promises rain but rain does not come. When the clouds lift the summer haze is gone. On the freshest days from high peaks near the monastery it is possible to see eastward 50 kilometers to the Gulf of Aqaba near Dahab and 100 kilometers to the mountains of northwestern Saudi Arabia. Poplar and almond leaves begin to turn yellow in mid-September. Above 2,000 meters, all wild perennial plants except ephedra (*'alda, Ephedra ciliata*) also lose their leaves and enter the condition the Bedouins call *yaabis*, "desiccated."[9] Only the palms and carobs of lower elevations lend green to the landscape. White storks (*wizz 'iraag, Ciconia ciconia*) plane overhead, sometimes in large numbers, on their journey from eastern Europe and western Asia to mainland Egypt and central Africa. Families who have tended high mountain orchards since May pack up their belongings and retreat to lower elevations. Ibex also descend to warmer places but prefer areas like Wadi Baghaabigh where people seldom come. Only the chukar partridge (*shinaar, Alectoris chukar*) lingers in the high mountains, seeking small, south-facing retreats in the rock. October brings cold nights. On cold November days Jabaliya Bedouins hike quickly from lowland residences to mountain orchards to harvest the year's last crop, the tangy quince fruit. Cirrus clouds sometimes thicken until cold rain falls.

By late November snow is on the highest elevations, sometimes in great depths. Many places are inaccessible. The Bedouins say it is impossible to reach the snowy summit of Jebel Katarina. Mahmuud Mansuur and his cousin Ibrahim Saalih were snowbound at 1,800 meters in Wadi Abu Tuwayta for three days one winter. Well-provisioned with food and fuel, they retired to a stone house and passed the time talking. A hungry fox barked and howled outside. They fed the animal, finally enticing it to eat from

their hands. In 1615 deep snow prevented Pietro Della Valle from ascending Jebel Musa.[10] A winter squall early in the 1980s blew the roof off the church on Jebel Musa's summit. The monastery does not always receive winter precipitation, but the monks say when it comes it is usually as snow. Up to 50 centimeters of snow fell in the winter of 1907–1908 at the monastery, which sits at the usual snowline of 1,600 meters. A monk who had resided there forty-three years described that as a year of "much snow."[11] Bedouins relate that a massive December 1972 snowfall remained on the ground at elevations as low as 1,800 meters until March and made the important pass route of Abu Jiifa unnegotiable. High Sinai's treacherous snowstorms lend beauty to the landscape. Entering upper Wadi ash-Shaykh on a winter day, archaeologist Flinders Petrie was impressed: "The higher hills were covered with snow, and there were fine effects of the light shining through the mists and the rain. Towards the close of the day we reached a grove of tamarisks that promised a fire and warmth. Clouds hung low down on the mountains, and held till another grey mass came along and took this waif of cloudland into its folds."[12]

The Jabaliya say that with its snows December is a transitional month. Winter truly sets in with the biting cold of January and February. In those months the high Sinai massif experiences a climate unparalleled anywhere in Egypt. Underscoring winter's unique character a Bedouin told me, "Our country is not like the rest of Sinai, you know!" At the monastery the mean minimum temperature during those months is 1 degree Centigrade, with extremes of minus 5 degrees. On Jebel Katarina's summit at 2,665 meters the January/February mean minimum is minus 4 degrees, with extremes of minus 14 degrees.[13] The well of Abu Jiifa at 1,800 meters freezes. In very hard winters like that of 1987 the voluminous swimming hole of al-Galt al-Azraq at 1,800 meters in Wadi Tala' freezes solid. Icicles, which the Bedouins call "columns" ('awamiid), hang from rocks. Only in winter are the black mountain areas inviting, the Bedouins say, because they retain more heat than red granite mountains. 'Awaad Ibrahim cursed the winter: "You stay in your house, you shut the door, you light a fire." The Jabaliya know winter as "the time when nothing moves" and as "the season of dispersal" when each family retreats to its own house and the migratory bird to its distant land. The Bedouins relate that their Christian neighbors, the monks of St. Katherine, choose the two coldest days of winter to immerse themselves in almost freezing water after lengthy praying and fasting, in order to demonstrate their rejection of earthly pleasures. The Jabaliya therefore call the coldest winter days "the dipping days" (al-ightayshaat). The extreme winter cold shocks many visitors, particularly those coming from temperate lowland Egypt. The night of January 13, 1926, was among the worst in the life of El Lewa Ahmed Shefik, Director-General of Egypt's Frontiers Administration. He and his companions arrived by car from Cairo and were settled in the monastery guest house. "It was extremely cold and I felt as if I were in a deposit of ice," this visitor wrote. "Everybody then went to bed. I went to my bed where there were 5 woollen blankets. I put one under me and the four over. And, in spite of all this and notwithstanding the fact that I was wearing plenty of night clothes and that the windows of the room had double glass panes, covered with curtains, I felt that I was sleeping in the open country and was never warm during the whole night. I impatiently waited for the morning to come. At day-break I hastened to see my companions to ask them how they had fared, and every one of them repeated the same complaint. When Rev. Polycarpos heard of this, he hastened to have our blankets increased." Later that morning Shefik and his companions marveled at a four-inch sheet of ice over the Spring of Moses on the pathway up Jebel Musa.[14]

The Jabaliya say that spring is a time of congregation, when people come together in the mountain gardens and the bird returns. They also recognize the season by the monks' celebration of Easter. Small waterfalls of snowmelt cascade from smooth red granite slopes. Most Bedouins regard it as the best season. 'Awaad Ibrahim mused, "I love spring because the ground is covered with green plants. The bottom of my *jalabiya* gets a green trim from brushing against the plants." The Jabaliya call the spring "the time of apricots, labors [in the gardens], and ghee."

By Egyptian desert standards the high Sinai mountains are exceptionally well-watered. The region overall has four to ten times the precipitation recorded at sea level in south Sinai. The mean annual precipitation at the monastery's elevation of 1,600 meters is 62 millimeters, falling in an average of ten days of the year.[15] Rainfall and snowfall amounts are more than 50 percent greater at the summit of Jebel Katarina.

Precipitation in south Sinai is seldom widespread but typically falls over very limited areas. On May 19, 1989, clouds promising rain spared Jebel Musa but dropped heavy rains on the settlement of Feiran 40 kilometers away. Three weeks earlier Jebel Musa received a shower but Feiran did not. Rainfall and snowfall figures for a given locale often fluctuate markedly from year to year. Average precipitation figures are therefore misleading. Floods and droughts occur and may be localized or widespread for short or long durations. In 1384 monks told visiting Tuscan pilgrims that six years had passed without rainfall.[16] In 1909 the monastery's archbishop, who had resided there since 1866, told a visitor that there were frequent drought periods of three to four years.[17] For every such account of drought there is one of copious rainfall. Sixty-one-year monastery resident Father Good Angel recalled the wet spring of 1929, the only time he ever saw the monastery's Well of Moses overflow. Abundant rains in 1989 broke a seven-year drought at the monastery.

Flood and drought cycles reveal little about long-term climate change, but Bedouin tradition suggests an overall drying trend. Mahmuud Mansuur recounted,

Sometimes nature was hard on us. Our grandfathers told us about terrible things that have happened seven times since the Jabaliya came to the Sinai. I know about one of these. It was a twenty- to thirty-year drought. When it happened the water dried up and people abandoned their gardens. Many families settled in Rafah and Cairo. The environment has changed. Look where the Byzantine remains are. They had gardens where now there could be none. Back then they had more rain, and the area could support many more people. You can see the natural "mortar" deposited on the walls of their stone huts by flash floods. And they were able to cultivate wheat and barley up here [on Jebel ad-Dayr] where this would be impossible now. They lived on what God provided.

Mansuur's notion of earlier wetter times seems reasonable. Since the region acquired its present general climate of hyperaridity in the third millennium B.C.E. there have been short-lived periods of more and less precipitation. Although authorities contest the exact sequence of wetting and

drying there are few who agree with C. C. Robertson that the area
was much more verdant at the presumed time of the Exodus, about
1500–1200 B.C.E. He asserted that "the coastal and mountain regions of
Southern Sinai, the Gulf of Suez, and the Gulf of Akaba were, at the Exodus period, intersected by watercourses where these are now marked by
dry river beds; and that these regions provided pastures for cattle."[18]

Rain sometimes falls heavily and destructively in southern Sinai. The
unbroken granite surfaces that comprise much of the area retain no moisture, deflecting water downslope where in increasingly large volumes it
searches for anything that might contain it. Trickles feed rivulets, then
rivers, and eventually raging torrents. On December 3, 1867, Reverend
F. W. Holland looked on in awe as in just thirty minutes a 300-meter-wide
stretch of dry Wadi Feiran became engorged with muddy floodwaters 2 to
3 meters deep. The flood killed thirty people and scores of sheep, goats,
camels, and donkeys. Large boulders swept the drainage with "the noise
of a hundred mills at work . . . something terrible to witness; a boiling,
roaring torrent filled the entire valley, carrying down huge boulders of
rock as though they had been so many pebbles, while whole families swept
by, hurried on to destruction by the resistless course of the flood."[19] On
May 10, 1872, rain and hail fell continuously for two hours at the Monastery of St. Katherine, almost destroying its garden.[20] In 1968–1969 the
worst flood in thirty years destroyed a large number of Jabaliya orchards.[21]
Most of the impressive stone walls surrounding orchards in Wadi Itlaah are
reconstructions of enclosures destroyed in that storm. Since that event
many Jabaliya gardeners have constructed low dams to prevent floods from
razing their orchards. In April 1989 an intense, localized storm dropped so
much rain between Shaykh 'Awaad and Abu Sayla, high in the Feiran watershed, that Wadi Feiran was flooded all the way to its mouth at the Gulf
of Suez, although no rain fell in Wadi Feiran itself. Local Bedouins who
visited Wadi Nugra after the event marveled at how radically its landscape
had been transformed. Water had scoured the wadi bed, uprooting and
transporting tamarisk and palm trees, stripping leaves from poplars, and
ripping weighted *shaduf* beams and buckets from their garden mountings.
The torrent carried a palm tree a distance of 1 kilometer and set it precari-
ously atop a 5-meter-high boulder. The flood filled hollow basins with
soil, destroyed stone garden walls 2 meters high and a half-meter thick,
deposited kilometers of plastic irrigation pipes kilometers from their original locations, and left new cutbanks and a flush of annual vegetation in its
wake. One of the greatest of all known storms destroyed the gardens of
Wadi Tinya one summer between two hundred and three hundred years
ago, the Jabaliya say. I asked some of the Bedouins how they knew this. A
couple tending a garden in the valley explained that when they excavated

an old well inside the garden enclosure they found remains of flowering rock-rose (*sirr, Helianthemum lipii*), along with almonds still encased in their shells. Rock-rose occurs only at elevations more than 200 meters above the garden site, so only a very heavy storm could have washed the plants this far down. The plants' flowering condition and the still-encased almonds told the Bedouins the storm had struck in summertime. They reckoned how long ago the event took place by the depth of the sediment.

Egyptian engineers have resigned themselves to the inevitability of having to rebuild Sinai roads after each destructive rain. They replaced long stretches of the Wadi Feiran and Taba to Nuweiba roads after a downpour on November 4, 1989, severed these Sinai arteries. In March of 1991 torrential rains fell in northeastern Egypt, dropping hail on Cairo and flooding western Sinai's watersheds. The settlement of Feiran was damaged heavily and an estimated 150 persons lost their lives there. No rain fell at the monastery.[22] Five months later the Feiran road was still impassable to motor vehicles.[23]

Jabaliya shepherds and gardeners seldom receive the kind of rains they hope for. Flash floods come from destructive, localized cloudbursts the Bedouins call "rockets" (*saruukh*) which drop moisture rapidly and excessively. The ideal is a lighter, steadier "irrigation" (*rayy*) rain which soaks the ground slowly over a wide area. This rain is most likely to fall between April and October, and the Jabaliya say it always comes from the south. It sends water flowing down the wadi without flooding it. It produces short-lived waterfalls and thin curtains of runoff on smooth red granite. It stimulates the germination of wild plants and irrigates the gardener's field. It produces the landscape envisioned in the Jabaliya expression "rice with lentils and waterfalls," meaning roughly "the good life."

In a good year snowmelt and rainfall splash down high mountain watercourses as late as June. Large valleys like Wadi Shi'g and Wadi Tala' carry water through even the driest summers and offer the most unexpected settings in this desert. The Jabaliya delight in the waterfall habitat they call "dripping-place" (*naggaat*). Water drips steadily over steep red granite walls on which hang a profusion of maidenhair ferns. Below the slide there is typically a pool surrounded by lush growth of rushes, suaeda, mint, bulrush, asparagus, wild grass, shave-grass, wild fig, and willow. These prolific habitats host a water-loving fauna of caddisfly larvae, water boatmen, dragonflies, crickets, and mosquitoes. These have been favored sites of human occupation for millennia. Near many of them are solitary, roofless round huts with rock walls typically 1 meter thick, 2 meters high, and 2 meters wide. These were the cells of Byzantine-period hermits who sealed their stone dwellings with natural mortar from the nearby waterfall faces.

Hikers in the area today indulge in red granite pools the Jabaliya call

*A pool in red granite
below al-Galt
al-Azraq in
Wadi Tala'.
September 9, 1989.*

galt, which often occur near dripping-places. The largest and most popular of these swimming holes is al-Galt al-Azraq, the "Blue Hole" of Wadi Tala', a basin of cold water 4 meters deep and 7 meters across shaded by cliffs and a sprawling willow tree. Where such pools occupy steep-walled canyons they are hazardous. Walkers are forced to take long detours around them. Those which have no shallows are deathtraps for poor swimmers like Saalih 'Awaad's eldest son, who perished in a basin in Wadi Tala' in 1979.

The surprising abundance of water in the high Sinai desert is manifested in the many Bedouin names for types of water sources. The *kharaza* or "bead" is an elongated pool in red granite which, unlike the *galt*, has no perennial source of replenishment. The mountain people sometimes construct a crude fence of rocks and tree limbs around these to prevent feral donkeys and ibex from muddying them. The *masak* or "gripper" is a water-eroded hollow in smooth red granite which "grips" water and holds it temporarily after rain. An *umshaash* or "soaker" is a soil- or gravel-filled depression that also holds standing water for a limited time after rain. Perennial water sources include the *thamiila* or "dregs," where a person can expose water by digging periodically in gravels of wadi floors. Places where such water might be obtained are often betrayed by the growth of mint. Small, permanent cliffside seeps called *ma'iin* do not yield enough water to be useful except where people have used cement and local materials to fashion small basins to collect runoff.

Inside the typical Jabaliya orchard is a large concrete *barka* or reservoir which the gardener irrigates his crops from. He fills it from an adjacent well (*biir*) which he and male members of his extended family have excavated in the wadi floor, typically to a depth of 4 to 6 meters. Although most wells are excavated and owned by families, an individual sometimes distinguishes himself by digging a public well. In 1986 Muhammad Mahmuud chiseled through 7 meters of solid rock to reach water on the heavily traveled Abu Jiifa camel route. Every day people honor his charity as they pause to drink from the well. The Jabaliya have known for centuries that the best place to dig a well is where a dike, a linear intrusion of soft igneous rock in harder parent rock, crosses the wadi floor. Dike rock is more porous than the ground around it, so it acts as a sponge and conduit for water. The Bedouins recognize that reddish-colored dikes (*jidda*) are softer and therefore more likely to yield water than the blackish, harder, less porous *hathruur* intrusions. The town of Katriin near the Monastery of St. Katherine owes its existence to water hoisted and pumped from a gigantic reddish dike which cuts a wide swath from one side of the al-Milgaa basin to the other. Eroding more readily than surrounding rock, many dikes have been scoured by wind and water to create passes and drainages. "The dike is all important around here," a Bedouin man told me. "Without it there are no gardens, no wadis, and no travel routes."

PLANT LIFE

Although it is desert, the Sinai is home to a surprising variety of plant life. Counts of the total number of plant species in the peninsula range from 812 to 1,000, or up to 45 percent of Egypt's flora.[24] Four hundred nineteen species occur in just 2 percent of the peninsula's territory, the high Sinai massif around Jebel Musa.[25] This high mountain ecosystem is a refuge for 27 of Sinai's 31 endemic plant species, which are found nowhere else in the world. With its biotic wealth this region is an "ecological island" in a depauperate desert.[26] The peninsula as a whole and the high mountain area in particular illustrate well the general rule that the more diverse are the habitats existing in an area, the higher are the numbers of species inhabiting the area.[27] Sinai's floral wealth has also been enriched by long-term changes in climate and by the peninsula's crossroads location.

The peninsula's plants have their origins in several floral regions: Saharo-Sindian, Sudano-Deccanian, Central Asiatic (Irano-Turanian), and Mediterranean, associated respectively with the deserts from the Sahara to Pakistan; the forest and steppe stretching from the Sahel to India; the high mountain forests of Turkey, Iran, and Afghanistan; and the cultivated landscapes and chaparral of the Mediterranean Basin.[28] Local factors such as weather, soil type, altitude, and human impact determine the distributions of these plants in Sinai. Following summer cloudbursts, tropical plants of Sudano-Deccanian origin germinate and develop into a short-lived savanna-like vegetation in the larger wadis surrounding the high Sinai mountains, particularly where they cross the coastal plains of the Gulf of Aqaba and the Gulf of Suez.[29] The other three plant regions are represented in the high mountains, with Saharo-Sindian desert vegetation prevalent in wadi beds below 1,300 meters, Mediterranean and Central Asiatic species in limited red granite habitats between 1,300 and 2,000 meters, and Central Asiatic steppe vegetation in the black volcanic districts above 1,600 meters.

Central Asiatic plant species were able to expand their range into Sinai from Turkey's Taurus Mountains, Iran's Zagros and Elburz Mountains, and Afghanistan's Paropamisus Range during much cooler and wetter times. During one or more episodes between 35,000 and 13,000 years ago precipitation was up to four times greater and temperatures two to five degrees Centigrade cooler than are characteristic of the Sinai and adjacent regions today.[30] These were ideal conditions for the growth of Central Asiatic shrubs and trees in a patchy or continuous steppe stretching for a distance up to 3,000 kilometers. As the climate dried and warmed, the ranges of most of these Asian plants retreated to their original cores in Central Asia.

The arrival of hot and dry conditions did not doom completely the Central Asiatic flora of the high Sinai mountains. As their ranges shrank back toward the northeast some individuals and communities of these Asian species persisted in south Sinai. The diverse array of habitats created by varying elevation, slope, aspect, soil, temperature, and precipitation allowed some of the stranded Central Asiatic shrubs and trees to survive in special places where they now serve as windows on the area's past environments. One of the most notable of these remnants in the Jebel Musa region is the wild pistachio tree (*butm, Pistacia khinjuk*), which survives in soil-filled cracks on north-facing slopes in the red granite of Jebel Na'ja, overlooking Wadi Tala'. Another is Moses stick (*yasar, Colutea istria*), popularly believed to have provided the staff which Moses used to obtain water from the rock, which grows in the red granite area below the 2,324-meter summit of Jebel 'Abbas Pasha. More than fifty such "relict" species remain in the high Sinai today, identical to their progenitors but separated from them by as much as 1,600 kilometers. On the summit of Jebel Abu Tarbuush I collected an ephedra (*'alda, Ephedra pachyclada*), whose nearest specimen outside this district is in Iran's Zagros Mountains.[31] Most of Sinai's relict species have members distributed spottily all the way to their places of origin; the Sinai hawthorn (*za'ruur, Crataegus sinaica*) grows on Mt. Hermon on the southern Lebanese/Syrian border, and the wild pistachio occurs at Petra in Jordan and is widespread in Iran and Afghanistan.[32] In their isolation in Sinai some of these relicts evolved gradually into endemics, or species found exclusively there. Among these is the rarest of all Sinai plants, the Sinai primrose (*Primula boveana*), whose nearest related species occur today in the Horn of Africa, Yemen, Turkey, Iran, and the Himalaya.[33] Another is *Rubus sanctus*, revered in the Monastery of St. Katherine as the original burning bush of the Exodus.[34]

The Central Asiatic steppic flora found on black volcanic peaks like Jebel Katarina and Jebel Musa reflects peculiar soil characteristics. The potential exists for a high steppe vegetation to occur at all elevations above 1,600 meters in the region, because average annual precipitation at these heights exceeds the 80 millimeters required to produce diffuse plant growth.[35] This potential is largely unrealized in the prevailing red granite areas because smooth-faced rock which sheds soil and water covers most of the area, and because people have cultivated most places where soil and water do settle. Diffuse steppe vegetation prospers in the high black volcanic areas. Unlike the red granites the volcanics have broken up to produce small rocks and soils which absorb and hold moisture, allowing little to run off. Because of a greater ratio of soil to exposed rock, snow falling on these soils stands longer than it does on red granite slopes at the same elevation. As snow melts it saturates the black rock soils, while on red granite it runs off.[36] These conditions of high altitude, cold, snow, and soil moisture found in Sinai black rock country are ideal for the growth of alpine Central Asiatic shrubs such as wormwood (*shiih, Artemisia inculta*), rock-rose, saltwort (*haamdh, Halogeton alopecuroides*), pyrethrum (*mirr, Pyrethrum santalinoides*), ephedra, and the endemic wick weed (*awarwar,*

Phlomis aurea). I collected these on the 2,113-meter black rock summit of
Jebel Abu Tarbuush in association with the Saharo-Sindian types articulated anabasis (*ujirim, Anabasis articulata*), *zaguuh* (*Pituranthos tortuosus*), and
thistle (*khashiir, Echinops galalensis*).

The very different flora found on the prevailing red granites also reveals
a distinct set of influences. The granites are largely impervious to moisture,
so plants can grow only where the rock has cracked and allowed soil to be
blown or washed in. The same rock that precludes vegetation on mountainsides nestles it in favored habitats farther downslope. Rainfall and
snowmelt run quickly off the smooth-faced granite into drainages and hollows below. There they saturate deep soils deposited by long periods of
wind and water erosion. Such runoff makes these drainages far more well-
watered than the region as a whole; while the ambient precipitation is 6 to
10 centimeters annually the water economy of red granite wadis is equivalent to 30 to 40 centimeters.[37] Such conditions represent a potential for
greater density and diversity of shrub and tree growth than exists on volcanic soils. In high mountain basins which people have not cultivated recently, there are as many as seventeen wild plant species per hundred
square meters.[38] However, because these soil-filled basins are relatively fertile, hermits, monks, and Bedouins have cultivated most of them for centuries. About 90 percent of all historical and modern orchards in the region
are in red granite wadis.[39] By 300 A.D. Christian ascetics began introducing
Mediterranean orchard and ornamental trees such as olive and cypress into
them. To appreciate the potential natural vegetation of the red granite districts one must look in the small cracks and hollows on mountainsides and
in the larger basins which are farthest and highest away from modern settlements. Central Asiatic species again dominate there.

Although heavily traveled by tourists today, Jebel Musa has not been
cultivated for many centuries and so has a flora which portrays the vegetative potential of the red granite areas. By the Stairway of Repentance
between the Monastery of St. Katherine (1,600 meters) and the Basin of
Elijah (2,000 meters), a surprising array grows in cracks and small basins in
the granite: the trees Sinai hawthorn and wild fig (*hammaat, Ficus pseudo-
sycomorus*) and shrubs including ephedra (*'alda, Ephedra sinaica*), the endemic wick weed, the endemic pyrethrum, the thistles *khashiir* and *khu-
shirif* (*Carduus arabicus*), lavender cotton (*gaysuum, Achillea fragrantissima*),
yellow gromwell (*libbayd, Alkanna orientalis*), wormwood, wild marjoram
(*za'tar, Origanum syriacum*, a Mediterranean species), lavender (*zayta, La-
vandula pubescens*), sage (*mardaguush, Salvia multicaulis*), *zaguuh*, and in a few
moist places mint (*habbak, Mentha longifolia*). Most of these shrub species
are very fragrant, which like spinosity in desert plants serves to deter herbivores. The Jabaliya say that the prevalence of such forbs has prompted

the Muzayna and other Sinai tribes to designate the Jabaliya homeland by the rhyme "*balad ash-shiih war-riih was-sirr wal-mirr*," the "land of wormwood and scent and helianthemum and pyrethrum." Visiting the monastery in the 1920s, Claude Jarvis thought the smell of these herbs was one of the place's "peculiar charms"; he wrote: "In the monastery region this strong aromatic scent that savours of incense and permeates everything gives an odour of sanctity in the literal sense to the surroundings that has, perhaps, a more impressive effect on one than anything else."[40] Previously cultivated and heavily traveled places on Jebel Musa also support *hinayda* (*Jasonia montana*), *khumkhum* (*Matthiola arabica*), roquette (*silla, Zilla spinosa*), *birkaan* (*Phaeopappus scoparius*), and wild rue (*haramlaan, Peganum harmala*). In the fertile basins at about 2,000 meters between the Basin of Elijah and Ras Safsaafa endemic wild thyme (*zaaytaraan, Thymus decussatus*), and in moist places bulrush (*diisa, Scirpus holoschoenus*) and rushes (*summaar, Juncus rigidus*) also occur. On Jebel Musa's 2,168-meter western summit of Ras Safsaafa I collected the rare nailwort (*Paronychia sinaica*). Other characteristic plants nearby are the endemic *gatu* (*Pterocephalus sanctus*), wound-wort (*gartam, Stachys aegyptiaca*), mullein (*khurmaa, Verbascum sinaiticum*), and plantain (*Plantago sinaica*).[41] At Mahashuur, elevation 2,120 meters on Jebel 'Abbas Pasha, I collected a steppic flora similar to that on Safsaafa which also included wild cotton (*wasbii-, Gomphocarpus fruticosus*), germander (*ja'ada, Teucrium leucocladum*), *jarad* (*Gymnocarpus decandrum*), milkvetch (*gaddas, Astragalus echinus*), *rifay'a* (*Bupleurum falcatum*), *dhafara* (*Iphiona scabra*), horehound (*gaasa, Ballota undulata*, a Mediterranean species), and the trees cotoneaster (*uruntil, Cotoneaster orbicularis*) and buckthorn (*shuhad, Rhamnus disperma*).

While these mountain perennial plants grow as diffused steppe, at lower elevations such as Shaykh 'Awaad (1,200 meters), where rainfall is less reliable, perennial growth is confined to a contracted pattern in wadi beds which receive runoff from the mountains. Diffused growth in these hot, hyperarid places is possible only after rare local rainfall. Short-lived communities of annual plants appear quickly and dormant perennials revive. The process begins almost instantaneously with rapid germination. A good measure of how readily seeds sprout after contact with moisture may be seen in a favorite Jabaliya children's game. Youngsters enjoy placing the seed of dhabb's spine (*shawk adh-dhabb, Blepharis ciliaris*) on their tongue. As soon as the seed meets saliva it pops loudly as the delicate tissue between the two halves of the fruit softens and releases the tension binding them. The greatest flush of annual plants usually occurs in May, or two to three months after the time rain is most likely to fall in this desert, and when temperatures are warming up. The often-colorful ephemeral display is a memory by mid-July. Perennials which remain in the wadi beds are generally of Saharo-Sindian and Sudano-Deccanian origin; at Shaykh 'Awaad I inventoried tamarisk (*tarfa, Tamarix nilotica*), acacia (*sayaal, Acacia raddiana*), common caper bush (*laysuuf, Capparis aegyptia*), caper bush (*lassaf, Capparis cartilaginea*), colocynth (*handhal, Citrullus colocynthis*), henbane (*saykaraan, Hyoscyamus muticus*), white broom (*retam, Lygos raetam*), *kibaath* (*Launaea spinosa*), *guurdhi* (*Ochradenus baccatus*), wild rue, and dhabb's spine. In floristic terms one walks from Afghanistan to the Sahel to the Sahara in the steep 8-kilometer descent from the Plain of ar-Raaha to Shaykh 'Awaad.

ANIMAL LIFE

The modern visitor to Jebel Musa is likely to come away with the impression that there is little animal life. This perception is misleading. There are no showy displays of wildlife in the world's deserts. In these difficult environments animals depend on camouflage, deception, rapid escape, and nocturnal activity to avoid detection. Observing desert animals is a time-consuming matter of careful tracking, listening, and waiting. Some of Sinai's animals are also difficult to see because of a long history of human persecution. People have hunted other species to local extinction. Pilgrims' and travelers' accounts written prior to the spread of firearms in the nineteenth century depict a wealth of animals that delighted some visitors and frightened others. Today old Bedouins recall from their youth large animals that to youngsters sound like mythical beasts of the past.

Sinai's unique birdlife reflects the peninsula's crossroads location and habitat diversity. A famous resident of the high mountain area is the Sinai rosefinch (*gazam, Carpodacus synoicus*). In its striking red plumage the male is one of the most easily observed and memorable birds of Sinai. In the 1970s Israeli naturalists noted that St. Katherine's monks fed the birds, causing the animals to lose much of their natural wariness of people.[42] The monks apparently discontinued this practice in the 1980s. Also common near the monastery and less shy there than elsewhere in the Sinai is the chestnut and jet black Tristram's grackle (*shahruur, Onychognathus tristramii*), whose song has been described well as "sweet, wild and weirdly melancholy."[43] Black-capped bulbuls (*bulbul, Pycnonotus xanthopygos*), chirruping "rich and fluty," often fraternize with these grackles.[44] Wild rock doves (*Columba livia*), indistinguishable from domestic pigeons, are common throughout the mountains. An important bird in monastic Christian folklore throughout Egypt, the brown-necked raven (*ghuraab, Corvus ruficollis*) usually occurs in pairs but sometimes in groups of fifty to one hundred individuals over the Plain of ar-Raaha, where they feed at the regional landfill. Early travelers to Sinai also noted large congregations at the monastery. In about the year 580 A.D. Antoninus Martyr saw monks feed nearly a hundred ravens every day at the monastery's kitchen in memory of Elijah, to whom ravens had brought food during his sojourn on Mount Sinai.[45] Sir John Mandeville related that "all ravens, choughs and crows of the district flew once a year in pilgrimage to the convent bearing a branch of bay or olive."[46] Fan-tailed ravens (*Corvus rhipidurus*) are also present. A characteristic small bird of Sinai's mountain wilderness is the indefatigable scrub warbler (*ifsay, Scotocerca inquieta*), which travels furtively among shrubs in high basins, repeatedly cocking its tail after it alights. Resident wheatears include the mourning wheatear (*bug'aa, Oenanthe lugens*), hooded wheatear (*abu al-'ala, Oenanthe monacha*), and white-crowned black wheatear (*umm suwwayd, Oenanthe leucopyga*). Bedouins say they know the resident hoopoe (*qubaara ummu wa abuu, Upupa epops*) as "the grave-digger of his mother and father," because if a young bird's parent dies it will not leave the deceased bird before burying it in a special place. Two gamebirds often seen running or in short bursts of flight are chukar (*shinaar, Alectoris chukar*) and the smaller sand partridge (*hajal, Ammoperdix heyi*). These birds are sympatric, occupying the same habitats from the lowest to highest elevations of Jabaliya territory. The Bedouins sometimes keep newly hatched chukar as pets. The birds imprint on their new "parents" and follow them around "like chickens," say the Bedouins. At the top of the food chain is the Verreaux's eagle (*'ugaab, Aquila verreauxii*), everywhere in its range a predator of hyrax. The Jabaliya also list hares and young sheep and goats among its prey. The Jebel Musa area is the only known breeding site for this bird in the western Palearctic region.[47] The Jabaliya sometimes see lammergeyer vultures (*Gypaetus barbatus*), but believe the once-common lappet-faced vulture (*Torgos tracheliotus*) has become locally extinct. Owls include the eagle owl (*hud/hud, Bubo bubo*) and one of the world's least-observed species, Hume's tawny owl (*buuma, Strix butleri*).[48] The Jabaliya say the tawny owl often alights near a person and begins its sharp clicking call, sometimes unnerving that person.

The Sinai is an important flyway in the Old World. Migrants in the high mountain area are less abundant than their counterparts in spectacular mass migrations across the peninsula's coasts. The Jabaliya have no knowledge of the quail (*Coturnix coturnix*), the migrant which in Biblical accounts miraculously alleviated the hunger of the Israelites in Sinai. Quail pass through the Sinai in autumn and spring but rarely stray into the high country of the southern peninsula. Common migrants in the mountains include white wagtails (*ra"iyy, Motacilla alba*) and red-backed shrikes (*Lanius collurio*). The largest migrant is the white stork (*wizz 'iraaq* or *naaja, Ciconia ciconia*). It is uncommon enough that the Jabaliya believe it never flies on Wednesdays.

Naturalist Stanley Smyth Flower regarded Sinai as "the richest part of Egypt herpetologically."[49] One of high Sinai's most characteristic reptiles is the deadliest, Burton's carpet viper (*hayya, Echis coloratus*). The snake is exceptionally well-camouflaged wherever it occurs. The Jabaliya have noticed that it varies in color from whitish in the lower sandy areas to pinkish in the higher red granites. It is armed with a venom which attacks the central nervous system. The Bedouins say it kills a man "instantly" and can dispatch a full-grown camel easily. Enough people have fallen to this snake that it is the only animal the Jabaliya invariably kill on sight. Climbing Jebel ad-Dayr I nearly put my hand on a specimen at 1,700 meters, and the Jabaliya say it ranges still higher up to the summits of Sinai's greatest mountains. The individual on Jebel ad-Dayr did not warn with the characteristic sawing of scales the Bedouins often hear. The area's other vipers are the greater Cerastes viper (*hanash, Cerastes cerastes*) and Field's horned viper (*turaysha, Vipera persica fieldi*). Jabaliya lore contends that one month the *turaysha* is blind, the next month deaf, the next blind, and so on. Perhaps the tradition of blindness derives from observation of the snake's inability to see when shedding its skin. Jabaliya shamans traditionally derived some of their medicines from the venom of this snake, reportedly after extracting fangs and venom sacs and releasing the then-harmless snakes alive. The Jabaliya insist that camels which have the opportunity to do so kill vipers deliberately with a quick backward strike of a front hoof. They say that the eagle is another effective viper killer, carrying the live snake high into the air and dropping it to the ground to be killed before eating it. The feline *gatt barri* (probably sand cat, *Felis margarita*) also kills vipers, according to the Bedouins. They do not believe that one viper can kill another, but they do regard the yellow scorpion as capable of killing even the virulent Burton's carpet viper. The region's rarest snake is Innes' cobra (*hanash iswid, Walterinnesia aegyptia*), which monks report having seen near the monastery in the late 1980s. Also preferring lower elevations is the non-venomous Jan's desert racer (*abu sayha, Coluber rhodorhachis*). The Jebel Musa area boasts the endemic Sinai banded snake (*abu murayra, Coluber sinai*), and with the Negev Desert shares the endemic Hoogstraal's cat snake (*Telescopus hoogstraali*).[50] Two agamid lizards (*hardhuun*) frequent red granite surfaces: Sinai agama (*Agama sinaita*), whose head becomes a brilliant blue after prolonged exposure to the sun, and the less ostentatious starred agama (*Agama stellio*). Their larger cousins the spiny-tailed agamids (*dhabb, Uromastyx aegyptius* and *U. ornatus*) occur at lower elevations on the margins of Jabaliya territory. More retiring than the agamids are two types of skink, eyed skink (*hadhaa, Chalcides ocellatus*) and gold skink (*wazaga, Eumeces schneideri*). The Jabaliya know all the fleet-footed lizards of the sandy floors of wadi beds and high soil-filled basins as *arabaana*. They include Bosc's lizard (*Acanthodactylus boskianus*) and the small-spotted lizard (*Eremias guttulata*). The most common gecko is the fan-footed gecko (*nataaga, Ptyodactylus hasselquistii*), which frequents Bedouin homes and rocky areas.

The Jebel Musa area has an abundant but secretive mammal fauna. Rodents, the most common mammals of the world's arid zones, are well-represented.[51] Below 1,800 meters the rough-tailed dipodil (*Dipodillus dasyurus*), silky jird (*Meriones crassus*), Egyptian spiny mouse (*Acomys cahirinus*), and garden dormouse (*Eliomys quercinus*) cohabit with monks and Bedouins. At higher elevations the golden spiny mouse (*Acomys russatus*) inhabits the most sacred places including the church and mosque atop Jebel Musa and the chapel on Jebel Katarina. The nocturnal bushy-tailed dipodil (*Sekeetamys calurus*) avoids people and their dwellings.[52] Hares (*arnab, Lepus capensis*) prefer open country at the feet of mountains in places like Wadi ash-Shaykh and the Plain of ar-Raaha. Larger mammals include two rarely seen species, Rueppell's sand fox (*abul husayn, Vulpes rueppelli*) and the rock hyrax (*wabr, Procavia capensis*). The latter is a rabbit-sized, very distant relative of the elephant. Recognizing it as a relative of man by virtue of its humanlike feet and lack of tail, some Jabaliya do not hunt or eat the animals. Others dismiss this taboo as superstition. Jabaliya shaykh Muhammad Abul-Haym quipped, "Well, there are sheep without tails, and you can eat those, can't you?" The Jabaliya have difficulty classifying the animal as a ruminant or non-ruminant, so have assigned it to a unique "betwixt and between" category.

One animal which is supremely well-adapted to life in the steep, difficult environment of the high Sinai has been persecuted mercilessly by Bedouins and is now rare. In the late 1970s Israeli researchers estimated the total ibex population in Sinai at two hundred to three hundred animals, of which perhaps half dwelled in the high southern mountains.[53] The number is certainly lower now. In seven months' walking in the mountains around Jebel Musa I rarely saw spoor and never saw the animal; in two years working in the Eastern Desert I saw evidence or animals almost daily. Delicious and defiant, the Nubian ibex (*badan, Capra ibex*) has always been the favorite game animal of the Jabaliya. Bedouins speak wistfully about the best chances of seeing the animal, during the November rutting season when bachelor herds of five to seven animals scour the countryside for mates. The Jabaliya believe a healthy population survives on the steep slopes of Jebel Mizna, well away from summer orchards and pastures. In winter these wild goats descend from such mountain heights to lower and warmer, wind-sheltered south-facing slopes where people find it relatively easy to hunt the animals. Jebel ad-Dayr provides ibex a rare refuge, and the Jabaliya occasionally sight herds of up to ten animals there. There is some

interaction between the wild goats and their domesticated counterparts. An ibex reportedly joined a Jabaliya herd of goats for three years before a wild ibex lured it away. The Jabaliya say their goats inexplicably "get tired" when they encounter a dead ibex.

A leopard burrow trap on the Abu Jiifa Pass. June 9, 1989.

One mystery is whether the leopard (*nimr, Panthera pardus jarvisi*), the ibex' chief natural predator, continues to live in the high Sinai mountains. The cat certainly was an ancient resident of the area. In the sixth century Mount Sinai's confessor St. Stephen is said to have guarded his garden from marauding hyenas with a leopard he raised from infancy.[54] This is a local counterpart of the many monk–leopard/lion interaction themes in the traditions of the Monasteries of St. Anthony and St. Paul in Egypt's Eastern Desert.[55] There is abundant evidence of historical leopard habitation around Jebel Musa in scores of burrow traps (*nusrit an-nimr*). The trap is a hollow loaf-shaped structure about 2 meters long, 1 meter high, and ½ meter wide, made of large rocks. It sprang when a leopard entered the burrow and gnawed on meat placed as bait at the far end. The bait was tied to a cord holding up a trip-stone that fell as the animal tugged on the meat. Bedouins today point out that their predecessors situated the traps in high mountain passes the leopards traveled frequently. In drier areas to the north people built the traps near the few water sources where leopards could drink.[56] It is not clear who built the earliest leopard traps. Similar traps in the Eastern Desert and rock art scenes of leopard hunts there probably date to Neolithic times when people began to keep domestic livestock. In Sinai the Jabaliya believe early monks built many of the traps, probably because they prized leopard skins for some unknown use; they had no sheep or goats so would not have killed the cats as competitors. Sinai Bedouins apparently used burrow traps as late as the 1950s to kill the animal they perceived as a constant threat to livestock.[57]

Travelers' reports and Bedouin oral history trace the plummeting fortunes of Sinai leopards. In 1844 German theologian Constantin von Tischendorf saw "tiger" tracks near Serabit al-Khadim in west-central Sinai.[58] Naasir al-'Afaali, at an estimated one hundred years of age the oldest Jabaliya person alive in 1989, as a boy had seen leopards near Jebel Musa. Jabaliya elders recall that in 1925 tribesmen killed one of a pair in Wadi Baghaabigh, just west of the circular dike. Saalih 'Awaad remembers having seen the skin of a freshly killed leopard in 1943 when he was fourteen years old. Cretan traveler Nikos Kazantzakis with his monk companions and a Bedouin escort came across "lion" (*kaplan*) tracks in the snow near the summit of Jebel Musa in February 1927.[59]

Bedouin accounts indicate that the animal was extirpated in the Jebel Musa area about 1955, when a Jabaliya man shot a leopard at Jebel Na'ja. The Bedouins admit that their own firearms and burrow traps ended this great cat's career in their homeland. A few leopards lingered elsewhere in Sinai. In 1959 Shaykh Muhammad Abul-Haym sighted a leopard on Jebel Serbal, 40 kilometers northwest of Jebel Musa. Most Jabaliya adults dismiss a ten-year-old boy's claim that he saw a leopard in 1981 8 kilometers west of Jebel Musa in Wadi Abu Za'atar. In 1987 two Jabaliya men claimed to have found a donkey which had been killed by a large carnivore at Jebel Umm Shumar, just 20 kilometers south of Jebel Musa. They followed the tracks and reportedly saw a leopard. Many Jabaliya believe the cat still lives in the Umm Shumar region. Members of the famous animal-trapping Tolba family of Abu Rawaash, a village near the Giza pyramids, told me they saw leopard tracks in 1988 in Wadi al-Akhdar, about 25 kilometers north of Jebel Musa. Egyptian biologist Ibrahim Helmy cautioned that their tracking records are unreliable. Jabaliya men rejected the account.

An Israeli visitor to Sinai supported the possibility of reclusive leopards surviving in the high mountains. "Who knows," he posed to me, "it was a long time before we figured out how many leopards we had and where they were." Despite spoor and reported sightings there was no hard evidence of leopards in modern Israel until October 1974.[60] Wildlife biologist Nael Abu Zayd of the Egyptian Wildlife Service believed in 1989 there were eight leopards in Israeli territory very close to the Egyptian border, and some of the animals might be straying into the Sinai. Israeli wildlife sources estimate their country's total population at ten to fifteen animals, all roaming the southern Negev Desert. At Metzoke Dragnot, a kibbutz north of Ein Gedi on the western shore of the Dead Sea, a leopardess took two domestic goats in the autumn of 1989, and could occasionally be seen sleeping on the lawn near the kibbutz' guesthouse.[61]

Although the leopard is probably gone its lore remains around Jebel Musa. Bedouins told Henry Palmer about leopard's origin. He was a man who performed his prayer ablutions using milk instead of water, and God punished him by turning him into a leopard.[62] At Farsh Umm Silla there is a famous rockshade known as Leopard Rock (Hajarit an-Nimr) because, tradition says, it was long a resting place for leopards. "It is better that there are no leopards left," 'Awaad Ibrahim told me, "they eat children." The Bedouins still tell this story which they date simply as "very old":

> There was once a young couple very much in love, and engaged to be married. They were together in Wadi Inshayl [south of Jebel Katarina]. He had to travel to at-Tur to trade and shop, and left her with the sheep and goats. While he was away a leopard mauled and killed his fiancée. People found her corpse and buried it nearby behind some boulders at the base of a cliff. He returned from his trip knowing nothing of what had happened. He fell asleep in a rockshade. He dreamed that his fiancée came to him and said, "O beautiful gazelle with antimony 'round your eye, do not be upset. Sweet things come and go in life. The last place we met, Inshayl, will be with us forever, though you will not see me again." When the man awoke the people told him what had happened. His heart was broken. He tracked the killer. He came across many other leopards, but wanted only the killer, for revenge. When he found the leopard he killed its mate, so that the leopard would forever suffer the kind of loss he had inflicted on the man.

The predatory niche occupied by the leopard has been taken over in part by the striped hyena (*dhab'a, Hyaena hyaena*), which is most common near the Sinai coasts but also occurs at the lowest elevations in Jabaliya territory, especially around Shaykh 'Awaad and Wadi Asba'iyya. The animal features in much Sinai folklore. Monastic tradition relates that in the sixth century John the Sabaite was approached by a mother hyena who laid her blind cub at his feet. He mixed his spit with some soil and applied it to the blind animal, giving it sight. The next day the sow returned to him, dragging an enormous cabbage which she laid at his feet. Smiling, he accused the animal of stealing it from another man's garden and demanded she take it back. She did.[63] Jabaliya greybeard Saalih 'Awaad told me this story about man and hyena:

A man shipwrecked in the Gulf of Suez and drifted ashore on a flimsy piece of wood, landing on a sandy beach. He knew he would die of thirst if he did not find water soon. A hyena soon came to investigate him. The man knew that before feeding on a carcass the hyena digs underneath the body, seizes the dead animal's tail in its mouth, and bears it away on its back. Hoping the hyena would carry him to the water it must drink from, the man attached a piece of cord to himself that would look like a tail, and played dead on the sand. The hyena investigated him, dug underneath him, seized the cord, and carried the man on its back to a nearby water source. There the ungrateful man slew the animal with his knife.

Despite some persecution and the general truth that the hyena throughout the Middle East is endangered, this animal's population in Sinai is apparently stable.[64] The peninsula's other predators are following the leopard's path. There are only rare Jabaliya accounts of caracal (*labwa*, *Felis caracal*) and sand cat. An intriguing question is whether wolves still live in the area. Mammalogists Dale Osborn and Ibrahim Helmy concluded that "wolves in Sinai could doubtlessly be considered as strays."[65] This was also the perception of wolves in Israel until extensive study revealed a stable resident population extremely wary of humans.[66] Some Jabaliya elders say a wild canid known as *dhiib* was resident until about 1950 and that animals known in the area today as *dhiib* which are responsible for killing sheep, goats, and chickens are in fact feral dogs. Other elders, however, insist that the "true" *dhiib* is still present. Saalih 'Awaad told me "it inhabits the area around Wadi Itlaah and Fray'a, and is very clever. It sleeps in caves by day, and comes out only at night. It has a long, thin nose, like a fox. It only needs to eat once a week. It hates and fears dogs because they attract people's attention to it. *Dhiib* and dog never mate, because they are bitter enemies. The *dhiib* is always careful to approach the dog from downwind. The *dhiib* often attacks and kills dogs, if no people are near." 'Awaad Ibrahim insists it was a "true" *dhiib* which killed a young donkey in Wadi Jibaal in 1988. Bedouins say the animal hunts singly or in small packs and is not reluctant to enter Bedouin dwellings to seize livestock.

What is the *dhiib*? Egyptian veterinarian Dr. Muhammad Sanhouri told me the wolf is still present near Jebel Musa. An animal classified as *Canis aureus lupaster* and commonly known as the jackal occurs in mainland Egypt and has been recorded in the western Sinai. For many years there has been a debate on identification of wild canids in Egypt; many "jackals" seemed to be misidentified as "wolves." Biologists concluded that it is simply difficult for many observers in the field to distinguish between jackals and wolves; a young wolf in particular resembles a mature jackal.[67] However, their food preferences seem to distinguish these species. Jackals take birds, small mammals, reptiles, amphibians, large insects, and carrion;

wolves eat these but also larger mammals including sheep.[68] This might make identification of the animals easier but for reports in Egypt of "jackals" taking sheep and goats.[69] Perhaps some "jackals" in Egypt are in fact wolves. Walter Ferguson contends that cranial, mandible, and dental measurements prove that the "jackal" of Sinai and mainland Egypt, *Canis aureus lupaster*, is actually a subspecies of wolf and should be reclassified as *Canis lupus lupaster*, the North African wolf.[70] Another subspecies of wolf, *Canis lupus arabs*, has been recorded close to the Sinai border in Israel's southern Negev Desert. Except for an incomplete skin without a skull, identified as a "wolf," there are no collection records of either *Canis aureus lupaster* or *Canis lupus arabs* in the Jebel Musa region that would help shed light on this puzzle, and all records of *Canis lupus* in Sinai are unverifiable "sight" records.[71] However, physical evidence of *Canis aureus lupaster* is available from the area between Jebel Musa and the Gulf of Aqaba.[72] Bedouin accounts of wild canid behavior suggest that either *Canis aureus lupaster* (now perhaps *Canis lupus lupaster*) or *Canis lupus arabs* or both are present. The wolf may live today around Jebel Musa.

Bedouin descriptions of some mammals confound ready identification, and there are at least two complete zoological mysteries in local oral tradition. One predator which the Jabaliya discuss either as extinct since about 1969 or as very rare today is the *namasa*. One man described the animal to me as "a short-legged black and white canid resembling a dog-fox hybrid, but large enough that an individual animal preys easily upon adult sheep and goats as well as hyrax." He admitted he had not seen the animal. Shaykh Muhammad Abul-Haym, although he had not seen the animal, had heard it was "like a fox but larger." He thought no person alive had ever seen the beast. Another man who had never seen one thought it resembled a cross between a dog and cat in size and general appearance. As a young man in about 1950 Saalih 'Awaad saw the animal from a distance. He depicted it to me as being "like a cat, but larger, with stripes on its legs and back, with a thin tail, not bushy like a fox's. It is whitish underneath and has long, thin legs. It lived in the mountains until about twenty years ago. No, it doesn't eat goats. It eats rodents. But it will suckle from goats to get milk. If you see a goat with a scratched-up udder you know the *namasa* has been at it. But this animal never kills a goat." Iftayh 'Awaad of the Muzayna tribe told me the beast certainly does kill sheep and goats, always with the rake of its sharp claw across the victim's throat, much as a man slaughters an animal. These descriptions do not point readily to any single known animal. The ratel or honey badger (*abu ku'ayb, Mellivora capensis*), which occurs in the Negev, has distinct black and white coloration but is white above rather than underneath.[73] In mainland Egypt *nimsa* refers to the mongooses and weasels, and the Bedouin descriptions of an animal intermediate between felines and canids point toward some member of their family Viverridae. The zoril (*Ictonyx striatus*), which occurs in the southern Eastern Desert of Egypt, is black and white, with black underneath, but has a bushy tail. The catlike genet (*Genetta genetta*), recorded recently in northern Israel and the southern Eastern Desert of Egypt, is another possibility, although it has short legs and a long bushy tail and could not be described correctly as "black and white." Even the aardwolf (*Proteles cristatus*), a member of the hyena family with stripes on its long, thin legs and its back, and recorded in the southern Eastern Desert of Egypt, is a candidate for the mysterious *namasa*.

Perhaps the most intriguing possibility of all is that bears lived in the high Sinai in this century. Grandparents of the oldest generation of Jabaliya people living today reported seeing the *shiib*, a carnivorous mammal they described as being "the size of a leopard, but rather doglike in appearance" and "between a lion and a dog." Ma'aza Bedouins of Egypt's Eastern Desert also have traditions about a large carnivore called *shiib* which occurred in the area rarely but as recently as 1947.[74] In northwest Arabia, Alois Musil heard accounts of a bizarre animal called *shiib* which is a "cross between a wolf and a female hyena . . . and attacks a man even when not provoked."[75] The doglike bear inevitably comes to mind, however farfetched its presence in Sinai may seem. Bedouin oral history suggests the *shiib* disappeared from the Sinai landscape around 1900, when Shaykh Muhammad Abul-Haym's father saw one. The animal's potential identification as a bear may be strengthened by monks' accounts. St. Katherine's eldest resident, Father Good Angel, told me that in about 1940 one of his fellow monks returned to the monastery in a panicked state from the peak of Jebel Katarina. Emerging from the summit's church during a snowstorm, he encountered a brown-colored bear! Like the monk the animal fled immediately in fright. The monks today relate that bears were a regular hazard to their predecessors before the monastery was built in the sixth century, and that this was one of the reasons Justinian ordered its construction. Augusta Dobson claimed the bear was "occasionally found" in the Sinai in the early 1920s.[76] Syrian bears (*Ursus arctos syriacus*) occurred in the woods of Galilee, the Carmel, and the Judean hills until the middle of the nineteenth century.[77] While there is no physical evidence that bears ever lived in the Sinai, oral tradition and the presence of habitats that have sheltered many unlikely plants and animals at least pose the possibility that monk and bear did meet on Mount Katherine.

Felix Fabri's party of pilgrims encountered a zoological mystery in 1483 north of Jebel Musa in the southern part of the at-Tiih Plateau. A creature which they thought at first was a wild camel looked down on them from a rock. The party's guide said it was "a rhinoceros or a unicorn."[78] En route from the monastery to mainland Egypt the party also met with a wild ass (probably Asiatic wild ass, *Equus hemionis onager*). Friar Fabri related a tradition that the animal brays twenty-four times in twenty-four hours, "and by this means the inhabitants tell the time in the night."[79]

Two

◆

"YOU WILL
WORSHIP GOD
ON THIS MOUNTAIN"

The captivity, exodus, and wandering of the Israelite nation related in the Pentateuch or Torah, the first five books of the Bible, is a compelling narrative. Central to the faith and identity of so many people of the world, this epic story has a trail which has attracted both skeptical and devout sleuths. Archaeologists have found little evidence on the ground or in non-Hebrew sources to prove that these events took place.[1] The faithful insist they did occur. "The first thing to be said about this Sinai experience of the Hebrews is that it actually happened," Murray Newman concluded unequivocally. "These Old Testament traditions . . . testify to the occurrence of a real historical event in which a real people and their real God were involved."[2] Some analysts believe the Exodus tale is so peculiar that it must have taken place. "What kind of people would invent for themselves a history of enslavement and escape from slavery?" challenged archaeologist Yigael Yadin.[3] Others argue there is no evidence that the events of Exodus did not take place, and therefore they probably did.[4] Some scholars occupy a middle ground, stating neither that the Exodus-Sinai narrative is purely fictitious nor that it is unadulterated truth.[5]

Whatever their veracity the events and places of the Exodus had a genuine impact on the identity of the Jewish people, and subsequently on the world's Christians and Muslims. God liberated the Chosen People and at Mount Sinai gave them a covenant or constitution to live by. The Giving of the Law at the Holy Mountain marks the real beginning of the Jewish nation.[6] The event is a fundamental reference for Christianity, too, because in dying Christ freed His people from the antiquated "law of sin and death" prescribed at Mount Sinai and created a new covenant (Romans 8:2).[7] Through the Angel Gabriel, God revealed the Mount Sinai tradition to the Prophet Muhammad, so that in the Quran it forms part of the bedrock on which Islam is founded.

The covenant between God and His people was established at a particular place, Mount Sinai, and that place is sacred. On that point Christians, Jews, and Muslims agree. But where is Mount Sinai? Members of the three faiths have approached this question very differently. For most Jews, it is not the mountain but the message which is important; the mountain should remain *terra incognita*, unlocated, unlocatable in no man's land.[8] There is no compulsion in Islamic tradition to prove the mountain's whereabouts, and most Muslims follow the popular Christian belief that Jebel Musa is Mount Sinai. Christians, however, have long sought to verify Biblical narratives with topographical realities. By the middle of the third century A.D., Christian ascetics in the Sinai were identifying the locations of Mount Sinai and other Biblical places and taking up residence near them to pray and contemplate. Soon pilgrims came and in their passionate reverence of these places helped fix them forever on maps of the Christian world. In the nineteenth and twentieth centuries scholars dissected Biblical passages and walked in deserts to "prove" they had at long last found Mount Sinai and other holy places. To understand why these places are so important to people even today one must begin with two sets of stories, the original Biblical narratives which established the names and traditions of these holy sites, and the subsequent explorations of the pathways of the Exodus.

THE SOURCE

The Israelites who followed Joseph and Jacob into the region of Goshen in Egypt were "fruitful and prolific; they became so numerous and powerful that eventually the whole land was full of them" (Exodus 1:7). A new pharaoh "who had never heard of Joseph" judged that " 'the Israelites are now more numerous and stronger than we are' " and determined:

"We must take precautions to stop them from increasing any further, or if war should break out, they might join the ranks of our enemies. They might take arms against us and then escape from the country." Accordingly they put taskmasters over the Israelites to wear them down by forced labor. . . . But the harder their lives were made, the more they increased and spread, until people came to fear the

Israelites. So the Egyptians gave them no mercy in the demands they made, making their lives miserable with hard labour; with digging clay, making bricks, doing various kinds of field-work—all sorts of labour that they imposed on them without mercy.

(EXODUS 1:8 – 14)

Among the measures Pharaoh took to stop the Israelites' growth was to command his people to "Throw every new-born boy into the river" (Exodus 1:22). After he gave the order a Hebrew woman descended from Levi gave birth to a boy whom she was able to hide for three months. "When she could hide him no longer, she got a papyrus basket for him; coating it with bitumen and pitch, she put the child inside and laid it among the reeds at the River's edge" (Exodus 2:3). Going to bathe in the Nile, Pharaoh's daughter discovered the basket and took mercy on the baby. Pretending not to know him, the boy's sister volunteered to find a nursemaid for the child. Pharaoh's daughter consented and the boy's own mother raised him. "When the child grew up, she brought him to Pharaoh's daughter who treated him like a son; she named him Moses 'because,' she said, 'I drew him out of the water' " (Exodus 2:10).

Although reared in the Pharaoh's court Moses remained at heart an Israelite. When he saw an Egyptian strike a Hebrew laborer Moses killed the Egyptian and hid his body in the sand.

When Pharaoh heard of the matter, he tried to put Moses to death, but Moses fled from Pharaoh. He went into Midianite territory and sat down beside a well. Now there was a priest of Midian with seven daughters. They used to come to draw water and fill the troughs to water their father's flock. Some shepherds came and drove them away, but Moses sprang to their help and watered their flock. When they returned to their father Reuel [Jethro], he said to them, "Why are you back so early today?" "An Egyptian protected us from shepherds," they said, "and he even drew water for us and watered the flock." "And where is he?" he asked his daughters. "Why did you leave the man there? Ask him to eat with us." Moses agreed to stay on there with the man, who gave him his daughter Zipporah in marriage.

(EXODUS 2:15 – 21)

During this exile in the desert Moses received the Call. God heard the Israelites "groaning in their slavery" and at "Horeb, the mountain of God"—throughout the Exodus narrative an apparent synonym of Mount Sinai—He appointed Moses to lead them to freedom:

Moses was looking after the flock of his father-in-law Jethro, the priest of Midian;
he led it to the far side of the desert and came to Horeb, the mountain of God.
The angel of Yahweh appeared to him in a flame blazing from the middle of a
bush. Moses looked; there was the bush blazing, but the bush was not being burnt
up. Moses said, "I must go across and see this strange sight, and why the bush is
not being burnt up." When Yahweh saw him going across to look, God called to
him from the middle of the bush. "Moses, Moses!" he said. "Here I am," he
answered. "Come no nearer," he said. "Take off your sandals, for the place where
you are standing is holy ground. I am the God of your ancestors," he said, "the
God of Abraham, the God of Isaac and the God of Jacob." At this Moses covered
his face, for he was afraid to look at God. Yahweh then said, "I have indeed seen
the misery of my people in Egypt. I have heard them crying for help on account of
their taskmasters. Yes, I am well aware of their sufferings. And I have come down
to rescue them from the clutches of the Egyptians and bring them up out of that
country, to a country rich and broad, to a country flowing with milk and
honey. . . . Yes indeed, the Israelites' cry for help has reached me, and I have also
seen the cruel way in which the Egyptians are oppressing them. So now I am
sending you to Pharaoh, for you to bring my people the Israelites out of
Egypt. . . . After you have led the people out of Egypt,
you will worship God on this mountain."
(EXODUS 3:1 – 12)

To give Moses confidence God invested him with miraculous powers;
here at the burning bush Moses first turned his staff into a serpent (Exodus
4:3). On divine instruction Moses' brother Aaron met Moses at the mountain of God and they discussed their plans to liberate their people (Exodus
4:27–28). Then they returned to the Nile. Moses was eighty years old at
the time, and Aaron eighty-three (Exodus 7:7). They had an audience
with Pharaoh, telling him, "This is what Yahweh, God of Israel, says, 'Let
my people go . . . ' " "Who is Yahweh," Pharaoh replied, "for me to obey
what he says and let Israel go? I know nothing of Yahweh, and I will not
let Israel go" (Exodus 5:1–2). Only ten plagues, concluding with the
deaths of all Egyptian first-born and the passover of Hebrew children, persuaded Pharaoh to relent to Moses and Aaron: "Up, leave my subjects,
you and the Israelites! Go and worship Yahweh as you have asked! And
take your flocks and herds as you have asked, and go!" (Exodus 12:29–31).
After 430 years in Egypt, "the Israelites left Rameses for Succoth, about
six hundred thousand on the march—men, that is, not counting their
families. A mixed crowd of people with them, and flocks and herds, quantities of livestock" (Exodus 12:37–41). God did not want the refugees to
encounter troops along their escape route: "God did not let them take the
road to the Philistines' territory, although that was the shortest. . . . Instead,

God led the people on a roundabout way through the Sea of Reeds [*yam suph*]. . . . They set out from Succoth and encamped at Etham, on the edge of the desert," guided there "by day in a pillar of cloud to show them the way, and by night in a pillar of fire to give them light," and pitched camp "in front of Pi-Hahiroth, between Migdol and the sea, facing Baal-Zephon" (Exodus 13:17–21;14:1–2). God had set a trap for Pharaoh's army, which pursued the Israelites and was drowned in the sea that had parted to let the chosen ones pass through safely (Exodus 14:21–28).

Moses then led his people "away from the Sea of Reeds, and they entered the desert of Shur." After three waterless days they reached the bitter water of Marah, which with God's intervention Moses made sweet (Exodus 15:22–25). Traveling on they arrived at Elim, "where there were twelve springs and seventy palm trees; and there they pitched camp beside the water" (Exodus 15:27). About forty-five days out of Egypt, the party set out from Elim into the desert of Sin, "lying between Elim and Sinai" (Exodus 16:1). The Israelites began to complain of deteriorating conditions, and God provided them with a steady diet of manna and quail (Exodus 16:13–14). The manna "was like coriander seed; it was white and its taste was like that of wafers made with honey" (Exodus 16:31).

Leaving the desert of Sin, the Israelites camped at Rephidim, where "there was no water for the people to drink" (Exodus 17:1). Fearing that his people would rise up in revolt, Moses appealed to God for help. God instructed him to:

> "Go on ahead of the people, taking some of the elders of Israel with you; in your hand take the staff with which you struck the River, and go. I shall be waiting for you there on the rock (at Horeb). Strike the rock, and water will come out for the people to drink." This is what Moses did, with the elders of Israel looking on.
> He gave the place the names of Massah and Meribah ["trial" and "contention"] because of the Israelites' contentiousness and because they put Yahweh to the test by saying, "Is Yahweh with us, or not?"
> (EXODUS 17:5 – 7)

The Amalekites then attacked the Israelite camp at Rephidim. Joshua and his men were able to defeat the Amalekite force because on a nearby hill Moses with the help of Aaron and Hur kept his arms upraised, giving Israel a miraculous battlefield advantage (Exodus 17:8–13). Moses traveled on to "the mountain of God" for a reunion with his father-in-law Jethro, his wife Zipporah, and their two sons. On Jethro's counsel Moses appointed judges to help distribute his stressful responsibilities (Exodus 18:5–27). Moses then rejoined his people on the eve of the fateful rendezvous with God on Mount Sinai:

Three months to the day after leaving Egypt, the Israelites reached the desert of Sinai. Setting out from Rephidim, they reached the desert of Sinai and pitched camp in the desert; there, facing the mountain, Israel pitched camp. Moses then went up to God, and Yahweh called to him from the mountain. . . . Yahweh then said to Moses, "Look, I shall come to you in a dense cloud so that the people will hear when I speak to you and believe you ever after . . ." Yahweh then said to Moses, "Go to the people and tell them to sanctify themselves today and tomorrow. They must wash their clothes and be ready for the day after tomorrow; for the day after tomorrow, in the sight of all the people, Yahweh will descend on Mount Sinai. You will mark out the limits of the mountain and say, 'Take care not to go up the mountain or touch the edge of it. Anyone who touches the mountain will be put to death. No one may lay a hand on him: he must be stoned or shot by arrow; whether man or beast, he shall not live.' When the ram's horn sounds a long blast, they must go up the mountain . . ." Now at daybreak two days later, there were peals of thunder and flashes of lightning, dense cloud on the mountain and a very loud trumpet blast; and, in the camp, all the people trembled. Then Moses led the people out of the camp to meet God; and they took their stand at the bottom of the mountain. Mount Sinai was entirely wrapped in smoke, because Yahweh had descended on it in the form of fire. The smoke rose like smoke from a furnace and the whole mountain shook violently. Louder and louder grew the trumpeting. Moses spoke, and God answered him in the thunder. Yahweh descended on Mount Sinai, on the top of the mountain, and Yahweh called Moses to the top of the mountain; and Moses went up. Yahweh then said to Moses, "Go down and warn the people not to break through to Yahweh, or many of them will perish. Even the priests, who do have access to Yahweh, must sanctify themselves, or Yahweh may burst out against them." Moses said to Yahweh, "The people cannot come up Mount Sinai, since you yourself warned us to mark out the limits of the mountain and declare it sacred." Yahweh said, "Away with you! Go down! Then come back bringing Aaron with you. But do not allow the priests and people to break through to come up to Yahweh, or he may burst out against them." So Moses went down to the people and spoke to them.

(EXODUS 19:1 – 25)

The sequence of Moses' encounters with God on the mountain is interrupted here by the insertion of the Decalogue, the "ten commandments":

Then God spoke all these words. He said, "I am Yahweh your God who brought you out of Egypt, where you lived as slaves. You shall have no other gods to rival me. You shall not make yourself a carved image or any likeness of anything in heaven above or on earth beneath or in the waters under the earth. You shall not bow down to them or serve them. . . . You shall not misuse the name of Yahweh

*your God, for Yahweh will not leave unpunished who misuses his name. . . .
Remember the Sabbath day and keep it holy. For six days you shall labour and do
all your work, but the seventh day is a Sabbath for Yahweh your God. You shall
do no work that day . . . Honour your father and your mother so that you may
live long in the land that Yahweh your God is giving you. You shall not kill. You
shall not commit adultery. You shall not steal. You shall not give false evidence
against your neighbour. You shall not set your heart on your neighbour's house.
You shall not set your heart on your neighbour's spouse, or servant, man or
woman, or ox, or donkey, or any of your neighbour's possessions." Seeing the
thunder pealing, the lightning flashing, the trumpet blasting and the mountain
smoking, the people were all terrified, and kept their distance. . . . So the people
kept their distance while Moses approached the dark cloud where God was."*
(EXODUS 20:1 – 21)

Within the cloud God elaborated to Moses upon the laws set out for
the people, addressing in this "Book of the Covenant" practical matters
such as treatment of women and slaves, murder, assault, theft, justice, sab-
batical and feast days, and concluding with a promise that an angel of God
would bring the people to the promised land (Exodus 21:1–23:23). The
sequence of Moses' meetings with God on the mountain is again disrupted
as God tells Moses, "Come up to Yahweh, you and Aaron, Nadab and
Abihu, and seventy of the elders of Israel and bow down at a distance.
Moses alone will approach Yahweh; the others will not approach, nor will
the people come up with him" (Exodus 24:1–2). Moses then told the
people all of what God had said. They promised to carry out the commandments. "Moses put all Yahweh's words into writing, and early next
morning he built an altar at the foot of the mountain, with twelve
standing-stones for the twelve tribes of Israel" (Exodus 24:3–4). Moses
then ratified the covenant with a sacrifice of bullocks. After reading to the
people the Book of the Covenant, Moses sprinkled the animals' blood
over the people, saying, "This is the blood of the covenant which Yahweh
has made with you, entailing all these stipulations" (Exodus 24:5–8).
"Moses, Aaron, Nadab, Abihu and seventy elders of Israel then went up,
and they saw the God of Israel beneath whose feet there was what looked
like a sapphire pavement pure as the heavens themselves, but he did no
harm to the Israelite notables; they actually gazed on God and then ate and
drank" (Exodus 24:9–11).

God invited Moses to come farther up the mountain to receive the
stone tablets which God himself had inscribed:

*Yahweh said to Moses, "Come up to me on the mountain. Stay there, and I will
give you the stone tablets—the law and the commandment—which I have written*

for their instruction." Moses made ready, with Joshua his assistant, and they went up the mountain of God. He said to the elders, "Wait here for us until we come back to you. You have Aaron and Hur with you; if anyone has any matter to settle, let him go to them." Moses then went up the mountain. Cloud covered the mountain. The glory of Yahweh rested on Mount Sinai and the cloud covered it for six days. On the seventh day Yahweh called to Moses from inside the cloud. To the watching Israelites, the glory of Yahweh looked like a devouring fire on the mountain top. Moses went right into the cloud and went on up the mountain. Moses stayed on the mountain for forty days and forty nights.

(EXODUS 24:12 − 18)

On the mountain God instructed Moses to "Make me a sanctuary so that I can reside among them [the Israelites]" (Exodus 24:8). This dwelling was to house the ark of the covenant, and God gave Moses precise construction details for the ark (Exodus 25:10−22). "Inside the ark you will put the Testimony which I am about to give you," He told Moses (Exodus 25:15). He gave Moses detailed instructions on how the sanctuary should be built and decorated, on how the priests of Israel should be consecrated, and on how offerings should be made in the temple (Exodus 25:23−31:17). "When he had finished speaking to Moses on Mount Sinai, he gave him the two tablets of the Testimony, tablets of stone inscribed by the finger of God" (Exodus 31:18).

During this long meeting the people of Israel had grown restless with Moses' absence, telling Aaron: "Get to work, make us a god to go at our head; for that Moses, the man who brought us here from Egypt—we do not know what has become of him" (Exodus 32:1). Moses' brother ordered the people to gather up all their gold jewelry. "He received what they gave him, melted it down into a mould and with it made the statue of a calf" (Exodus 32:4). Aaron built an altar before the statue and proclaimed, "'Tomorrow will be a feast in Yahweh's honour.' Early next morning they sacrificed burnt offerings and brought communion sacrifices. The people then sat down to eat and drink, and afterwards got up to amuse themselves" (Exodus 32:6). Up on the mountain, God told Moses to climb down to his errant people: "Go down at once, for the people whom you brought here from Egypt have become corrupt" (Exodus 32:7). God threatened to destroy them but Moses pleaded with Him and won leniency; "Yahweh then relented over the disaster which he had intended to inflict on his people" (Exodus 32:14). Moses was to inflict his own wrath on them:

Moses turned and came down the mountain with the two tablets of the Testimony in his hands, tablets inscribed on both sides, inscribed on the front and on the back.

The tablets were the work of God, and the writing on them was God's writing,
engraved on the tablets. . . . And there, as he approached the camp, he saw the
calf and the groups dancing. Moses blazed with anger. He threw down the tablets
he was holding, shattering them at the foot of the mountain. He seized the calf
they had made and burned it, grinding it into powder which he scattered on the
water, and made the Israelites drink it. . . . When Moses saw that the people were
out of hand—for Aaron had let them get out of hand to the derision of their ene-
mies all around them—Moses then stood at the gate of the camp and shouted
"Who is for Yahweh? To me!" And all the Levites rallied round him. He said to
them, "Yahweh, God of Israel, says this, 'Buckle on your sword, each of you, and
go up and down the camp from gate to gate, every man of you slaughtering brother,
friend and neighbour.' " The Levites did as Moses said, and of the people about
three thousand men perished that day. "Today," Moses said, "you have
consecrated yourselves to Yahweh, one at the cost of his son, another of his brother;
and so he bestows a blessing on you today."
(EXODUS 32:15 – 29)

Moses added a topographical detail in a subsequent recollection of this
event: "That work of sin, the calf you had made, I took and burned and
broke to pieces; having ground it to the finest dust, I threw its dust into
the stream that comes down the mountain" (Deuteronomy 9:21).

The next day Moses told his people, "I shall go back up to Yahweh:
perhaps I can secure expiation for your sin" (Exodus 32:30). "Moses then
went back to Yahweh"—apparently on Mount Sinai—where God assured him that those who sinned "I shall blot out of my book. So now go
and lead the people to the place I promised to you. . . . Move on towards
a country flowing with milk and honey, but I myself shall not be going
with you or I might annihilate you on the way, for you are an obstinate
people" (Exodus 32:33–33:3). God ordered that the Israelites should remove their jewelry, "So, from Mount Horeb onwards, the Israelites
stripped themselves of their ornaments" (Exodus 33:6). Moses pitched the
Tent of Meeting, a place to meet with God "outside the camp, far away
from the camp." As a "pillar of cloud" descended on the tent God spoke
to Moses "as a man talks to his friend." Moses pleaded with Him to show
his people the way to the promised land, and again God acceded to Moses'
request (Exodus 33:7–17). Moses then asked to see more of God:

"Please show me your glory." Yahweh said, "I shall make all my goodness pass
before you, and before you I shall pronounce the name Yahweh; and I am gracious
to those to whom I am gracious and I take pity on those on whom I take pity."
"But my face," he said, "you cannot see, for no human being can see me and
survive." Then Yahweh said, "Here is a place near me. You will stand on the

*rock, and when my glory passes by, I shall put you in a cleft of the rock and shield
you with my hand until I have gone past. Then I shall take my hand away and
you will see my back; but my face will not be seen." Yahweh said to Moses, "Cut
two tablets of stone like the first ones and come up to me on the mountain, and I
will write on the tablets the words that were on the first tablets, which you broke.
Be ready at dawn; at dawn come up Mount Sinai and wait for me there at the top
of the mountain. No one may come up with you, no one may be seen anywhere
on the mountain; the flocks and herds may not even graze in front of this mountain." So he cut two tablets of stone like the first and, with the two tablets of stone
in his hands, Moses went up Mount Sinai in the early morning as Yahweh had
ordered. And Yahweh descended in a cloud and stood with him there and
pronounced the name Yahweh. . . . He then said, "Look, I am now making a
covenant: I shall work wonders at the head of your whole people as have never
been worked in any other country or nation, and all the people round you will see
what Yahweh can do, for what I shall do through you will be awe-inspiring.
Mark, then, what I command you today . . ." Yahweh then said to Moses, "Put
these words in writing, for they are the terms of the covenant which I have made
with you and with Israel." He stayed there with Yahweh for forty days and forty
nights, eating and drinking nothing, and on the tablets he wrote the words of the
covenant—the Ten Words. When Moses came down from Mount Sinai with the
two tablets of the Testimony in his hands, as he was coming down the mountain,
Moses did not know that the skin of his face was radiant because he had been
talking to him. And when Aaron and all the Israelites saw Moses, the skin on his
face was so radiant that they were afraid to go near him. But Moses called to them,
and Aaron and all the leaders of the community rejoined him, and Moses talked to
them, after which all the Israelites came closer, and he passed on to them all the
orders that Yahweh had given to him on Mount Sinai.*
(EXODUS 33:18 – 34:32)

The Israelites then constructed the Dwelling, the ark of the covenant
and other ritual furnishings according to God's specifications. "On the first
day of the first month in the second year the Dwelling was erected. Moses
erected the Dwelling . . . He took the Testimony and put it in the ark . . .
He brought the ark into the Dwelling . . ." (Exodus 40:17–21). When he
finished his work "the cloud then covered the Tent of Meeting and the
glory of Yahweh filled the Dwelling" (Exodus 40:34). The Israelites finally
set out for the promised land, erecting the Dwelling at each camp. "At
every stage of their journey, whenever the cloud rose from the Dwelling,
the Israelites would resume their march. If the cloud did not rise, they
would not resume their march until the day it did rise" (Exodus 40:
36–37).
   The departure from Mount Sinai after approximately a year's stay there

is related in the books of Numbers and Deuteronomy. The Numbers account reveals the date on which the Israelites broke camp at "Yahweh's mountain": "In the second year, in the second month, on the twentieth day of the month, the cloud rose from where the Dwelling of the Testimony was, and the Israelites set out, in marching order, from the desert of Sinai. The cloud came to rest in the desert of Paran . . . They set out from Yahweh's mountain . . ." (Numbers 10:11–33). Many years later in Moab, Moses recalled the order God had given to break camp at Mount Sinai:

> Yahweh our God said to us at Horeb, "You have stayed long enough at this
> mountain. Move on, continue your journey, go to the highlands of the Amorites,
> to all those who live in the Arabah, in the highlands, in the lowlands, in the
> Negeb and in the coastland; go into Canaan and to Lebanon as far as the great
> River Euphrates. Look, that is the country I have given you; go and take
> possession of the country that Yahweh promised on oath to give to your ancestors,
> Abraham, Isaac and Jacob, and to their descendants after them" . . . So, as
> Yahweh our God had ordered, we left Horeb and made our way through that vast
> and terrible desert, which you saw on the way to the Amorite highlands,
> and arrived at Kadesh-Barnea.
> (DEUTERONOMY 1:6 – 19)

The entire itinerary of the Exodus is recounted in Numbers 33:1–49, a passage subjected to the intense scrutiny of those who would retrace the route:

> These were the stages of the journey made by the Israelites when they left Egypt in
> their companies under the leadership of Moses and Aaron. Moses recorded their
> starting-points in writing whenever they moved on at Yahweh's order. The stages,
> from one starting-point to another, were as follows: They left Rameses in the first
> month. It was the fifteenth day of the first month, the day following the Passover,
> when the Israelites confidently set out, under the eyes of all Egypt. . . . The Isra-
> elites left Rameses and camped at Succoth. Then they left Succoth and encamped
> at Etham which is on the edge of the desert. They left Etham, turned back to
> Pi-Hahiroth, opposite Baal-Zephon, and encamped at Migdol. They left
> Pi-Hahiroth, crossed the sea into the desert, and after marching for three days in
> the desert of Etham they encamped at Marah. They left Marah and reached Elim.
> At Elim there were twelve springs of water and seventy palm trees; they encamped
> there. They left Elim and encamped by the Sea of Reeds. They left the Sea of
> Reeds and encamped in the desert of Sin. They left the desert of Sin and
> encamped at Dophkah. They left Dophkah and encamped at Alush. They left
> Alush and encamped at Rephidim; the people found no drinking water there.

They left Rephidim and encamped in the desert of Sinai. They left the desert of Sinai and encamped at Kibroth-ha-Taavah.

Even while Moses lived, the events at Mount Sinai acquired enormous historical significance and became a constant reference for identity and admonition. The prophet reminded his people of the duties of their covenant:

But take care, as you value your lives! Do not forget the things which you your-selves have seen, or let them slip from your heart as long as you live; teach them, rather, to your children and to your children's children. The day you stood at Horeb in the presence of Yahweh your God, Yahweh said to me, "Summon the people to me; I want them to hear me speaking, so that they will learn to fear me all the days they live on earth, and teach this to their children." So you came and stood at the foot of the mountain, and the mountain flamed to the very sky, a sky darkened by cloud, murky and thunderous. Yahweh then spoke to you from the heart of the fire; you heard the sound of words but saw no shape; there was only a voice. He revealed his covenant to you and commanded you to observe it, the Ten Words which he inscribed on two tablets of stone. Yahweh then ordered me to teach you the laws and customs that you were to observe in the country into which you are about to cross, to take possession of it. Hence, be very careful what you do. Since you saw no shape that day at Horeb when Yahweh spoke to you from the heart of the fire, see that you do not corrupt yourselves by making an image in the shape of anything whatever
(DEUTERONOMY 4:9 – 16)

Moses told his people that because they had earned God's wrath God would not allow him to accompany them into the promised land. He prophesied that they would not remain long in the promised land, but because of idolatry

"you will be utterly destroyed. Yahweh will scatter you among the peoples . . . You will suffer; everything I have said will befall you, but in the final days you will return to Yahweh your God and listen to his voice. For Yahweh your God is a merciful God and will not desert or destroy you or forget the covenant which he made on oath with your ancestors. Put this question, then, to the ages that are past, that have gone before you, from when God created the human race on earth: Was there ever a word so majestic, from one end of heaven to the other? Was anything like it ever heard? Did ever a people hear the voice of the living God speaking from the heart of the fire, as you heard it, and remain alive? Has it ever been known before that any god took action himself to bring one nation out of

another one, by ordeals, signs, wonders, war with mighty hand and outstretched
arm, by fearsome terrors—all of which things Yahweh your God has done for you
before your eyes in Egypt? . . . Hence, grasp this today and meditate on it
carefully: Yahweh is the true God, in heaven above as on earth beneath, he and
no other. Keep his law and commandments as I give them to you today, so that
you and your children after you, may prosper and live long in the country that
Yahweh your God is giving to you for ever." . . . Moses called all Israel together
and said to them, "Listen, Israel, to the laws and customs that I proclaim to you
today. Learn them and take care to observe them. Yahweh our God made a cove-
nant with us at Horeb. Yahweh made this covenant not with our ancestors, but
with us, with all of us alive here today. On the mountain, from the heart of the fire,
Yahweh spoke to you face to face, while I stood between you and Yahweh to let
you know what Yahweh was saying, since you were afraid of the fire and
had not gone up the mountain."
(DEUTERONOMY 4:26 − 5:5)

Moses retold the commandments to his people, recalling again the divine fury of the setting in which God delivered them: "These were the
words Yahweh spoke to you when you were all assembled on the mountain. Thunderously, he spoke to you from the heart of the fire, in cloud
and thick darkness. He added nothing, but wrote them on two tablets of
stone which he gave to me" (Deuteronomy 5:6−22). Moses promised the
people that God would reward them if they followed the covenant made
at Sinai: "Listen to these ordinances, be true to them and observe them,
and in return Yahweh your God will be true to the covenant and love
which he promised on oath to your ancestors. He will love you and bless
you and increase your numbers; he will bless the fruit of your body and
the produce of your soil, your corn, your new wine, your oil, the issue of
your cattle, the young of your flock, in the country which he swore to
your ancestors that he would give you. You will be the most blessed of all
peoples" (Deuteronomy 7:12−13).

After elaborating upon the covenant made at Sinai with the Deuter-
onomic code of law and reminding his people to follow it, Moses prepared
for his death and his people's final passage into the promised land. He
recited the "Song of Moses" God had dictated to him (Deuteronomy 32:
1−43). God then asked Moses to climb his last mountain:

"Climb this mountain of the Abarim, Mount Nebo, in the country of Moab,
opposite Jericho, and view the Canaan which I am giving to the Israelites as
their domain. Die on the mountain you have climbed, and be gathered to your
people." . . . Then, leaving the Plains of Moab, Moses went up Mount Nebo,
the peak of Pisgah opposite Jericho, and Yahweh showed him the whole

*country. . . . Yahweh said to him, "This is the country which I promised on oath
to give to Abraham, Isaac and Jacob, saying: I shall give it to your descendants. I
have allowed you to see it for yourself, but you will not cross into it." There in the
country of Moab, Moses, servant of Yahweh, died as Yahweh decreed; they buried
him in the valley, in the country of Moab, opposite Beth-Peor; but to this day no
one has ever found his grave. Moses was a hundred and twenty years old when he
died, his eye undimmed, his vigour unimpaired.*

(DEUTERONOMY 32:49 – 50; 34:1 – 7)

Another Biblical tradition linked with holy places on Jebel Musa is the
account of the prophet Elijah's sojourn on Mount Sinai. In the book of
1 Kings, Horeb occurs in a context unrelated to Moses and the covenant,
set in the reign of Ahab (874–853 B.C.E.). This king of Israel "did what is
displeasing to Yahweh": he "married Jezebel daughter of Ethbaal, king of
the Sidonians, and then proceeded to serve Baal and worship him"
(1 Kings 16:30–31). The prophet Elijah warned Ahab that God would
punish him with a drought. God ordered Elijah to flee to Cherith, east of
the Jordan, where God had commanded ravens to bring him food, and
where he could drink from a stream (1 Kings 17:1–6). During the ensuing
drought and famine Jezebel "was butchering the prophets of Yahweh"
(1 Kings 18:4). Elijah boldly ordered Ahab to assemble the four hundred
prophets of Baal on Mount Carmel, where Elijah performed a miracle
while Baal's prophets could not. Elijah ordered his people to seize the
prophets of Baal. "They seized them, and Elijah took them down to the
Kishon, and there he slaughtered them" (1 Kings 18:40). When the king
told his wife what Elijah had done, Jezebel sent a message to Elijah threatening to have him killed within twenty-four hours. Elijah fled into the
desert near Beersheba. An angel came to him to refresh him for his journey
to Horeb.

*So he got up and ate and drank, and strengthened by that food he walked for forty
days and forty nights until he reached Horeb, God's mountain. There he went
into a cave, and spent the night there. Then the word of Yahweh came to him
saying, "What are you doing here, Elijah?" He replied, "I am full of jealous zeal
for Yahweh Sabaoth, because the Israelites have abandoned your covenant, have
torn down your altars and put your prophets to the sword. I am the only one left,
and now they want to kill me." Then he was told, "Go out and stand on the
mountain before Yahweh." For at that moment Yahweh was going by. A mighty
hurricane split the mountains and shattered the rocks before Yahweh. But Yahweh
was not in the hurricane. And after the hurricane, an earthquake. But Yahweh
was not in the earthquake. And after the earthquake, fire. But Yahweh was not in
the fire. And after the fire, a light murmuring sound. And when Elijah heard this,*

he covered his face with his cloak and went out and stood at the entrance of the cave. Then a voice came to him, which said, "What are you doing here, Elijah?"

(I KINGS 19:8 – 13)

Elijah again explained his flight and God ordered him to return by the same route to the desert of Damascus to anoint new kings of Israel and Aram, and to anoint Elisha son of Shaphat to be his own successor as prophet (1 Kings 19:14–16). "Leaving there, he came on Elisha son of Shaphat as he was ploughing behind twelve yoke of oxen, he himself being the twelfth. Elijah passed near to him and threw his cloak over him. Elisha left his oxen and ran after Elijah. 'Let me kiss my father and mother, then I will follow you,' he said. Elijah answered, 'Go, go back; for have I done anything to you?' " Elijah could not dissuade Elisha, who destroyed his oxen, "rose and, following Elijah, became his servant" (1 Kings 19: 19–21).

PLACES IN THE WILDERNESS

The search for Mount Sinai must begin with scrutiny of the natural setting depicted in these Biblical passages. What is the countryside of the wandering like? Does the Biblical narrative provide topographical or environmental clues about precise conditions, locations, and seasons that would point to particular places, or even to the general region where these events may have taken place? A tantalizing mixture of accurate natural history and vague depiction makes it difficult to answer these vital questions.

The general aspect of Sinai as desert wilderness (Hebrew, *midbar*) is well-developed in the Bible and fits the environment of much of the peninsula today. The names "Sinai" and "Horeb" themselves suggest a rugged desert landscape. Horeb may mean "arid mountain," "disintegrating mountain," "desolate place," "waste," "ruin," or "heat."[9] Richard Pocke supposed that the neighboring peaks of Jebel Musa and Jebel Katarina might have been likened to human breasts, in Persian "sine."[10] Bedouins of south Sinai today assert that the name came from the Arabic word for "tooth" (*sinn*), because the jagged mountains of their homeland resemble canine teeth. Some scholars have proposed that the mountain's name derived from the Hebrew word for a bush or the burning bush (*seneh*), either because the shrub occurs there or because treelike patterns of pyrolusite are common in the rocks of Jebel Musa and its neighbors.[11] Perhaps in reference to its spectacular relief, Sinai may also mean "to shine."[12] Other scholars have argued that the mountain or peninsula was named for the Mesopotamian moon god Sin after the Assyrians came to dominate the eastern Mediterranean in the eighth century B.C.E.; the high peaks of Sinai are thus the "mountains of the moon."[13] Alternatively, Sinai may have come from the addition of the suffix "the one of" (*ayu*) to the root "Sin," which referred to a wilderness area in the peninsula; Sinai would mean "the one (the mountain) of the Wilderness of Sin."[14] The holy mountain of Sinai and the peninsula eventually became synonymous, with the peninsula by most accounts deriving its name from the mountain.

The Biblical people who perceived the desert as hostile or forbidding clearly were not indigenous to that environment but came from a much greener place. At Kadesh the Israelites complained of Sinai: "It is a place unfit for sowing, it has no figs, no vines, no pomegranates, and there is not even water to drink!" (Numbers 20:5). They saw a deathlike land separating two lifegiving areas. "Think of the fish we used to eat free in Egypt, the cucumbers, melons, leeks, onions and garlic," the Israelites recalled at Taberah, in hunger forgetting their bondage (Numbers 11:5). Their hopes turned east to "a fine country, a land of streams and springs, of waters that well up from the deep in valleys and hills, a land of wheat and barley, of vines, of figs, of pomegranates, a land of olives, of oil, of honey" (Deuteronomy 8:7–8). In their long captivity the Hebrews had acquired that essential Egyptian dread of the desert.

In the Biblical accounts of Sinai there is a vagueness about the environment that fits a people with little knowledge of the desert. There are also reliable observations of Sinai's natural history. The account of quail (*Coturnix coturnix*) coming into camp at Kibroth-ha-Taavah depicts a scene which may be witnessed on a reduced scale today on Sinai's Mediterranean coast during the autumn migration: "A wind, sent by Yahweh, started blowing from the sea bringing quails which it deposited on the camp. They lay for a distance of a day's march either side of the camp, two cubits thick on the ground" (Numbers 11:31).[15] The abundance of the birds might have been only slightly exaggerated. As recently as the 1930s Alexandria and Port Said were sometimes "absolutely invaded by quails."[16] In early September men seated at sidewalk cafes in Port Said netted the birds as they flew by, and on the Sinai coast the birds landed in such numbers that they literally covered the ground so that there was no room for more birds unless they alighted on others' backs.[17] The Hebrews' suffering as they ate quail may have been more a chemical than a moral consequence. "The meat was still between their teeth, not even chewed, when Yahweh's anger was aroused by the people. Yahweh struck them with a very great plague . . . they buried the people who had indulged their greed" (Numbers 11:33,34). David Trocki proposed that on spring migration northward through the Nile Valley the birds may have fed on a poisonous ergot fungus, to which they are immune.[18] My father recalled from his upbringing in rural Florida the conventional wisdom that no one could eat one quail daily for thirty days and survive. Aficionados of quail in Egypt told me that if you eat more than a dozen birds at a sitting you are likely to "suffer from the richness." The Israelites who "indulged their greed" paid a high price.

Like quail, the Biblical manna may have been a genuine resource of the Sinai. Many researchers have concluded that manna is secreted by two insect species, *Trabutina mannipara* and *Najacoccus serpentinus*, which infest tamarisk trees in the mountainous south and the lowland north of the Sinai, respectively. Fritz Bodenheimer explained that in early summer following good winter rains, these scale insects suck the carbohydrate-rich sap of the tamarisk and excrete a surplus onto the tree's twigs as small globules that crystallize and fall to the ground.[19] People must collect the edible, sticky substance before the day's heat comes on or ants find it. In 1844 Constantin von Tischendorf was delighted to be able to eat the "excrescences hanging like glittering pearls or thick dewdrops" from tamarisks in Wadi Feiran:

> These thickish lumps were clammy, and had the same powerful scent emitted by the shrub. I tasted it, and its flavour, as far as I could find a suitable comparison, greatly resembles honey. My Bedouins told me that no manna had been collected for three years, but that this year a rich harvest was expected. In the month of July, the Bedouins, and also the monks of St. Catherine's monastery, collect it in small leathern bags, chiefly from the ground, whither it drops from the branches upon hot days. As it is not produced in very large quantities, it is sold tolerably dear, and chiefly to the pilgrims to Mecca and Mount Sinai. Yet do the Bedouins themselves indulge in it; they eat it spread upon bread, like honey.[20]

In 1483 Felix Fabri saw St. Katherine's monks selling vials of this substance at a very high price to pilgrims, while local Bedouins offered counterfeit manna for sale.[21] As recently as 1922 the monks more generously bestowed small tins of manna on pilgrims and travelers.[22] The Bible indicates that whatever this unusual substance was that sustained the Israelites for forty years, it was such a prized symbol of their miraculous delivery and survival that God ordered Moses to keep about a gallon of it for posterity: "Fill a *homer* with it and preserve it for your descendants, so they can see the bread on which I fed you in the desert when I brought you out of Egypt" (Exodus 16:32). Aaron placed the manna in the ark of the covenant next to the tablets of the law.

The paths and places of the Exodus are among the most frequently studied yet least agreed upon subjects of Biblical geography. If the date of the Exodus were established, existing knowledge of ancient travel and trade routes might shed light on the probable route of the fleeing Israelites.

Biblical scholars acknowledge that there are no reliable clues about the
length of time the Israelites stayed in Egypt, but recognize indications of
when they might have departed.[23] These date the Exodus to between 1500
and 1200 B.C.E. The most favored theory, based on mention of the cities
Pithom and Rameses in Exodus 1:11, depicts Seti I (1302–1290) as Pharaoh of the oppression and Ramses II (1290–1224) as Pharaoh of the
Exodus.[24] Others label Ramses II the Pharaoh of the oppression and
Merneptah (1224–1214) the Pharaoh of the Exodus; or Tuthmosis III
(1490–1436) and Amenhotep II (1439–1406), respectively.[25] Giza Plateau
archaeologist Mark Lehner contends that Tuthmosis III was the Pharaoh
of the Exodus, and Queen Hatshepsut (1486–1468) was the woman who
salvaged Moses from the reeds.[26] To know how many people fled Egypt
might also help in tracing their route, based on assumptions of the varying
carrying capacities of places. Some observers assume as truth the figure of
600,000 men fleeing with their families, to arrive at a total of 2 to 3 million
Israelites on the Exodus.[27] They look, therefore, for large camping places.
Others insist the total could not have exceeded 25,000–30,000.[28]

Scholars use varying assumptions about the date, the number of people
traveling, the political situation, and the environmental context of the
Sinai to argue for one of three possible routes of the Exodus. One argument is that the Israelites traveled across northern Sinai, close to the Mediterranean coast.[29] The heavily garrisoned mining region of Serabit al-
Khadim would have deterred the refugees from traveling to the south. The
dry southern Sinai could not have supported their livestock. The tamarisk
trees which yield manna and the abundant quail of the autumn migration
are typical of northern rather than southern Sinai. Others insist on a southern route through the high Sinai mountains, arguing that only in the south
were there adequate water supplies and pastures for people and their herds.
Too many of Pharaoh's troops would have been using the northern "Way
of the Philistines" (also known as the "Way of Horus" and "Way of the
Sea") along the Mediterranean coast for the Israelites to pass along it
safely.[30] According to a third school of thought the route least-used by the
Egyptians and therefore safest for the Hebrew people was the central pas-
sage along the "Way of Shur" leading almost due east from present-day
Ismailiya to Bir Gafgafa in north-central Sinai, across the plain north of
Jebel Halaal, to Ein el-Qudeirat in northeastern Sinai.[31]

Biblical places should correspond with contemporaneous Egyptian sites
known through archaeology. The corroboration is scant. Most students of
this problem agree that only two places named in the Exodus and wanderings accounts can be securely identified: Kadesh-Barnea is Ein el-Qudeirat
in northeastern Sinai, and Ezion-Geber is Tell el-Kheleifeh near Eilat.[32]
All other stations of the Exodus remain uncertain. Their identifications are

based on authors' convictions, particularly about which route the fleeing Israelites chose. The following litany is just a brief synopsis of the massive literature on this topic which, as Augusta Dobson complained, "can grow very weary."[33] The land of Goshen is generally presumed to be the northeastern Nile Delta region, though some have equated it with all Egypt. Pithom may have been 55 kilometers west of Ismailiya at Tell er-Retabeh, or a site just west of Lake Timsah.[34] Rameses may have been on the eastern fringe of the Delta either at Tanis (San el-Hagar) or farther south at Qantir.[35] Succoth may have been 30 kilometers southwest of Port Said, or 40 kilometers southwest of Ismailiya at Tell el-Mashkuta.[36] Etham, "on the edge of the desert," may have been between the Great Bitter Lake and Lake Timsah, or west of the Great Bitter Lake.[37] Pi-Hahiroth may have been just west of the western tip of Lake Bardawil at Muhammadiya, on the west-central shore of the Great Bitter Lake, on the southeast shore of the Gulf of Suez just south of modern at-Tur, or modern Ismailiya.[38] Baal-Zephon may have been just southeast of modern Suez, between the Great Bitter Lake and Suez, west of the modern Suez canal at the southern tip of Lake Manzala, in the northeastern Delta at Tell Defneh, or on the narrow spit separating Lake Bardawil from the Mediterranean Sea.[39] Migdol may have been just west of the western tip of Lake Bardawil, or west of the southern end of the Great Bitter Lake at Gineifa, or between Suez and the Great Bitter Lake, or on the west coast of the southern Gulf of Suez just north of Jebel az-Zayt.[40] Marah may have been just southeast of the eastern tip of Lake Bardawil at Mazar, or north of Wadi Gharandal in west-central Sinai at Ain Hawara.[41] Elim, with its twelve springs of water and seventy palm trees, may have been on the Mediterranean coast west of al-Ariish at Masaid, near the northeast tip of the Gulf of Suez at 'Uyun Musa, a site in lower Wadi Gharandal near central Sinai's west coast, or just north of modern at-Tur as the monks of St. Katherine believe.[42] The Sea of Reeds may have been the southern part of Lake Manzala, Lake Bardawil, Lake Timsah, a marshy area north of Lake Timsah, the Gulf of Suez, the Gulf of Aqaba, or the southern part of Lake Manzala.[43] Dophkah may have been in southwestern Sinai, either at Serabit al-Khadim or in the upper reach of Wadi Feiran.[44] Alush may have been modern al-Ariish, or a site northeast of Jebel Serbal.[45] Rephidim may have been the cape of Ras as-Sudr on the northeast coast of the Gulf of Suez, Wadi Feiran, north of Aqaba in the Wadi 'Araba, or a site just northwest of Jebel Musa in Wadi ash-Shaykh as St. Katherine's monks believe, and where they erected a chapel in 1981 to mark the place where the Israelites defeated Amalek.[46] The desert of Sinai may have been the granite district from Jebel Musa north to the border of the Plateau of at-Tiih.[47] The desert of Sin may have been this same area, or the entire upper Sinai massif, or the coastal region of the Gulf of Suez

near the mouth of Wadi Feiran, or the area along the central part of the
modern border between Egypt and Israel.[48] The desert of Shur may have
been the extreme northwest Sinai or the entire eastern coastal area of the
Gulf of Suez.[49] The desert of Paran may have been the Plateau of at-Tiih,
but may also have been synonymous with the wilderness of Zin, which
would place it in southern Wadi 'Araba or in the western Negev Desert.[50]

And where is Mount Sinai? What does the mountain look like? The
Bible provides few clues. It is in "the desert of Sinai" (Exodus 19:1). The
passages do not reveal its relative height or even its general appearance.
Only subsequent interpretations give earthly dimensions to the mountain.
The first-century Jewish historian Flavius Josephus wrote that lofty and
forbidding Mount Sinai "is the highest of all the mountains thereabout."[51]
In contrast the Babylonian Talmud describes Mount Sinai as low: "God
left all mountains and hills and caused His Divine Presence to rest on
Mount Sinai, which was not high."[52] In the Babidbar Rabha, a treatise on
Numbers written by Rabbis of the Talmud, other great Biblical peaks
dwarf Mount Sinai: "Tabor and Carmel came from the end of the world,
priding themselves on their height and saying 'We are high, and the Holy
one, Blessed be He, will give upon us His Torah' (the Law). But Sinai
humbly says 'I am low,' and therefore God put His glory upon it and gave
the Torah on Sinai, and it merited all that great honour."[53]

The vagueness of Biblical depiction of Mount Sinai may be deliberate.
Perhaps people are not meant to know where this mountain stands and be
tempted to revere it rather than the message it stands for. Historically most
Jews have avoided assigning an earthly location to Mount Sinai.[54] It is a
celestial place which God placed off-limits to ordinary people: "Take care
not to go up the mountain or touch the edge of it. Anyone who touches
the mountain will be put to death" (Exodus 19:12). As a sacred precinct
Mount Sinai has a counterpart in the Holy of Holies of the Temple; owing
to its sanctity Jews today are admonished to not ascend Temple Mount in
Jerusalem where the sanctuary once stood.[55] Contact with the sacred
would transform an ordinary person, with fatal results. Whoever climbed
Mount Sinai "would himself become holy, and would have to be put to
death not so much as a punishment, but in order to prevent the holiness
which he contracted being dispersed into the profane world," explained
Ronald Clements.[56]

Most of the scholars who have "proven" the location of Mount Sinai
are Christians. They have used secular criteria from archaeology, geography, history, and geology to pinpoint about twenty mountains as the
"true" Sinai. Lina Eckenstein documented rich artwork and other remains
of occupation in west-central Sinai's Serabit al-Khadim to argue that this
is Mount Sinai.[57] However, this was an active Egyptian turquoise mining

site during the presumed time of the Exodus, making it an improbable retreat for the Hebrew refugees. The real Mount Sinai according to Italian archaeologist Emmanuel Anati is Har Karkom, also known as Mount Saffron and Jebel Ideid, in the Israeli Negev Desert 80 kilometers northwest of Eilat, just 6 kilometers from the Egyptian border. The base of this modest mountain of 851 meters is embellished with abundant rock art and stone monuments which Anati interprets as evidence that Har Karkom "must have been a sacred mountain in ancient times, a place of worship of very great importance" for a period of about a thousand years.[58] The remains date to the Bronze Age of 2900–2000 B.C.E., and the site was abandoned at least seven hundred years prior to the date at which most Biblical scholars begin to date the Exodus. If Har Karkom is Mount Sinai the traditional Exodus chronology would have to be overthrown. That cannot or should not be done, William Stiebing argues, for once the generally accepted date of the Exodus is revised radically, so is the entire sequence of Biblical archaeology including the settlement of Canaan, the building of Solomon's Temple, and the Temple's destruction.[59]

Some Mount Sinais are far afield of the Sinai. Charles Beke and A. Lucas placed Mount Sinai at Jebel Shaykh Muhammad Bagir (Jebel Baghir or Jebel an-Nuur), just northeast of Aqaba.[60] Nielsen put Mount Sinai at Petra.[61] Identifying the Strait of Tiran as the body of water in which Pharaoh's army drowned, and pointing to the blackened summit of Jebel al-Lawz as possible evidence of a divine conflagration, Larry Williams identifies this mountain in northwestern Arabia as Mount Sinai.[62] C. C. Robertson placed Mount Sinai between Wadi 'Araba and Wadi Ithm in northwest Arabia, admitting that its location cannot be determined exactly, but "it was probably one of the lower spurs of the as-Sera ridge of Mount Seir."[63] He cited the apostle Paul as proof that Mount Sinai is in that vicinity: "Now Sinai is a mountain in Arabia . . ." (Galatians 4:25). Others who place Mount Sinai in northwestern Arabia argue that the land of Midian described in the Bible corresponds with Midian as it is known today; however detractors point out that Antoninus Martyr (c. 530 A.D.) placed the city of Pharan—assumed to be modern Feiran in southwest Sinai—in "the land of Midian."[64]

Those who argue for a northern route of the Exodus presume that Mount Sinai must be one of the lower peaks of northern Sinai or southern Israel. Claude Jarvis identified Jebel Halaal in northeastern Sinai as Mount Sinai.[65] Geographer Menashe Har-El regards diminutive 618-meter Jebel Sin Bisher just 50 kilometers southeast of Suez as the Holy Mountain.[66] Other "true" Sinais in the north are Jebels Kharif, Yeleq, and Maghara.[67]

Most Biblical geographers believe that Mount Sinai is one of the high peaks of the southern Sinai Peninsula. They assume that the fleeing Israelites took the southern route and that Sinai must be an imposing peak along that route. They have combed the region with the basic topographical sketch Edward Robinson made in 1849.[68] Mount Sinai must have three elements:

1. A mountain-summit, overlooking the place where the people stood. 2. Space sufficient, adjacent to the mountain, for so large a multitude to stand and behold the phenomena on the summit. 3. The relation between this space where the people stood and the base of the mountain must be such, that they could approach and stand at the nether part of the mount; that they could also touch it, and that further bounds could appropriately be set around the mount, lest they should go up into it, or touch the border of it.[69]

Using these criteria most scholars have identified either Jebel Serbal or Jebel Musa as Mount Sinai, while a few have chosen Jebel Katarina.

Jebel Serbal is a beautifully wild, many-pinnacled mountain dominating the landscape around Wadi Feiran. On his 1845 journey Richard Lepsius visited both Serbal and Musa and concluded that the former was Sinai, adding that "On this point I find all the most important voices unanimous."[70] John Lewis Burckhardt, Flinders Petrie, and Carl Ritter were among those voices.[71] Naturalist Edward Rüppell climbed the 2,070-meter peak in 1831 and observed that the Bedouins of the vicinity who had revered the mountain "from time immemorial" still took off their shoes to pray at the summit. Its ruggedness, its geographical position, and its importance in Bedouin faith made it a most likely Mount Sinai: "The wild, craggy rocks of Serbal, and the isolated position of this mountain is much more remarkable and grand than any other group of mountains in Arabia Petraea, and it was peculiarly adapted for the goal of religious pilgrimages."[72] Nabataean inscriptions dating to the second and third centuries B.C.E. in the Jebel Serbal region may support the notion that pilgrims came here between the presumed time of the Exodus and the arrival of Christian anchorites in the region.[73]

Despite its many competitors Jebel Musa endures as the favorite Mount Sinai of Biblical geography. With his criteria of what the mountain must look like Edward Robinson insisted that to the exclusion of all other possible plain-mountain combinations in south Sinai only the Plain of ar-Raaha adjacent to Jebel Musa could have accommodated the Israelites, whose number he estimated at 2 million.[74] Edward Hull, too, was satisfied that this "traditional Sinai in every way meets the requirements of the narrative of the Exodus."[75] Charles Wilson, Edward Palmer, and Dean Stanley agreed. Hull found the capacity of the Plain of ar-Raaha especially persuasive: "For myself I have never had a doubt, after traversing this great amphitheatre leading up to the very base of the stupendous granite cliff of Ras Sufsafeh, that here indeed was the camp, and there the mount from whence Jehovah gave forth His laws amidst the thunders and earthquakes which caused the mountain to rock from its foundations."[76] Biblical scholars have disagreed about which extremity of Jebel Musa is the summit where Moses met with God. Robinson identified the place of the giving of the Law as Ras Safsaafa, the lower western summit of Jebel Musa overlooking the Plain of ar-Raaha.[77] Hull disagreed with Robinson's thesis that the spot must be visible from the Israelites' camp. He argued that the peak of Mount Sinai is in fact the highest summit of Jebel Musa, which Ras Safsaafa blocks from view from ar-Raaha. This "is in entire accordance with the account in the Bible. Once Moses and Joshua had disappeared in their ascent of the mount behind this rock they were lost to view."[78] Geographer Carl Ritter and Reverend W. Arthur agreed with Robinson that the place of the lawgiving must have been visible from the camping ground, but they, too, favored Jebel Musa's highest eastern summit as the sacred spot. The camping ground was not the Plain of ar-Raaha, they argued, but the basin of Wadi Asba'iyya at the eastern foot of Jebel Musa.[79] Reverend Arthur observed that the vegetation on the Plain of ar-Raaha was not as rich as in Wadi Asba'iyya; therefore, the latter certainly was where the Hebrew multitudes kept their flocks.[80]

This scholarly debate over Mount Sinai has always been lively. In the nineteenth century the experts undertook considerable hardship to reach southern Sinai. They walked hallowed ground with Bible in hand. Each experienced a special sense of revelation about the exact places where the divine events occurred. Each was unyielding in his convictions and attacked the others for not yielding to his. Edward Robinson and Dean Stanley, for example, reportedly were so certain that the Plain of ar-Raaha was the camping place that they would not set foot in rival Wadi Asba'iyya. Reverend G. S. Drew was indignant: "It is a shame for men like Robinson and Stanley to profess to inform the public about valleys which they have never traversed, but have judged of them from the tops of mountains."[81] The scholarly pilgrims heaped scorn on those like Carl Ritter who identified the places of Sinai from maps and manuscripts alone. "Only those who have visited personally this wonderful region can realize to their full extent the harmony between the narrative and the physical conditions present to his view," Edward Hull huffed.[82]

One of the most paradoxical dimensions of scholarship on the geography of Mount Sinai and the Exodus is an enduring compulsion to explain scientifically the supernatural events of the Bible. The following arguments provide only a sample of a vast literature dedicated to this effort.

A celestial mishap explains the plagues and the rain of manna. Jupiter ejected a large comet-like object which later became Venus, explained physician and psychoanalyst Immanuel Velikovsky. Earth passed through the object's tail as Moses was preparing for the Exodus, and a chain of cataclysms—the plagues—began. Reactions between carbon and hydrogen from the comet's tail produced carbohydrate material that rained down as manna.[83]

The burning bush (*sneh*) was a real shrub so rich in natural oils that the sun set it aflame. Philip Haney misidentified the reputed burning bush in the Monastery of St. Katherine as the fraxinella or "gas plant" (*Dictamnus albus*), explaining "the bush produces an oil so volatile that it can be ignited by the sun. The oil quickly burns up but the bush itself is not damaged."[84] This plant is apparently unknown in the Sinai today. The burning bush has also been identified as *Loranthus acacia*, a crimson-flowered parasite of acacia trees "which, when the sun shines through it, may look like flaming fire."[85] Alternatively the desert may have played a perceptual trick on old Moses: "It is possible to imagine a situation in which refracted light waves transmitted an image of a flame burning in some distant place and superimposed the image onto the *sneh* that Moses saw. The singularly low probability of such a coincidence puts it in the category of a miracle."[86]

The parting of the sea to allow the Israelites to pass and the subsequent demise of Pharaoh's army had a meteorological basis. Oceanographer Dr. Doron Nof of Florida State University in Tallahassee and atmospheric scientist Dr. Nathan Paldor of the Hebrew University in Jerusalem proposed that at the shallow northernmost extremity of the Gulf of Suez winds of 40 knots (74 kilometers per hour) blowing steadily for ten to twelve hours might have pushed water a mile or two to the south, causing a 10-foot drop in sea level and exposing a large swath of sea floor over which the Israelites passed and on which Pharaoh's troops were drowned. "Our physical and mathematical analysis shows that both values for the drop in sea surface height and withdrawal distance for the water are more than sufficient to cause the calamity that befell the Egyptians," Dr. Paldor concluded.[87] Weather phenomena also explained for Claude Jarvis the pillar of cloud by day and pillar of fire by night which led the Israelites: "In Sinai when heavy weather is impending there is a most remarkable cloud formation—namely, a huge column of cumulus, black in the center with hard white edges. This column, which begins at the sky-line and is most impressive, extends to the zenith, constantly emitting lightning, and at night is an intermittent blaze of fire. This cloud . . . to the superstitious Israelites no doubt appeared to be a sign from the Almighty to show them the way. It also proved their salvation, as it heralded the heavy weather that accounted for the engulfing of the host."[88]

Moses used an old trick to obtain water from rock: "The limestone rock in Sinai has been known—and Moses may have known this from his previous sojourn in Midian—to give forth water when struck, the broken surface exposing the soft and porous rock underneath," explained Harry Orlinsky.[89] In the Sinai Jarvis witnessed one of his own camels corpsmen accomplish this miracle by striking weathered limestone with a shovel.[90]

Mount Sinai could not be a very high or steep mountain; if it were, Moses at his venerable age could not have conquered it. Lord Lindsay was certain old Moses could not possibly have ascended formidable Jebel Musa two or three times a day; therefore, Mount Sinai must be Jebel Munayja, the little hill at the head of Wadi ad-Dayr.[91] Har-El concurred that neither Moses nor his elder brother Aaron nor seventy elders could have negotiated the high peaks of Jebels Musa, Serbal, and Baghir; therefore, none of these is Mount Sinai.[92] C. C. Robertson agreed: "The idea of Moses with the seventy elders of Israel scaling this great height is not a reasonable proposition. It is accessible to ibex and the wild goat, but ceremonial dignity is not associated with violent physical exertion."[93] Lepsius could not agree with Edward Robinson that Ras Safsaafa is the peak of Mount Sinai, because it would have been too steep for the octogenarian to climb.[94]

Jebel Musa cannot be Mount Sinai because its granite would be too hard for God to carve the commandments into; therefore, Mount Sinai must be made of softer sedimentary rock such as found at geographer Har-El's Mount Sinai, Jebel Sin Bisher.[95] Whatever rock they were made of the tablets must not have been highly prized, Emmanuel Anati suggests: "The act of breaking the tablets he had received from God makes one wonder about the actual value of these tablets."[96]

As for the pyrotechnical theophany on Mount Sinai: the mountain must have been a volcano, probably in geologically active northwestern Arabia. "It is on this assumption, and on this only, that the Pillar of Cloud and Fire, the lightnings, thick smoke, convulsive tremblings, and flaming summit of the mountain, and, finally, the mysterious Tables of the Covenant 'written by the hand of God,' are capable of any rational explanation," concluded Reverend W. J. Phythian-Adams. Mount Sinai is the volcano Hala al-Bedr on the table mountain of Jebel Tadra southeast of Tabuk, where "we find without difficulty the locality and the mountain we are seeking. In an extraordinary number of particulars, they fit precisely the conditions of Israelite tradition."[97] There is even a modern parallel to the ancients' reluctance to approach the mountain: Bedouins have regarded al-Bedr as a holy volcano ever since it "vomited fire and stones, destroying many Bedouins and their camels and sheep. Since then the Bedouins have been afraid to ascend this volcano and they drive away their animals, not allowing them to graze upon the slopes or upon the gray ridge of Tadra."[98]

The apparent theophany on Mount Sinai may actually have been an elaborate theatrical event staged by Moses' in-laws, the nomadic Kenites, to boost Moses' standing among his people: "The descent of the god of fire, needed for the authority of Moses, was arranged by the Kenites for a fixed day. On this day no one was allowed to go unto the Mountain. They kindled one or more big fires, causing much smoke. They hammered on metal plates, moved torches in the smoke, and gave the signal to bring the people to the nether part of the Mount by blowing a trumpet (shofar) repeatedly, louder and louder. As Moses spoke, he was answered by the sound of gongs. The purpose was to hold the people in awe."[99]

These explanations are ironic. They strip away the wonder that must have called their proponents to investigate the mountain in the first place. Sinai is a mountain of faith and mystery.

Three

♦

THE
HEAVENLY
CITIZENSHIP

One of the great spiritual themes in the Judaeo-Christian and Muslim traditions is the holy man's transformation in the wilderness. From the flaming bush at Horeb God revealed His name to Moses and assigned his mission, changing the course of his life from fugitive shepherd to patriarch and liberator. After God made the covenant with Moses atop the desert mountain of Sinai the prophet descended a new man, his face glowing with an unearthly radiance. With the power of the Spirit in Him after His ordeal in the desert, Christ returned to Galilee, where His reputation "spread through the countryside . . . and everyone glorified him" (Luke 4:14–15). Muhammad retreated for weeks at a time to a cave on the rugged desert mountain of Hiraa near Mecca to contemplate and eventually to hear the Angel Gabriel recite the words of God. "And now, behold! A dazzling vision of beauty and light overpowered his senses . . . And his soul was filled with divine ecstasy. When this passed, and he returned to the world of Time and Circumstance and this world of Sense, he felt like one whose eyes had seen a light of dazzling beauty, and felt dazed on his return to common sights. The darkness now seemed tenfold dark; the solitude seemed tenfold empty." [1]

These transformations of spirit and perception did not come easily. The desert is a difficult environment. It is "the place where jackals live" (Psalms 44:19). It is a land of evil spirits like "the Beast" (Psalms 72:9). "When an unclean spirit goes out of someone it wanders through waterless country looking for a place to rest, and cannot find one," Christ said (Matthew 12: 43). There is hunger, temptation, and self-doubt. Moses and Christ were weakened by fasting. Christ was "put to the test by the devil" in the desert where the Spirit led Him (Matthew 4:1–2). Muhammad thought he was going mad at his first revelation at Hiraa. If prophets might fail in the desert, ordinary people would certainly suffer there. "And the whole community of Israelites began complaining about Moses and Aaron in the desert, and said to them, 'Why did we not die at Yahweh's hand in Egypt, where we used to sit round the flesh pots and could eat to our heart's content! As it is, you have led us into the desert to starve this entire assembly to death!' " (Exodus 16:2–3).

Paradoxically the desert is also a land of newfound freedom, of rebirth from deprivation and of measured nurturing. In this difficult setting Moses found a guardian: "In the desert he finds him, in the howling expanses of the wastelands. He protects him, rears him, guards him, as the pupil of his eye" (Deuteronomy 32:10). The Israelites never had too much in Sinai, but their diet of manna and quail was never too little either.[2] Near the end of his life Moses reminded his people of the desert's role in shaping them:

> *Remember the long road by which Yahweh your God led you for forty*
> *years in the desert, to humble you, to test you and to know your inmost heart—*
> *whether you would keep his commandments or not. He humbled you, he made*
> *you feel hunger, he fed you with manna which neither you nor your ancestors had*
> *ever known, to make you understand that human beings live not on bread alone*
> *but on every word that comes from the mouth of Yahweh. The clothes on your back*
> *did not wear out and your feet were not swollen, all those forty years.*
>
> (DEUTERONOMY 8:2–4)

The desert life of the Exodus would come to be remembered as a lost ideal, a time when Israel was a child.[3] Christ would recall the lesson of the desert of the Exodus to answer the devil who tempted Him: "Human beings live not on bread alone, but on every word that comes from the mouth of God" (Matthew 4:4).

Christian monasticism is a spirituality of the desert, founded on the proposition that because the desert is a hard place one might meet God there.[4] The Monastery of St. Katherine at Mount Sinai was established upon a tradition of seeking the most remote and blessed places of that spiritual realm.

"A LAND SET BY ITSELF"

The word "hermit" comes from the Greek *eremites*, "he who lives in the desert."[5] Monasticism arose and first flowered in the spiritual heartland of the Judeo-Christian and Muslim world, the desert within a 300-kilometer

radius of Jebel Musa. Conditions there are ideal for solitude, contemplation, and deprivation. Water, vegetation, and even shade are in short
supply. There is extreme heat and bitter cold. There are threatening animals. People are few. Most importantly it is quiet. The desert is the quietest
realm on Earth, rivaled only by the icy polar regions. Resting after strenuous walking in Sinai and the Eastern Desert I would hear only the inner
sounds of my pulse. In full rest I would listen for any sound at all and hear
nothing. I grew disassociated physically and perceptually from what I had
been accustomed to in urban living. Returning to the cities of the Nile I
found noise overwhelming. Every step felt like a large, quick stride. I felt
improved.

The early hermits who went into the wilderness were pioneers redis-
covering human senses. One of the first to enter this new world was the
Egyptian St. Anthony (251–356 A.D.). At about age twenty Anthony had
been inspired by Christ's instruction to the rich young man, "If you wish
to be perfect, go and sell your possessions and give the money to the poor,
and you will have treasure in heaven; then come, follow me" (Matthew
19:21).[6] Near the Nile the sexagenarian ascetic had been "beset by many"
and could not find the peace he needed for prayer and contemplation. As
he sat by the river one day considering ways to extricate himself,

> *a voice came to him from above, "Antony, whither goest thou and wherefore?"*
> *"Since the multitude permit me not to be still, I wish to go into the upper Thebaid*
> *on account of the many hindrances that come upon me here, and especially because*
> *they demand of me things beyond my power." "But if you wish really to be in*
> *quiet, depart now into the inner desert." And when Antony said, "Who will*
> *show me the way for I know it not?" immediately the voice pointed out to him*
> *Saracens about to go that way. So Antony approached, and drew near them, and*
> *asked that he might go with them into the desert. And they, as though they had*
> *been commanded by Providence, received him willingly. And having journeyed*
> *with them three days and three nights, he came to a very lofty mountain, and at*
> *the foot of the mountain ran a clear spring, whose waters were sweet and very cold;*
> *outside there was a plain and a few uncared-for palm trees. Antony then,*
> *as it were, moved by God, loved the place, for this was the spot which he*
> *who had spoken with him by the banks of the river had pointed out.[7]*

The place Anthony loved was the labyrinthine 1,200-meter-high South
Galala Plateau in Egypt's northern Eastern Desert. Beginning around
313 A.D., he spent much of the remainder of his life in what he called "the
inner mountain," apparently well within the deeply dissected plateau.[8] In
1983 I came across the retreat of an early hermit in the plateau interior.

The cave resembles written depictions of Anthony's "inmost shrine."[9] It is yet another world removed from the isolated grotto on the north escarpment of the plateau which is popularly identified today as Anthony's refuge. The cave is in a wildly beautiful wadi of water-polished marble. There are wild fig trees and abundant ibex and sand partridges. In a nearby cave I found remains of many leopards, some of which may have lived in Anthony's time. The great cats made an impression on early anchorites in the area. Monks knew the plateau as Mount Climax and Mount Kolzim, but also "Leopard Mountain" (Jebel Nimora).[10] The area's natural history acquired a dreadful reputation, providing the challenging spiritual habitat which hermits sought. Anthony's biographer wrote that demonic animals tormented and tempted the saint: "As he was watching in the night the devil sent wild beasts against him. And almost all the hyenas in that desert came forth from their dens and surrounded him; and he was in the midst, while each one threatened to bite . . . Surely it was a marvellous thing that a man, alone in the desert, feared neither the demons who rose up against him, nor the fierceness of the four-footed beasts and creeping things, for all they were so many."[11] Anthony made peace with the animals. Along with his extraordinary physique despite sustained fasting, this suggested to observers that Anthony had truly returned to Adam's natural condition before the fall.[12]

Among the beasts which taunted Anthony was a half-man half-ass that tempted him to return to civilization.[13] But civilization would find Anthony. In the broad Wadi 'Araba fronting the plateau's northern escarpment Anthony permitted his followers to erect the individual tents, perhaps resembling those of contemporary nomads, that served as their cells. Anthony's words about the blessings of solitude had "persuaded many to choose the solitary life; and so henceforth there arose monasteries even in the mountains, and the desert was made a city by monks coming out from their own and enrolling themselves in the heavenly citizenship."[14] This "city" was a prototype of the monastery, a colony of anchorites, literally "those who withdraw."[15]

"What leads a man to live in the middle of nowhere for the sake of prayer?" I heard a teacher from West Virginia ask one of St. Katherine's monks. It was certainly not heredity. Father Makarios' twin brother was a blackjack dealer in a Nevada casino. The monk paused and responded: "Some men feel the Call in a strange, different way than other men do, and must take extraordinary steps to remove the buffers and distractions separating them from God." Explaining to me that men become monks today for the same reasons articulated by Mount Sinai's sixth-century saint John Klimakos, Father Makarios said:

There are three reasons why a person goes into a monastery: one is to be near to God, the other is to recognize your sinfulness, and the other one is to be in Paradise. If you are in the monastery for any other than those three reasons, you do not belong there. We are at all times in our minds in remembrance of God. Everything we do transposes itself into a God-like mentality or state of mind, if that is possible to do. We also know that the human mind wanders. Those who achieve that God-like state of mind—those people are the saints.

St. Katherine's monks believe they are following the God-seeking paths of Anthony and John the Baptist. "The first monk was St. John the Baptist, who went out into the desert and prepared himself to come back into society and announce the coming of the Messiah," Father Makarios explained. "'Someone is coming greater than I,' St. John said, 'prepare yourself.' That idea transposed itself into monasticism. So the fathers of the church in the tradition see St. John as the paragon of monasticism." St. John established a pattern of simplicity and denial: he "wore a garment made of camel-hair with a leather loin-cloth round his waist, and his food was locusts and wild honey" (Matthew 3:4). Father Makarios described St. Anthony as "the *par excellence* example of monasticism as far as contemporary people are concerned," but added that "Anthony was simply following the example of St. John the Baptist." Their discipline, deprivation, and asceticism in the desert wilderness were exemplary, but Father Makarios suggested theirs was a difficult path to follow today:

Monks would gain reputations because they were spiritual people. You and I have a very hard time understanding what it means to be spiritual because we don't know. We never came across anybody who was spiritual, to be able to understand, to intellectualize and experience what it means, what this terminology means. We just don't have the experience at all. So when people came along who were gifted and able to extricate themselves from the hubbub of society, they had to go off by themselves. They could not maintain their spiritual dignity in the world by staying close to the people. They had to get away. So they would wander off. These days you cannot go anywhere and be by yourself from that point of view, using those concepts, because the world is just too small anymore.

St. Katherine's monks are successors to a pattern of settlement that began to be established in the fourth century as increasing numbers of ascetics wandered into the wilderness to get away. In mainland Egypt, Sinai, and the Judean Desert the most dedicated and admired ascetics, beginning with Anthony, became "gurus" surrounded by disciples.[16] Anthony's biographer portrayed an impromptu community in the South Galala area that became, by the will of its citizens, a spiritual paradise set in the wilderness:

> So their cells were in the mountains, like tabernacles, filled with holy bands
> of men who sang psalms, loved reading, fasted, prayed, rejoiced in the hope of
> things to come, laboured in almsgiving, and preserved love and harmony one
> with another. And truly it was possible, as it were, to behold a land set by itself,
> filled with piety and justice. For then there was neither the evil-doer, nor the in-
> jured, nor the reproaches of the tax-gatherer: but instead a multitude of ascetics;
> and the one purpose of them all was to aim at virtue. So that any one beholding
> the cells again, and seeing such good order among the monks, would lift up his
> voice and say, "How goodly are thy dwellings, O Jacob, and thy tents, O Israel;
> as shady glens and as a garden by a river; as tents which the Lord hath pitched,
> and like cedars near waters."[17]

Such loose-knit communities formed the cores of what would become monasteries. Most began as an unwalled, dispersed community of ten to twelve recluses, the "cell-dwellers" (*kelliotai*), who lived solitarily in their individual cells but met on weekends for mass and communal prayer at a central place consisting of a church and service buildings, often inhabited by an abbot (*hegumen*) and steward (*oikonomos*). This arrangement, which provided for the material and security needs of its members, was called a *laura* or "lane," probably after the paths connecting the hermits' distant cells with the central church.[18] By the fifth century the prototype of the monastery, the coenobium, had developed as a preparatory center for and alternative to the laura. The coenobium was a walled enclosure in which monks worked, prayed and ate communally, and sheltered the needy. There was less opportunity for contemplation in the coenobium, so many of its inhabitants aspired to move on to the laura. Only those who had thrived through a long period of training in the coenobium were allowed to do so.[19]

Inevitably it became increasingly difficult to live the reclusive, contemplative, God-nearing life that the paragons of monasticism had. One problem was certainly logistical. In the deserts of Sinai, Palestine, and mainland Egypt adequate water supplies and food sources were few and dispersed. Competition for choice hermitage sites grew. In the fourth century a monk from Feiran reportedly visited the monk Sisoeis at the retreat of St. Anthony in the Eastern Desert, boasting that he had not seen a human being in ten months. Sisoeis replied that it had been eleven months since he had seen one himself.[20] Before long the wilderness was more crowded and sightings of people were more frequent. "And the farther away they got, the more people would have the tendency to follow them," Father Makarios explained. The hermits must have resented the world closing in on them. In about the year 400 a devout Italian pilgrim named Postumianus admired the resolve of those few men who still kept the world at bay:

> *I saw the Red Sea, and Mount Sinai, whose summit almost touches heaven and is utterly unapproachable. In the midst of its remote valleys, it is said, there is an anchorite: I tried long and hard to find him, but could not set eyes upon him. For close on five years now he has been far from all human intercourse, and knows no clothing except that, by a special gift of grace from above, he covers his nakedness with the hair of his head. Everytime the monks wished to visit him, he made off with all speed to trackless places, and shunned all human encounter. Five years before, I was told, he showed himself to a single person who, as I believe, had deserved this visitation by the strength of his faith. On this occasion, when asked the question, why in fact he so strenuously shunned mankind, he answered the visitor by saying that he who receives visits from men, cannot expect to be visited by angels. Hence the opinion has spread, not without reason, among many, that that holy man is visited by angels.*[21]

As the monastic movement matured the communal lifestyle became the norm. The occupation of hermit was frowned upon or at least became more difficult to undertake. Father Makarios noted that in view of the community structure of monastic life, it was ironic that the word "monk" derived from the Greek *monachos*, "a person who is alone." But, he said, there were good reasons for monks not to try to emulate the severe asceticism of their prototypes, and for abbots only rarely to grant permission for monks to become hermits:

> *Monasteries are very well organized. There is an infrastructure within the monastery itself, and because it is a shared existence nothing is done without permission. No person who is in a monastery for a very short period of time with very little experience within the parameters of monasticism is allowed to live alone by himself out in the wilderness. It just is not done because there are dangers involved. Not physical dangers. It is not a threat to the person's life from that point of view, but from a spiritual point of view.*

I asked whether it took an extra spiritual strength to be alone.

> *Of course it does. It takes time. You do not do it when you are young. There are all kinds of stories that can be told about monks who were young*

*who wanted to go and live off somewhere by themselves to try and become the
great spiritual lights of Christianity. They were not saints first of all. They were
idealistic in mentality. And the admonition is insanity. And it happens.
It happens inside the monasteries as well as outside. So a young person who is
not well-trained, not well-steeped in the traditions of monasticism and the
personal regimen for developing an ascetic life, is going to be in danger because of
it. So it is always older monks, with more experience, that is not age-wise but
seniority-wise, who do these things, these days.*

Today the Monastery of St. Katherine boasts only one hermit. Father
Adrianos lives much like the anchorites of the laura did, returning from his
retreat at the Monastery of St. Galaktion and St. Episteme on nearby Jebel
ad-Dayr to the Monastery of St. Katherine each Saturday night to pass that
evening and Sunday in prayer and communal meals with the monks, and
to obtain his week's provisions, including sardines, olive oil, and painting
supplies. Some of his peers believe Father Adrianos has spent too much of
his forty years in the Sinai alone and has succumbed to the dangers. He
speaks of a giant "cloud-sucking machine," which Israeli soldiers installed
soon after their occupation of the Sinai began in 1967, designed to reduce
rainfall in the peninsula. He insists he saw soldiers setting up the device,
but his fellow monks say he saw only Israeli soldiers firing flares in war
games.

However far they have diverged from their most austere origins, monasteries must be appreciated in relative terms as refugia from worldliness.
Monks still struggle to stave off the mental and spiritual distractions felt by
ordinary men, especially men of the urban "flesh-pots" of the world. Monasticism is a retreat to a different kind of city, a kind of "anti-city" established away from the worldly city.[22] Monasteries may, however, serve the
people of the city. In their communal isolation monks are supposed to
develop a unique and separate relationship with God before joining the
world again. The monk's paradoxical spiritual mission is "*a withdrawal in
order to return. A monk must first withdraw, and in silence must learn the
truth about himself and God. Then, after this long and rigorous preparation in solitude, having gained the gifts of discernment which are required
of an elder, he can open the door of his cell and admit the world from
which formerly he fled.*"[23] The accomplished monk may travel out to
meet the world. In the fourteenth century St. Sabas visited Palestine,
Mount Sinai, Anatolia, and Cyprus on a spiritual quest. Such odysseys
were not unusual in the Christian eastern Mediterranean.[24] Monks are also
required to allow the world in. Father Makarios spoke of their responsibility: "The monastery is there as much for other people as it is for yourself." Monks instruct that men do not live by bread alone. Guarding what

they see as its earthly portal, they remind people that the Kingdom of God is not of this world.

Although their mission was blessed, monasteries were populated by many people who were not motivated primarily by prayer and good deeds. Many early fourth-century monks of Sinai and Palestine were refugees from religious persecution in Egypt at the hands of then-pagan Romans. After Rome became Christian in 313 this pressure ceased, but there were new incentives for people to flee to the wilderness. Monasteries offered a better, easier, and more satisfying way of life to poor people, a shelter from taxation for those who suffered at the hands of oppressive collectors, and asylum for criminals.[25] Although the picture of early monastic society is not entirely pious, monks today emphasize as they must have then that spiritual outcome rather than original motivation is most important. Father Makarios spoke:

> *There were sociological reasons for why monks went into the desert. The people who became monastics in the early days, like St. Episteme and Galaktion, were in the desert as much to avoid paying taxes as they were there for Christ. There were three basic groups of people who became monastics. There were people who avoided taxation, who would escape into the desert because they were fairly assured that they would not be pursued. And taxation was a big problem. It was a major source of revenue under the Romans. Another group of people were people who were trying to avoid military service. They would flee into the desert because they would not get drafted. The Bedouins still do it. The other group were people who broke the law. They had secular reasons for getting away, but at the same time when they got into that environment with other people around them, who may not have had as colored or checkered a past as they might have had, their lives were affected, from a spiritual point of view. A lot of these people became saints. St. Moses the Egyptian was a brigand. He had a band of thieves who ran around with him attacking caravans. He fled, went into the desert and became a monk, and then was revered as a saint in the church. Galaktion and Episteme were avoiding paying taxes. These three characterizations of people—draft dodgers, tax evaders, and criminals—they were not the majority; they were the minority. People were in the desert for legitimate reasons, for spiritual growth: that is why they went there.*

Pilgrimage also helped fill the monasteries of the eastern Mediterranean region. Some pilgrims joined monasteries to further the spiritual blessings they began to experience on pilgrimage.[26] They had begun their journeys as ordinary and in some cases very sinful people. The monks of St. Katherine today recite this account of a prostitute turned ascetic to explain the legitimacy of the eremitical mission, regardless of the individual's origin:

*There was a prostitute named Mary in Alexandria in the fifth century. She saw a
lot of activity on the docks, and talked to the people there. They said they were
going to Jerusalem for the Feast of the Elevation of the Holy Cross, and she went
with them, working her way to Jerusalem on a boat. When she got there, all the
other pilgrims with great joy and great celebration were participating in the festivities, and they went into the Church of the Holy Sepulchre, where the cross was
kept. She could not go in the door. She was physically barred by some invisible
presence from going inside. And everybody else in the meantime was just passing
her, going around her on either side and going right in the door with no problem
whatsoever. The Virgin Mary appeared to her at the door and told her that she
could not go in because of her background. She was a working girl going to Jerusalem on a pilgrimage, making her living on the ships, getting there and having this
experience occur. Then she went off into the desert by herself where she remained
for forty years. The Virgin Mary had told her to take five altar breads with her as
a means of sustenance, and she used that bread for forty years. That is what she
ate for food. She was discovered at the end of that time by a certain monk from
another monastery nearby in the desert and he could not recognize her. Her body
was emaciated through fasting. And this monk found her at the end of the time,
and she said, "Come back here next year and bring me holy communion."
So he did and he found her in the same place at that time, and did not even
recognize her as being a female, because of the emaciation of her body from her
fasting, her asceticism. And then she said again, "Come back next year." When
he came back the second year and brought holy communion to her, she had died.
And the lions, the wild animals of the area who were caring for her, wrote her
name in the sand with their paws, "Mary," and they buried her.*

In telling this story today, monks emphasize the significance of their
predecessors' presence in Mary's wilderness:

*But what was the monk doing out there? He was from a monastery in the
Transjordanian Desert, near Jericho. The monks of this particular monastery
were sent out every year for the forty days of the great fast, the fast leading up to
the celebration of the resurrection of Christ. The monastery emptied: the abbot
would send all the monks away into the desert because the forty-day fast is taken
very seriously in the Orthodox Church as a period of fasting and penance. In order
to become more spiritually tuned-in the monks would go out by themselves for this
forty-day period and return for the celebration of the resurrection at the monastery.
So that is what he was doing out there, and that is when he bumped into her,
accidentally. He had no idea what was going to happen until he found her in the
desert. So that is what was going on.*

St. Mary the Egyptian became one of the most popular saints of eleventh-
and twelfth-century Europe.[27] Many who admired this sinful working

woman turned pilgrim and saint made pilgrimage to the place where tradition said she crossed the Jordan to enter the wilderness. It was the same place tradition held that John had baptized Christ.[28]

MONASTICISM AND MOUNT SINAI

From its origin in Anthony's Eastern Desert monasticism spread rapidly eastward into Sinai and the Levant. In 250 A.D. Dionysus of Alexandria reported that Egyptian Christians were fleeing from persecution into the Sinai, the wild frontier region the Romans knew as Palestina Tertia on the southwestern flank of Arabia Petraea or "Rocky Arabia."[29] Persecution was severe during the reign of Decius Quintus Traianus (249–251), when 144,000 Christians were reportedly killed in Egypt. A subsequent wave of persecutions took the life of St. Katherine, the namesake of the monastery that would be built at the foot of Jebel Musa.[30] Lacking Roman garrisons, Sinai was a logical and accessible place of retreat. Wadi Feiran at the base of Jebel Serbal had only the small Roman administrative post of Pharan, which Christian refugees skirted as they sought refuge farther south.[31] When the persecutions ceased, fertile and well-watered Feiran became the most attractive magnet in all Sinai for the monastically inclined. One of St. Anthony's disciples, Hilarion (291–371 A.D.), spent the years 360–363 in the area.[32] Many more inspired by Anthony's example would follow.

Feiran is a hospitable place and nearby Serbal is an imposing mountain. By the middle of the third century at least some Christians who took up residence in southern Sinai apparently regarded Serbal as the Mountain of God. But Jebel Serbal was a short-lived Mount Sinai, eclipsed by the growing belief that Jebel Musa was the true mountain. There may have been rival Mount Sinais for some time, with Coptic Egyptians believing in Jebel Serbal while Syrian and Byzantine Christians turned to Jebel Musa.[33] Today's monks of St. Katherine believe their predecessors recognized Jebel Musa as the true Mount Sinai in the fourth century. Support for this view may be found in a record of Julianus Sabus, a Syrian monk from Osrhoene who around 360 A.D. with a few devoted followers traveled from Odessa to Jebel Musa to build a chapel on its peak.[34] Ammonius described a settlement of monks at the foot of the mountain in about 372, and in about 400 the pilgrim Etheria visited this site "lying under the slope of the mount of God."[35] In 449 Nilus likewise depicted this settlement as being "at the foot of the mountain where God conferred with the people."[36] About a century later when the Emperor Justinian founded a great monastery at the foot of Jebel Musa the mountain's status as Mount Sinai for most Christians was forever sealed, and the cultural fulcrum of Christian life in the peninsula shifted there.[37] Until Islam swept into the peninsula in the seventh century Feiran nevertheless persisted as a large Christian community and as the Episcopal See of Sinai.[38] One of St. Katherine's monks explained to me that there were so many hermits living "like mice" in the area's caves that the wadi was named after them; *fayraan* in Arabic means "mice."

How Jebel Musa came to be Mount Sinai for Christian monks is not clear. John Lewis Burckhardt concluded that the move was strictly strategic; the more remote Jebel Musa was more defensible than Wadi Feiran, so that Jebel Serbal lost the honor of being Mount Sinai.[39] Menashe Har-El, too, speculates that Christians could not defend Feiran from Muslims and so transplanted their holy places to Jebel Musa.[40] Daniel Silver supposed that Jebel Musa's identification as Mount Sinai was "probably based on little more than the vision of a desert monk who had settled himself near the spot and had a revelation that this was the famous Mount Sinai where Moses had spoken with God. Others heard of his vision, and soon the height came to be named Jebel Musa. Centuries later an established order of monks learned of the tradition, found that place able, and built here their fortress monastery."[41] The monks of St. Katherine consider such explanations cynical, even heretical. They say that trustworthy Bedouin oral tradition has provided them with the uninterrupted truth about Sinai's holiest places:

> *The first monks coming to this area did not know where these sites were. They knew they wanted to find them, if they could, but they did not know exactly where they were. They were instructed about these locations by the Bedouins themselves, whose ancestors were the eyewitnesses to the events of the Exodus. Of course they had no written language. The only means they had of obtaining any historical record was by storytelling. So between the times of the events themselves, and the time the Christian monks showed up, all these sites were being cared for, at least were known about, by the Bedouins, who themselves had no religion whatsoever. And the Israelites themselves, not being much interested in this area, did not leave any shrines or markers anywhere to indicate where they had been or where they had not. They were very transient people at the time.*

Monks today say their predecessors knew with certainty they had found Mount Sinai when Bedouins showed them a very special bush at the foot of Jebel Musa. Its presence above all else distinguished this from other Mount Sinais; there was never a burning bush tradition at Serbal or elsewhere.[42]

The site that was to be occupied by the Monastery of St. Katherine at the foot of Jebel Musa was known for a long time as "the Bush." Ammonius mentioned the Bush as a settlement of ascetics in about 372. In about

380 the Palestinian monk Silvanis with a few followers came there from Scetis in Egypt's Wadi an-Natrun, and stayed for some time before moving on to Gaza.[43] By a unique living bush they regarded as the original burning bush, anchorites built a tower into which they could retreat when enemies threatened them.[44] They also constructed a church there dedicated to the Virgin Mary. A popular but probably untrue tradition relates that they built the tower and church in 330 at the order of Empress Helena, mother of Emperor Constantine, who visited the site and responded to monks' pleas for protection from marauding nomads.[45]

The tower and church were standing in about 400 A.D. when Etheria, a noblewoman from Spain or Gaul, visited Jebel Musa as a pilgrim to Mount Sinai. The buildings by the bush were the core of a laura: ascetics were scattered in the mountains around Jebel Musa, except on Saturdays and Sundays when they congregated by the bush to celebrate mass and exchange provisions.[46] Etheria described the setting:

It was necessary for us to come out at the head of the valley, because there were very many cells of holy men there, and a church in the place where the bush is, which same bush is alive to this day and throws out shoots. That is the bush . . . out of which the Lord spake in fire to Moses, and the same is situated at that spot at the head of the valley where there are many cells and a church. There is a very pleasant garden in front of the church, containing excellent and abundant water, and the bush itself is in this garden. The spot is also shown hard by where holy Moses stood when God said to him: "Loose the latchet of thy shoe." [47]

These early monks at Jebel Musa thrived on orchard agriculture. Etheria depicted the industry of these early Christian horticulturalists:

As we were coming out of the church [on the summit of Jebel Musa], the priests of the place gave us eulogiae, *that is, fruits which grow on the mountain. For although the holy mountain is rocky throughout, so that it has not even a shrub on it, yet down below, near the foot of the mountains, around either the central height or those which encircle it, there is a little plot of ground where the holy monks diligently plant little trees and orchards, and set up oratories with cells near to them, so that they may gather fruits which they have evidently cultivated with their own hands from the soil of the very mountain itself.*[48]

These small, dispersed orchards were the forerunners of modern Bedouin gardens in the Sinai mountains. In high, often remote, soil-filled basins, hermits planted fruit and nut trees introduced from as far away as Greece and Anatolia. They practiced well-established techniques of grafting, selecting, and breeding these orchard crops. They dug wells to irrigate small crops of wheat, barley, and vegetables.⁴⁹ Today many of these remote refuges may be reached by stone stairways these pious gardeners assembled painstakingly. Nearby are the ruins of stone dwellings and natural rock shelters in which the hermits slept. There are living reminders of their tenure here, including the giant, still fruitful walnut tree of Wadi Abu Juruus, cleft in the middle as if struck by lightning.

The recluses may have lived relatively well around Jebel Musa. Their environmental circumstances were certainly friendlier than those of their counterparts across the Gulf of Suez in Egypt's Eastern Desert. Some measure of Jebel Musa's relative hospitality is provided in a fifteenth-century pilgrim's comparison of this good mountain with St. Anthony's dreadful South Galala Plateau:

> *It is said that in the country near the Red Sea there is a mount named Climax, where there are said to be women who are notable for long beards. These women pass their time most cruelly in hunting, have tigers instead of dogs, and breed leopards and lions; wherefore no one dares go near that mount for fear of those cruel women, who even charge naked against armed men and overthrow them, with the help of the beasts which they tame. No such beings dwell upon the holy mount, but only a few hungry wretches, all of whose rage can be quieted by the gift of a morsel of bread. I could tell many tales of the terrors of other mountains, which cause men to dread and fear them, whereas Mount Sinai is altogether free from all such; on the contrary, it is so desirable in all respects that it is pleasant to mankind, so much so that men of the highest ranks flock thither from the uttermost parts of the world. Let this suffice for Mount Sinai.⁵⁰*

Some writers point to the amenities of Jebel Musa to explain why this mountain came to be Mount Sinai. Four of the five centers of monastic settlement in the southern Sinai correspond with exposures of red granite at elevations between 1,200 and 2,000 meters above sea level, where human ecologists Aviram Perevolotsky and Israel Finkelstein noted agricultural potential was greatest. "If the red granite had not been exposed in these wadis, Jebel Musa might never have been identified as Mt. Sinai," they concluded.⁵¹ Father Makarios had read this. It made him angry.

The cultivated wilderness of Jebel Musa exerted a strong draw on a growing population of ascetics in the eastern Mediterranean region during the Byzantine era. In about the year 420 a wealthy man of Constantinople named Nilus left his position and family to answer Sinai's call:

> *A powerful longing towards Sinai seized me, and neither with my bodily eyes nor with those of the spirit could I find joy in anything, so strongly was I attracted to that place of solitude. Indeed, when love of a thing lays hold of the heart, it dis-*

tracts the heart from even the dearest persons, and leads it so powerfully away that
neither sorrow nor grief nor disgrace form any obstacle. Since the desire for solitude
drove me irresistibly, I took my two children with me and went to their mother,
gave one to her and kept the other with me, and told her of my decision. . . .
It was only with a heavy heart and with tears that she agreed.[52]

Men like Nilus who went to Mount Sinai praised the quality of environment there for what they called quietude or *hesychia*, named for the Armenian-born monk John Hesychast (454–559), who lived in seclusion for more than fifty years.[53] Monks insisted this special state of stillness existed only in isolation and solitude.[54] They struggled for spiritual perfection in some of the most remote, wild, and beautiful places of the Old World: the Eastern Desert, Cappadocia, the Pontic Mountains, Mount Athos, and the Judean Desert. For quality of spiritual life no place would surpass Jebel Musa.

Four

◆

THE
MONASTERY OF
SAINT KATHERINE

A monk at the Monastery of St. Katherine told me that in the sixth century some of his predecessors protested the Byzantine Emperor Justinian's construction of the monastery, saying, "'Who needs this place? We can pray without these stone buildings and this big church.' Some of the monks complained about it and actually left." Why then was the monastery built? The monastery's official version is that marauding nomads identified as "Ishmaelite Arabs" or "Saracens" had tormented the monks, "plundering their food stores, invading and emptying their cells, and entering their churches where they devoured the eucharist."[1] Unable to tolerate this situation and mindful of Justinian's reputation as a great builder and defender of Christendom, monks at Mount Sinai petitioned the ruler to build them a defensible monastery. Justinian consented.

While pious concern for the monks' safety may have been one of Justinian's motives in building the Sinai monastery, he had greater strategic reasons. His realm of 527–565 A.D. stretched from Gibralter to Mesopotamia. Its eastern and southern flanks from Armenia to Egypt comprised a vulnerable frontier region which Justinian tried to secure by building fortresses to serve as defensive outposts and forward positions. Some of these fortresses were also monasteries in which monks served even if unwittingly as agents of empire. The Monastery of St. Katherine was one of these. Nearby Justinian also had monasteries built at Kolzim (Clysma, modern Suez) and at Raithu (modern at-Tur).[2] These filled an especially important role, because with the decline of the bishopric of Petra in the fifth century no outpost of Byzantium stood between Jerusalem and Cairo.[3]

The Monastery of St. Katherine is full of paradox. For such a small and remote place it has always commanded a surprising amount of global concern and influence. From prosperity to near-calamity the fortunes of this isolated monastery have been tied to events in Europe and the eastern Mediterranean region. Its isolated setting is at global crossroads, placing it to benefit and suffer with changes in world trade. Required to be men of few possessions, its inhabitants have been endowed with enormous communal wealth. They still lead frugal lives in what one observer described as the "most perfect relict of the 4th century left in the world," but not without a diesel generator, a telephone, a fax machine, a photocopy machine, tape cassette stereos, and shortwave radios.[4] They have been saints and scoundrels. These holy men and their timeless, otherworldly institution have reflected the realities of an uncertain and changing world.

A GREEK ISLAND

The monastery appears today much as it did on its completion in 565 A.D., when workers placed marble inscriptions in Greek and Arabic on the west wall: "This holy monastery was erected on Mount Sinai, where God spake unto Moses, by the humble king of the Romans, Justinian, unto the everlasting remembrance of himself and of his wife Theodora."[5] Defining an area of 70 by 80 meters or as today's monks reckon "about the size of a city block," the monastery's walls of native granite are 12 to 15 meters high and 2 to 4 meters thick.[6] The monastery has succeeded as a fortress. A large earthquake in 1312 failed to bring the structure down. Napoleon's forces rebuilt the wall's damaged upper portions in 1801.[7] Defenses included a cannon which visitors described and photographed as late as 1927.[8] As recently as 1909 it was difficult to get in and out of the place. Its main door, located in the western wall, was usually kept closed. From 1600 until about 1920, people and supplies were drawn in on a basket suspended on a 10-meter long, 6-centimeter thick rope from a windlass on the north wall.[9] This "first passenger elevator in the world" was put to use again for the 1954 film *The Valley of the Kings,* starring Robert Taylor and Eleanor Parker.[10]

The institution was consecrated as the Monastery of St. Mary. Monks today explain that this original name had a special relationship to its location: like the bush here that did not burn, the Mother of God was a virgin. The monastery wall enclosed the bush and the church and tower which the pilgrim Etheria described.[11] Justinian's builders converted the church to a basilica which would incorporate the area's holiest site, that of the bush itself. This structure was dedicated as the Basilica of the Transfiguration, its apse bearing a lovely mosaic of the appearance on Mount Tabor of Christ flanked by Moses and Elijah. The monastery, therefore, came to be known also as the Monastery of the Transfiguration. Monks today boast

The Monastery of
St. Katherine.
August 28, 1993.

that the basilica's doors are the world's oldest functioning doors and that they lead into the world's oldest active Christian church. A Greek inscription over the doorway invokes the sanctity of this site: "In this place the Lord said to Moses, I am the God of thy fathers, the God of Isaac, and the God of Jacob. I AM THAT I AM. This is the gate of the Lord: let the righteous enter in thereby." [12] Monks say the figures carved on the doors depict the animals and plants of Paradise described in the books of Genesis and Exodus. Woods used in the doors and other parts of the monastery came from the immediate environment and include date palm, poplar, cypress, almond, tamarisk, olive, acacia, and pistachio. [13]

The construction of this fortress-monastery in the Sinai wilderness was an extraordinary feat. Architects, workmen, and materials had to be dispatched from as far away as eastern Europe for the project. The monastery would be built to last. Anyone with an eye for the landscape might, however, question why it was built in the exact spot it was. The structure sits in a narrow valley trough and is vulnerable. Anyone armed with stones, arrows, or more sophisticated weapons can threaten the inhabitants from the heights above. Justinian's court historian offered a supernatural justification for not placing the monastery on Jebel Musa's peak: the Emperor Justinian "built this church, not on the mountain's summit, but much lower down. For it is impossible for a man to pass the night on the summit, since constant crashes of thunder and other terrifying manifestations of divine power are heard at night, striking terror into man's body and soul." [14] Not only is the monastery not situated high on a mountain, but it appears to sit unnecessarily low in a drainage. It is perilously close to a wadi bed that in times of exceptionally high rainfall becomes a river. Unlike the summit this site had water, but water sources were plentiful in less precarious places. There is a legend that Justinian had his legate Doulas beheaded for choosing the site so unwisely. [15] Why then here?

Strategic concerns were sacrificed in the interest of building the monastery around a sacred place, the site of the burning bush, which was situated unfortunately in a low place. One might imagine the architect and builders pleading unsuccessfully with the anchorites to allow them to transplant the living bush to some other location near the holy mountain. The monastery would have to enclose the bush where it grew and yet escape potential flash flooding. [16] So the monastery stands in an unlikely place, its northeastern corner reaching dangerously close to the floor of Wadi ad-Dayr to take in the burning bush.

The bush might not have survived a transplant to some distant place. The living shrub which monks today identify as the original burning bush is a specimen of *Rubus sanctus,* a water-loving perennial that thrives here only because of its proximity to a permanent water source. Its presence

betrays the monastery's good fortune of being compensated for an unfor-
tunate topographical situation by a generous endowment of water. Three
water sources, known as the wells of Moses, St. Helena, and St. Stephen,
are within the monastery walls, and a fourth is just outside the northern
wall. A nearby cistern collects rainwater that courses through monastery
alleys after rare storms. The water quality is good. After relying on "salt-
ish" sources on their journey from Gaza, Tuscan pilgrims arriving at the
monastery in 1384 praised its sweet water.[17] A spiderlike network of pipe-
lines introduces water into the monastery from more distant sources. One
pipeline follows a channel built by monks at least three hundred years ago
to carry water from a reservoir near the Basin of the Almond on western
Jebel Musa to the monastery far below, where it is stored in a cistern.[18]
Another storage tank atop the monastery's library holds water carried
6 kilometers by a twenty-year-old pipe from a prolific well in the monastery's garden in Wadi al-Arba'iin. Monks complain that the Jabaliya Bedouins often puncture this 8-centimeter metal pipeline to water their
livestock.

Water has provided sustenance to monastic life at Jebel Musa. Since its
founding the monastery's inhabitants, aided by their Bedouin employees,
have enjoyed a harvest of irrigated fruits and vegetables. Today the young
monk Dorotheus, working shoulder-to-shoulder with a full-time Jabaliya
gardener named Jimaya', tends an assortment of crops in the gardens just
west of the monastery. There are tomatoes, squash, wheat, oranges, wal-
nuts, peaches, apricots, figs, mulberry, and a struggling guava. The men
care for a number of olive trees, including some they planted recently with
stock imported from Crete. Spires of dark green cypress trees, some
brought from Mount Athos and Cyprus more than a thousand years ago,
tower incongruously against the native red rock.[19] The monastery complex appears like a Mediterranean isle in a Saharan sea.

On this Greek island the monks have usually led lives of comfortable
deprivation with occasional hard times. Late in the fourth century "their
aspect and also their discipline was like that of angels. Their bodies were
all of them very pallid, as one might say, incorporeal; for they possessed
nothing for the wants of the body; no wine, no oil, no bread was to be
found at once belonging to them, except a few dates, and what was suitable for them."[20] Tuscan pilgrims of the late fourteenth century depicted
the monks' lives as "strenuous and hard; each day they have a loaf . . .
Wine they drink not, nor do they eat meat."[21] Mid-nineteenth-century
travelers found them less abstemious, eating salt-fish, eggs, bread, and
boiled vegetables, and drinking date brandy and a "delicate wine" produced in Sinai.[22] In 1816 Burckhardt called the brandy, which monks dis-
tilled from dates grown in their gardens at at-Tur, "the only solace these

recluses enjoy."[23] The monks nevertheless enjoyed good health. "Nor did I trace in any of the brethren the least indication of want," wrote Tischendorf.[24] M. Léon de Laborde found the monks in unexpected condition: "When we entered the convent we were surprised, after having just quitted the desert, where we had seen only a wretched and unsettled people, to find the interior so neatly arranged and in such excellent order, and inhabited by so many cheerful and healthy looking monks."[25] Burckhardt credited the environment: "The excellent air of the convent, and the simple fare of the inhabitants, render diseases rare. Many of the monks are very old men, in the full possession of their mental and bodily facilities."[26]

Monks recognized resources in the Sinai flora and fauna. Hermits in particular had extensive knowledge about edible and other useful plants, in part through association with local nomads. In the Byzantine era hermits were known as "grazers" for their meager diet of dry bread, kidney beans, wild plants, and water.[27] As late as the 1820s travelers observed monks at Jebel Katarina exercising their knowledge of plants: "In the month of June, when the herbs are in blossom, the monks are in the habit of repairing to this and the surrounding mountains, in order to collect various herbs, which they dry, and send to the convent at Cairo, from whence they are dispatched to the archbishop of Sinai at Constantinople, who distributes them to his friends and dependents; they are supposed to possess many virtues conducive to health."[28] The monks have more recently helped impoverish plant life around the monastery. Father Good Angel recalled that when he came to the institution in 1928 there were many more trees and shrubs in the immediate environs. Over the years Bedouins cut these to supply the monastery's fuel needs.

On their desert island, many of St. Katherine's modern monks have lost touch with the natural environment surrounding them. Most lack wayfinding abilities and occasionally venture into the surrounding area with distressing results. In May 1989 two monks set out on foot for at-Tur and became lost. They credit their survival to a rescue by Bedouins. Most monks walk no farther than the summit of nearby Jebel Katarina. The monastery's only hermit has the most contact with nature. In his refuge perched high on the southwestern slope of Jebel ad-Dayr, Father Adrianos keeps a small garden and stocks a crowded bird feeder. But he is no modern St. Francis. He regards hyraxes and foxes as agricultural pests in his garden of tomatoes, squash, almonds, grapes, and carnations. He sets a steel trap for the fox and calls the hyrax "a destroyer." He complains of how the birds he attracts damage his grapes and olives.

As death comes the monks are ready. They lay the deceased to rest in a cemetery limited to six graves to conserve the precious soil of the monastery's garden. He enters the longest-occupied of the six graves. Monks

wash the bones of its former occupant and separate them into large
mounds of skulls and bones in the nearby charnel house. More distinguished brethren like St. Stephen remain whole in special niches in this
ossuary. The Jabaliya insist that not all of the bones in the charnel house
are those of monks. They explain that long ago the monks instructed their
Jabaliya employees to fetch the bones of all monks and hermits from distant
cells in the St. Katherine region. The Bedouins did so, but also brought
skeletal remains from many other burial sites, including pre-Christian
rockshade graves. Whomever the remains belong to, they serve monks and
visitors alike as a statement about the transitory nature of this life.

An image of a flourishing island independent and alone, filled with
monks living and dying in satisfied self-sufficiency, does not match the
reality of the Monastery of St. Katherine. Apart from water and garden
produce, the monastery derives little sustenance from its immediate environment. Circles of dependence upon the wider world begin right outside
the walls and have grown to include today the most distant points of the
globe. For both good and ill the monastery's fortune has been tied to
Europe and other faraway places by an odd connection with a young girl
from Alexandria.

THE REALM OF ST. KATHERINE

The Sinai monastery was well-known in the early Byzantine world as the
place of Moses' encounters with God, but after 1000 A.D. it become more
wealthy, renowned, and interdependent with the wider world from association with another sacred figure, St. Katherine. Born to a high-ranking
official of Roman Alexandria late in the third century A.D., Katherine
became a woman of exceptional intelligence ("all who saw and heard
Katherine marvelled at her scholarship"), appearance ("tall in stature, in-
comparably beautiful"), and character ("exceedingly kind").[29] Numerous
suitors sought her hand in marriage as she challenged her anxious relatives
to find a mate who would match her four reputed virtues of rank, wealth,
wisdom, and beauty. Katherine turned them all away as unworthy. Her
mother, who in this period of Christian persecution kept her faith secret,
introduced the girl to an ascetic living in the desert near Alexandria. The
holy man told Katherine, "I am acquainted with a unique Man who in-
comparably transcendeth all those attributes thou has mentioned and
countless others." In subsequent prayer and visions Katherine met and
mystically married Christ. The young convert became so zealous that she
tried to persuade the Emperor Maximanus, a notorious persecutor of
Christians, that he should forsake his idol-worship for the true God. Finding her attractive, the emperor met with her frequently until he grew tired

ΗΑΔΙΚΑ · ΤΕΡΙΝΑ

of her attempts to convert him, and imprisoned her. He invited 150 scholars and rhetoricians to match wits with his prisoner. She overwhelmed them with her faith and knowledge. The emperor had them executed. When Katherine, insisting that she was the bride of Christ, refused to marry Maximanus and renounce Christ the emperor ordered her execution. Her death was to be particularly gruesome: four wooden wheels

studded with steel blades and sharp spikes would mutilate the girl. But at
the execution an angel released her unharmed from the device, which
spun out of control and killed many pagan bystanders while others converted on the spot. Katherine would become the patron saint of clock-
makers, carnival ride attendants, carmakers, and others who work with
wheels.[30] The emperor would continue to insist she marry him, until on
November 25, 305, he finally had her beheaded successfully, "Whereupon,
that hour, her revered and precious relics were devoutly translated by holy
angels and deposited on Mt. Sinai in a secret place."[31]

According to the inhabitants of the monastery that would bear her
name, Katherine's body came to rest not on Mount Sinai (Jebel Musa),
but on the summit of a nearby mountain which they named and is still
known today as Mount Katherine (Jebel Katarina). There are conflicting
versions of when monks found her body and how long they allowed it to
remain on the mountaintop. In 1216 monks told the visitor Magister
Thietmar:

> A certain hermit who dwelt in another part of Mount Sinai from that on
> which the body of St. Katherine was laid by the angels, frequently saw, by day
> and by night, a light of great brightness in or near the place where the body lay.
> Wondering what it was, he went to the church at the foot of the mountain, and
> described the sight that he saw and the place where he saw it. The monks, after
> fasting, ascended the mountain, in a procession that was led by him. When they
> found the body, they greatly wondered who it was, whence it had come, and how it
> was taken there. As they stood there wondering, an aged hermit from Alexandria
> declared, like Habakkuk the prophet who spoke to Daniel, that the body had
> been brought to Sinai by the grace of God, and he assured those who doubted,
> that it was the body of the blessed Katherine, and had been carried there by angels.
> At his instigation, the bishop and the monks translated the body to the church
> because the place where it lay was quite inaccessible.[32]

According to other reports monks built a chapel on the summit of Mount
Katherine to house her remains, and until at least 1096 climbed the mountain to say mass and tap the healing oil of her bodily remains.[33] In about
the year 1025 a Sinai monk from Sicily named Simeon (or Pentaglossus for
his linguistic talents) climbed Mount Katherine to pray there and collect
some of the oil. He tilted the reliquary too far and three of Katherine's
fingers fell into it. Simeon had been charged with the monastery's routine
chore of traveling to Normandy and Brittany to collect alms from noble
benefactors, and he set out on his journey with Katherine's relics in hand.
Pirates attacked his ship but Simeon escaped overboard. He reached An-

tioch, traveled with pilgrims to Belgrade and Rome, and finally arrived in Normandy.[34] In the reliquary of Rouen's newly built Abbey of the Trinity he deposited Katherine's fingers.

The end of Simeon's odyssey with Katherine's remains marked a turning point in the Sinai monastery's career. Abbot Isambert of the Rouen church suffered terribly from toothache and was divinely advised to seek a cure from Katherine's relics. It worked. The Abbey of the Trinity became the Abbey of St. Katherine.[35] News of miracles spread as Katherine's remains continued to heal the sick. Her reputation and her relics grew. Small amounts of the precious oil were deposited in reliquaries in Montoire and in Paris' Sainte-Chapelle.[36] The spirit of Katherine counseled Joan of Arc. Churches, chapels, hospitals, and even an order of knights dedicated to Katherine spread throughout Europe. Consecrated in 1148, St. Katherine's Church stood near the Tower of London until it was razed in 1825.[37] King Louis built Paris' Church of St. Katherine in 1229. St. Katherine was the patron saint of the universities of Paris and Padua. In 1307 the Doge Pietro Gradenigo founded Venice's Festa dei Dotti in her honor.[38] With increasing success Sinai monks continued to seek donations in Europe, and growing numbers of Europeans made pilgrimage to far-off Sinai in homage to St. Katherine. By the twelfth century the Sinai monks had relocated Katherine's remains from the mountaintop to a golden casket in the monastery's basilica, and rededicated their institution as the Monastery of Saint Katherine.[39]

The Monastery of St. Katherine acquired the culture and doctrine of Byzantine Orthodox Christianity, but by virtue of its fame and its remote setting developed an extraordinary degree of autonomy. It stayed out of the fray that split the Roman and Orthodox churches in 1054 and retained good relations with Rome.[40] Nominally subject to the Orthodox Patriarch of Jerusalem until 1782 and still ordained by him, the monastery's archbishop and abbot in fact acts independently of the Patriarchates of Jerusalem, Constantinople, Tanta, and Alexandria.[41] Its relative neutrality and autonomy were enormously profitable to the Monastery of St. Katherine. It was not obliged to share the huge sums of cash and material wealth brought by pilgrims and knights during the Crusader period of the thirteenth century. Even the fall of Constantinople (1453) and then Sinai (1517) to the Turks did not stop the flow of income. The monastery did pay an annual tribute of three hundred ducats to the Turks, but this was more than offset by the two thousand ducats France's King Louis XI (1461–1483) and his successors granted the monastery each year. Queen Isabella of Spain (1474–1504), her successor King Phillip, Holy Roman Emperor Maximilian I (1493–1519), and the King of Hungary also gave generously. Every pilgrim to the monastery was compelled by tradition to place two ducats in the chest of St. Katherine.[42]

The monastery profited also from endowments of land granted by crusaders and others who had owned or conquered territory in the Near East. Fretellus of Antioch in about 1130 A.D. remarked that St. Katherine's monks "from the confines of Ethiopia to the utmost bounds of the Persians, were venerated in every tongue, possessing their property freely and quietly among themselves. They had cells throughout Egypt and Persia, around the Red Sea and Arabia, from which all they required flowed most liberally."[43] These "cells" were the Sinai monastery's *metochia* or "daughter-houses," which the monks today call "satellites." Eventually totaling 105 separate properties, these endowments were most extensive in the thirteenth century on the eve of the monastery's period of maximum prosperity. Four were in Sinai, 5 in mainland Egypt, 4 in Palestine, 2 in Syria, 3 in Lebanon, 6 in Cyprus, 28 in peninsular Greece, 13 on the Greek Islands, 4 in Crete, 11 in Turkey, 1 in Georgia, 1 in Kiev, 1 in Bessarabia (modern Moldova), 8 in Romania, 4 in Serbia, 2 in Bulgaria, 3 in Italy, 3 in France, and 2 in India.[44] These so-called "dependencies" supplied monks, money, and cultural wealth to a remote desert monastery that in fact depended upon them for its welfare.

The monastery's most important daughter-houses have always been in Crete. These were established through donations as early as the tenth century, but most date to 1203, when the Archbishop of Crete, "a lover of St. Katherine, the Virgin," bestowed local properties worth an annual income of four hundred ducats on the Sinai monks.[45] After the Venetians acquired Crete in 1204, archbishops of Sinai traveled to Venice to renew the doges' guarantees of the safety of the monastery's properties in Crete. After 1669, when the Turks occupied Crete, the monks obtained the good will of Istanbul. From its prosperous possessions in Crete the Sinai monastery took on a strongly Cretan ethnic and cultural character.[46] This heritage is prominent in the monastery's collection of some two thousand icons, often described as the world's oldest and largest.[47] The monastery escaped the iconoclasm that destroyed Christian art in Europe from 726–843 A.D., retaining an unsurpassed inventory that included about fifteen hundred Cretan icons and also Palestinian, Byzantine, and locally produced works.[48]

The cult of St. Katherine declined with the Reformation of the sixteenth century.[49] The Sinai monastery might have become poorer but for the intervention of Russia's czar, who from the "third Rome" assumed the role of Orthodoxy's protector. Petitioned in 1547 by a Sinai monk named Gregorius, Ivan the Terrible responded with gifts to the churches of Sinai and Alexandria. He also arranged for a caravan of food to be sent each year at his expense from Cairo to the monastery. Russian czars continued to bestow magnificent gifts on the monastery and on churches throughout the Orthodox world until World War I and the Russian Revolution. With those events the monastery's fortunes declined. Its properties in Russia, Serbia, Turkey, and Bessarabia were confiscated or closed.[50] The two *metochia* in Cyprus and one at Tripoli in Lebanon became casualties of war in the 1970s. Today the monastery's only remaining satellites are two in Crete, one on the Greek island of Zakynthos, three in peninsular Greece, one in Istanbul, two in mainland Egypt, and the monasteries of Feiran and at-Tur in the Sinai.[51]

The monastery's fortunes fluctuated with the career of East-West trade as well as with changing political events. When Medina's port of Djar was closed to Egyptian traders in 775 A.D. and the Egyptian port of Kolzim (Suez) silted up, the region's best port for exchanging Egyptian agricultural products and Eastern goods became Raithu, later known as Porta Santa Katerina (modern at-Tur). St. Katherine's monks at the Raithu monastery probably controlled the landing stage of this port and by the middle of the fifteenth century levied a 10-percent tax on goods shipped through it. The monastery's financial welfare received a serious blow when the Portuguese developed the sea route to India at the close of the fifteenth century. The Mameluke Sultan al-Ghuri was reportedly so disturbed by Portuguese disruption of the trade routes that had been so profitable to him that in a letter to the Pope in 1503 he threatened to destroy the Church of the Holy Sepulchre and the Monastery of St. Katherine unless the Church intervened on his behalf.[52] At-Tur did not regain any of its former glory until 1858, when the International Quarantine Board established a station there where westbound pilgrims returning from Mecca were required to lay over for forty-eight hours.[53]

Many of the flesh and blood needs of the Sinai community have historically been met by reliable, routinized contacts with Cairo. In 1816 John Lewis Burckhardt observed the monks receiving supplies on an irregular basis from Cairo.[54] In the 1920s visitors found them reliant on large imports from Egypt of corn, wheat, rice, and oil.[55] As recently as the 1950s Bedouin caravans organized by Father Good Angel transported these goods from the port of at-Tur to the isolated monastery. The monastery's principal food supplies now arrive by truck in a weekly delivery from its enclave on northeast Cairo's Midan adh-Dhaahir. The driver is the monastery's lawyer, Antonios. During the Israeli occupation of 1967–1980 the monastery established an office in Jerusalem to fulfill this supply function. To reach their Cairo property monks had to fly from Israel via Cyprus or Athens.

The monastery's welfare has always relied in part on resources scattered throughout the Sinai Peninsula. It is monks' lore, upheld nominally even today, that all land within a three-and-one-third-day camel ride from the monastery belongs to the monastery. In 1926 monks boldly told this to the Director-General of Egypt's Frontiers Administration, insisting they had the title-deeds to prove their claim.[56] In the mid-nineteenth century the monastery asserted rights to all palm and fruit trees on the Gulf of Aqaba coast.[57] I asked septuagenarian Father Good Angel what the monastery's property boundary is today. "It has no borders," he replied firmly, restating the ancient claim. The monks' mystical sovereignty over the Sinai land-scape was stated in an ancient tradition about a hidden monastery between Jebel Musa and at-Tur which no man could find, and to which some of St. Katherine's monks were miraculously transported.[58] In reality all that remain today of the monastery's Sinai properties are seven outlying estates: the gardens and chapels of the Monastery of the Forty Martyrs in Wadi al-Arba'iin on Jebel Musa's south slope; the gardens and chapels of the Mon-astery of the Holy Apostles or St. Apostolos (Arabic, al-Bustaan) and the Monastery of the Virgin Mary (Arabic, Dayr ar-Rabba) in the al-Milgaa basin west of Jebel Musa; the monastery and garden of the "Poor Doctors" Cosmas and Damianos (Greek, Anargyres; Arabic, Dayr Tala') in Wadi Tala', 4 kilometers west of the Monastery of St. Katherine; Dayr Rum-haan, between the Monastery of St. Katherine and Wadi Feiran; the con-vent in Wadi Feiran; and the Church and Monastery of St. George in at-Tur.[59]

The small number of monks and nuns now in the service of St. Kath-erine find it difficult to assert the monastery's sovereignty over these out-lying properties. Father Dorotheus commutes from the Monastery of St. Katherine to tend the Dayr Tala' garden several times a week. He rides there on a she-camel named "Diriisa" he purchased for fifteen hundred Egyptian pounds from a Suwalha Bedouin breeder in Wadi Feiran. He complains of the animal's temperament and once referred to it as a "son of a dog," warning me to keep out of biting distance. Nevertheless this animal and a donkey he bought at market in al-Ariish for seven hundred Egyptian pounds are indispensible to him and to the monastery. The donkey carries Dayr Tala's annual olive harvest back to the monastery, from where it is shipped to al-Ariish to be pressed. Two nuns who are siblings represent the monastery at the Feiran property. With the assistance of a Jabaliya Bed-ouin gardener and watchman, the sisters tend the convent's arbors of grapes, orange, grapefruit, pomegranate, Zizyphus fruit, olives, and dates. One of the nuns, Constantia, is a talented painter who replicates the mon-astery's icons on occasional demand for about $200 per work.

The monks of St. Katherine believe that after centuries of tolerance and respect from ruling Muslim authorities they are now being subjected to official hostility. They say the Egyptian government is simply confiscating the lands which belong by tradition to the monastery. One monk reported that government officials challenged them to "prove that the land within three days' camel ride of the monastery is yours." The monastery could not, this monk claimed, "because there were no documents: there were only traditions. So the government said, 'You can have 60 meters beyond the monastery gate only.'" The monks claim that their properties and rights have been violated excessively in at-Tur. In 1985 the Egyptian Ministry of Antiquities began excavating the Monastery of St. John the Baptist there, where tradition holds that Blemmys nomads massacred the monks of Raithu in the fourth century, and where the great Sinai saint John Klimakos wrote some of his works. To the monks' dismay the Ministry is sending all artifacts recovered from the site to the Coptic Museum in Cairo. They are angry that stories of the excavation printed in Egyptian newspapers identified the site as a Coptic monastery. They complain that to reach the ruins the Muslim excavators dug through a Christian cemetery and disposed of the exhumed bodies in a mass grave 2 kilometers to the east. "They just brutalized the corpses," one monk said. "Damned people!" another said of the excavators as we toured the site. "It's like watching your life pass in front of you. It's disgusting. But what can we do about it? Can the bishop of the monastery tell them not to dig here anymore?" One body that the monastery was able to recover was in an extraordinarily good state of preservation. "It's almost like he could get up and walk away," one monk remarked as we viewed the corpse in its glass case in the nearby Church of St. George. Some 150 years old, the clergyman's shocking red beard, wrinkled face, and gnarled hands suggest to the monks today that if not a saint he was at least a very holy person. They say the body gives off a sweet fragrance, a sign to them that he was blessed. "We don't know what he did in his lifetime, but for the body to be in this state is exceptional," the monk said. "The other bodies in the cemetery were nothing but bones."

North of at-Tur, a few kilometers from the ruins of the Monastery of St. John the Baptist and close to the shore of the Gulf of Suez, is a fine palm grove which the monks identify as Elim, of the "twelve springs and seventy palms," where Moses and his people "pitched camp beside the water" on their way to the Holy Mountain (Exodus 15:27). There are many more than seventy palms today, but the monks say that prior to a large construction project undertaken by Egyptian contractors twelve separate springs were discernible. Promoting it as the "Bath of Moses" (Hammaam Musa), Egyptian developers in the late 1980s built a recreation complex bounded by a rock wall and containing a parking lot, clubhouse, and cafeteria, with its centerpiece a swimming pool—presumably the

Bath of Moses. An Egyptian flag flies over it. The monks condemn it as illegal, claiming that the entire palm grove belongs to the Monastery of St. Katherine, and pointing out that a monastery building had long occupied one corner of the property. Acting on information that this project was about to begin, the monastery in 1988 spent twenty thousand Egyptian pounds to construct a wall delimiting its property. As we stood viewing the site an angry monk described to me what happened then:

The "Bath of Moses" (Hammaam Musa) development near at-Tur. November 7, 1989.

The wall was three-fourths of the way completed before the mayor [of at-Tur], who is a fanatic Moslem, sent the bulldozer here in the middle of the night and leveled the wall completely. They destroyed everything. It was three-quarters of the way finished and they came with a bulldozer and leveled it. They destroyed the springs, because they built this parking lot and cut off all their water supplies. Ruined everything. This is disgusting. They said, "You don't have permission to build this wall here, because this is not your garden." What do you mean it's not our garden? This garden has been in the possession of the monastery since the fourth century A.D., and you're telling me now it's not our garden? What proof do you need? With that building on the corner over here? They said that building dates from the time of the Israelis, after 1967. That building is at least two hundred years old. So the compromise was in the end that they would give us that corner. They marked off a certain number of meters over there and said, "Okay, here's your garden back." What use is that to the monastery, or to society in

general, or to history regarding this important site here? None whatsoever.
And now I see tents pitched over there. I wonder what that means.

The monastery produced Ottoman-era documents in an effort to convince Egyptian authorities that its claim to the land was legitimate. According to the monks the officials rejected the claim outright. The monks protested that to recover the tourist complex in Sinai's disputed Taba from Israeli control the Egyptian government used similar Ottoman archives as legal claims. The monks also complained to the authorities that a number of dwellings on the beach north of this site which belong to the monastery are pounded by Egyptian artillery in military exercises.

The monks believe that such incidents at at-Tur occur primarily because they are too few people to maintain a presence that might deter other claimants. The last resident monk left here in 1967 when Israeli troops forced him and many of his parishioners to evacuate the area. They blame their own archbishop for not having dispatched at least one monk to stave off Egyptian encroachment, and blame themselves for being unwilling to serve in what one called this "Godforsaken place." "We need to show the cloth and collar around here," one said. A monk from the Monastery of St. Katherine says mass each Sunday in the Church of St. George to a dwindling congregation of five or six persons. One of the monks described the fifteen-member Christian enclave in at-Tur, which once numbered in the thousands, as a "dead community." The Boulos household, led by a resolute eighty-year-old patriarch, is one of the last remaining Orthodox families in at-Tur. They occupy a decaying residence just outside the Church and Monastery of St. George in a neighborhood lacking piped water. Soon Egyptian authorities would resettle them and their neighbors so that their homes could be blown up to make space for a seaside park. Old Boulos boasts that his family has a five-hundred-year history as fishermen in at-Tur. Since 1967 most of his neighbors had fled for better opportunities in the cities of Egypt, the United States, and Australia. All but one of Boulos' six children followed them. Emil was intent on becoming a monk of St. Katherine. If he were to join those ranks he would be only the second of the monks now in residence to have come from the Egyptian Greek Orthodox community. For now he was enrolled in an auto mechanics training program in at-Tur, where he contemplated his future from the doomed remains of a once thriving community. "I hate to come down here," said the monk who was translating the family's Greek for me. "I get depressed. Every time I come down here I get a headache."

To counter what they insist is a deliberate confiscation of their land, the monks of St. Katherine are trying to reassert themselves on the landscape. They claim to have attempted to purchase back at market price some lands confiscated by the government but that the government refused bitterly to sell to them. Northwest of Jebel Musa, near Wadi at-Tarfa, the monastery did purchase a small new plot of land from the government, dug a well, and began building a small monastery. It will not have a resident monk but will declare the monks' presence. The monks also built a new church in the garden of the convent in Wadi Feiran. In 1988 Jabaliya workmen of the monastery built a small chapel on Jebel Musa over the grotto where St. Stephen of Sinai is said to have died. During the following year Jabaliya laborers under monastery orders extended the walled perimeter of the orchard at Dayr Tala' by about 100 meters. The monks hope these efforts will slow their losses.

THE SOCIETY

At times in its long history the Monastery of St. Katherine has been a thriving and cosmopolitan place. In its library collection of more than three thousand volumes, which monks claim is "second only to the Vatican," there are works by Syrian, Georgian, and Slavic monks who resided here with the ethnic Greek majority. The bilingual Greeks produced both Greek and Arabic manuscripts, and their colleagues created texts in Syriac, Georgian, Armenian, Slavic, Latin, and Ethiopic.[60] The eleven chapels within the monastery's walls also reflect diversity; some were founded by Syrian, Armenian, Coptic, and Latin monks.[61]

That kind of diversity was possible when Sinai was a mecca for monks. According to the monks' tradition, there were as many as 3,000 brethren in and around the monastery during the Byzantine period.[62] Reliable reports of the monastery's population date to about 1000 A.D., and suggest more modest numbers. Table 1 reflects a general trend of decline, with occasional brushes with oblivion.[63]

The monks' ranks fluctuated dramatically for several reasons. Tradition relates that early in the eleventh century the cruel Muslim Caliph al-Hakim decimated the population as part of an overall policy of genocide against Christians.[64] By 1384 a prosperous community hosted pilgrims: 150 monks lived within the monastery walls and another 50 in Jebel Musa's chapels.[65] Then the plague struck Egypt.[66] One hundred years later a visitor to the monastery found "nothing that did not speak of dire poverty."[67] "Hostile Arabs" were blamed for a purge that by 1565 left the monastery completely empty and its gates walled up. The single monk who inhabited the place in 1600 was reportedly starving.[68] When their population rose

POPULATION OF MONKS

AT THE MONASTERY OF ST. KATHERINE

Year	Number	Year	Number
1000	300	1844	18
1336	400	1845	25
1384	200	1871	28
1435	50	1888	30
1485	30	1909	28
1512	40	1912	25
1546	60	1922	22
1561	40	1926	21
1565	0	1929	31
1600	1	1938	19
1620	3	1957	12
1700	50	1964	17
1783	50	1975	12
1793	50	1983	14
1800	28	1989	12
1816	23	1993	15
1838	21		

above 20 the monks prospered. Burckhardt wrote, "They have all taken to some profession . . . Among the twenty-three monks who now remain, there is a cook, a distiller, a baker, a shoemaker, a tailor, a carpenter, a smith, a mason, a gardener, a maker of candles, &. &. Each of these has his workshop, in the worn-out and rusty utensils of which are still to be seen the traces of the former riches and industry of the establishment."[69] Sartell Prentice explained why only a score of monks lived there in 1912: "Life and the pay are not sufficient inducements for young recruits to join the forces that year by year are growing smaller." He predicted direly that "in the course of a few years, the treasures of the monastery will no doubt be removed, and the Mount Sinai Monastery will be only a memory."[70] When Nikos Kazantzakis visited in 1927, 20 monks resided there. Then-Archbishop Porphyrios III told the Cretan novelist of his ambitious plans to attract bright Greek monks and scholars who would work on the monastery's precious manuscript collection. Kazantzakis was skeptical: "I did not speak. I was uneasy. The Monastery of Sinai is in danger. Since the war, young men no longer come here who are learned and useful and can give it support. It, too, will be swept away by the descending squall."[71]

These most dire predictions have not come true, but the monastery today hovers perilously close to abandonment. Monks claim that the Egyptian government has imposed a ceiling of 50 on their number, but if such a restriction exists it is generous. The handful now living there see themselves carrying a special cross. One monk said, "We are here to preserve and protect this monastery. The monks here now are very few in number. In the past there were 3,000 monks. All we can do now is be here and be representative of Christianity and monasticism." The pressures of great numbers of tourists visiting the monastery are one reason for the declining population; dedicated ascetics do not want to become hosts and objects of mass secular visitation. Public relations are another problem. The monastery traditionally recruited from its far-flung daughter-houses. With this system defunct the archbishop travels the world to plead with young men of Orthodox parishes. Few respond. Standards of eligibility have therefore had to change. The monastery long observed an unwritten rule that its monks must be ethnic Greeks. But these are in short supply because of a general exodus of Greeks from Egypt and from competition between Egypt's Greek Orthodox churches over the remaining two to three thousand souls. In the 1980s some of the monks proposed that the Greek-only policy was misguided, insisting that Orthodox members of other ethnic groups should be admitted. The monastery elders consented, and by 1989 the tiny population of 12 included clergymen of varying ethnic backgrounds from France, Italy, Yugoslavia, Australia, and the United States in addition to those of Cypriot, Cretan, and mainland Greek origins. The monks are even considering augmenting their ranks with Coptic Christians who do not share Orthodoxy's dogma of the two natures of Christ.

Monks who do come to Sinai vary in their commitment and ability to tolerate a demanding way of life in a difficult environment. Some reside here only briefly, sometimes as veterans of several monasteries. "This should *never* be done. A monk should *never* leave his monastery," one lamented. This is an ancient admonition to Sinai monks. John Cilix, abbot and seventy-six-year resident of the monastery at at-Tur, advised his brethren to always remain there. He praised a fellow monk who had lived at Raithu for seventy years on a diet of green meat and dates.[72] Although the church discouraged it from the fifth century on, peregrination became a common practice among Near Eastern monks. Some traveled to visit other monks or to make pilgrimage, but as a special kind of asceticism some wandered for the sake of wandering, carrying no possessions and relying on charity.[73] Others moved on because of the stresses of monastic life. In the mid-nineteenth century the typical monk stayed at the Monastery of St. Katherine for six years.[74] In 1990 one of the monks observed, "Novices come, postulates come, all the time. They don't stay. The attrition rate is really very high, 90 percent. People might come to the Sinai looking for monasticism and might not find it here. They might travel to another monastery which may suit them better than our monastery. Others just go back into the world and carry on with their lives."

An outstanding monk by measure of length of residence is Father Good Angel, who came to the Sinai in 1928. Agathangelos served three years at the monastery in at-Tur, where one of his duties was organizing regular caravans of up to one hundred camels to deliver provisions to the Monastery of St. Katherine. These included dry goods and fresh foods sent by boat from Suez, and fried and salted fish from the Gulf of Suez and Red Sea. On the eve of the Second World War, St. Katherine's archbishop sent him on a brief mission to Crete. German soldiers captured him and sent him to Dachau concentration camp, where he survived for three years until British troops liberated the camp. During his internment the Nazis performed experiments on his brain. A longtime associate of the monastery told me he had been in a vegetative state for many years and only recently had become reanimated.

Outside observers and even some resident monks have regarded the Monastery of St. Katherine at some periods in its history as the home of some of Orthodoxy's worst characters. Augusta Dobson depicted the monastery of the early 1920s as "a sort of penal settlement, where monks guilty of criminal offences, those troublesome to the Church by reason of unorthodox opinions, or lunatics were sent, to keep them safely out of the way."[75] A German pilgrim described it similarly in the nineteenth century as "a kind of asylum for the rascally priests of the Greek Church."[76] The monks confess that along with meditation, prayer, and self-denial at Mount Sinai there are jealousy, contempt, and deceit. "There are monks to avoid," one monk warned me. They complain of a "Judas" in their ranks who reports regularly to Egyptian intelligence on the comings and goings of monks and visitors. One monk described another as an "unintelligent" man who "cannot conceptualize"; he was "a hippie and a drunk" before coming to Sinai from Rhodes, but he was "good with animals." Another monk was "an arrogant fool," a proud product of privileged upbringing in Greece. A "wacky" monk had come to Sinai only "because he was in trouble at Mount Athos." His peers accused the monastery's hostel keeper of "wheeling and dealing" with guests and accepting gratuities from them instead of praying and doing his other duties. The only Egyptian-born monk was an orphan raised in the Cairo monastery, where the clerics recall him as being "nothing but a trouble-maker." He has not yet overcome that legacy at the monastery, where his peers distrust him. They are also concerned about the apparently low mental ability of a novice who came into the monastery from the Orthodox community in at-Tur. He had failed his university examinations. Did he come to the monastery because he could not succeed elsewhere? The monks questioned the spiritual credentials of a Greek-American novice who came to the monastery after seeing visions and hearing a voice. The monastery elders met to discuss whose voice, God's or Satan's?

From the inside and outside alike there have always been detractors of monastic life. "Their conception was a wrong one," Augusta Dobson wrote of the monks, "for to flee for ever from an angry and sinful world was not what their Master taught. They came from one hopelessness to another."[77] Visitors peering through different perceptual lenses have found only merit in the monks' sacrifice and tenacity. "Earlier visitors have described the monks of Sinai as dirty and drunken," wrote Maynard Williams. "Quite aside from their cordial hospitality, we found none who were not neat and not even by a casual breath did any monk betray a predilection for alcohol."[78] In 1336 Ludolf von Suchem found that the monastery's four hundred residents "follow very strict rules; live chaste and modestly; are obedient to their archbishop and prelates; drink not wine but on high festivals; eat never flesh; but live on herbs, pease, beans and lentils, which they prepare with water, salt, and vinegar; eat together in a refectory without a table-cloth; perform their offices in the church with great devotion day and night; and are very diligent in all things; so that they fall little short of the rules of St. Anthony."[79] Tuscan pilgrims of the late fourteenth century also observed discipline and denial: "In appearance they look devout and holy men, of great penance and of great abstinence, and very mortified in demeanor."[80] Bishop Richard Pococke saw the monastery as a place of spiritual perfection: "The service of the Greek church is perform'd here with much greater decency than ever I saw it in any other place, and, it is probable, most agreeably to the ancient customs of the Greek church."[81] Today it would be difficult not to admire the monks' resolve to practice their spiritual mission. Despite their growing obligations to service tourists and to actively resist forces of change and development around them, they find time for their principal occupation of prayer, beginning with a four-hour service that starts at 4:15 A.M. "There are three eight-hour periods of the day in the monk's life," Father Makarios explained. "Eight of prayer, eight of work, and eight of rest. Rest does not mean sleep. There is one thing we have learned in thousands of years of monastic tradition: when you are sleeping you are not praying. And when you are sleeping, we are praying."

Against great odds the monks of St. Katherine struggle to emulate the exemplary past of their institution. They speak often of St. John Klimakos, "John of the Ladder" (570–649 A.D.), who spent forty years in utter silence in a cave overlooking the gorge of Wadi Itlaah (ancient Thola), 5 kilometers northwest of Jebel Musa. From his experience, which he called the "ordeal" of following and imitating Christ, this saint was able to describe the thirty steps or rungs of a ladder which a monk may climb to attain spiritual perfection. The goal of the ordeal, he wrote, was "holy silence"—the elusive *hesychia*.[82] "The friend of silence," he explained, "draws near to God and, by secretly conversing with Him, is enlightened by God."[83] John's writing on the heavenly ladder had a powerful influence on spiritual life in the West through the end of the Middle Ages, and contributed many proverbs to vernacular speech in the Orthodox world.[84] Monastic life at Jebel Musa became such an inspiration that ascetics of monasteries in the most inaccessible mountain regions of Europe came to be known as "Sinaites." The last great Sinaite was an Anatolian monk named Gregory who revived Hesychasm in the thirteenth century. He learned quietude by spending three years at Jebel Musa and climbing the mountain each day.[85]

I asked Father Makarios whether as models of Hesychasm, John Klimakos and Gregory still have lasting influence on the monks of St. Katherine. "Of course. They are a very important part of the life of the monastery." He emphasized that they also spread the blessings of spiritual life in the Sinai throughout the Orthodox world:

Although St. Gregory did not spend a lot of time in the Sinai he was a brother of the monastery. He traveled to Greece and one of the things he realized when he got there was that the monks were not praying properly. So he taught them the tradition of prayer that was so much a part of the monastery of Sinai. The monastic tradition of Mount Sinai, the prayer life there, was much more enhanced than it was even in Greece in those days. So when he went to Mount Athos and found this deplorable situation there, he taught the monks there to pray the way the monks in Sinai pray. So the spiritual life was rejuvenated in those days because of Gregory, because of the spiritual tradition that he came from. He was able to transpose that into the lives of the monks that he came in touch with in Greece. John of the Ladder left his writings behind him. Those are his legacy. His brother was the abbot of the monastery in at-Tur, in Raithu, and asked him to please send him something to help inspire the monks of his monastery in at-Tur. That was the book that he wrote, that Ladder of Divine Ascent. *That is where that book came from. He was writing a letter to his brother, simply to give him instructions.*

Monks still retire to the sanctuary of John Klimakos as a place where they might find spiritual inspiration from the past. John himself had come to Mount Sinai to contemplate at its holy places. Layers of meaning and experience are still accumulating on the sacred sites around Jebel Musa.

Five

◆

THE
CHRISTIAN
LANDSCAPE

Jebel Musa is an earthly interpretation of heavenly Mount Sinai. Over nearly two thousand years of occupation and visitation devout Christians have shaped the face of the land in an image befitting the miraculous events they believe occurred there (Map 2). Their beliefs explain why the landscape appears as it does; why, for example, paths, chapels, and crosses are where they are. Their beliefs also explain what has not been done to the land; why, for example, there are large stretches of ground unmodified by human activity even after two thousand years. The long tradition of pious stewardship of the land at Jebel Musa also offers people today a perspective on how the land might be used in the future.

THE PLAIN OF ASSEMBLAGE

Pilgrims and travelers who made their way across sea and desert with the goal of Mount Sinai in their hearts approached their destination with hope and anticipation. They would not be disappointed. Awaiting them was one of Earth's most dramatic vistas and a landscape crowded with divine associations.

Historically most visitors to Jebel Musa came from the northwest. They spent some time in Cairo securing provisions and arranging transport to the Sinai. They crossed the Isthmus of Suez and made their way slowly down the windy coastal plain of the Gulf of Suez. They entered the mountainous country at the mouth of Wadi Feiran, visited the oasis of Feiran, and started up one of Feiran's principal tributaries, Wadi ash-Shaykh. That drainage leads all the way to the monastery, but only after a final turn of almost 90 degrees that before the era of the motorcar would cost the traveler extra time. The pilgrim's caravan, therefore, took the shortest route, leaving Wadi ash-Shaykh about 25 kilometers northwest of the monastery to cross a sandy plain and low hills to reach what is now Shaykh 'Awaad, just outside of the circular dike ringing the high Sinai massif. At that 1,200-meter elevation cameleers secured baggage to their animals and walkers checked their footwear before the final steep approach to the monastery. They passed up a dramatic gorge called Nagub al-Haawa, "Pass of the Wind," which slices right through the circular dike to create what Franklin Hoskins described as "mysterious effects that would have bewildered the pencil of Dante himself."[1] It was hard going. "I never found a path so rude and difficult as that we were now ascending," Edward Robinson wrote in his 1838 journal.[2] For the first three hours out of Shaykh 'Awaad the steep incline blocked the far view. Finally the path leveled off and the gorge widened, giving way suddenly to a broad plain leading uninterrupted for a distance of 5 kilometers to the Monastery of St. Katherine and the foot of Jebel Musa. In about the year 400 the pilgrim Etheria made this entrance into the Plain of ar-Raaha. "In the meantime we came on foot to a certain place where the mountains, through which we were journeying, opened out and formed an infinitely great valley, quite flat and extraordinarily beautiful, and across the valley appeared Sinai, the holy mountain of God."[3] "The view beyond the pass from the crest of Er Raaha is extremely beautiful," Edward Palmer agreed fifteen hundred years later. "The plain seems enclosed by lofty mountain walls, and the gorge itself is like a narrow gate, through which the open country and distant hills appear in the perfection of aerial perspective."[4] Arthur Stanley also entered ar-Raaha this way:

We reached the head of the pass; and far in the bosom of the mountains before us, I saw the well-known shapes of the cliffs which form the front of Sinai. At each successive advance these cliffs disengaged themselves from the intervening and surrounding hills, and at last they stood out—I should rather say the columnar mass, which they form, stood out—alone against the sky. On each side the infinite complications of twisted and jagged mountains fell away from it. On each side the sky encompassed it round as though it were alone in the wilderness. And to this giant mass we approached through a wide valley, a long continued plain, which, enclosed as it was between two precipitous mountain ranges of black and yellow granite, and having always at its end this prodigious mountain block, I could compare to nothing else than the immense avenue,—the "dromos," as it is technically called,—through which the approach was made to the great Egyptian temples. One extraordinary sensation was the foreknowledge at each successive opening of

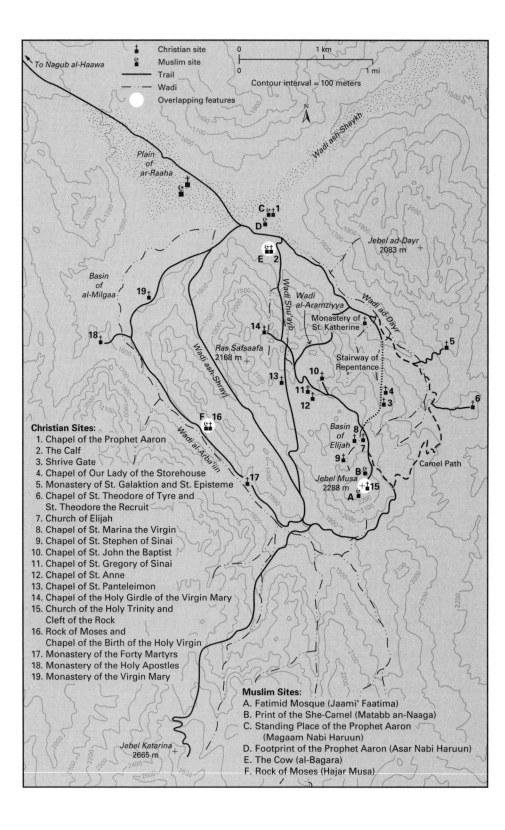

Christian site
Muslim site
Trail
Wadi
Overlapping features

0   1 km
0   1 mi
Contour interval = 100 meters

To Nagub al-Haawa

Plain
of
ar-Raaha

Wadi ash-Shaykh

Jebel ad-Dayr
2083 m

Basin
of
al-Milgaa

Wadi Shu'ayb

Wadi
al-Aramziyya

Wadi ad-Dayr

Monastery of
St. Katherine

Stairway of
Repentance

Ras Safsaafa
2168 m

Wadi ash-Shrayl

Wadi al-Arba'iin

Basin
of
Elijah

Camel Path

Jebel Musa
2288 m

Christian Sites:
1. Chapel of the Prophet Aaron
2. The Calf
3. Shrive Gate
4. Chapel of Our Lady of the Storehouse
5. Monastery of St. Galaktion and St. Episteme
6. Chapel of St. Theodore of Tyre and
   St. Theodore the Recruit
7. Church of Elijah
8. Chapel of St. Marina the Virgin
9. Chapel of St. Stephen of Sinai
10. Chapel of St. John the Baptist
11. Chapel of St. Gregory of Sinai
12. Chapel of St. Anne
13. Chapel of St. Panteleimon
14. Chapel of the Holy Girdle of the Virgin Mary
15. Church of the Holy Trinity and
    Cleft of the Rock
16. Rock of Moses and
    Chapel of the Birth of the Holy Virgin
17. Monastery of the Forty Martyrs
18. Monastery of the Holy Apostles
19. Monastery of the Virgin Mary

Jebel Katarina
2665 m

Muslim Sites:
A. Fatimid Mosque (Jaami' Faatima)
B. Print of the She-Camel (Matabb an-Naaga)
C. Standing Place of the Prophet Aaron
   (Magaam Nabi Haruun)
D. Footprint of the Prophet Aaron (Asar Nabi Haruun)
E. The Cow (al-Bagara)
F. Rock of Moses (Hajar Musa)

the view of every object that would next appear; as cliff and plain, and the deep
gorges on each side, and lastly the Convent with its gardens burst before me. . . .
But the whole impression of that long approach was even more wonderful than
I had expected. Whatever may have been the scene of the events in Exodus,
I cannot imagine that any human being could pass up that plain and not
feel that he was entering a place above all others suited for the
most august of the sights of earth.[5]

Their approach up Nagub al-Haawa to the Plain of ar-Raaha and Jebel
Musa awed Edward Robinson and his companions in 1838:

Here the interior and loftier peaks of the great circle of Sinai began to open upon
us,—black, rugged, desolate summits; and as we advanced, the dark and frowning
front of Sinai itself began to appear. . . . I had never seen a spot more wild and
desolate. As we advanced, the valley still opened wider and wider with a gentle
ascent, and became full of shrubs and tufts of herbs, shut in on each side by lofty
granite ridges with rugged shattered peaks a thousand feet high, while the face of
Horeb rose directly before us. . . . Reaching the top of the ascent or watershed, a
fine broad plain lay before us, sloping down gently towards the S.S.E. enclosed by
rugged and venerable mountains of dark granite, stern, naked, splintered peaks
and ridges, of indescribable grandeur; and terminated at the distance of more than a
mile by the bold and awful front of Horeb, rising perpendicularly in frowning maj-

A view
southeastward from
the top of Nagub al-
Haawa pass to the
entrance of the Plain
of ar-Raaha and
Jebel Musa, the
apparently lower
mountain at left. By
Arthur Sutton,
1912.

MAP 2
Christian and
Muslim sacred places
around Jebel Musa.

esty, from twelve to fifteen hundred feet in height. It was a scene of solemn gran-
deur, wholly unexpected, and such as we had never seen; and the associations
which at the moment rushed upon our minds, were almost overwhelming.[6]

Towering above the plain, Mount Sinai stirred deep emotions in the
weary and exhilarated traveler. Justinian's court historian Procopius saw it
as a "precipitous and terribly wild mountain."[7] Franklin Hoskins regarded
the view as "among the most sublime mountain prospects in the world."[8]
"A stately, awful-looking, isolated mass it is," Edward Palmer wrote,
"rearing its giant brow above the plain, as if in scornful contemplation of
the world beneath."[9] "When facing its awful, stately grandeur, I felt as if I
had come to the end of the world," wrote Edward Wilson.[10]

Pious visitors called the flat expanse at the foot of the mountain the
"Plain of Assemblage" because they believed the Israelites were camped
there when Moses received the commandments. Its Arabic name ar-
Raaha, "the Resting Place," also honors this belief. Pilgrims walked on it
reverently. "On the very plain we were crossing the tents of the people of
God were once pitched," Augusta Dobson wrote of her 1922 approach to
the monastery. "It seemed impossible to realise that we were on this holy
ground at last; we moved on in silence, the 'speaking silence of a
dream.'"[11] Most visitors continued directly to the monastery and later
returned to the plain with monks who escorted them to its sacred sites.
Etheria took this tour:

> *Now this is the great and flat valley wherein the children of Israel waited during*
> *those days when holy Moses went up into the mount of the Lord and remained*
> *there forty days and forty nights. . . . The holy men showed us each place that we*
> *came to in the whole valley. They showed us the place where the camps of the*
> *children of Israel were in those days when Moses was in the mount. They showed*
> *us where they all had their dwelling places in the valley, the foundations of which*
> *dwelling places appear to this day, round in form and made with stone. They*
> *showed us also the place where holy Moses, when he returned from the mount,*
> *bade the children of Israel run from gate to gate. They showed us also the place*
> *where the calf which Aaron had made for them was burnt at holy Moses' bidding.*
> *They showed us also the stream of which holy Moses made the children of Israel*
> *drink, as it is written in Exodus. They showed us also the place where the seventy*
> *men received of the spirit that was upon Moses. They showed us also the place*
> *where the children of Israel lusted for meat. They showed us also the place which is*
> *called a Burning, because part of the camp was consumed what time holy Moses*
> *prayed, and the fire ceased. They showed us also the place where it rained manna*
> *and quails upon them . . . At the very end of the valley we saw the graves of*
> *lust . . . Thus were shown to us (the sites of) all the events which in the sacred*

books of Moses are recorded to have occurred there, viz., in the valley which, as I have said, lies under the mount of God, holy Sinai.[12]

Etheria's itinerary on the plain remained as the classic pilgrim's tour until late in the twentieth century when hotel construction on the Plain of ar-Raaha obliterated most of these places.

As visitors left the Plain of ar-Raaha and entered the Wadi ad-Dayr less than 2 kilometers below the monastery they passed a small hill on their left. The promontory is known as Nabi Haruun ("Prophet Aaron") because of one tradition that Aaron ordered the golden calf to be installed at its southern foot, where today there is a Jabaliya Bedouin cemetery, and another tradition that Aaron was consecrated in the tabernacle which Moses erected on its summit.[13] Today the hill is crowned by two stark white shrines. The larger Christian chapel is a 1911 restoration of a much earlier edifice. At a spot 1 kilometer southwest of Nabi Haruun in the mouth of Wadi ash-Shrayj, monks in the eighteenth and nineteenth centuries showed visitors a rock depression resembling the shape of a calf's head, explaining that Aaron had used it as a mould for the idol.[14] In the fourteenth and fifteenth centuries monks showed pilgrims an extraordinary feature about 500 meters to the south of Nabi Haruun in the mouth of Wadi Shu'ayb. A granite formation there bears striking resemblance to the head and forequarter of a cow, and monks explained this was the

The Cow (al-Baqara) in the mouth of Wadi Shu'ayb. August 27, 1993.

place of the Israelite heresy.[15] "You see something exactly like a calf which they say was the calf," the Tuscan pilgrim Gucci wrote.[16] From there monks pointed out to Etheria and later pilgrims the large boulder in Wadi Shu'ayb where the furious Moses broke the tablets of the Law.[17] A rival tradition put this site in Wadi al-Arba'iin. In 1844 Tischendorf noted that Bedouins had been digging around the rock in Wadi Shu'ayb with the "hope of discovering the rare fragments of the tables."[18] In the fourteenth century monks showed pilgrims the place on a ridge above Wadi ash-Shrayj where on God's instruction Moses erected the bronze serpent that would cure his people of snakebite, as related in Numbers 21: 6–9.[19]

THE BURNING BUSH

At the place where Nagub al-Haawa enters the Plain of ar-Raaha travelers' senses were overwhelmed both by the mountain vista and by the appearance of their destination, the Monastery of St. Katherine. "We could see its cypresses and its walled enclosure," Augusta Dobson wrote, "it looked like a strange anomaly, a garden in the desert, a house of habitation set amid bare, barren mountain ranges; to those of us who now saw it for the first time it far surpassed our highest expectations in its strong, solitary beauty and impressiveness."[20] Claude Jarvis wrote of its unlikely presence, "It comes as a surprise and a shock—albeit a pleasant one—to see anything that savours of civilisation in this rugged wilderness."[21] After entering the monastery some reverent visitors reeled at the jolting sensation of being at Mount Sinai. "I was affected by the strangeness and overpowering grandeur of the scenes around us," Edward Robinson wrote in 1836, "and it was for some time difficult to realize, that we were now actually within the very precincts of that Sinai, on which from the earliest childhood I had thought and read with so much wonder. Yet, when at length the impression came with its full force upon my mind, although not given to the melting mood, I could not refrain from bursting into tears."[22]

After settling within the monastery pilgrims made a solemn visit to the holiest place on the landscape of Mount Sinai, the piece of ground occupied by the Chapel of the Burning Bush. Father Makarios and his fellow monks regard it as the most sacred place on Earth: "It is the holiest site in the world," he said. "If you consider the event that took place there, you cannot—there is no way—that you could compare that location with any other in anybody else's religion, because of what occurred there, and never happened before anywhere, to anybody." The ground is more sacred than the bush which stood on it; God had told Moses, "Take off your sandals, for the place where you are standing is holy ground" (Exodus 3:5). Early Christians must have made this distinction between the bush and its location as the monastery complex took shape. Etheria had seen growing at this site "Which same bush is alive to this day and throws out roots."[23] The Chapel of the Burning Bush probably began as an open outdoor courtyard, accessible from the basilica, where a living bush grew. By 1216 the roofed Chapel of the Burning Bush had been built over the courtyard, with its altar situated exactly where the bush had stood.[24]

What happened to the bush? In 1216 German pilgrim Magister Thietmar saw no bush at all, testifying "there is also in a chapel of this monastery the spot where stood the bush venerated by all, as much by Saracens as by Christians . . . The bush has indeed been taken away and divided among Christians for relics."[25] The monastery's tradition denies any hiatus in the life of the bush, which flourishes a few meters away from its original location. Monks today claim their predecessors transplanted the bush when they built the chapel. I had this exchange with one of them:

"If the chapel is on the site where the bush originally was, was the bush transplanted?"

"Yes."

"So the roots aren't considered to be under the chapel today?"

"They are. They are still there."

"The roots are under the chapel, so they extend . . ."

"The pious tradition of the monastery is that the replanted bush rejoined the roots that were there from the original planting. It is only a
matter of 5 meters or so. It is not very far."

"Do you know when the replanting was supposed to have taken
place?"

"About the tenth century or so. The reason it was moved was because

it was inside an open-air enclosure, and that area became a chapel, and the
monks covered the roof, cutting off sunlight to the plant. So, in order for
it to survive, they had to move it to a place where there was still adequate
sunlight. So that transplanting worked, but others since then have not."

For the monks the ecology of the bush testifies to its sanctity. They
claim that it is the only specimen of its kind anywhere in the world and
cannot be transplanted again. As we stood at the foot of the retaining wall
below the shrub Father Makarios explained to me, "This bush is what the
whole thing is all about. This is what attracted the monastics to come to
this area in the very beginning. It is unique. No other plant like this is alive
anywhere in the Sinai. This plant will not grow anywhere else. It has been
tried. Efforts have been made to transplant the bush. They have all
failed." [26]

The monks are closer to the truth about this plant than most observers
realize. Botanist Nabil El-Hadidi of Cairo University told me that *Rubus
sanctus* is an extremely rare endemic species of Central Asiatic origin whose
range is limited to the immediate environs of Jebel Musa. How long could
it live? "For thousands of years," El-Hadidi said. It is quite plausible that
the bush growing in the monastery today is the very one Etheria described—and it could have lived in Moses' time. I could not bring myself
to tell the fathers that in my months of walking in the Sinai mountains I
did see other specimens of *Rubus sanctus*. In respect for the monks the
Jabaliya Bedouins do not discuss other members of this species with them,
either, though they know it well by its Arabic name *'allayg*. There are only
a handful of the plants in this area. One is at the swimming hole of al-Galt
al-Azraq; there is another at a place higher up in Wadi Tala'; and a third
grows unrecognized by the monks outside the retreat of St. John Klimakos
in Wadi Itlaah. Despite their faith the monks are open-minded about the
bush. Father George asked me to write down its Latin name for him. Another asked me pointedly whether I had seen any others of its kind. "I
have seen bushes *like* it," I said, referring to a related member of the rose
family, *Rosa arabica*, another Sinai endemic I had collected.

The monastery's bush never fruits. Father George waters the shrub
from the nearby Well of Moses, which he explains is the place where
Moses met Zipporah, and which he says miraculously "never goes dry, no
matter what the climatic conditions." He prunes the bush regularly, giving
the foliage to Greek pilgrims to carry away as mementos. Nevertheless it
sometimes reaches prodigious size and spills out of its embankment onto
the walkway below, as it did prior to 1984 when the monks met to discuss
its condition and elected to crop it close. It had become "long and sickly,"
they said. There were not enough visitors at the time to carry all the foliage

away. The monks' solution to the disposal problem? They set fire to it. "Yes, well, it did burn," confessed a monk who had watched.[27]

CLIMBING MOUNT SINAI

Many of the world's sacred mountains distinguish themselves by their physical presence. Mount Kailas of the Hindu and Buddhist worlds boasts one of the highest summits on the Tibetan plateau. It is isolated from other peaks and has a shape "so regular as if it were the dome of a gigantic temple."[28] Four of south Asia's greatest rivers rise near it and radiate from it "like the spokes from the hub of a wheel."[29] Jebel Musa has no such qualities. It is not the highest. From the summit of nearby Jebel Katarina it looks insignificant. The objective observer entering the Plain of ar-Raaha from Nagub al-Haawa might be struck equally by the awesome presence of all the mountains ringing the plain. Only knowledge of which one is Mount Sinai inspires special reverence and sets Jebel Musa apart. "Sacred place is ordinary place, ritually made extraordinary," wrote Beldon Lane.[30] Monks, Bedouins, pilgrims, and travelers recalling the events of Exodus have fixed through ritual the places which sanctify Jebel Musa.

Jebel Musa does have some odd physical properties. It is unusual in the south Sinai for such a high mountain to rise directly out of a plain, and from the Plain of ar-Raaha, Jebel Musa appears to do so more steeply and symmetrically than its neighbors. "The combination was satisfying—convincing," Edward Wilson concluded. "This must be the 'true Sinai,'—the very mountain upon which the glory of the Lord rested in the sight of the people."[31] It has an exceptional summit, a sharp cone of dark volcanic material perched assymetrically atop the easternmost extremity of a red granite ridge. There are other examples of extrusive and intrusive igneous rocks situated together in the region, but they occur usually in horizontal beds rather than in this peculiar configuration. There are more alluvial basins suitable for orchard agriculture on the Safsaafa portion of the mountain than on surrounding peaks, and the higher elevations of the mountain are therefore more habitable for people. There are more water sources on and around the base of this mountain than any other in the region.

The faithful see no need to weigh arguments in favor of or against Jebel Musa. It is Mount Sinai. It is a sacred mountain. It is as Buddhist Lama Anagarika Govinda defined the sacred mountain, referring to Tibet's Mount Kailas, a "mountain with personality," a "vessel of cosmic power," a "celestial temple, the throne of the gods, the seat and centre of cosmic powers, the axis or hub which connects the earth with the universe, the super-antenna for the influx and outflow of the spiritual energies of our planet."[32] It is a sacred mountain as Martin Lev defined Calvary in Jeru-

A view eastward from the summit of Jebel Abbas Pasha to Jebel Musa. The summit is at the extreme right, with Ras Safsaafa in the center. Wadi ad-Dayr meets the Plain of ar-Raaha at the extreme left center. In the foreground is the settlement of Katriin. July 15, 1989.

*A view
northeastward from
Jebel Katarina to the
conical summit of
Jebel Musa, with
gardens of Wadi
al-Arba'iin just
below center.
June 11, 1989.*

salem's Church of the Holy Sepulchre, symbolizing "the meeting place of
the three cosmic levels of the universe: heaven, earth and the underworld,"
the "universal axis, or *axis mundi*, which connects these three worlds, and
makes communication between them possible. Since it was only through
this axis that influences could pass from one world to another, it was always
at the site of its earthly image that the great events of our own world took
shape." [33]

The monks of St. Katherine call it "the God-Trodden Mountain"

(*Theobadistan Oros*), "the Mountain of God," "the Mountain of the Giving of the Law," "the Holy Mountain," and "Horeb" (*Choreifa*). Believers say the hierophany left tangible marks for all to see. Both monks and Bedouins for centuries have explained to visitors that the plantlike patterns which appear on some rocks (and which today geologists identify as dendritic pyrolusite) were caused by the divine conflagration on Mount Sinai; the light was so intense that it imprinted shadows of living plants on stone.[34] A fourteenth-century Tuscan pilgrim believed the limited distribution of these stones verified this was the Mountain of God: "It is said that these stones to which the rays of God extended, took the print of a palm; and this is proved by the fact that in other parts, save on this mount, stones of this kind are not found."[35] In 1216 pilgrim Magister Thietmar noted that monks and Bedouins prescribed these marked stones against all infirmities.[36]

Both Bedouins and monks believe that God has repeatedly manifested Himself in spectacular atmospheric and seismic events on the mountain. An account of a Blemmys nomad attack on the monks around 400 A.D. relates that after clergymen took refuge in the tower near the burning bush, the mountain glowed in flame and repelled the invaders.[37] A fifth-century monk explained how the theophany at Sinai again saved the monks during a Saracen nomad attack on the Bush settlement. He wrote,

Plantlike patterns of the "rays of God"— or dendritic pyrolusite—on a rock by the Well of Moses. August 25, 1993.

"I came, I know not how—excited as I was—to the top of the Mount, and, the rest of the monks ran as fast as they could over the rocky ravines in order to reach the Mount, since they know that it was characteristic of the Saracens that they never go up that Mountain since that is where God appeared and spoke to the children of Israel."[38] In 1010 A.D. the Caliph al-Hakim reportedly decided not to attack the monastery when he learned the mountain was once again in flame.[39]

Sacred places may induce a feeling of serenity or well-being but may also exert violent and terrible forces; the sacred landscape is a landscape of fear.[40] One of the oldest Christian traditions associated with Mount Sinai is that because of divine manifestations it should not be climbed, at least not by the spiritually uninitiated. In about 400 A.D. Nilus noted that people avoided the mountain "since God conferred there with the people."[41] In the fourth century Etheria and in the sixth century Antoninus Martyr observed that no hermit ever spent the night there.[42] Today no such prohibition exists. Father Makarios spent a night there in the autumn of 1989 with soldiers of the Multinational Force and Observers. His fellow monks interpret the restriction in Exodus 19 as relevant only to the time when Moses was meeting with God on the mountain. However, they also insist that when God said "not to go up the mountain or touch the edge of it" He meant that nothing inappropriate should be done there. To the monks this means that no secular dwellings should be built on the mountain, and that people should always walk reverently upon it.

The monks have always believed that the mountain should be ascended only by those with proper ritual preparation. One way to earn this right is to endure climbing it by the "Stairway of Repentance." Known to Bedouins as "the Path of Our Lord Moses" (Sikkat Sayyidna Musa), this route begins just southeast of the monastery and traces a steep, short route up Jebel Musa. The monastery's tradition is that pious monks carved and layed in its steps in a single fifty-year period in the sixth century. Just how many steps there are is disputed. To many weary walkers the figure of 50,000 calculated by de Laborde in 1836 seems correct.[43] There seem in fact to be about 3,750 steps today, of which the final 750 lead from the Basin of Elijah to Jebel Musa's summit. No one would dispute that the climb is difficult. Father Michael suggested I must have committed some grave sin for wanting to climb the stairs one August day. Tourists prefer walking up the longer but more merciful camel path to the Basin of Elijah and using the stairs for an easy and swift descent.

Monks previously used the stairway to test pilgrims' piety and determine whether they were worthy of continuing on to the summit. At a place about two-thirds of the way up this route are two stone arches. An ancient tradition relates that Elijah built the upper one and Moses the

The Stairway of
Repentance with the
Shrive Gate of
St. Stephen.
October 12, 1989.

lower one.[44] At the lower or Shrive Gate the sixth-century St. Stephen, who now rests in the charnel house, took pilgrims' confessions and tested their knowledge of the Bible. He granted certificates to the pure and the knowledgable and allowed them to continue upward through the second gate unchallenged.[45] In the fifteenth century monks told pilgrims that "by terror or by miracle" no Jew could pass through the lower gate and continue up the mountain; for example, one Jew who disguised himself as a Christian was repelled by a vision of the crucified Christ above the arch.[46]

In the 1880s monks related that a Jew had refused to step through the Shrive Gate because a cross was above it. Attempting to scramble around the gate's left on a steep rock wall he slipped and broke his neck.[47] In the early 1800s monks were fond of telling visitors that a Jew had once tried to pass through the gate but an iron cross above it mysteriously repelled him. The man then had himself baptized just below the gate at the Spring of Moses and passed unchallenged up the mountain.[48] St. Stephen had reportedly baptized many Jews in this spring and then allowed them to proceed up the mountain, but turned back those who would not be baptized.[49] This water source has been known variously as 'Ayn Musa, the Fountain of St. Sangarius and the Fountain of the Shoe or 'Ayn el Kontarai.[50] In the early nineteenth century monks told visitors it appeared miraculously to a pilgrim shoemaker who resolved at this spot to become a hermit and pass the rest of his days here.[51]

Between the Spring of Moses and the Shrive Gate is the Chapel of Our Lady of the Storehouse (*Oikonomissa*), a brilliant white shrine dedicated to a miraculous event that occurred here. The Monastery of St. Katherine had once become so infested with "flies, ants and fleas, in such size and number that they could not stay there nor preserve the corn they had there." All but two monks fled their deteriorating monastery. These two finally decided to abandon the place after one final prayer on the summit of Mount Sinai. On their ascent they encountered at this spot an apparition of the Virgin Mary, the "honest woman" who made a pledge to them:

"I wish that you return back and not go any farther, and I promise you
that henceforth you will not lack what you need for your living, and neither flies nor ants nor fleas will again torment you, nor shall they destroy
your corn."[52] In the 1380s monks told pilgrims about another miracle the
two men beheld:

*Having returned to the monastery they found a very great number of camels laden
with food brought from Cairo of Babylon by a grace begged from God by the prayers of Our Lady and Moses. Which miracle was made manifest by a child who
came with the camels, for when the monks asked the cameleers who had sent the
food, they replied that a good man had bought them in Cairo, and had paid them
for the transport, and had preceded them through the desert to that place. Having
taken inside the food, a child who had come with the cameleers, seeing an image of
Moses, began to cry out: This is the man who did thy buying and who guided us
as far as near here and who told us to unload the camels in this place; and this boy
said that he wished to remain in this place and to become a religious, and to be a
Christian; for which thing the cameleers took him and quartered him.*[53]

Legend relates that St. Mary of the Pledge kept her word to the Sinai
monks for many centuries: "From the day Our Lady made the said promise, always they have had their living, and never has anything been wanting; and then, that very spot is free of flies, ants and fleas, which are very
few or not at all, while, as said, the country around is entirely infected
with insects."[54] Pilgrims marveled at this miracle into the 1850s: "Certain
unclean creatures like flies, wasps, hornets, fleas, and others of that sort,
cannot live there, nor come into the monastery from outside. And it has
been observed, that if such creatures are introduced into the monastery,
they instantly die. All this the brethren have obtained by virtue of their
saintly and upright life."[55]

Most visitors to Jebel Musa today climb the mountain by a camel path
which begins immediately behind the monastery and leads southeast up
Wadi ad-Dayr. On the walker's left is Jebel ad-Dayr (also known as Jebel
Baraka, Jebel Mugaffa, and Mount Episteme), a multisummited red granite
ridge rising to 2,083 meters.[56] From the camel path an ancient walkway
rises steeply on its slope to a whitewashed structure overlooking Wadi ad-
Dayr that monks claim is Sinai's oldest monastery, the Monastery of
St. Galaktion and St. Episteme (Arabic, Dayr Mugaffa). The nun Episteme
and her husband the monk Galaktion were said to have had a small following of ascetics on the mountain during the Roman persecutions of the
third century. Roman soldiers made the couple Sinai's first martyrs.[57] Like
many other significant places in the area, the hermitage dedicated to

A view northeastward from near the Chapel of St. John the Baptist to the Monastery of St. Katherine at the foot of Jebel ad-Dayr. July 17, 1989.

St. Galaktion and St. Episteme owes its existence to a vertical dike in which early monks were able to excavate a permanent water supply. Today the water is impounded clear and cold in a shaded reservoir within a cave, guarded ominously by a white spray-painted skull crowned by a cross. This was painted by the monastery's resident, the hermit Adrianos. From his refuge there is an exceptional vista of the eastern portion of Jebel Musa, including its summit. Near Jebel ad-Dayr's own broad crown are several basins in which ancient hermits cultivated wheat and barley. Several of their strongly built stone dwellings and a network of pathways and stone stairways they developed to link the basins remain in good condition. The most spectacular of the basins is the Basin of the Rock Dove (Arabic, Farsh Himaami), which occupies an eroded dike at the source of Wadi Ariiba. One of its early Christian tenants built a small check dam to soak the ground where he planted wheat and barley. In the granite wall flanking the basin's western side is a V-shaped cleft which affords a dramatic view of the Monastery of St. Katherine 400 meters directly below.

Continuing up the camel route past the trail to the Monastery of St. Galaktion and St. Episteme, the walker reaches the head of Wadi ad-Dayr. To the left or east is Jethro's Mountain or Jebel Munayja ("Conversation Mountain" or "Mount of the Conference"), a greenish hill with a sharp peak of 1,857 meters. On its summit is a white church dedicated to St. Theodore, a martyred Roman soldier, and to St. Theodore of Tyre.

Monks' tradition holds that it stands on the site where Jethro and his daughters were camped when Moses first came to the Holy Mountain.[58] In the fifteenth century monks told pilgrims that this is where Moses, Aaron, and the seventy elders saw God standing on what looked like "a sapphire pavement pure as the heavens themselves," and where God invited Moses to come farther up the mountain.[59] Disoriented in the predawn darkness, many walkers accidentally climb this peak rather than Jebel Musa. The correct path cuts out of the head of Wadi ad-Dayr into a series of steep switchbacks up the northeastern flank of Jebel Musa. Rock retaining walls strengthen the path in several places. These were built by laborers who developed this route for Ibrahim 'Abbas Pasha, ruler of Egypt from 1849 to 1854. In 1853 the pasha visited Sinai and made plans to build a palace on Jebel Musa's summit. Bedouins tell visitors that the scheme "so inflamed Moses that he dealt the Pasha a shaking"; the leader was assassinated the following year.[60] In fact by that time workers had begun construction of a palace for 'Abbas Pasha on the 1,300-meter summit of a nearby mountain known today as Jebel 'Abbas Pasha, reportedly after placing meat on all the region's peaks and observing that it spoiled least there.[61] Reinforced camel routes leading up that mountain and through the Nagub al-Haawa pass testify to his resolve to create a home in the high Sinai. Along the pasha's route on Jebel Musa a German benefactor, Bassilia

115

•

The

Christian

Landscape

A view

southwestward from

Jebel ad-Dayr to the

Monastery of

St. Galaktion and

St. Episteme and the

peak of Jebel Musa,

with the camel path

winding up Wadi

ad-Dayr and

Jebel Musa.

September 6, 1989.

*A view
southwestward from
the Basin of the
Rock Dove on Jebel
ad-Dayr to the
Monastery of St.
Katherine at the foot
of Jebel Musa. The
summit of Jebel
Katarina is in the
distance in the
upper left.
September 6, 1989.*

Schlink of the "Marie Sisters" or Darmstadt Sisters, erected a plaque in 1979 citing Deuteronomy 5:2, "The Lord our God made a Covenant with us in Horeb," and continuing: "Blessed are they whom God encounters here, to make the covenant of love with them, to unite Himself with them, to take them into His Heart and Being, on His path, the path of His commandments."[62] As the route reaches the ridge dividing the drainages of Wadi ad-Dayr and Wadi al-Arba'iin, a narrow footpath known to pilgrims as the Road of God drops quickly into Wadi al-Arba'iin.[63] Camels can continue on another kilometer into the Basin of Elijah, where this route joins the trail leading from the Stairway of Repentance.

The Basin of Elijah (Arabic, Farsh Iliyahu), also known as the Plain of the Cypress Tree, creates a real geological break in the mountain.[64] This flat bowl at 2,000 meters provides sudden and welcome relief from the steep Stairway of Repentance. The rest is short-lived because the steepest part of the climb lies ahead in the final 750 steps leading 250 meters in elevation to the summit. Standing in the basin the climber may appreciate that Jebel Musa has two distinct parts. The cone-shaped summit is dark and its rocks fragmented; it is made of volcanic and metamorphic materials. Underfoot and spreading in all directions but south is the more gentle landscape of red granite. Most walkers continue on to the summit and miss the most beautiful portion of Jebel Musa, a series of basins extending 2 kilometers to the northwest as far as Ras Safsaafa, where the mountain comes to an abrupt end overlooking the Plain of ar-Raaha. In the past some monks, Biblical scholars, and travelers have insisted that the Safsaafa portion of Jebel Musa is "Horeb," while the summit area is "Mount Sinai" proper.[65] Monks today make this distinction to refer to the different parts of the mountain, but not to argue where the events of Exodus took place.

The Basin of Elijah is the natural centerpiece of Jebel Musa. It is a beautiful place. Flanked by six small cypress trees and a lone olive tree, a giant

A view southward to the Basin of Elijah and the summit of Jebel Musa. The Church of Elijah and ancient cypress trees are in left center. July 17, 1989.

cypress tree more than five hundred years old towers over the basin, with a dark green crown that creates a striking contrast with the gentle pink of the surrounding granite. This unlikely tree invites much curiosity. In 1835 Wilhelm Philipp Schimper measured its circumference a meter above the ground as 2.6 meters.[66] At least one Bedouin has climbed to the top of the tree. At its foot is a cistern the Jabaliya call the "Well of Our Lord Moses" (Bir Sayyidna Musa), which collects rain and snowmelt, yielding excellent water from a depth of about 6 meters.[67] Jabaliya shepherds take water from it to fill a small rock hollow nearby so that their livestock and ibex may drink. Below the well and overlooking the top of the Stairway of Repentance is a dam built recently by Jabaliya laborers to prevent floodwaters from damaging the monastery below.

Elijah's story dominates the basin that bears his name. Monastic tradition regards this as the place to which Elijah fled after slaying the prophets of Baal. Over the tiny grotto where they believe Elijah stayed for forty days and nights while ravens fed him, early monks built the Church of Elijah (Arabic, Kaniisat Iliyahu). Since Etheria's time monks have occasionally celebrated mass in the church and opened its doors to pilgrims.[68] Above the church monks showed pilgrims the rock where ravens fed Elijah.[69] Within the church is a chapel dedicated to Elisha, who left this place to follow Elijah and become his successor. Edward Hull believed that St. Paul fled to this very place when he "went into Arabia" (Galatians 1:17).[70] Opposite the church is a smaller chapel of St. Marina the Virgin (Arabic, Bayt al-Gasiis, "house of the priest"), which was rebuilt after falling into ruin early in the eighteenth century.[71] It commemorates a young woman who disguised herself as "Brother Marinus" to live in a monastery and was convicted wrongly of seducing a woman.[72] About 500 meters to the southwest of the Church of Elijah is the chapel marking the spot where St. Stephen perished in 580 A.D. Somewhere in this vicinity, perhaps within the Basin of Elijah, is a holy place which has been forgotten.[73] In the fourth century Etheria "came to another place not far off, which the priests and monks pointed out to us, where holy Aaron had stood with the seventy elders, when holy Moses was receiving the law from the Lord for the children of Israel. In that place, although it is not covered in, there is a great rock which has a flat surface, rounded in shape, on which those holy men are said to have stood; there is also in the midst of it a kind of altar made of stones."[74] Monks today do not know where this place is.

SAFSAAFA

The Safsaafa portion of Jebel Musa sprawls northwest from the Basin of Elijah. There are no sites commonly identified with the Exodus narrative on this part of the mountain, but it has a distinct aura of sanctity. Beginning in the fourth century hermits lived, prayed, and cultivated orchard trees and wheat and barley in small soil-filled basins there.[75] Later monks built chapels to honor their devout predecessors and other holy figures. The substantial-looking chapels that stand today next to the ruins of early Byzantine dwellings are no older than the nineteenth century. All of the chapels are connected by pathways. Where these are steep there are stone steps which remain in excellent condition as testimony to the extraordinary dedication of the pious men who carved them. A path leading northward over a low pass from the Basin of Elijah forks, with the right branch leading to a chapel dedicated to St. John the Baptist (Arabic, Kaniisat al-Yuhanna). Near the chapel an early hermit enjoyed the fruits of a domestic fig he had grafted onto wild fig stock, and grew wheat in a plot now overtaken by wild hawthorn trees. Tristram's grackles roost in a poplar tree here, and olive and cypress trees add an air of fertility to the place. Just east of the chapel and garden monks built a dam to prevent flooding of the Monastery of St. Katherine below, but it later broke and water inundated the monastery. Above the dam stands a cross built in memory of martyred monks. From it there is a breathtaking view of the monastery 400 meters below.

Turning left at the fork on the path leading from the Basin of Elijah, one reaches a chapel dedicated to St. Gregory of Sinai. Monks today say

The abandoned garden and Chapel of St. Panteleimon on Jebel Musa. The peak of Jebel Katarina rises over the chapel. July 17, 1989.

this thirteenth-century ascetic lived in a rock shelter where the chapel now stands and climbed to the summit of Jebel Musa to pray each day. He cultivated wheat in a small basin now overgrown by argel plants, and drew sweet water from a well there as Bedouin shepherds do today. Next to the well is a very old, twisted almond tree (Arabic, *lawz*) for which the Bedouins have named Gregory's chapel the "Chapel of the Almond" (Kaniisat al-Lawz). At the northeastern end of Farsh al-Lawz, the Basin of the Almond where the chapel stands, a path terminates after a steep and circuitous ascent from Wadi ad-Dayr via the drainage of Wadi al-Aramziyya. Ancient monks used this route frequently and improved it in places, but monks today avoid it as too dangerous. Tucked away in a narrow drainage beyond the southeastern end of Farsh al-Lawz is the Chapel of St. Anne, known to the Jabaliya as "the Hidden Chapel" (al-Madsuus).

The main path leading from the Basin of Elijah continues northwestward from the Chapel of the Almond and again forks. Bearing left or southwestward the walker soon reaches the Chapel of St. Panteleimon, known to Bedouins as the "Red Church" (Arabic, Kaniisat al-Ahmaar). Like Jebel Musa's other chapels this one is closed and locked, but it is possible to peer through a window to view the altar. Outside is a broken-down wall that once protected a garden in which hermits grew wheat. It is now overgrown with secondary growth plants, suggesting the ascetics

were here recently in ecological terms. East of the chapel on a high promontory are numerous rock structures which ancient cenobites dwelled in.
In 1739 monks told Bishop Pococke that two brothers, the sons of some
king, had lived in one of them as hermits.[76] From the Chapel of St. Panteleimon the path continues southward, meets another track leading up
from Wadi al-Arba'iin, and drops quickly into Wadi ash-Shrayj, the drainage which defines Jebel Musa's northwest flank and empties out into the
Plain of ar-Raaha. Early monks told pilgrims that this "Derb Seritch" was
the Path of Moses, the route the prophet used to climb Mount Sinai.[77] It
is, as they advised ambitious pilgrims, the easiest of all routes up the
mountain.

Retracing one's steps from the Chapel of St. Panteleimon and taking
the other path at the last fork, one climbs over a pass and approaches Jebel
Musa's most remote basin, just below its northwestern extremity at Ras
Safsaafa. From the right or east the main path is joined by the "Way of
Jethro" (Arabic, Sikkat Shu'ayb), an alternative but extremely difficult
route up Jebel Musa which begins opposite Nabi Haruun at the mouth of
Wadi ad-Dayr. Beyond this junction, Byzantine-era steps lead down into
a basin graced with a lone willow tree (Arabic, *safsuuf*), from which this
part of the mountain acquired its name. The Jabaliya regard the tree as
"very ancient" and therefore revere it. Almost within its shade is a well-
built chapel of local granite known to the Jabaliya as the Willow Church
(Kaniisat as-Safsaafa), and to St. Katherine's monks as the Chapel of the
Holy Girdle of the Virgin Mary because of a tradition that the Mother of
Christ appeared to a fourth-century hermit at the site and gave him her
belt as evidence of her visit.[78] On the natural rock wall between the tree
and chapel are two hollows where early monks probably burned votive
candles. Above and behind this place is the Ras Safsaafa peak of Jebel
Musa, marked with a vertical wooden post that once supported a cross.

From the 2,168-meter summit of Safsaafa the entire Plain of ar-Raaha
is visible. It is a dramatic view. The American Edward Wilson wrote, "The
beauty of the scene is very great. No accessories of snow or river or foliage
are there, and none are needed—nor distance, to 'lend enchantment to
the view.' Would that I could picture what I saw! The rugged 'Rock of
Moses' lay at my feet, as black as the shadow at its side. Across the plain,
on each side, the crag-crowned mountains were glowing with streams of
ruby color. Nature seemed preparing for some great spectacle."[79] Some
early Biblical scholars were so touched by the physical drama of this setting, and so willing to match it point-by-point with Biblical narrative, that
they insisted it must have been here that Moses met with God while his
people camped below. Edward Robinson and Eli Smith read the relevant

*A view westward to
the Chapel of the
Holy Girdle of the
Virgin Mary and its
lone willow tree,
with Ras Safsaafa
rising above.
July 17, 1989.*

passages from Exodus as they stood here. "We gave ourselves up to the
impressions of the awful scene; and read with a feeling that will never be
forgotten, the sublime account of the transaction and the commandments
there promulgated, in the original words as recorded by the great Hebrew
legislator."[80] To Edward Palmer, this was without doubt the "nether end
of the mount" cited in Exodus 19:17.[81] Arthur Sutton wrote, "So close
does the plain Er Raha come to Mount Sufsafa that one can at once un-

derstand the need of 'setting bounds about the mountain' to prevent the people from touching it." [82] This proximity of mountain and plain still invites incursions: Ras Safsaafa was to be the terminus of the aerial cable car envisaged for development on Mount Sinai.

If there is one setting in the Jebel Musa region that has the natural presence one might expect of a sacred place, it is the Safsaafa portion of Jebel Musa. Stairways, chapels, and crosses are only the most obvious manifestations of this very special area. There is an easiness to the terrain, with only low ridges separating the bowls smoothed in its red granite. The path moves readily underfoot, especially after the labor of the climb from the monastery. Ibex, birds, and other wild animals are more abundant here than anywhere else in the area. The vegetation is rich because this high altitude receives maximum potential rain and snowfall, because the soil-filled basins hold much water, and because hermits left behind cypress, poplar, and olive. Thyme, sage, and oregano are the dominant wild shrubs, creating a natural incense that adds to an atmosphere of sanctity. Bedouin girls in colorful adolescent dress bring their sheep and goats up here from distant lowland camps. The girls' flute (*shabaaba*) is the only sound of human presence on Safsaafa: the Jabaliya obey the monks' prohibition of camping on the sacred mountain and are gone by dusk. It is a shock after the quiet sanctity of Safsaafa to step back into the Basin of Elijah, which although beautiful seems commercial and profane. Tourists of many tongues converse and shout, Bedouin peddlers sell Cokes, trailsides are lined with litter, and graffiti spoil the rock faces.

THE PEAK

The most heavily traveled portion of Jebel Musa is the most sacred: all trails finally converge on the final 750 steps to the summit. To reach the top from the Basin of Elijah visitors unknowingly pass the stone marking the spot where monks say Aaron was turned back as unworthy to tread the holy ground above. [83] At the summit, after the difficult two-and-a-half- to three-hour climb from the monastery, the first sensation is relief or triumph. Then comes the pleasure of the view. Photographer Franklin Hoskins recorded his impression: "The view from the top is wild and imposing beyond the power of any pencil or camera." [84] Two decades earlier Edward Hull had written, "Nothing can exceed the savage grandeur of the view from the summit of Mt. Sinai. The infinite complication of jagged peaks and varied ridges, and their prevalent intensely red and greenish tints . . . The whole aspect of the surroundings impresses one with the conviction that he is here gazing on the face of Nature under one of her most savage forms, in view of which the ideas of solitude, of waste, and of desolation connect with those of awe and admiration."[85] From the summit many observers have seen a sea of petrified waves. For Francis Henniker "all the rest is a sea of desolation. It would seem as if Arabia Petraea had once been an ocean of lava, and that while its waves were running literally mountains high, it was commanded suddenly to stand still."[86] "The eye sought in vain to catch some prominent object amid the chaos of rocks which were tumbled round the base, and vanished in the distance in the form of raging waves," Léon de Laborde wrote. "If I had to represent the end of the world, I would model it from Mount Sinai."[87] Even the most secular visitors are moved. "The view, though not so extensive nor so picturesque as that from Jebel Katarina, can never in its solemn desolation be forgotten, even should one be callous and steeled against all its sacred associations," wrote Charles Wilson.[88]

Not all visitors see a beautiful landscape from the summit. The naturalist Edward Rüppell saw "the whole aspect of Sinai, destitute of brooks, and of verdure in the ordinary sense, as exceedingly gloomy."[89] James Wellsted perceived "nothing to give an interest to the scene except the mighty Recollection of the Past: this throws over it all a dark and deep and mysterious charm."[90] Jebel Musa's heights displeased Edward Robinson: "My first and predominant feeling while upon this summit, was that of disappointment."[91] Lesley Hazleton was discouraged: "I have never seen such ugly mountains as those of Santa Katerina. I feel . . . if I were just to touch any one of those jagged peaks, it would draw blood. My heart caught with the heaviness of doubt and disappointment; where I had expected majesty, I saw only a bleak deformity."[92] I met Ian White, a well-traveled Australian who had spent the night on Jebel Musa's summit from which, he said, "everything looked more or less the same." He preferred the American Southwest.

The faithful focus their attention on the summit not for its vista but as the place of the great hierophany described in Exodus. In the fourth century the Spanish pilgrim Etheria depicted a church which stood over the traditional site where Moses received the Law from God: "In that place there is now a church, not great in size, for the place itself, that is the summit of the mountain, is not very great; nevertheless, the church itself is great in grace."[93] The Emperor Justinian had a new church erected on the site in 532 A.D.[94] Early pilgrims and monks knew it as the Chapel of Moses, Chapel of St. Michael the Archangel, and Chapel of the Latins.[95] In the 1700s a separate Greek Church of Our Savior stood just south of the main Latin or Catholic church, apparently north of where the mosque is today.[96] The summit churches have fallen into ruin and been repaired many times. In the mid-1980s a windstorm blew the roof off the church

and Jabaliya workmen repaired the structure quickly. Monks today claim that the existing Church of the Holy Trinity which was built in 1934 on this site incorporates some of Justinian's original components. The stone is recognizable as granite quarried in the nearby Basin of Elijah. According to monks today the altar of this church is built over the very rock from which God hewed the tablets of the Law. Earlier monks told pilgrims that the marks left by Moses' knees were still imprinted in rock beneath the church floor.[97]

The church's western wall abuts a large rock which is rich in sacred associations. In 1384 monks told pilgrims that "Atop this rock God the Father stood when he gave the ten commandments to Moses" and that the wind-eroded hollow beneath it was the "cleft in the rock" in which Moses hid himself as God's glory passed by.[98] The pilgrims had no doubt that God created the crevice for Moses to retreat into:

The Church of the Holy Trinity on Jebel Musa's summit. At left, adjoining its western wall, is the traditional "cleft in the rock." October 11, 1989.

> *Then the rock, parting, divided: and one part raised itself up a good bit, and leaned on that rock from which it was parted, and remained suspended so that three men could easily enter beneath it. And really to see that rock and the way it stands, it well appears to be a thing done by divine miracle, because truly it would be impossible for Moses to stand beneath this rock, because that place beneath the rock where he was standing was just under where God the Father stood on the rock above. There it is said he remained 40 days with God.[99]*

"Out of devotion we all laid ourselves in the hollow place wherein the Lord laid down Moses upon his belly," pilgrim Felix Fabri wrote. "In imitation of the prophet we laboriously wormed ourselves into this hole." Two hundred fifty years later Richard Pococke also investigated the grotto:

> *To the north of these churches, and adjoining to the church of the Latins, is the great rock about nine feet square, which is almost as high as the top of the church. Under the west side of this rock is a cavity, in which one may conveniently lie, and from it there is a crack in the rock to the east, thro' which one may see the light. This is said to be the place from whence Moses saw the back parts of the Lord, when he told him "that he would put him into a clifet in the rock." The common people say the rock inclined forward, that Moses might not see, and that lifting himself up to look, he left the impression of his back in the top of the cell.*[100]

In the cleft monks showed Edward Palmer "something like the impression of a man's hand and head" left there by Moses.[101] Bedouins believe these marks were created when "Moses shrank back into the rock while the glory of the Lord passed by."[102] Monks in 1844 showed Tischendorf a stone "immediately behind the chapel" which they said Moses sat upon after he had received the tablets. Tischendorf sat on it for a long time writing letters home.[103]

In deference to the sanctity of this place monks have never lived on Jebel Musa's summit. "No one, however, dwells on the very summit of the central mountain," Etheria reported in the fourth century. "There is nothing there excepting only the church and the cave where holy Moses was."[104] Only the dead could reside there; as recently as 1384 the church contained remains of deceased monks and saints, reputedly including Elijah's successor Elisha.[105] Traditionally monks have visited the summit only briefly but as often as possible to commemorate the events that took place there. A Romanian monk who died at an old age at the monastery in the early 1980s is said to have climbed to the summit one hundred times. Most monks still aspire to climb once a month, despite their reluctance to mix with the tourists who frequent the summit. In former times there were no secular distractions and monks and pilgrims mingled happily. Visitors attended the masses which monks celebrated routinely in the church.[106] Each September 3 monks honored the feast of Moses with a special mass there, after which they distributed food to Bedouins and anyone else present.[107] They drew their water from a cistern constructed sometime prior to 1739 about 100 meters south of the summit.[108] When the festivities concluded they retreated to the monastery.

WADI AL-ARBA'IIN AND
MOUNT KATHERINE

127

•

The
Christian
Landscape

Jebel Musa is flanked by two large drainages running northwestward into
the Plain of ar-Raaha. On the mountain's north side is Wadi ad-Dayr, in
which the monastery sits, and on its south is Wadi al-Arba'iin, "Valley of
the Forty," also known as Wadi al-Leja and Wadi Layan. All of Wadi al-
Arba'iin is off-limits to visitors today because the headquarters of the local
secret police is located at the valley's mouth, just above the village of Katriin. In former times the valley was an important destination for pilgrims.
At its mouth monks as recently as 1836 showed visitors the spot where the
earth opened to swallow up the unfaithful Korah, Dathan, and Abiram, as
related in Numbers 16:32−33.[109] About halfway up the valley they visited
the "Rock of Moses" (Arabic, Hajar Musa), a large granite boulder which
monks and Bedouins believe is the "rock at Horeb" which Moses struck
to water the Israelites, and which he named Massah and Meribah (Exodus
17:5−7). Water no longer runs from beneath the rock, but when it did
pilgrims drank from it. They carved crosses into the rock and marveled at
its twelve peculiar indentations. The Jabaliya believe these are the "twelve
springs" referred to in the Quranic account of Moses striking the rock
(Sura 2:60; see also Sura 7:160).[110] Monks told Edward Palmer about the
rock's markings and its wondrous properties: "There are sundry niches, or
fissures, in this stone which are construed by the credulous into twelve
mouths, whence they say that water gushed forth to supply the twelve
tribes. Monkish legend has it that this rock followed the children of Israel
throughout their wanderings."[111] In 1974 the monks built the small Birth
of the Holy Virgin Chapel adjacent to the rock.[112] They still marvel at the
site. One told me: "The marks in the stone there were not manmade.
They cannot detect how those marks got in the stone. Well, you see the
stone, you cannot explain—no one can explain—scientists have examined
those stones. They cannot find any instrument made by human hands that
would make those marks. The Bedouin tradition is that water ran from
the site all the way to Wadi Feiran above ground. That is how much water
there was. It ran above ground for 60 kilometers. They say the reason Wadi
Feiran is so verdant is because water ran from here and supplied water to
the area." I was not able to confirm Bedouin belief in this tradition. In
1739 Richard Pococke and in 1816 John Lewis Burckhardt saw Bedouins
placing herbs in the rock's twelve "mouths" and then feeding them to
their camels "as a sovereign remedy, as they think, in all disorders."[113]
Bedouins also discern in the rock the imprint of Moses' back, made when
he rested against it. Nearby is his footprint. In 1837 monks showed Gotthilf

Jabaliya children by
the herb-blessed
"mouths" of the
Rock of Moses in
Wadi al-Arba'iin.
August 27, 1993.

von Schubert another holy place in Wadi al-Arba'iin, the stone on which an angry Moses broke the tablets of the Law. Lord Lindsay reportedly saw a Bedouin kneeling and praying by this rock while stroking it with his hand.[114] Palmer learned that the entire Wadi al-Arba'iin "is looked upon by the Arabs as particularly sacred. They believe that no robbery can be perpetrated there without immediate detection, and that if a man afflicted with any malady whatever were to sleep within its precincts he would experience instant relief. Here the 'spirits' are said to hold nightly revel, and celebrate *fantasias* to the sound of sweet music."[115] Pococke's guides told him that this valley was the Rephidim of Exodus 17:1, where the Israelites defeated Amalek.[116]

About 2 kilometers above the Rock of Moses is the bright green enclave of the Monastery of the Forty Martyrs (Arabic, Dayr al-Arba'iin). It is dedicated to forty Christians martyred at Cappadocia in distant Asia Minor. Father Makarios told me the story of their sacrifice:

> *They were from an area known as Sebaste. They were Christian soldiers in the Roman army in the third century* A.D. *They were asked to worship the pagan gods, and of course they refused. It was wintertime. The pagan soldiers forced the forty into the freezing waters of a lake. They went in gladly. The pagans thought that by morning the Christian forty would be dead from the cold. They were not. However, during the night, one of the forty backed out and went ashore. He was killed. Another of those standing by saw what was happening, took off his own tunic, and joined the others in the water. Because they never did freeze to death, they were all killed by the bystanders. A monastery was erected to their memory in the Sinai.*

The Monastery of the Forty also honors a link with the earliest Christian habitation of Mount Sinai. At the north end of the monastery's olive gar-

The Monastery of the Forty Martyrs in Wadi al-Arba'iin, with the northeastern flank of Jebel Katarina rising behind. August 26, 1993.

den is a rock shelter where the hermit St. Onophrius was said to have lived for seventy years after coming to this lonely place from Upper Egypt.[117] Tradition holds that before Onophrius died in 390 A.D. his mentor St. Anthony visited him here.[118]

Today the monastery gardens and its Church of St. Mary of Mercy are looked after by the family members of a Jabaliya man named Faraji. They tend the olive trees in an orchard shared with great cypress and poplar trees, and raise their beans and other vegetables just outside the monastery enclosure.[119] Farther up the wadi, near the divide leading into Wadi As-ba'iyya, there is a small Jabaliya settlement. The young girls of this hamlet pasture their families' sheep and goats on Jebel Musa, climbing the Byzantine path to the Chapel of St. Panteleimon. The same children one sees on Jebel Musa one day may be seen the next on the high, windy slopes of Mount Katherine.

Jebel Katarina rises precipitously to the southwest from Wadi al-Arba'iin and presents one of Sinai's steepest climbs. Many weary pilgrims have shared Sigoli's conviction that he was able to reach the top only because of the "grace of God and the Virgin spouse of Jesus Christ, St. Katherine."[120] Fortunately about halfway to the summit on the path from Wadi al-Arba'iin there is a water source. Monks today call it Perdika, Greek for "partridge." They explain that in the twelfth century when their predecessors climbed the mountain to fetch St. Katherine's body, they began to falter from thirst. A partridge appeared miraculously to lead them to this small water source.

Traditions associated with St. Katherine have left a mark on the mountain named after her. When Felix Fabri and his companions climbed the mountain in 1483 they saw a depression on the summit made miraculously by the pressure of the saint's body. Their guide, a monk, explained that birds respected this spot and would not even defecate on it.[121] A Tuscan pilgrim marveled at a scent which wafted miraculously from this spot: "Again I say to you, reader, that big stone on which lay this blessed body, which has been open to rain and wind, emits such a great odour that it is an incredible thing to him who with bodily eyes has not seen."[122] Monks displayed to pilgrims two other marks in the stone nearby they said were made in the fifteenth century by the posteriors of angels.[123] They also showed visitors an outline in the native rock they believed to be St. Katherine's footprint.[124] All of these sacred signs are enclosed today within a small chapel complex on the mountain's summit. Monks still point out the impression left in the rock as St. Katherine's body lay there in a fetal position. The stone is discolored by what they say was St. Katherine's blood spilled at the moment her body came to rest there. Monks rarely visit this place, but are well-equipped to stay when they do. There is a kitchen and

sleeping area. The structure is built to withstand the rigors of Egypt's highest place (2,665 meters), with a sturdy roof of sheet metal and red tile
manufactured in Marseilles. Four hundred meters away is Jebel Katarina's
twin summit of Jebel Zebir. On its peak is the ruin of a weather station
erected by the Smith Meteorological Institute of California in 1932 and
manned in summers by British scientists until the outbreak of World
War II.[125] After 1967 Israeli soldiers built a jeep road to the summit and
used it as a military observation post.

*The Chapel of St.
Katherine on the
summit of Jebel
Katarina.
June 11, 1989.*

THE FACE OF HOLY LAND

For the monks of St. Katherine the landscape around Jebel Musa is
crowded with sacred places, rich in stories. For centuries they have depicted these places and symbols of the stories they tell on icons. Until the
early 1920s monks awarded all visitors a "pilgrim certificate" which verified they had visited Mount Sinai, and which at home would remind them
of the sacred sites they had seen.[126] The tattered remains of these mementos
posted by returning pilgrims may still be seen in Orthodox churches
throughout Russia.[127] The certificate was a reproduction of an icon a resident monk named Theodosius painted in 1778.[128] At the lower right a
procession of monks receives the archbishop. Arab archers besiege the
monastery. The Virgin and Christ child appear in the flame of the burning

bush as a barefooted Moses kneels before it. A raven brings food to Elijah. Above him is Jebel ad-Dayr with its Monastery of St. Galaktion and St. Episteme and other chapels. Moses is depicted as a shepherd in the valley between Jebel ad-Dayr and the central peak of Mount Sinai. The Stairway of Repentance, with its gates of St. Stephen and many chapels, appears on the mountain. At the summit God delivers the tablets to Moses from a cloud, attended by trumpeting angels. On the neighboring peak of Mount Katherine angels lay the saint's body to rest. Below her is the Perdika fountain. At the foot of the mountain in Wadi al-Arba'iin some of the forty martyrs meet their death.

Such images of Mount Sinai had a profound impact throughout the Christian world, particularly in the Middle Ages. As the fame and influence of the Sinai monastery spread, the Byzantine depiction of rugged, holy Mount Sinai became a prototype for the motif of sacred landscapes everywhere. In a fifteenth-century painting, for example, St. Francis of Assisi receives the stigmata in a valley surrounded by rocky, bare, pointed mountains reminiscent of the high Sinai massif.[129]

The monastery's iconography is not naturalistic; there is no consideration of real scale or topography. The art conveys a general attitude of the monks. They know sacred places with exacting detail but take little interest in their broader setting. In 1849 Karl Graul observed this paradox: "The monk who was our guide hardly ever knew the name of a wadi or a mountain, but he knew these [Biblical] localities perfectly and never failed to impart to us the relevant tradition of the Fathers."[130] Perhaps the monks have felt that intimate knowledge of the Holy Mountain would diminish its mystery. "God said not to touch this mountain," they often say. They even avoid the excessive contact with the mountain that climbing it alone would provide. "I go up there with people," Father Makarios said. "I would not go up alone. I never go up there alone, ever." I asked why. "It is not safe," he said. "Physically it is not safe?" He answered cryptically, "Always travel with somebody else up that mountain."

The places of the Exodus are real for these devout men and until quite recently have provided them with an ideal setting for prayer. When I asked about one of these sites Father Makarios grew defensive, as if I were challenging his faith. "Is the hollow by the north side of the church the site where your tradition says Moses hid from God?" I asked. "Yes, that is true. We take all those things for granted. How can we dispute those things? We cannot do it. It is going against our own tradition if we deny those sites there." "Are those sites meaningful to you?" I continued. "Of course they are, extremely meaningful. Not only to me, but to the church at large. To any religious tradition. And I think that is why people come here today, generally speaking, the average person who is on a bus with a lot of other people. Those people are searching for places like these for reassurance." The monks see themselves as guardians of places which belong to the spiritual heritage of humankind, and wince with a burden of historical responsibility when skeptical visitors and secular changes threaten them.

With words, drawings, and photographs, travelers and pilgrims for centuries have tried to capture the spiritual essence of places around Mount

"The Convent of St. Catherine, Mount Sinai." By David Roberts, 1856. The view is northwestward down Wadi ad-Dayr to the Plain of ar-Raaha.

Sinai. It was not a particularly difficult task. The stark simplicity of a desert, its dramatic mountains and valleys, the romantic appearance of monks and Bedouins in traditional garb, the antiquity of chapels, and the verdant aspect of gardens lent themselves well to images of spiritual rhapsody. Sacred places generally represent images of the way the world should be; here was that would-be world on this Earth.[131] David Roberts' 1856 lithograph of the monastery and the Plain of ar-Raaha is a perfect snapshot of a real landscape. The sanctity of this setting is manifest here with accuracy rather than artistic embellishment. A caravan of Bedouins or pilgrims is approaching Mount Sinai across the pristine Plain of ar-Raaha, where the children of Israel once camped. In words Edward Palmer painted a picture of the divine landscape of Mount Sinai: "What scene so fitting to witness the proclamation of the primeval law as those hoary primeval rocks? Surely it was not accident which determined the choice, but rather that universal harmony of the Moral and the Physical in Nature which attest so plainly the unity of purpose in God's creative scheme." [132] "There is a magnificent correspondence between the granite cliffs of Sinai and the unchangeable walls of moral truths," agreed photographer Franklin Hoskins. "It is no accident that the promulgation of the Divine Law, the fundamental principles of all the best moral and legal systems of the world, are linked with the oldest geological formation of our planet." [133] Standing on the summit of Jebel Musa Tischendorf felt that

> Prayer—fervent intense prayer—was necessary here. It seemed as if the Almighty were nearer here than anywhere else on earth. His sublimity, his reverential majesty, his love, his mercy, all combined with one superb ideal. As a throne which God has raised for himself upon the earth; unchangeable since the day of the creation; and built by the same hand that formed the heaving ocean, and arched the eternal heavens: this is Sinai. It stands there like a holy fortress removed from the forums of the world, far from the habitations of man, alone amid the desert and the sea, towering upwards to the clouds.[134]

To understand why the landscape at Jebel Musa appears as it does one must return to the monks' iconography. The wild scenery only lightly embellished by human activity is not accidental. The monks of St. Katherine and their Jabaliya Bedouin neighbors have kept it that way to reflect their vision of sacred space. They have always forbidden the building of any structures on the Plain of ar-Raaha and allowed only churches and chapels to be built on Jebel Musa and neighboring mountains. No Bedouin dwellings or other secular structures have been permitted, except recently for refreshment stands to service pilgrims and tourists. The Jewish historian Flavius Josephus wrote that Mount Sinai was already so sacred in

A view northwestward down Wadi ad-Dayr to the Monastery of St. Katherine and the Plain of ar-Raaha. By H. Fenn and C. Cousen, 1880.

Moses' time that nomads would not even graze their animals on it: "Taking his station at the mountain called Sinai, he drove his flocks thither to feed them. Now this is the highest of all the mountains thereabout, and the best for pasturage, the herbage there being good; and it had not been before fed upon, because of the opinion men had that God dwelt there, the shepherds not daring to ascend up to it." [135] While this account might be mythological and might not in fact refer to Jebel Musa, it is clear that the sacred landscape of Jebel Musa has appeared exactly as devout people have wanted it to, and they have kept it that way as long as they have been able. Travelers' and pilgrims' depictions of the Jebel Musa environs are remarkably consistent from the fourth through mid-twentieth centuries. The Plain of ar-Raaha is sweeping and bare. Wadi ad-Dayr and the mountains embracing it dwarf the monastery and the shrines of Nabi Haruun, the only apparent signs of human handiwork. Jebel Musa's towering flanks rise into the heavens.

Skeptics have presented evidence to prove that Sinai's sacred sites are ordinary after all, inadvertently promoting an attitude that opens doors for change and development on the landscape. "The legends of St. Catharine's monks are palpably worthless," Henry Palmer concluded flatly. "With characteristic effrontery, the holy fathers have grouped together in a preposterous jumble, within easy reach of their own gates, the sites of many of the chief events of the Lawgiving and the Exodus." [136] A monk showed

Tischendorf the mould of the golden calf. The German scoffed, "I could not make up my mind to investigate critically these ridiculous traditions: and yet, among European travellers, more than one enthusiast has given himself to the task." [137] On their 1927 automobile trip Ralph Bagnold and his companions were "thrilled to identify on the way all the camping places of the Israelites," but they sneered at how others located sacred places: "This craving for identification leads people to great lengths away from common-sense. Places seem to be moved about to suit convenience, each spot being fixed with much exactness on quite imaginary evidence. The odd thing is that even in the minds of intelligent people the doubts of common-sense seem to detract nothing from the gratification of being at the place tradition has appointed." [138] The great German geographer Carl Ritter felt it was the geographer's duty to set the record straight by invalidating falsely proclaimed sacred places:

We know how difficult it is in our familiar home scenes to disentangle that which is authentic from that which is fable; and how readily many accept the false, rather than search for the true. And still more is this the case in a land so ancient as that which we are now studying, where undisputed traditions have long clothed each cleft in the rocks, and each splintered summit, with some idle monkish fancy, not allowed to die, but taken up by the credulous Arab, and be-

come more widely spread, and more ridiculously, if one may not say seriously, distorted. The whole region swims before the eyes with fantastic legends, and it requires more effort to break through them than it does to climb the steep hills or wander over the arid plains.[139]

Doubters have also comforted themselves by denying that miracles have taken place around the sacred mountain. Edward Palmer, for example, related the account of the Virgin Mary ridding the monastery of vermin, adding that "such a thing as a flea has never been seen within the convent walls. But they have been *felt*, as I can testify."[140] The unbelieving may view a specimen of *Rubus sanctus*, climb Jebel Musa, and return home without having seen the burning bush or Mount Sinai; sacred space may be trod upon without being entered, as theologian Beldon Lane contended.[141]

The monks of St. Katherine have both a privilege and a burden in living with sacred places, where they see and hear constant reaffirmation of the Divine Presence. A bush which burned but was not consumed still lives and cannot be transplanted. Water comes from stone and a well does not go dry in the worst drought. At these rare places on Earth where miracles have occurred, miracles continue to happen at them and only at them, protecting the places themselves and the people who guard them with faith and ritual. Monks and Bedouins believe that God's presence lingers in perpetual protection of Mount Sinai and the Monastery of St. Katherine. They say that no earthquake will ever harm the monastery. A mysterious plague called the "yellow pest" which struck down travelers elsewhere in the nineteenth century would not harm them at the Holy Mountain.[142] The Jabaliya have long believed that the monastery is "under the special protection of heaven, and that no evil designs against it can ever prosper, but will recoil upon the aggressor's head."[143] The monks relate that the monastery had been on the verge of capture many times, "but always at some critical moment there had been some act of God that had saved it."[144] Their faith is undiminished today. "The monks see a connection between the burning bush and their lives," Father Makarios explained. "The monastery is protected. We always say that the hand of God is protecting the monastery. So that nothing untoward is going to happen to the monastery itself, or whatever belongs to the monastery." As pressures grow to develop Mount Sinai his faith is reassuring.

Six

◆

THE
PEOPLE
OF THE MOUNTAIN

Isolated in a sea of Islam and unlettered in the ways of the desert, the monks of St. Katherine have depended upon the good will and physical assistance of Sinai's Bedouin tribes. Their reputation as marauding desert pirates makes Bedouins unlikely benefactors of helpless Christians. Pastoral nomads, however, have themselves always depended upon enclaves of settled people for supplies and services, and the Monastery of St. Katherine has filled that function. Traffic of supplies and pilgrims and requirements for manual labor in the monastery's properties have also created many employment opportunities for Sinai's Bedouins. It has been in the interest of all parties that no harm should come to the monks. An extraordinary symbiotic relationship has developed between the Christian ascetics and their Muslim neighbors.

The monks have an especially close relationship with one of these Bedouin tribes, the Jabaliya. This group originated as a diverse collection of serfs from Europe and the Near East sent to build and maintain the monastery. Intermarrying with local nomads and converting to Islam, they evolved into a distinct culture. Nevertheless they continued to share the monks' beliefs about the sacred places of Mount Sinai, and they donated new Muslim traditions of their own (see Map 2). The Greek Orthodox monks and the Muslim Jabaliya Bedouins have lived in peace side-by-side, leaving distinct but completely compatible signs of their beliefs on the landscape. These unlikely partners have cultivated the face of this sacred land carefully and remain as its principal defenders today.

The Sinai Peninsula is a patchwork of territories belonging to some seventeen tribes and also inhabited by a score of less powerful and populous groups. Two large confederations of Bedouin tribes have prevailed in the Sinai, the Tiyaaha or "People of the Plateau of Wandering" and the Tuwaara or "People of Mount Sinai."[1] The Mount Sinai alliance is composed of major tribes of the southern peninsula: the 'Alaygaat; the Muzayna; the Suwalha and its constituent subtribes al-'Awarma, Awlaad Sa'iid, and Gararsha; and the tribe which lives around the mountain itself: the Jabaliya, literally "the people of the mountain."[2] By their own estimates there are about three hundred families or fifteen hundred souls in the tribe. Perhaps eight hundred live within a 5-kilometer radius of Jebel Musa, while nearly half live in settlements 15 kilometers away in at-Tarfa and 40 kilometers distant in Wadi Feiran.[3]

The Jabaliya are not "true" Bedouins in the usual sense of claiming descent from a common Arab progenitor who was a nomad in the Arabian Peninsula. They are instead the descendants of about two hundred families from Alexandria in Egypt, Walachia in what is now southern Romania, Bosnia, and the Black Sea coast of Anatolia.[4] According to documents in the Monastery of St. Katherine, in 527 A.D. the Emperor Justinian sent the first contingent of one hundred families from eastern Europe to help build the monastery and to be "slaves of the monastery, obedient to the monks, they and their descendants, until God regain possession of the world and all that is upon it."[5] Egypt's governor Theodosius supplemented the workforce with another hundred families from Alexandria.[6] The men were servants rather than slaves. They prepared meals for the monks, maintained the physical plant of the monastery, and tended crops in orchards belonging to the monastery throughout the south Sinai. They also developed a family life and culture independent of the institution they worked for. These attendants of the monastery intermarried with local Bedouin Arabs, particularly of the Bani Wassil tribe, and converted to Islam after the mid-seventh century. Between 1517 and 1520 the Ottoman Sultan Salim I dispatched another already-Muslim group from al-Matariya in the northeastern Nile Delta to provide security for the monastery.[7] These troops added to the ethnic mix of the developing Jabaliya culture.

Like that of other Sinai Bedouins the Jabaliya kinship system is a tribal segmentary lineage organization composed of subsets of membership in groups of people descended from common ancestors. The system is patrilineal, requiring that descent be traced through male offspring of male progenitors. Within the Jabaliya tribe there are four clans or "quarters" (*rub'a*): the Awlaad Jindi, Wuhaybaat, Hamayda, and Awlaad Saliim, which take their names from male ancestors. Clans in turn are composed of lineages (*'ayla*), generally encompassing about ten to twenty-five households. Each lineage is named for a male founder or for some distinguishing trait; for example, a Diguuniyiin clansman told me his "bearded people" once grew beards "long and thick, like the monks'." Aside from the family household the only subset of the lineage is "the five" (*al-khams*), a group consisting of all members of the five most recent generations.

In Bedouin society throughout the Middle East it is a matter of personal pride and ethnic integrity to be able to recite one's ancestry through males in these tribal subgroups all the way back to the single great tribal progenitor. With their complex origins the Jabaliya cannot reasonably do so, and their oral genealogies appear weak in comparison with those of other tribes. While the typical Ma'aza tribesman across the Gulf of Suez in Egypt's Eastern Desert can readily recite at least twelve patrilineal ancestors, his Jabaliya counterpart recalls only four. There is much uncertainty in Jabaliya oral history. A Jabaliya man asked me whether it were true that his ancestors came from Romania. Another shrugged, "Some say we came from Romania, but I do not know if that is true." He could not name a tribal patriarch. Jabaliya informants told anthropologist Emanuel Marx that their ancestor was a Greek slave named Constantine.[8] Others say all Jabaliya tribespeople are descended from a man named Bakhiit and his brother al-Jindi, who came from the Black Sea region. Bakhiit, who they say is buried in Wadi Asba'iyya in a tomb the Bedouins still honor today, had two sons, Sulaym and Humayd. Humayd was the progenitor of the Humayda clan. Humayd also begat Wuhayb, founder of the Wuhaybaat, and Saliim, founder of the Awlaad Saliim. Awlaad Jindi clansmen told me they descended from Bakhiit's brother al-Jindi, whose name means "the soldier"; he was head of the only body of soldiers Justinian sent with the laborers who built the monastery. The anthropologist Ben David recorded a Jabaliya family tree in which Sulaym and Humayd are depicted as sons of Bakhiit, and al-Jindi is named as Ahmad, a man who attached himself to the tribe but was not a blood relative.[9] Some Awlaad Jindi clansmen confided in me that their ancestors might have been more recent arrivals from Egypt rather than ancient soldiers from the Black Sea region. Jabaliya shaykh Muhammad Abul-Haym recited yet another genealogy to anthropologist Clinton Bailey, pinpointing Bakhiit as an ancestor who lived only eight generations ago, or around 1645 A.D.[10] Such conflicting accounts leave the true history of the Jabaliya unwritten, but reinforce the monastery archive's portrayal of them as people of diverse origins.

This tribe created by the mingling of European, Egyptian, and Bedouin cultures has always had a special classification in Sinai Bedouin society. Physical differences are barely noticeable; compared with their neighbors the Jabaliya tend to have broader noses and fairer skin that burns more easily. In the past anthropologists and travelers even discerned Berber and Negroid features among the Jabaliya, proposing that this mixture of ethnic types made Jabaliya women the most beautiful in all Sinai.[11] However attractive they might be to outsiders the Jabaliya today claim they "never" marry other tribespeople or foreigners, and they discredit other Sinai tribes like the Muzayna for doing so. In the past the Jabaliya were themselves scorned. Other Sinai tribespeople called them a "bastard" race and labeled them contemptuously as "the sons of the Nazarenes."[12] A shaykh of the Awlaad Sa'iid told anthropologist Henry Field that the Jabaliya were "Ruumi," literally meaning "Roman" or "Byzantine" and connoting infidel Christendom; no true nomad would marry one of them.[13] Muzayna tribespeople still classify the Jabaliya as "Hiteim" or outcast.[14] To learn whether the Jabaliya might acknowledge having been classified this way I asked a Jabaliya man who the Hiteim are. He replied, "They are not exactly Arab [Bedouin], but 'half-and-half' people." I asked where they live. "In the sands of north Sinai." He asked where I had heard the term, but did not suggest his tribe ever had this appellation. He volunteered that the Gararsha tribe was the worst traditional enemy of the Jabaliya, but added, "We have not had very many enemies. We have kept to ourselves and the monastery."

The Jabaliya have invested themselves with all the offices and properties characteristic of a Sinai Bedouin tribe, including tribal territory, tribal leadership, and tribal brand. They have the smallest of the Sinai's tribal territories, but its great diversity compensates for its size. Encircled by possessions of the Awlaad Sa'iid, the Jabaliya territory corresponds almost exactly with the geological boundary of the circular dike defining the high Sinai massif. The Jabaliya call their homeland al-Jibaal, "the mountains," and take their identity and their livelihood from this landscape. However rootless outsiders may perceive nomads to be, most are in fact attached deeply to particular places. The Jabaliya believe their territory has the best climate, water resources, animal and plant life, and people anywhere in the Sinai. A Jabaliya man told the anthropologist Emanuel Marx, "I do not leave because my country is dear to me. I am tied to it by my navel-string. For when a child is born, the father buries the navel-string and the placenta deep in the ground."[15] Late in the nineteenth century Henry Palmer learned that as soon as a Bedouin woman bears a child she lays the naked baby for a few moments in a hole (*girbuus*) in the ground, and then swaddles the infant.[16]

Two essential components of Bedouin identity, women and land (*'uura wa buura*), nominally "belong" to the larger units of clan and tribe. A clans-

man may sell his land to a member of another clan, or give his daughter in
marriage to a member of another clan, but only with the permission of the
"owning" clan. Both transactions are common, although interclan mar-
riages are frowned upon. Similarly, a Jabaliya tribesman may sell land or
betroth his daughter to a member of another tribe, but only with the approval of Jabaliya tribal leaders. Marriage is rarely transacted between
tribes, but land more often is. About twenty Awlaad Sa'iid households
own gardens in Jabaliya territory and pass their summers there. Members
of the two tribes are buried side-by-side in the cemetery of Wadi al-Birka.

The Awlaad Jindi, the second largest Jabaliya clan after the Wuhaybaat,
owns more Jabaliya land than the other three clans together. Awlaad Jindi
clanspeople claim this is because they have an undivided inheritance from
al-Jindi, while the other three clans had to divide their inheritance from
Bakhiit. While all clan members in theory collectively own such resources
as water and garden plots, in practice control of these resources falls to
lineages and families. A man spoke to me about his paternal uncle's sister's
garden, his paternal uncle's garden, and his paternal uncle's brother's garden, but hastened to add "all of the gardens are ours, collectively." The
tribal signature (wasm) serves as symbol of the important fiction of collec-
tive ownership. Whatever their clan or lineage, all Jabaliya tribespeople
mark their camels, water sources, and most prized trees with this tribal
brand, which resembles a backwards "E."

Leadership among the Jabaliya functions at both the clan and tribal levels. Each clan has a headman (omda). His main function historically was to
distribute economic opportunities fairly among clan members, deciding,
for example, who would work at the monastery. The headman role is
almost entirely nominal today. The Awlaad Jindi omda Tayyib Musa Far-
rayj resides in Wadi Feiran where few of his clansmen live, and plays little
active role in clan affairs other than organizing the annual feast at Shaykh
'Awaad. The Egyptian government did acknowledge his office by jailing
him in 1989 as a responsible party when one of his clansmen fired a gun
near some Egyptian soldiers and refused to surrender to authorities. In
protest of the government action the Jabaliya canceled the Shaykh 'Awaad
festival that year.

The actual arbiter of almost all Jabaliya matters is the tribal shaykh, an
office created in the 1890s.[17] Since 1961 that position has been held by
Muhammad Mardhi Sulimaan Abul-Haym of the Awlaad Saliim clan.[18]
His main function is to intercede on behalf of his constituents in their
affairs with non-Bedouin people. He acts as liaison with the government
and with the monastery, in the latter capacity replacing the traditional role
of the headmen in delegating Jabaliya workmen to the monastery. Follow-

ing a stroke in 1984 he was unable to perform his duties fully. The stroke paralyzed his right side completely for several years, but he eventually recovered sensation in that orbit. General weakness, a dysfunctional eye, and other troubles of a sixty-five-year-old man linger. On advice of an Israeli physician he takes weekly injections of vitamin B-12 and daily doses of ginseng. "Well, they won't hurt him," British physician John Cohen told me of this regimen. When he was incapacitated the shaykh accepted the assistance of a young relation, Musa 'Awaad. "Shaykh" Musa still carries out most of Abul-Haym's duties and has earned the respect of Egyptian authorities and tourists for his good judgment and easygoing style. Many of his own people would like to see Abul-Haym replaced by Musa 'Awaad or another man. They believe Abul-Haym has become wealthy by taking too much of a percentage from the fee charged to tourists for hiring Jabaliya guides and camels. They blame him for the shortage of backcountry tourists originating from Egypt, because in order to take enough money for himself he demands an exorbitant fee that Egyptians and poorer foreigners cannot afford. "He thinks only of money," complained one Jabaliya man. His greed is so profound, said another, that he spends little time with his family members 15 kilometers away in at-Tarfa; being away from the town of Katriin would mean losing money. His tribespeople, who also complain that Egyptian government decisions rather than tribal consensus have kept him in power, continue to call for a younger, more vigorous, and less avaricious shaykh.

Traditionally the Jabaliya looked to the monastery for leadership. Until the twentieth century the Jabaliya had said they did not need a shaykh: the monastery was their shaykh. The headman and shaykh offices were created recently to meet requirements of the Bedouins' changing relationships with the monastery.[19] The monastery appointed four omdas and paid them salaries for their principal duty of deciding which of their clan members would work at the monastery. The omda office declined in importance as wage labor opportunities increased outside the monastery after 1967. One shaykh rather than four omdas was sufficient to discharge the go-between role. The headmen went off the monastery payroll and the shaykh came on.[20] This functional change accompanied a general weakening of very strong links that had existed for centuries between the two communities. Monastery literature still claims that Bedouin allegiance is unwavering: "The Archbishop of St. Katherine is considered by them to be their judge and leader, and they bring to him all their affairs and problems."[21] This is no longer true, but to understand the historical appearance of the landscape around Mount Sinai and the social environment in which landscape change is now taking place, it is necessary to appreciate the relationship that existed between these cultures until very recently.

The Jabaliya have always dealt with the monastery quite literally as a parent institution. They still call themselves *Awlaad ad-Dayr*, "Children of the Monastery." Their subservient position in this relationship dates to their original exclusive role as European and Egyptian serfs performing manual tasks for the monastery. As a distinct Jabaliya culture evolved, the monks refused to change the basic rules governing their relations. The Jabaliya acquiesced because the monastery provided them with sustenance and security. At the same time the monks' welfare depended upon Jabaliya labor and good will. In a difficult environment each group helped the other, even if on uneven terms.

The Jabaliya recall today with surprising reverence that their ancestors were solely and completely dedicated to the service of the monastery and lacked anything of their own: all livestock, orchards, and territory belonged to the monastery. A sixth-century Byzantine imperial decree awarded the monastery sovereignty over all land within a radius of three-and-one-third days' camel ride from the monastery, or as a Jabaliya man delimited this to me, the land bounded on the east by the Gulf of Aqaba and the west by the Gulf of Suez.[22] This effectively made all of south Sinai monastery property and allowed the monks to decide exactly and exclusively how the land should be used. The Jabaliya obeyed, allowing the land around Jebel Musa to be shaped as the monks wanted it to be, and providing the labor to shape it. The monastery prohibited its subjects from building any dwellings or orchard enclosures on sacred Mount Sinai, the Plain of ar-Raaha, Wadi ad-Dayr, and Jebel ad-Dayr. To ensure compliance the monastery insisted that homes of its Jabaliya employees must be located at least a half-day's walk away from the monastery. With monks' permission the Jabaliya erected a few Muslim shrines within the sacred precinct, but the landscape was predominantly a Christian image of Mount Sinai. It was a sacred landscape that could not be altered for any secular purpose. Bonds between the monks and Bedouins maintained it in a pristine state until late in the twentieth century.

Outside of the restricted area the Jabaliya could build homes and orchards, but they were obliged to obtain the monastery's permission and to register all subsequent construction at the monastery. Until 1967 they were also compelled to share half of their harvests with the monastery.[23] This sharecropping arrangement appeared to some outsiders to be disadvantageous both to monks and Bedouins; Edward Palmer described it this way:

To these [gardens in neighborhood of monastery] the monks of Sinai claim an exclusive right, allowing a certain percentage of the produce to the Arab families who tend them. As they take no measures to ensure their cultivation, and only demand that their Arab tenant should bring them a few vegetables or fruit from time to time, this arrangement tends to prevent rather than promote horticulture—an occupation which, if only properly encouraged, might be made an important instrument in ameliorating the condition of the Bedawin, especially in the well-watered valleys around Jebel Musa. But what do the Greek monks care whether the Bedawin starve or no? A Christian community—Heaven save the mark!—they have resided here for centuries without learning one jot of the language or life of their neighbors, without teaching them one word of religion or truth.[24]

The monks took from their subservient neighbors but also gave to them. The most important symbol of the monks' role in this symbiotic relationship was the regular ration of bread they provided to the Bedouins. This bread dole (*tubaara*) began as early as the ninth century and persists in modified form today.[25] In 1393 the monks dispensed two loaves daily to every Bedouin and pilgrim who sought it.[26] Nine years earlier pilgrims supposed that "this they must do from force rather than good will, because, if they did not, these would take that and other things by force, and they would molest them and harm the pilgrims who come there."[27] In 1483 Felix Fabri saw eighty to one hundred Bedouins take a daily quota of the bread.[28] In 1615 Pietro Della Valle "arrived in the night, and the door was closed. Hundreds of Arabs were encamped under the walls, and were begging for bread."[29] In 1658 Jean Thévenot saw as many as four hundred Bedouins clamoring for bread outside the wall.[30] In the 1920s and 1930s the bread ration was five loaves to a man, three to a child, and eight to a headman, every other day except in some years when it was distributed daily.[31] The output of bread was prodigious. "If you were to stay for no more than a couple of days in the convent, you might easily carry away the impression that the place is a sort of holy bakehouse and bread-shop, and that the monks are a race of holy grocers," wrote Louis Golding. "In one way or another they seem to be busy with grain or bread at most hours of the day. You have a feeling that they might be doing something a little more exalted with their spare time."[32]

If abundant and lifegiving, the bread, made of maize imported from the Nile Valley, was often not very good.[33] In 1844 Tischendorf regarded the bread distributed to the Jabaliya "of an inferior quality to that consumed within" the monastery.[34] Edward Palmer wrote facetiously that he gave a loaf to a geologist who identified it as "a piece of metamorphic rock containing fragments of quartz imbedded in an amorphous paste." He supposed that "no decently brought up ostrich could swallow one without endangering his digestion for the term of his natural life."[35] By all accounts the bread was hard, but kept well. The Jabaliya reconstituted it easily by soaking it in water.[36]

This bread ration kept Bedouins dependent upon the monastery, and inevitably monks used it for political purposes. In about 1920 a Jabaliya family tried to assume ownership of one of the monastery's gardens. The monks halted the bread supply to the entire tribe and only government intervention restored it.[37] On one occasion a dispute over the bread ration resulted in political reform in favor of the Jabaliya. In 1958 Jabaliya girls were caught cheating by posing as pregnant women and thereby collecting additional loaves. The monks insisted that from then on all women should be accompanied at the bread line by their husbands. The Jabaliya, who recognize distinct male and female realms, protested because this would require men and women to stand together. Demanding that the new law be dropped, Jabaliya shaykh Saalih Abu Msa'ad ordered Jabaliya employees of the monastery to strike. The monastery backed down and granted other concessions, including allowing Jabaliya leaders to decide which of their tribesmen would work at the monastery.[38]

In the 1950s the Egyptian government introduced into the Sinai a system for distributing subsidized basic goods such as flour, rice, cooking oil, tea, and sugar. The Israeli administration perpetuated this system. These sources dramatically reduced the historic dependence of the Jabaliya on the monastery for bread and other staples.[39] Bread survives today only as a symbol of ties between monks and Bedouins. The Jabaliya uphold the fiction that the monastery must give them bread whenever they ask for it. Now, in fact, the monks distribute bread on a regular basis only to their full-time Jabaliya employees. Father Michael explained that it was nevertheless important that monks and Bedouins worked together on Saturdays preparing the standard pita-like loaves and the special round breads of Easter: "It is the one thing all of us in the monastery do together." The work has been easier since the early 1980s, when the Bishop of Crete donated a mixer to the monastery.

At any given time about thirty men appointed by Shaykh Abul-Haym have temporary manual jobs at the monastery paying twelve Egyptian pounds per day, a rate competitive with wages offered elsewhere in Sinai. The monks also employ seventeen full-time Jabaliya workmen at the monastery and six in its outlying properties. The low ratio of Bedouins to monks contrasts markedly with what the monks remember as "good days" as recently as the 1930s, when there were three Bedouins to a monk, including one who was in effect the monk's servant. At the monastery Bedouins have many duties monks do not want to fill, and some they could not. They drive the monastery's work truck, maintain its diesel generator,

do routine chores on the grounds, clean and service the guest hostel, and cook for the monks. These full-time Jabaliya employees earn seventy Egyptian pounds monthly, or about half what they would earn as contracted manual laborers in the nearby town of Katriin. Monastery employees acknowledge, however, that they have much "hidden" income from the institution in the form of bread, clothing, holiday gifts, and other gratuities. The monastery also provides two meals daily for its Jabaliya workmen. Monks admit that the fare is inferior to their own and seldom includes chicken or meat. Jabaliya employees may leave the monastery premises only with monks' consent, and typically are allowed to do so only once each week.[40] They have a one-month vacation each year. While such working conditions may sound grim I found the Bedouins generally content and in some cases very pleased with their occupation, describing it as good, viable work for decent people. Ahmad, a man in his fifties who had worked at the monastery since 1959, told me, "This is the best place anywhere." He spoke of enjoying pleasant weather, fresh air, and thousands of stars in the night sky. He would not want to work in Katriin or in Cairo, he said. For their part the monks exalt the advantages their Jabaliya workmen enjoy. One told me, "They regard it with very high status because there are so few who can work here."

In their everyday contacts there is often apparent good will between these two very different peoples. They have reached an odd linguistic

compromise that seems to produce mostly lighthearted exchanges.[41] All the full-time Bedouin employees speak some Greek and most of the monks speak some Arabic. In his youth Father Good Angel was able to read and write Arabic. A good place to see what appears to be heartfelt symbiosis between monk and Bedouin is in the garden of the Monastery of the Poor Doctors in Wadi Tala'. Father Dorotheus works side-by-side in mundane chores with Hussayn, the Jabaliya caretaker. They converse in Arabic because Dorotheus thinks a monk should defer to the region's predominant language. The men remained friends even after an incident nearby in 1988 strained relations between their communities. Just above the Tala' monastery in Wadi Nakhala the monks built a concrete reservoir to retain springwater and rainfall runoff to irrigate the orchards below. Monks welcomed Bedouins to share the water, but say the Bedouins took too much. The monks then had a plastic waterpipe installed to divert all waters directly to the monastery, forcing the Jabaliya to seek water elsewhere.

Their differences sometimes produce disharmony between the two groups, and there is an undercurrent of incompatibility even after centuries of cohabitation. The Jabaliya are strongly family-oriented and view the celibate monks as a little odd. At the same time they understand the sacrifice involved and believe truly pious and ascetic monks are good men. However, they think as a group the monks today are not as devout as their

Father Dorotheus (seated, lower right), his camel, Diriisa, and a Jabaliya boy, Muhammad, in the garden of the Monastery of St. Katherine. Beneath the cypress trees at the right is the charnel house; above them is the Stairway of Repentance approach to Jebel Musa's summit. May 23, 1989.

predecessors. For their part some monks view the Muslim Jabaliya as heathens and as uncouth. They grudgingly respect Bedouin stamina but rarely praise the intellect and skills by which the Bedouins have thrived in this difficult environment. "They overgraze the land and throw their trash around," one monk identified as the principal occupation of the Jabaliya. Like most settled people the monks regard the Bedouins as thieves. "They steal any construction wood left outside the monastery," one complained. Some monks believe the proper station of the Jabaliya should always be as servants of the monastery. Embarrassing a younger peer, the elderly Father Good Angel spoke to me of the Jabaliya as "slaves." The younger father explained that this was a pejorative term and did not reflect how other monks felt about the Bedouins. "I would never say that about them or to them. I would not call them slaves. Their ancestors were slaves," he said. Later he admitted, "They help us a great deal. We would not be able to function in any normal sense of the word if it were not for the Bedouins." With their own ranks very small, the monks are indeed heavily dependent upon the Jabaliya both to perform vital everyday services and to assert what remains of the monastery's authority in the area. Bedouins are doing the construction work that the monastery hopes will save the Christian landscape from systematic dismantling by Egyptian developers. Loyal Jabaliya employees are the monks' eyes and ears in the broader world. The monks, for example, visit the chapel on top of Mount Katherine only once a year to celebrate mass, but they dispatch a Jabaliya watchman there once each week to check on the integrity of the locked building.

With the Israeli occupation of Sinai in 1967 the relationship between monks and Bedouins began to change. A growing wage labor economy gave the Jabaliya many more opportunities for employment outside the monastery, and the Bedouins experienced an increasing sense of independence from their historical patrons. At first the Jabaliya took only tentative steps away from the monastery, even continuing to register all real estate transactions with the monastery, and reiterating their ancient saying that "the government of the Sinai is with the monastery."[42] This position was expedient: circumstances continued to arise in which the Jabaliya benefited by deferring to the monastery's historical authority. For example, in the late 1970s an Awlaad Sa'iid tribesman claimed that some land held by the Jabaliya on Jebel Fray'a belonged rightfully to his family. The Jabaliya denied his claim, and both parties asked Archbishop Damianos to settle the matter. The monastery produced a document proving that a Jabaliya man of the Awlaad Jindi clan named Abu Garayshaan had purchased the land from Awlaad Sa'iid tribesmen nearly five hundred years earlier! The monks continue to insist that they are the most reliable mentors and protectors Bedouins could have. One explained:

We have an outreach program with the Bedouins. We help them as much as we possibly can with food, clothing, and medicine, and many of them work here. They don't have confidence in the government from the medical point of view, so they come to the monastery. They come from all over. Not just the Jabaliya: all the Bedouins come from everywhere in the Sinai. Some of them travel great distances. They respect the monastery because it is an institution that has been around for a long time, has not gone anywhere, and has not failed them yet. The political situation in Sinai has changed four times only in this century. Every time they turned around there was a new government to deal with. The political infrastructure presence in the Sinai was nil up until 1967. There were no political appointees in the Sinai. Do you know who the governor of Sinai was? The Archbishop. He adjudicated all the problems the Bedouins had: someone stole my wife, my goat fell down a cliff, whatever problems the Bedouins had. They all came to the monastery, because they knew the Bishop would help them with their problems. Not just the local Bedouins, all of the Bedouins. They recognized the monastery as being their political base. And the Abbot of the monastery, who resided in the monastery itself, was their chief for every practical purpose.

After the Sinai returned to Egyptian control in 1980 more ties between monks and Bedouins were broken, and the monastery's outreach role is minimal today. While Cairo historically accepted the monastery's claim to much of the Sinai because it meant the monks had to exercise responsibility for security of caravan routes, after 1980 the government nullified all such claims.[43] Perceiving Bedouin deference to the monastery in such matters as territorial ownership as service to a non-Egyptian political entity, the Egyptian government forbade the Jabaliya to register their properties with the monastery. Bedouins are now required to file all real estate transactions with the city council office in Katriin. Egyptian authorities generally view fraternization between monks and Bedouins with suspicion. The Jabaliya are aware that Egyptian security men are scrutinizing their contacts with the monastery, and fear retribution if Egyptian authorities perceive them as disloyal to Egypt. Since 1980 the Bedouins have therefore had to distance themselves physically from the monks. Both parties nevertheless still speak privately about the importance of their close, symbiotic relationship. They know that if circumstances change they might need one another more than ever.[44]

THE BARBARIANS

To ensure their survival and prosperity the monks of St. Katherine had to be mindful of public relations with their Bedouin neighbors. In order to attract financial support from benefactors in the West they had to portray themselves as vulnerable to the nomads. To avoid intervention from Cairo they had to convince governments there that the monastery's authority kept Sinai stable. They had to buy sufficient protection from the nomads without giving away all they had. They had to favor some tribes without alienating and making enemies of others. The monastery's presence today suggests the monks succeeded in their public relations efforts. There are no Bedouin records of these relations, but monastery archives indicate they were difficult at times.

Christian records suggest that trouble between holy men and desert "barbarians" began as soon as ascetics began to populate the Sinai. In about 250 A.D. Bishop Dionysius of Alexandria reported that Christians fled into the desert to escape persecution where "many were seized in the Arabian mountains by the heathen Saracens and carried off into captivity."[45] The most famous altercation between the groups purportedly took place sometime between 373 and 410 A.D. and was witnessed and recorded by a monk named Ammonius from Canopus, near Alexandria. He had recently arrived at Mount Sinai with a group of Egyptian pilgrims after an eighteen-day journey from Jerusalem when, on January 14, a band of "Saracens" reacting to the death of their leader attacked the community of monks living in cells around the Holy Mountain.[46] While the raiders killed thirty-eight monks, others including Ammonius took refuge in the tower by the bush at the foot of the mountain.

And they killed in Geth-rabbi all those whom they found there; and in Choreb; and people in Codar; and all those whom they found near to the Holy Mountain. And they came also as far as ourselves; and were also nearly killing us; for no man stood up against them; except the merciful God; He who stretched out His hand in conjunction with those who call upon Him from their whole Heart. And He commanded and a flame of fire was seen on the summit of the Holy Mount, and it was a wonder; and all the mountain was smoking, and the fire bursting out up to the sky. All being seized with terror, we became insensible through the fear of the vision. And falling on our faces, we worshipped God, and supplicated that He would carry us over the present necessity, which lay heavy on us, to a prosperous issue. Nay, even the Barbarians also, terrified by this new and unwonted sight, by a sudden impulse took to flight, many of them even leaving their arms with their camels, nor did they brook a moment's delay. And now when we saw that they were scattered in flight, we poured out our thanks, and glorified God, who had not over-looked His suppliants, until the end.[47]

This martyrdom is remembered in an inscription of the monastery's south chapel reading: "The Holy Fathers lie here, equal in number to those who were killed on the 14th of January, and imitating them through a baptism of blood. Theirs is the joyous and true Burning Bush; through them, O God, save us." [48] Jabaliya men told me their own account of Sinai's martyrs in which they named the Bani Saalih, a pre-Muslim Arab people, as the priest-killers. To force the murderers' retreat God made fire appear on Ras Safsaafa.

The monastery account relates that after the survivors emerged from the tower to mourn the deaths of their comrades they received news that the fathers at Raithu (modern at-Tur) had come under attack from a band of Blemmys nomads from eastern Egypt who had landed in a pirated vessel. [49] To defend their families 200 Arabs described as Pharanites (residents of Feiran) went out to meet the raiders; 147 of them died in the ensuing battle. Raithu's monks retreated to a fortress, pursued by the Blemmys horde:

They ran fast like wild beasts and came upon us to the fortress where we had fled; and they were expecting that they would find much hidden treasure. As they were walking round the walls screaming, and filling the air with wild howls, and threats in barbarous languages, we all spent the time in much sadness of spirit, quite destitute of counsel, with our eyes fixed on God, prostrate in mind, overflowing in prayer. . . . Then the Barbarians, as no one opposed or retarded their onrush, climbed up over a heap of tree trunks, piled up like a wall, and the door being opened, ran in like ravening wolves, huge, rough animals, with their swords firmly grasped in their hands. [50]

Finding no treasures but only men in loincloths, the furious bandits killed all but two of the monks and retired to their vessel intending to sail away to Clysma (modern Suez). But the watchman they had left at the ship was secretly a Christian and had sabotaged the craft. The enraged Blemmys now killed the women and children of Raithu and burned its famous palm trees. In the final battle which followed Arab Pharanites killed all of the Blemmys, losing 84 of their own men. [51]

There is a parallel tradition of another incident around 420 A.D. between monks and Bedouins at Mount Sinai. An educated man named Nilus traveled with his son Theodolus from their home in Constantinople to visit the Holy Mountain. In Sinai they met the indigenous Saracens, a people who lived from the Red Sea to Jordan by hunting game and attacking travelers. These nomads worshiped the Morning Star. On stone altars they burned game animals, white camels, and young boys in sacrifice to this star. Their rites required them to drink the sacrificial victim's blood and eat its flesh before the sun appeared above the horizon. [52] After father and son arrived at the settlement of the Bush these pagans attacked the place. They seized the monks' winter food stores and ordered them to strip and stand in groups according to age. They killed some of the older monks, took the young ones and Nilus' son into captivity for sacrifice, and dismissed the rest. Some had already survived by fleeing to the heights of Mount Sinai, knowing the superstitious Saracens would not follow them onto the mountain where God had appeared in flame. Theodolus survived the sacrificial pyre, was sold into slavery, and eventually escaped to live out his days at Mount Sinai with his father, St. Nilus.[53]

Who were these "marauding Bedouin" of the monastery records and what was their impact on the monks of Sinai?[54] It is possible that these attacks never actually took place. The accounts of Ammonius and Nilus may have been literary fabrications created after the monastery was founded to justify its construction or to endow it with martyrs of its own.[55] It is also possible that even if the stories are not true they reflect genuine circumstances that would have justified the monastery's construction. The Near East was inhabited by Saracens, the Arab "Easterners" who were the ancestors of Bedouins and other Arabs of the region today.[56] There is reliable evidence that a truce between Rome and the Saracens broke when the Saracen leader died about 370 A.D., and the Saracens attacked Roman interests in Egypt, Palestine, and Arabia.[57] The dispute between Rome and the nomads was settled in about 380 A.D. when a Saracen who had converted to Christianity was consecrated as Bishop Moses of Feiran.[58] Some of the Saracens controlled East-West trade routes while others, like many pastoral nomads until recently, enjoyed raiding. They may have attacked monastic populations in the belief—perhaps well-founded—that pilgrims had brought precious gifts to the fathers.[59] The Blemmys, Hamitic ancestors of the modern Beja-speaking Bishariin and other tribes of northeastern Sudan, did threaten Egypt in the fourth century as far north as modern Luxor, where Roman forces repelled them. They pushed into Egypt again in the fifth century.[60] Disparate nomadic groups and Sassanian troops were active on the eastern margin of the Eastern Roman Empire, and Justinian's tacticians may have had reason to fear they would attack Palestine and regroup in Sinai's wilderness, possibly even to assault Christian ascetics there.[61]

Whether or not the accounts of Ammonius and Nilus are true they became a real part of the monastery's legacy and continue to shape the views of its inhabitants today. They portray the monks' non-Christian neighbors as a threatening force which required the monastery to be built. The monastery's official version is that "The monks of Mount Sinai, having heard of the good will of the emperor Justinian, and how he took pleasure in the foundation of churches and monasteries, went to him and complained that the Ishmaelitish Arabs were doing them injury, in that they consumed their stock of provisions, and destroyed their settlements.

When the emperor asked what they desired of him, they answered: 'We beg you, Sire, to build us a monastery, wherein we might find protection.' "[62] The image of hostile Bedouin neighbors continued to serve the monastery long after that protection was granted.

At times the threat was real. There are several reliable accounts of Bedouin attacks upon the monastery. The period following Islam's penetration into the Sinai in the seventh century was especially volatile, as revealed in part by a low output of only crude volumes in the monastery library.[63] Several centuries of relative calm followed, but in the Middle Ages some Muslims, apparently including Bedouins of the Sinai and adjacent regions, resumed attacks on the monastery. Incidents reportedly occurred in 1479, 1516, 1565, 1600, 1618, 1632, 1656–1660, and 1731–1733.[64] In 1484 a Venetian pilgrim found monks mourning the death of their abbot, whom "Arabs" had murdered. He saw tribesmen bullying the monks "like starved dogs," making "such an uproar that it seems like Hell," and keeping the monks busy satisfying their demands.[65] During the same century Arab treasure-seekers reportedly tore up a mosaic on the floor of the monastery's basilica and on another raid broke into the marble chest containing the relics of St. Katherine, where they found only bones.[66] In 1598 Harrant de Polschitz was "obliged to visit Mounts Sinai and St. Katherine, accompanied only by some Arabs, none of the monks daring to attend him through fear of being molested or made prisoners by the Bedouins."[67] When Thévenot visited in 1658 he found the monastery in "a dilapidated state: the monks who remained there were in a constant quarrel with the Bedouins, but the most of them had fled for greater security to Tor."[68] In 1762 no one could be admitted to the monastery without a written certification of being Christian, reportedly because of Bedouins' repeated efforts to capture the monastery.[69] In 1798 the army of Napoleon Bonaparte attempted to impose order, decreeing that henceforth no Bedouins had any claim on the monks, who should be left unmolested to pursue their faith.[70]

Unstable relations between monks and Bedouins continued into the nineteenth century. In 1816 Swiss explorer John Lewis Burckhardt saw that "the monks live in such constant dread of the Bedouins, who knowing very well their timid disposition, take every opportunity to strengthen their fears, that they believe a person is going to certain destruction who trusts himself to the guidance of these Bedouins anywhere but on the great road to Suez or to Tor."[71] Burckhardt depicted the ambivalence but essential gratitude the monks felt about their nomadic neighbors:

The Arabs, when discontented, have sometimes seized a monk in the mountains and given him a severe beating, or have thrown stones or fired their musquets into the convent from their neighbouring heights; about twenty years ago a monk was killed by them. The monks, in their turn, have fired occasionally upon the Bedouins, for they have a well furnished armory, and two small cannon, but they take great care never to kill any one. And though they dislike such turbulent neighbours, and describe them to strangers as very devils, yet they have sense enough to perceive the advantages which they derive from the better traits in the Bedouin character, such as their general good faith, and their placability. "If our convent," as they have observed to me, "had been subject to the revolutions and oppressions of Egypt or Syria, it would long ago have been abandoned; but Providence has preserved us by giving us Bedouins for neighbours."[72]

Tension between the communities persisted. In 1822 nervous monks stoned Edward Rüppell and his Bedouin escorts, thinking that as they approached the walls they were preparing to attack the monastery.[73] Later that century Edward Palmer related that Bedouins took advantage of the monastery's vulnerable topographical situation: "The Bedawin, who have from time to time manifested a laudable antipathy to monastic institutions, were in the habit of occasionally stoning or shooting the reverend fathers from the heights above."[74] At times the monks reportedly became hostage to their policy of dispensing bread and other staples, because whenever they declined to distribute these goods on demand, the shunned Bedouin

immediately displays his hostility to the monks, lays waste their garden, and makes prisoners of them when they are on their walks outside the walls. Even murder has been committed on them, and huge stones hurled down on the convent from the high cliffs above. It was for this reason that Volney, who visited most of the convents of the Holy Land, all of which are surrounded by hostile Beduins, called them cages, where the monks live like prisoners, and depend even for their daily bread upon the good-will of the wild hordes that encompass them.[75]

In 1807 a traveler found the chapel on Jebel Musa's summit "half fallen," a condition monks at that time attributed to Bedouin retaliation for not receiving an allowance from the monastery.[76] Bedouins reputedly even extorted fruits from the monastery garden: "[A]nd some years, when there is the promise of a plentiful harvest, the Beduins ravage it, carrying off all the produce, and compel the monks to buy it back from them."[77] Monks today claim an enormous historical sum of casualties at the hands of Bedouins and other enemies. One told me, "The monks often were killed, individually or in groups. Seven thousand monks have lost their lives in this monastery over the past fourteen hundred years. Killed. Seven thousand! By Bedouins, by armies, by barbarians."

In all these accounts Bedouin enemies of the monastery are nameless.

The nearest suspects, the Jabaliya, were the least likely culprits. They had
the most to lose by making enemies of their Christian patrons. The monastery even made special arrangements to safeguard the Jabaliya from attacks by more powerful Sinai tribes; in 1088 A.D., for example, the monastery gave some gardens in Wadi Fray'a to the Mahasna, a clan of the
'Awarma, in exchange for Mahasna protection of the Jabaliya.[78] Both the
monks and the Jabaliya were vulnerable to the interests of a number of
Bedouin tribes, many of which owned small slivers of the peninsula. The
monastery depended for its sustenance and its pilgrimage traffic on long,
vulnerable overland routes that passed through a number of these territories. To keep them open the monks had to establish and maintain economic and political relations with numerous tribes. Tribes which were not
included in such arrangements, or which felt the monks had violated terms
of agreement, were probably the perpetrators of raids on the monastery.
Their identities remain a mystery.[79]

The monastery had formal contracts of employment and security with
Sinai tribes. These stipulated that the monastery would provide specified
tribes with bread, cash, or a regular share in transport of supplies and pilgrims. The contracted tribes were responsible for protecting the monastery
and its supply lines from attack, and for compensating the monastery for
any losses. The monastery gave Jabaliya caravaneers $\frac{1}{12}$ of the value of the
provisions they transported between at-Tur and the monastery. This was a
smaller share than the monastery gave to other tribes working the caravan
routes, but the Jabaliya were compensated for this shortfall with exclusive
rights to the escort of pilgrims and travelers in the immediate monastery
environs.[80] The monks were obliged to pay all Jabaliya men who reported
for available work. Edward Palmer described the system:

*When they are on the point of departure, every Arab who presents himself with his
camel can claim a certain portion of the hire, whether he be employed or not. This
custom has long been established, and is kept up to the present day. The monks,
moreover, are bound to give notice to their ghufara, or "protectors," of the presence
of pilgrims at the convent, and this is done in the following manner. A man is
despatched to the well in Wadi Nasb, on the upper route, who plants two foot-
marks in the direction of the convent, and places in front of them the Jibaliyeh
tribal-mark. Any Arab who happens to pass that way and see the sign may
present himself at the convent and share in the profits of the transport.*[81]

The monastery bursar (*oikonomos*) paid headmen of the other "guardian" (*ghufara*) tribes contracted to protect caravan routes an annual payment called a *ghafra*. In the early sixteenth century this amounted to
twenty halves of silver.[82] Tribes contracted in this manner included at vari-

ous times the Ahaywaat, 'Alaygaat, 'Awarma, Awlaad Sa'iid, Huwaytaat, Masa'iid, Muzayna, Rutaymaat, Suwalha, Suwarka, and Wuhaydaat.[83] In the 1930s Father Good Angel personally negotiated with members of the 'Awarma, Awlaad Sa'iid, and Muzayna tribes to transport goods by camel caravan from at-Tur to the monastery.

Three particular tribes other than the Jabaliya had a special historical relationship with the monastery. They were guaranteed preference for employment and given unobstructed access into the monastery precinct. According to the Jabaliya these were the Awlaad Sa'iid, the Suwalha, and a confederation of the Muzayna and Gararsha, and their names were once inscribed on three now-faded roundels above the western entrance to the monastery.[84] Monastery documents list the Awlaad Sa'iid, Suwalha, and 'Alaygaat as the three special tribes.[85] In 1988 the Awlaad Sa'iid tried to reinstate their ancient status in an incident that recalled dark days in relations between the monks and Sinai Bedouins, and once again demonstrated the thoroughness of monastery records. A delegation of about 250 Awlaad Sa'iid tribesmen arrived unexpectedly at the monastery, where they demanded to be employed, suggesting that they could supply guides and camels to tourists around Jebel Musa. Jabaliya tribesmen replied that the Awlaad Sa'iid had no such right. To resolve the conflict both parties consulted the archbishop (*batraan*) in his ancient capacity as arbiter. Consulting old records, Archbishop Damianos located a document stating that the environs of the monastery (Arabic, *dhawaahi ad-dayr*) were the exclusive realm of Jabaliya labor. The document was apparently drafted about two hundred years ago to strip the Awlaad Sa'iid of their privileges after one of their tribesmen stabbed a monk just outside the monastery walls.

BETWEEN CHRISTIANITY AND ISLAM

In 639 A.D. Islam swept across Sinai and into Egypt. The monks at Jebel Musa resisted the new faith but their serfs, Christian ancestors of the modern Jabaliya, eventually embraced it. Jabaliya oral tradition today relates that the Caliph 'Umar (634–644 A.D.) imposed a decree ordering all of Sinai's inhabitants except the monks to convert to Islam, and that copies of this decree survive in the monastery. Some of the early Jabaliya may have converted quite willingly to protest what they regarded as oppressive monastic rule, or to establish some degree of independence from their parent institution.[86] Monastery documents, however, suggest the conversion process may not have been entirely voluntary. During the reign of the Caliph 'Abdul Maalik Ibn Marwan (705–708 A.D.) Muslim forces reportedly attacked the monastery, killing many of its Jabaliya attendants and pressuring the survivors to convert. Some did but others "sought refuge in the holy

mountain," including one man who slew his wife and children rather than
allow them to be converted. He retreated to Mount Sinai, "where he lived
with the wild beasts until death approached."[87] It was a long time before
all of the Jabaliya became Muslim. In 1517 when the Ottoman Sultan
Salim I conquered Egypt the Jabaliya reportedly sent a message to him
promising that the entire tribe would convert to Islam if the sultan would
release them from their servitude to the monks. He did not, but insisted
they must convert anyway.[88] By most accounts the last Jabaliya Christian
was a woman who died in 1750 and was buried in the monastery garden.[89]
However, an English missionary reported that in 1821 the monastery's Father Kaliston baptized several Muslim Jabaliya tribespeople into the Christian faith.[90]

There are conflicting accounts of the Prophet Muhammad's contact
with the monastery, and there are questions about whether contact took
place at all. Some monastery records say that a delegation of monks traveled to Medina in 625 A.D. and met with the Prophet in an effort to obtain
his patronage and protection. Both the monks and Bedouins say Muhammad had already visited the monastery before his revelations began, on one
of his journeys as a merchant.[91] By some accounts the Prophet granted his
protection of the monastery on that visit. As he rested with his camels on
Jebel Munayja at the head of Wadi ad-Dayr, "an eagle was seen to spread
its wings over his head, and the monks, struck by the augury of his future
greatness, received him into their convent, and he in return, unable to
write, stamped with ink on his hand the signature to a contract of protection, drawn up on the skin of a gazelle, and deposited in the archives of
the convent."[92] One monk explained to me why Muhammad wanted to
protect the monks: "Muhammad was here before he was a prophet. He
was treated well here. Muhammad and his companions were taken in by
the monastery and treated very well by the monastery, as well as was possible in those days. For that reason he guaranteed the safety and protection
of this place. That is one of the reasons for its longevity."

The guarantee came in the form of a document, which the Jabaliya
believe was written by the Caliph 'Umar Ibn al-Khuttab and signed with
the Prophet's hand, exempting the monks from military service and taxation, advising Muslims to assist the monks and threatening Muslims with
damnation if they interfered with the monastery or the pilgrimage routes
leading to it. The document itself claims to have been dictated by the
Prophet and written by his cousin and son-in-law 'Ali in 623 A.D.:

*To all whom it may concern this letter is addressed by Mohammed, son of Abdul-
lah, he who proclaims and admonishes men to take knowledge of the promises of
God to his creation, in order that men may raise no claim of right against God or*

against the Prophet, for God is almighty and all-wise. It is written to people of his
faith and to all in the world who profess the Christian religion in East and West,
near and far, whether they are Arabs or non-Arabs, unknown or known, as a writ
which he has issued for their protection. If any person henceforth violates the pro-
tection hereby proclaimed, or contravenes it or transgresses the obligations imposed
by it, he forgoes the protection of God, breaks his covenant, dishonours his religion
and deserves to be accursed, whether he be a sultan or any one soever of the faithful
of Islam. If a monk or pilgrim seeks protection, in mountain or valley, in a cave or
in tilled fields, in the plain, in the desert, or in a church, in such case I am with
him, and defend him from everyone who is his enemy—I, my helpers, all men of
my faith, and all my followers, for these people are my followers and my protégés.
I wish to protect them from interference with the supply of victuals, which my pro-
tégés have procured for themselves, and also from the payment of tax over and
above what they themselves approve. On none of these accounts shall either com-
pulsion or constraint be used against them. A bishop shall not be removed from his
bishopric, nor a monk from his monastery, nor a hermit from his tower, nor shall a
pilgrim be hindered in his pilgrimage. Moreover, no church or chapel shall be
destroyed . . . They shall not be obliged to serve in war, or to pay the poll-tax . . .
These people shall be assisted in the improvement of their churches and religious
dwellings; thus they will be aided in their faith and kept true to their alliance.
None of them shall be compelled to bear arms, but the Moslems shall defend them;
and they shall not contravene this promise of protection until the hour comes and
the last day breaks upon the world. . . . This promise of protection was written in
his own hand by Ali ibn Abu Talib in the Mosque of the Prophet on the third of
Muharram in year 2 of the Prophet's Hegira. Praise be to all who abide by its
contents, and cursed be all who do not observe it.[93]

When Ottoman troops occupied Sinai in 1517 they sent the original
firman to the palace of Sultan Salim I in Istanbul and replaced it with a
copy the monks display in one of the most heavily traveled corridors in the
monastery, where all visitors may see it.[94] This may be the most important
document in the monastery's vast collection. The Jabaliya have always
honored it, citing it frequently to reaffirm what they view as the special
status of the monastery and of Mount Sinai in their own Islamic universe.
The firman has probably deterred some Muslim forces from harming the
monastery. Whenever a new sultan acceded to the Ottoman throne he
ritually instructed the Pasha of Egypt to protect the monastery.[95] The pasha
renewed this protection by reissuing the firman each year. About one hundred of these certificates remain in the monastery archives.[96] They testify
to the success of what may have been a ploy by the monks; several observers believe that monks rather than the Prophet Muhammad drafted the

original firman of protection when a Muslim army threatened the monastery in about 1010 A.D.[97]

A real threat may have caused the monks to take such an extraordinary step to protect themselves, and they have certainly taken others. In 1009 in an assault on Christianity the allegedly psychotic Caliph al-Hakim of the Tunisian Fatimid dynasty destroyed the Church of the Holy Sepulchre in Jerusalem.[98] His forces then reportedly set out to raze the Monastery of St. Katherine. There are several versions of what followed. One is that the Prophet's firman—perhaps freshly written—repelled his army. Another account is that the caliph decided not to attack the monastery and even repented when he learned the mountain was once again in flame.[99] In another version a party of monks met the caliph as he was on his way to destroy the monastery, imploring him to save it as a holy place for Muslims. As they met, another party of monks worked feverishly to erect a mosque within the monastery walls atop a spot where they would say the Prophet Muhammad had stood.[100] This is the account today's monks relate. Yet another version is that al-Hakim, initially bent on the monastery's destruction, was talked out of his plan by the monks, and then ordered the monks to build a mosque where Muhammad had stood in order to "pacify his soldiers' thirst for Christian blood." In fact the mosque was apparently constructed around 1106 during the reign of al-Hakim's successor, the Fatimid Caliph al-Afdal.[101] The Crusaders had taken Jerusalem in 1099; the mosque may have been built to service a Muslim detachment sent to defend the site against the Crusader army, or perhaps as a device to ward off an attack by Ottoman troops. Its minaret is of inferior construction, suggesting the mosque was built in a very short time.[102] Nevertheless it remains incongruously aside the basilica bell tower on the monastery skyline. The monks keep the mosque closed and locked today. Muslims worshiped there in the fourteenth century, and in the mid-nineteenth century travelers observed that "even now Moslem pilgrimages sometimes come to this place; and when any one of eminence is a guest, the call to prayer is given from the minaret."[103] By the 1930s it was less accessible: "It is only during the month of Ramadan the Beduin are allowed to enter it, which they do so daily, and light a lamp there, and so keep it sanctified."[104] Muslim guests and Jabaliya employees of the monastery used the mosque until the mid-1980s, when a chill in relations between the monks and Egyptian authorities forced its closure.[105]

The monks say that some years ago a cross appeared atop the mosque's minaret, placed there by Jabaliya Bedouins as a symbol of their unspoken faith. The Jabaliya are certainly Muslims. Bedouin workmen at the monastery seem to pray more regularly and at an earlier age than their counterparts in the neighboring mountains, as if to strengthen their faith in a setting where it is vulnerable. However, they undoubtedly retained a substratum of Christianity as they made the transition to Islam. Early this century Claude Jarvis described them as a "strange race" whose religion "is of a vague variety as, though they profess to be Moslems, they appear to have distinct Christian leanings."[106] In the late nineteenth century Edward Palmer saw Bedouins making ritual use of the cross: "The monks are supposed to owe their security to the potency of a charm they possess, to wit, the cross; and so convinced are the Bedawin of the efficacy of this, that they themselves make frequent use of the same emblem, wearing it in their turbans, carrying it in their religious processions, and even occasionally placing it at the head of a tomb."[107] In 1927 traveler Maynard Williams claimed that "before lying down, these retainers make a sign of the cross. At a circumcision ceremony, the leader has a knife in one hand and a cross in the other. In their religious processions the cross is carried, and it sometimes stands upon the headstones of their graves."[108] Until very recently the Jabaliya unabashedly participated in Christian celebrations with the monks. "Their presence, in their Bedouin costume, and officiating at the Whitsun service of the church of the monastery, perfectly astonished me," wrote Tischendorf in 1844.[109] Today the Jabaliya do not participate fully in church ritual, but some of them have a special relationship with the monks and their traditions. Some of the Bedouins told me they had seen the relics of St. Katherine, and monks told me they blessed some of the Bedouins. I had this exchange with Father Makarios:

"When you say they get blessings from the monastery, are you talking about blessings from Allah, or Christ?"

"Well, they have this association with the monastery and this close relationship with the monks, so depending on your outlook it is either a blessing or a curse."

"But do you bless them with a Christian blessing?" I asked.

"They pray in front of the icons and in front of the coffin of St. Katherine."

"They pray Muslim prayers?"

"We read prayers from the Christian prayer book over their heads. The bishop does it all the time."

"At the Feast of St. Katherine?" I asked.

"Anytime."

Bedouins and monks have traditionally met on Easter and on the Feast of St. Katherine not to pray together but to exchange gifts and reaffirm their friendly relations. The Jabaliya recall Easter (Arabic, *Iftaar an-Nasraani*) as the most important gathering. Each Easter they had a formal conference (*majlis*) during which both groups spoke about their relation-

ship and negotiated a date for the annual Jabaliya pilgrimage of Nabi Haruun. This meeting also allowed the Jabaliya simply by attending to express
their loyalty to the monastery. The monks remembered their presence
when it came time to choose Jabaliya employees.[110] A large-scale exchange
of gifts between the monks and Jabaliya men, women, and children followed their meeting. Jabaliya attendance at the Easter gathering declined
as the wage labor economy replaced the monastery as a principal source of
employment. Today there is no *majlis* but only a low-key, lightly attended
ritual exchange in which monks offer Bedouins bread, dates from at-Tur,
and colored Easter eggs, and the Jabaliya reciprocate with dehydrated
cheese (*'afiig*), goat ghee, pears, almonds, and a kid goat.

In these uncertain times when the monks have greatly reduced interaction and influence with their Jabaliya neighbors, they are comforted by
their belief that the Bedouins are at heart Christians loyal to the monastery.
"They keep crosses in their homes," one monk told me:

*They have a lot of superstitions that their welfare is tied to that of the monastery,
and they know their ancestry is connected with it, so they never would harm it.
The Bedouins have a certain understanding about their lives and their connection
with the monastery. It's a very close assimilation. They are very close to the monastery and have always had a certain rapport, more of a reverence for the monastery
than the average Bedouin who is a member of the Moslem faith. And certain
things have happened in the past that would have a tendency to give them a special
status in terms of their religious beliefs and their close links with the monastery that
other Bedouins would not share at all, under any circumstances.*

The monk did not reply when I asked him what things had happened.
Many months later he told me about an event involving a photograph of
Farhaan, the Jabaliya watchman of the monastery, which he said revealed
the Bedouin's faith. The West German tourist who took the picture in
1988 gave it to Farhaan, who brought it to the monk after noticing an
unusual feature in it. The monk explained:

*I as a casual observer would have looked at the photo without noticing anything
unusual—just a Bedouin standing in the sunshine having his picture taken. But
on close scrutiny of the photograph, you would notice, slightly below the left knee,
a very distinct and very, very prominent, very clear image of a cross. Not just any
kind of a cross, a so-called Byzantine cross that was designed and used as symbol
of the Byzantine Empire and its presence in the world for one thousand years.
That is the style and shape of the cross. There is no question about it. The art
historian could confirm that very clearly, and yet without any other artificial means
of any kind whatsoever, that image—that cross—appears just below the left knee*

The miracle of the robe. Courtesy of the Monastery of St. Katherine.

as the Bedouin is standing in the sunshine posing for this photograph. It is not a double exposure, or something the photographer set up deliberately, or something the Bedouin did by himself. The cross appeared there at the time that photo was taken, and is captured there on film. Farhaan was speechless about it. All the monks have seen the photo. They cannot believe it. There is only one explanation I can think of. These men are crypto-Christians. They believe in Christ although they cannot worship Him openly at all. I have seen a lot of weird things in my life, but I have never seen anything as weird, as inexplicable, as this. It cannot be explained.[111]

If the Jabaliya converted to Islam only half-heartedly or were satisfied to practice a religion that contained elements of the monastery's Christianity, it may have been because they believed they obtained substantive benefits from this faith. Pilgrims and travelers for centuries have related the Jabaliya belief that St. Katherine's monks could produce rain for Bedouin crops and herds. Edward Palmer wrote:

They say that once upon a time the Book of Moses, which had been delivered to him by God on the top of Sinai, was kept upon the summit of the mountain, and then the rain fell round about for alternate periods of forty days and forty nights. But the monks, wishing to obtain greater control over the Arabs, brought down the mysterious book, which was engraved upon stone, and built it into the walls of the

church [the Chapel of the Burning Bush], leaving this little window through
which it might be occasionally seen. Whenever they desire rain, they have only to
open the window to procure it at once, and they can even bring wind and storms
and locusts upon the country by the same means.[112]

Burckhardt added that Bedouins attributed drought to the monks' refusal
to exercise their powers. They also blamed monks for a devastating surplus
rain which flooded the area, sweeping away livestock and date trees: "You
have opened the book so much that we are all drowned," one angry Bedouin protested to the monastery.[113]

Bedouins today are nostalgic about the days before 1967 when monks
produced rain for them. Modern developments, particularly related to
tourism, brought a stop to the practice. Many things have changed. The
face of the land is different. The Jabaliya speak reverently of a landscape
that once evoked a sense of eternity and proximity between God and man.
It was the monastery nestled at the foot of Mount Sinai under a starry sky:
"the monastery, and the night, and the mountain" (ad-dayr wal-layl wal-
jabal). The Jabaliya believe these are the first words in the Prophet's firman
of protection for the monastery. As we sat high on Jebel Musa I asked
Mahmuud Mansuur what the words meant. He explained that God had
created a sacred realm around the monastery. Ordinary people could feel
the power of this place, he said: "In the old days, there was no town, only
pure desert, the monastery, and the mountain. When the night came the
view in the darkness was spellbinding. You would sit here at night. All was
quiet. The world was completely dark. It was a special feeling. The night
was powerful."

THE MUSLIM LANDSCAPE

The Jabaliya revere Mount Sinai because they share deep historical ties
with the monks' beliefs, but also because Islam has endowed them with a
parallel set of traditions about the mountain. Mount Sinai has an exalted
status in the Quran, where its principal synonym is "the Mountain" (at-
Tur and al-Jabal). A chapter in the Quran, "The Mount" (Sura 52), bears
its name. God prefaces a statement on the creation of Mankind by swear-
ing to four sacred symbols: "By the Fig and the Olive, and the Mount of
Sinai, and this City of security [Mecca]" (Sura 95:1–3; see also Sura 52:
1).[114] As in the Bible, Mount Sinai is most significant as the place where
God made a covenant with His people. The Exodus account in the Quran
parallels that in the Bible, beginning with Moses' journey into Sinai after
killing an Egyptian. At an unspecified watering place "in Midian" he met
two daughters of a man who is unnamed. Popular tradition identifies the

man as Shu'ayb, another figure in the Quran, and in Jabaliya beliefs Shu-'ayb is the same person as the Judaeo-Christian Jethro. Moses married one of his daughters and encountered the burning bush:

> *Now when Moses had fulfilled the term, and was travelling with his family, he perceived a fire in the direction of Mount Tur. He said to his family: "Tarry ye; I perceive a fire; I hope to bring you from there some information, or a burning fire-brand, that you may warm yourselves." But when he came to the Fire, a voice was heard from the right bank of the valley, from a tree in hallowed ground: "O Moses! Verily I am God, the Lord of the Worlds."*
> (SURA 28:29 – 30)

A parallel passage in another chapter reveals the name of the valley in which God spoke from the bush: "But when he came to the fire, a voice was heard: 'O Moses! Verily I am thy Lord! Therefore in My presence put off thy shoes: thou art in the sacred valley Tuwa" (Sura 20:11–12).

Moses returned to Egypt to lead his people to freedom. Pharaoh challenged him and met his end in the Biblical fashion: "We sent an inspiration to Moses: 'Travel by night with My servants, and strike a path for them through the sea, without fear of being overtaken by Pharaoh, and without any other fear. Then Pharaoh pursued them with his forces, but the waters completely overwhelmed them and covered them up" (Sura 20:77–78; see also Sura 2:50). The subsequent sojourn of the Israelites in Sinai parallels the Biblical account, but the events of the wandering are compressed. The people have the same volatile relationship with a wrathful God who nurtures and punishes them. "O ye Children of Israel! We delivered you from your enemy, and We made a Covenant with you on the right side of Mount Sinai, and We sent down to you manna and quails, saying: 'Eat of the good things We have provided for your sustenance, but commit no excess therein, lest My Wrath should justly descend on you: and those on whom descends My Wrath do perish indeed!' " (Sura 20:80–81; see also Sura 2:57, and 7:160 and 20:80 for manna and quail). Water appeared miraculously in the desert to save the people: "And remember Moses prayed for water for his people; We said, 'Strike the rock with thy staff.' Then gushed forth therefrom twelve springs. Each group knew its own place for water. So eat and drink of the sustenance provided by God, and do no evil nor mischief on the face of the earth" (Sura 2:60; see also Sura 7:160). Moses ascended the mountain to meet with God. "And We called him from the right side of Mount Sinai, and made him draw near to Us, for mystic converse" (Sura 19:52). The prophet fasted there forty days: "We appointed for Moses thirty nights, and completed the period with ten more: thus was completed the term of communion with his Lord, forty nights" (Sura 7:142). The sky grew stormy and the mountain crumbled as God met with Moses: "When Moses came to the place appointed by Us, and his Lord addressed him, he said, 'O My Lord! Show Thyself to me, that I may look upon Thee.' God said, 'By no means canst thou see Me direct; But look upon the mount; if it abide in its place, then shalt thou see Me.' When his Lord manifested His glory on the Mount, He made it as dust, and Moses fell down with a swoon. . . . Ye were dazed with thunder and lightning even as ye looked on" (Sura 7:143; Sura 2:30). God then gave Moses the Law:

God said: "O Moses! I have chosen thee above other men, by the mission I have given thee and the words I have spoken to thee: Take then the revelation which I give thee, and be of those who give thanks." And We ordained laws for him in the Tablets in all matters, both commanding and explaining all things, and said: "Take and hold these with firmness, and enjoin thy people to hold fast by the best in the precepts: soon shall I show you the homes of the wicked, how they lie desolate."
(SURA 7:144 – 145)

The mountain continued to tremble and the people grew fearful. "When We shook the Mount over them, as if it had been a canopy, and they thought it was going to fall on them, We said: 'Hold firmly to what We have given you, and bring ever to remembrance what is therein; Perchance you may fear God' " (Sura 7:171). As Moses conversed with God his people erred.

And remember We appointed forty nights for Moses, and in his absence ye took the calf for worship and ye did grievous wrong. . . . The people of Moses made, in his absence, out of their ornaments, the image of a calf, for worship. It seemed too low: did they not see that it could neither speak to them, nor show them the way? They took it for worship and they did wrong. . . . When Moses came back to his people, angry and grieved, he said "Evil it is that ye have done in my place in my absence: did ye make haste to bring on the judgment of your Lord?" He put down the Tablets.
(SURA 2:51; SURA 7:148,150)

Some of the people repented and God spared them, but others paid with their lives: "And remember We took your Covenant and We raised above you the towering height of Mount Sinai, saying: 'Hold firmly to what we have given you, and hearken to the Law.' They said, 'We hear, and we disobey.' And they had to drink into their hearts of the taint of the Calf, because of their Faithlessness. Say: 'Vile indeed are the behests of your Faith if ye have any faith!' " (Sura 2:93; see also Sura 20:83–97 for the events of the Calf). Moses did not break the tablets but took them up in his arms and returned up the mountain with the seventy elders. He left them some distance away and as the mountain quaked violently he spoke again with God, begging His forgiveness (Sura 7:154–155).

The location and general aspect of Mount Sinai are even less precise in the Quran than in the Bible. References to events on the "right side" of the mountain do not provide any clues. In Islamic scholarship and popular culture there is no strong tradition of searching for Mount Sinai, and most of the world's Muslims have always accepted the pre-Islamic belief that Jebel Musa is the mountain.[115] Muslims seem to accept this identification with less awe than most Christians, perhaps because the Quranic account does not carry the Bible's injunctions against ordinary people approaching the mountain. Gamaal Sharif, a Muslim peasant of Luxor, told me it was well known that God spoke with Moses there, but that the mountain was not "sacred" in the sense of being an object of reverence or worship. Today there is no great tradition of Muslim pilgrimage to the site, but Muslims who visit this overwhelmingly Christianized landscape recall its Islamic associations. A few have expressed apparent contempt or competition, superimposing the spray-painted slogans "God is Great" and "There is No God but God" over painted crosses marking the route to Jebel Musa's summit. In the mid-1980s someone broke into the church on the summit through a glass window and threw icons and furniture around. The monks blamed "Muslim fanatics" but were certain these were not Bedouins. A devout Cairene woman who paints the monastery as a hobby drops its prominent mosque from her scenes in apparent retribution.

Only the Jabaliya and other Bedouins of Sinai have carefully marked the mountain's events as related in the Quran. Bedouins probably named the mountain Jebel Musa, "Moses Mountain," in the eighteenth century.[116] At the same time they referred to all the south Sinai mountains as the "Mountains of Moses," and used the Quranic name "Tuur Sinai" as a synonym for Jebel Musa itself.[117] Bedouins today say their ancestors knew the mountain as "Horayb," which they recognize as being close to the Arabic word for "war." Perhaps it was called this, they venture, because the lightning and storms that God made on it were like the sights and sounds of battle. Jabaliya Bedouins told Henry Palmer that as Moses ascended the Stairway of Repentance to meet with God, "the world became subject to his command, mountains were rent asunder, and hard rocks melted like wax before him."[118]

While the monks say the Bedouins informed them of many of the places of scripture, the Bedouins say it was the monks who told them about many of these sacred sites. On the summit the Jabaliya recognize the same grotto acknowledged by Christians as Moses' retreat when God's glory passed by. "The Mahometans have a great veneration for this plais, and it is said they offer sacrifice at it," Bishop Pococke observed in 1738.[119] In 1507 Gregor von Gaming and Martin Baumgarten spent a sleepless night near the grotto, disturbed by Bedouin couples copulating within it, "a beastial service in the belief that children who were here conceived were endowed with a holy and prophetic spirit."[120] Lina Eckenstein supposed this behavior was the real reason most Christians avoided climbing the Holy Mountain.[121]

Near the church on Jebel Musa's summit Bedouins in 1926 showed Ahmed Shefik the spot where Moses "fell down with a swoon." Shefik led his Muslim guides in prayer there.[122] Early in the nineteenth century John Lewis Burckhardt reported that Bedouins believed the tablets of the covenant were hidden beneath the church, so they "made excavations on every side in the hope of finding them."[123] Later visitors supposed this caused the church to finally collapse.[124] Ten meters south of the church is the small Fatimid Mosque (Arabic, Jaami' Faatima), a successor to an original mosque built probably between 1101 and 1130 A.D.[125] The Jabaliya believe it dates to the rule of the Caliph 'Umar (634–644 A.D.). Monks today say scornfully that Muslims built it by quarrying stone from the first church that stood on the summit. For many observers, however, the proximity of church and mosque on Mount Sinai has been a hopeful symbol of peace and reconciliation. Reverend Sartell Prentice wrote, "Here on this mountain, sacred to Christian and Mohammedan alike, in silent friendliness, chapel and mosque lie side by side, as if ignorant or fearful of the antagonisms of their servants in this world."[126] The mosque is situated above a site sacred to the Jabaliya, a cave in which they say Moses lived and fasted during his forty days and nights on the mountain—a tradition shared by fifteenth-century monks—and where the Prophet Muhammad spent a night when he visited the area as a caravaneer.[127] Ten steps lead down into the cave, where there is a small altar and a *mihrab* niche indicating the direction of Mecca.[128] Today the cave serves as a storeroom for the Jabaliya cafe-keeper who runs a brisk business for tourists on the mountaintop. The man periodically opens a locked door leading into the cave, emerging moments later with tea cups, Pepsis, or biscuits. Upon request he shows visitors the impression on a nearby stone left by Moses' hand.[129]

Approximately 200 meters northwest of the summit is a hollow in the rock which in size and shape is remarkably like the hoofprint of a camel. The Jabaliya claim it is the Print of the She-Camel (Matabb an-Naaga) of Nabi Saalih Rashiid, a man they believe was either an early Muslim prophet or the progenitor of the Bani Saalih tribe. Earlier Bedouins told travelers that the hoofprint belonged to the Prophet Muhammad's she-

The Print of the
She-Camel (Matabb
an-Naaga) on
Jebel Musa.
October 11, 1989.

camel, an animal of such stature that its other legs rested in Mecca, Jerusalem, and Damascus or in Mecca, Cairo, and Damascus.[130] Nonbelievers have long challenged its authenticity. In 1658 Thévenot observed that this hoofprint "was reverently kissed by the Arabs," and he attributed its formation to the monks, "in order that they might find favour with the Mohammedan inhabitants of the land."[131] Arthur Stanley in 1853 related that "it is true that the monks themselves, in the seventeenth century, declared to the Prefect of the Franciscan Convent that this mark had been made by themselves, to secure the protection of the Bedouin tribes. But it has more the appearance of a natural hollow, and it is more probable that they were unwilling to let the Prefect imagine that such a phenomenon should be accidental, than that they actually invented it."[132] One of the monks told me that he believed someone had chiseled it, but he did not say who. Tischendorf scorned it: "[T]his is nothing more than a satire—an ironical sneer at the Christian worship of relics. It struck me that the Koran, by many a trait, had the same relation to the Bible as the imitator has to an original genius: this admirably illustrates the much-worshipped footstep of the dromedary of Mahomet."[133] Such views are in marked contrast to the absolute respect Bedouins have for monks' and Christian pilgrims' beliefs in Sinai's sacred places.

The summit area of Jebel Musa was always the most important ritual place in all Sinai for the Jabaliya and the other tribes of the Tuwaara Confederacy. It was a powerful place where God would listen to them and bless them. Throughout the year individuals and families traveled there to redeem vows they had made when they had been in danger, to increase offspring, and to ask God to help them accomplish other goals.[134] Family members paraded their livestock in several circles around the Matabb an-Naaga to ensure the herd's fertility. To boost milk production they milked their goats directly into the impression. The eldest male of the family led prayer by reciting the opening chapter of the Quran while others burned incense and placed aromatic wormwood and other herbs in the stone semicircle around the print. Infertile women walked around the site to obtain or restore fecundity.

The summit of Jebel Musa was vital to the ritual life of the entire Jabaliya tribe. On the two most important occasions in their religious calendar, the Feast of the Sacrifice ('Iyd al-'Adha) and the Feast of the Prophet Saalih (Nabi Saalih), almost all the able-bodied members of the Jabaliya congregated there in local pilgrimage (ziyaara). On the eve of the Feast of the Sacrifice they gathered there to pray in honor of the Standing on Arafat in Mecca. The Jabaliya recall that clouds always gathered overhead, indicating that storms were forming 1,000 kilometers away over Mecca, too, to wash away the blood of the sacrifice there. The tribe slept that night in the Basin of Elijah and arose to slaughter their sheep and goats in an atmosphere of devotion and revelry. Late in the day in a gesture symbolic of their ties with this sacred landscape they descended the mountain on all its major pathways.[135]

The Feast of Nabi Saalih took place in the spring on a prearranged date and was attended by the Jabaliya and members of neighboring tribes, especially the Awlaad Sa'iid, Muzayna, and the 'Alaygaat. It began 10 kilometers distant from the summit in Wadi ash-Shaykh at the shrine dedicated to this mysterious pre-Islamic figure.[136] The celebrants marched together from the shrine of Nabi Saalih, sometimes having already sacrificed animals there, to the summit of Jebel Musa, where the major sacrifice in honor of Moses took place.[137] At times the Bedouins slaughtered their animals atop the Matabb an-Naaga.[138] Their custom was to smear the doorposts of the nearby mosque with the blood of the sacrifice.[139] "The Arabs look with profound veneration upon Jebel Musa," Edward Palmer wrote. "Once in a year they sacrifice a sheep or goat upon it to the Israelitish Lawgiver, and the doorway of the little mosque upon the summit is all stained and blackened with the blood of victims."[140] In 1738 Richard Pococke "saw the entrails of beasts near the mosque."[141]

The ceremony of Nabi Saalih may have a remote link with an ancient pre-Muslim ritual on or near the peak of Jebel Musa. In about the year 580 Antoninus Martyr wrote:

Mount Syna is stony, and there is little earth, and in its neighbourhood are many cells of men who serve God, the same in Horeb. And in this part of the mountain the Saracens have an idol of marble white as snow. A priest of theirs dwells there, who wears a dalmatica and a linen cloak. And when the time of their festival comes previous to the appearance of the moon, before it appears on the festive day, the marble begins to change its colour, and when they begin to adore it, the marble is black as pitch. The time of the festival being over, it returns to its former colour. At this I wondered greatly.[142]

Another place of great sanctity in Jabaliya tradition is Nabi Haruun, literally "the Prophet Aaron," the hill at the mouth of Wadi ad-Dayr where the monks believe Aaron fashioned the golden calf. The Jabaliya remember Aaron on the hilltop with a special shrine located adjacent to its Christian counterpart. In this unlocked building a green shroud covers a box which resembles a grave. However, Aaron is not buried here, the Bedouins insist: it is simply a "standing place" (*magaam*) marking the site where Aaron supervised the building of the calf (*'ijl*). South of the shrine is a hollow in the red granite which they regard as Aaron's footprint (Asar Nabi Haruun). The Bedouins venerate this holy site by placing wormwood and other herbs in a ring around it. The Jabaliya also revere the odd granite formation in the mouth of nearby Wadi Shu'ayb recognized by fourteenth- and fifteenth-century monks as the place of the golden calf. The Bedouins call it "The Cow" (al-Bagara) and explain either that the Children of Israel used it as a mould for their idol, or that it is the petrified calf.[143] From here Bedouins point out Jethro's Water (Maayit Shu'ayb), the watering place in this steep valley on the northeastern flank of Jebel Musa where Moses met Shu'ayb's daughters as they watered their livestock.

Until recently Nabi Haruun was the starting point for a local pilgrimage that linked the Bedouins and the monastery in a single ritual event. This was the visitation (*ziyaara*) of Nabi Haruun, held each summer at a date mutually arranged by the monks and Bedouins on the previous Easter. For three days nearly all Jabaliya tribespeople camped around Nabi Haruun, culminating their celebration with a sacrifice at Nabi Haruun and a procession to the monastery. The monks were always involved in some ceremonial way. In the late eighteenth century the Jabaliya sacrificed a camel after marching it three times around the monastery.[144] More recently the feast ended with the Bedouins walking in procession three times around the monastery while chanting hymns to Moses and St. Katherine. While the women remained outside the men went into the monastery to view with the monks the relics of St. Katherine and to receive their archbishop's blessings.[145]

On their ritual journeys of Nabi Saalih and Nabi Haruun the Bedouins

Filling the Footprint
of the Prophet Aaron
(Asar Nabi
Haruun), with the
shrines of Nabi
Haruun in the
upper right.
September 6, 1989.

reaffirmed friendly relations with one another and settled debts and disputes.[146] They kept alive their ancient bonds with the monastery. They
restored the fertility of women and livestock. Through these rituals the
Jabaliya were able to celebrate and maintain their balance with the social
and physical environment around Mount Sinai. This harmony would not
survive the momentous changes introduced by the Israeli occupation and
a booming tourism industry. The last occasion on which the entire Jabaliya
tribe gathered was for the final feast of Nabi Haruun in 1966.[147] This was

also the last time they participated as a group in a joint ritual with the monastery. Until 1973 the Bedouins climbed Mount Sinai on feast days to sacrifice at its sacred places, but finally gave up these vital rituals because they attracted too many tourists. Today the visitor who knows where to look will find a few herbs placed gently around the Matabb an-Naaga. On the mountain that is all that remains of the ancient traditions of the People of the Mountain.

Seven

◆

THE

BEDOUIN

WAY OF LIFE

There are about a dozen monks but nearly a thousand Bedouins in the region of the Monastery of St. Katherine; the dominant way of life around Mount Sinai is Bedouin. Their unique European origins and their association with the monastery in no way hindered the Jabaliya from becoming Bedouin. Like the other Sinai tribes the Jabaliya have come to know their desert environment extremely well. Like the other tribes they have learned to take advantage of all possible opportunities to survive and persist in this desert. The mountains' diversity has created more opportunities for them than other Sinai Bedouins enjoy. The Jabaliya have incorporated all of the best information, techniques, and strategies available to them: the orchard agriculture of Byzantine Christianity, the pastoral nomadism of Arabian Bedouins, the hunting and wayfinding skills of preagricultural peoples, and the entrepreneurial spirit of Israeli and Egyptian merchants. They are a creative and flexible people, carrying an ancient way of life into a changing world. They are changing, too, and in the process are searching for ways to retain an intimate knowledge of the local environment and a value system that resists the less attractive aspects of modernization.

Some of the Jabaliya say their tribal name means not "People of the Mountain," in reference to Mount Sinai, but "the Mountain People," in tribute to their ability to live in a rugged and challenging land. They pride themselves on ancient skills of living off the land and on the physical strength and spiritual freedom the outdoor life engenders. "Look at plants that grow in the shade: they are spindly and weak and produce little fruit, while those in the sun are strong and fruitful," a Jabaliya man told me. "They benefit because the sun is a problem. We say 'Whoever strives for something grows; whoever has difficulty becomes strong.'" The Jabaliya are a people strengthened by sun and mountain.

PASTORALISM

The people who came from southeastern Europe and northern Egypt to serve the monastery absorbed Sinai's dominant Bedouin culture. This was a pastoral nomadic way of life: pastoral in that people kept livestock, and nomadic in that they moved with these animals between seasonal pastures. The Jabaliya raise sheep, goats, and camels. Camels are the least significant members of this livestock trilogy; the Jabaliya estimate there are only 100 to 110 individuals in the Jebel Musa region. These animals are adapted to life on open plains. Their range and utility is quite limited in this high country, where they must remain on stable, well-worn paths of wadi floors. Several major pedestrian routes are altogether closed to them. Camels are most useful in carrying the summer harvest of fruits and vegetables from Jabaliya gardens into the town of Katriin far below for sale. Males, which can carry larger loads, are in greatest demand. Females are often left to their own devices for periods of ten days to two weeks. The Jabaliya say that camel's milk is so nutritious that a person could exist on it without any supplemental foods, but camels are too few for this to be a common item in their diet. Although limited in its utility the camel is a prized possession. It is the only animal in the livestock trilogy that bears the Jabaliya tribal brand (*wasm*), resembling a backward letter "E" on the animal's left cheek. Each animal has a personal name such as Subhaan ("Majesty") or Zarraag (the name of an energetic insect). Many families own donkeys, which are especially useful at carrying baggage on steep slopes. Despite Islam's classification of donkeys as unclean some Bedouins are fond of the animals. An old woman of the Awlaad Jindi has a close companion in her donkey, whose name is Zagharuuti ("Ululator"). The animals sometimes escape from their owners to join one of many herds of feral donkeys in the area. Periodically a family requires a donkey but cannot afford one, and must resort to capturing one of these semi-wild animals. It is a difficult chore requiring three or four men working together to chase, corner, and harness the animal. Then the trying breaking-in period begins.

Sheep and goats were the backbone of the Jabaliya pastoral economy. Before 1967 when wage labor opportunities began to grow, the typical family had a herd of about sixty animals divided almost equally between sheep and goats. By selling an annual surplus of these livestock to villagers and townspeople the family earned enough cash to cover its expenses for four to five months of the year.[1] Only a few families own dogs and they never use them to herd livestock. For the Ma'aza Bedouins of Egypt's Eastern Desert dogs are very useful in hunting ibex.[2] Unlike the Ma'aza the Jabaliya are armed, and the availability of guns probably accounts for the rarity of dogs among them. As I petted a man's dog and told him we had an expression that the dog is man's best friend, he replied that the Jabaliya regard the camel, dog, and sheep as man's friends. I asked if the goat were in this category also. It is not.

The crying of house cats and crowing of roosters are common sounds in the high mountain gardens of summer. Both animals attest to the unusually sedentary nature of the Jabaliya. Their tribal territory of 200 square kilometers is small and their historical connection to the monastery close; both factors historically reined in the tribe. Fortunately it has not been necessary for the Jabaliya to search far for resources; their mountains' complex topography and vegetation offer Jabaliya shepherds a wide variety of pasture types. These Bedouins historically were nomadic, but only in moving from one residence to another within their resource-rich confines. They practiced a vertical migration pattern, relocating between low winter and high summer pastures. From their lowland winter homes they grazed their animals on Saharo-Sindian vegetation in the wadis and south-facing slopes below 1,300 meters, and on Central Asiatic plants between 1,300 and 1,600 meters. In their highland summer range they pastured livestock on Central Asiatic vegetation flourishing above 1,600 meters, particularly where snowmelt created a flush of growth they call 'ushaab ar-rabii'a ("spring pasture") on the north-facing slopes of black rock mountains like Jebel Abu Tarbuush and Jebel Katarina. Summertime also found the herds feeding on perennial plants in soil-filled hollows of red granite areas.[3]

Low temperatures, blustery wind, and snow prevent the Jabaliya from wintering in the high mountains. They sit out the cold in extended-family bungalows in warmer elevations below 1,600 meters. The village of Abu Sayla, 6 kilometers northwest of the monastery, developed as a winter quarters of the Jabaliya. When most of the Bedouins were pastoralists it was nearly a ghost town in the summer. The settlement is perched just above a gorge that floods frequently, giving the village its name "Father of the Torrent." This dispersed collection of sixty single-story homes is built entirely of native granite. From a distance it is difficult to distinguish the site, so perfectly does it blend with its parent landscape. It is as suitable an adaptation to this environment as the black wool tents which typify Bedouin habitation elsewhere.

Summer is the time of the Jabaliya. Many abandon winter residence in Abu Sayla, Shaykh 'Awaad, and Katriin to take possession of Sinai's high places. They retire to a mountain kingdom blessed by the inability of motor vehicles to pass into it from any direction. For most Bedouins the gateway to this realm is just south of Katriin on the route of Abu Jiifa, "Father of Odors," named for the dung of camels that struggle with its switchbacks. On the Katriin side of the Abu Jiifa pass there are several small walled enclosures overgrown with apricot and quince trees. These surprising islands of greenery among red granite are only small hints of the treasure that lies beyond. "When you drink from Abu Jiifa you are about to reach the freedom of the mountains," a Jabaliya companion smiled as we paused on the route. At the top of the pass is an old leopard burrow trap and an extraordinary view southward into the large at-Tbuuk valley. This drainage and most of its tributaries are lined nearly continuously with walled orchards, creating a leaflike pattern of green veins set in red granite. There are about four hundred separate orchards in the high valleys of the Jabaliya territory. The average plot is about a half-acre (one-fifth hectare) in size and contains fifty fruit-bearing trees and a wide range of vegetable crops.[4] The existence of these gardens is a complete surprise to anyone who thinks of Mount Sinai as an area of monks and chapels only, or of Bedouins as a people who hate farming, or of summer in the Egyptian desert as a kind of hell.

The Jabaliya orchard is a paradise. Water trickles, sputters, and splashes from pipes and channels to irrigate fava bean, onion, watermelon, canteloupe, red pepper, eggplant, tomato, string bean, mallow, tobacco, basil, purslane, spearmint, rosemary, carob, two almond varieties, olive, two apricot varieties, six varieties of pears, walnut, three varieties of plums and prunes, peach, five apple varieties, orange, pomegranate, lemon, fig, date, three types of grapes, guava, and quince. Different combinations of these crops succeed at different elevations. At his 1,800-meter gardens in Wadi Abu Tuwayta and Wadi Tinya, Saalih 'Awaad and his sons Sa'ad, Ahmad, and Ibrahim lovingly tend almond, pear, apple, and peach trees and raise zucchini, sorghum, watermelon, canteloupe, tobacco, red pepper, eggplant, tomato, onion, string bean, mallow, basil, spearmint, rosemary, and purslane. In winter Saalih and family reside in the village of Abu Sayla and work their garden at 1,450 meters in nearby Wadi Itlaah, where they raise winter crops of wheat, fava bean, and onion. Date palm, carob, guava, fig, and lemon also thrive here. There are odd species, too. In his Abu Tuwayta orchard Saalih 'Awaad looks after a rare avocado tree he planted during the Israeli occupation. Israelis also introduced the geraniums that decorate

A walled Jabaliya
orchard in
Wadi at-Thuuk.
June 9, 1989.

many gardens. Although it is a weed the Jabaliya let the attractively flowering wild hollyhock (*khutmii, Alcea striata*) grow. The Jabaliya prize mulberry fruits but no gardener would plant and care for one in his enclosure: it would grow too large and crowd out important orchard crops. The Jabaliya, however, revere trees and would not cut down a mulberry that appeared in a garden. Instead, they would neglect it and hope it might not mature.

These Bedouins mark the passage of summer days by the changing harvest. The apricots of late May and early June usher in the summer season. It is one of the busiest times because men and boys must pick the delicate fruits and transport them with care and haste to market in Katriin, and slice and dry those they will not sell. One memorable June day I assisted in the apricot harvest, recklessly consuming a large number of the ripe fruits. I spent much of the late afternoon and evening running from my hosts to the shelter of nearby boulders. "Oh yes," my companions said, "apricots are famous for causing stomach troubles. The skin does this." In a typical year at 1,800 meters, "istambuuli" grapes and the "ifsayli" apple variety mature in mid-July; figs in mid-August; almonds, peaches, pears, prunes, and "amrikaani"-type apples and green grapes in the peak harvest season from late August to mid-September; dates, pomegranates, and "shitawi" or "winter"-type pears in October; and "shitwaani" apples, some grapes, and quince in November, with quince the last to be picked. In his garden in Wadi Abu Tuwayta, Saalih 'Awaad has a "shitawi" pear tree so reliable that he reckons his calendar by it: its fruits always ripen on October 25. That event marks for Saalih the impending end of the gardening season in the high Sinai. The entire family packs up and relocates to Abu Sayla until the following May. During the winter orchard owners periodically hike into the mountains to irrigate trees to prevent freezing temperatures from drying them out. When the trees begin to bloom in February they must be watered once weekly, by April twice weekly, and by June on alternate days if they are to produce a good harvest.[5]

The Bedouins eat some of these fruits as they come into season and dry others for later use. They reconstitute dried apricots with water and sugar. They slice, dry, and powder tomatoes as an additive for rice and soups. Raisins, particularly of the "istambuuli" grape variety regarded as most nutritious, and dried string beans are welcome items at wintertime meals. Jabaliya women prepare a jam from quince fruits. From the carob bean they make a sweet called *ma'atuul.* Dried rosemary leaves flavor tea throughout the year. To earn the cash they need to buy other supplies, the Bedouins also sell limited quantities of their harvest in Katriin. Dried apricots fetch eighteen Egyptian pounds per kilogram, fresh apricots two pounds, unshelled almonds seven pounds, pears six pounds, grapes two pounds, pomegrantes two pounds, and apples three pounds. In earlier times middlemen transported Jabaliya produce by camel for sale and trade in distant at-Tur, Suez, and Cairo.[6] Agriculture generated up to 60 percent of the family's expenses for the grain and other staples they were obliged to purchase from towns and villages.[7] Unlike almost all other Bedouins in the Middle East, the Jabaliya established farming as a significant, regular, and reliable source of sustenance.

Most Egyptians of the Nile Valley and many Israeli visitors to the Sinai perceive Bedouins as drug cultivators and smugglers. "How else can they live except by smuggling and dealing narcotics?" a Cairene asked me. An Israeli tour leader explained to me that the Jabaliya were not growing sufficient food crops because they had diverted most of their water and best agricultural land to the drought-intolerant opium poppy. He claimed that the environmental impacts were dramatic, especially on the few "dripping place" (*naggaat*) habitats in the region. At the waterfall of Wadi Nugra, he said, poppy growers had used plastic pipe to divert water that previously fed the falls and large pools below. Following up this report I found that water had indeed been diverted from the Nugra falls, but for cultivation of vegetables. My Bedouin companion was upset that the diversion was destroying maidenhair ferns below the waterfall, so he disconnected the pipe. There seemed to be a political statement in the Israeli man's story; "there was no such harvest under the Israelis," he boasted, "but the Egyptians never come up here." In fact opium cultivation is all but nonexistent in Jabaliya territory; poppies were grown in one garden there in 1987. Fear of the Bedouins as drug addicts and smugglers nevertheless has a strong hand in Egyptian policy toward the Jabaliya. Local government officials in the settlement of Katriin speak of halting the drug trade as one of their top priorities. Local security forces feel inadequately equipped to apprehend and prosecute the alleged violators, and in one instance tried to secure the services of an Egyptian anthropologist as an informant. She had earned the confidence of Jabaliya women in her research and refused the offer. St. Katherine's monks also perpetuate a stereotype of their neighbors as drug smugglers. When a wealthy Jabaliya man purchased a garden plot from the monastery in Wadi Feiran, the monks attributed his fortune to the drug trade.

The Jabaliya do cultivate stimulants, but not to the extent that their reputation suggests. Many grow tobacco for domestic use, but very discreetly because of a government monopoly on its production. They roll and smoke it green and its odor is so pungent that early on I thought it was marijuana, and I could not understand how men could smoke so many "joints" in a day and remain standing. I was not the only outsider who misidentified the substance. Police in the town of Katriin detained Mahmuud Mansuur when they saw him rolling what they thought was a marijuana cigarette. Some men do grow marijuana for personal use. In September 1989 an interclan dispute arose when authorities in Katriin arrested an Awlaad Jindi clansman for smoking marijuana. The accused named his supplier as a Humayda clansman, who was then jailed.

Jabaliya orchard agriculture today is a remnant of a much more extensive network of gardens which monks and hermits established beginning about 300 A.D. They literally carried the seeds of this system from the Mediterranean world along with the techniques to maintain it, including grafting and irrigation.[8] Bedouins acknowledge this inheritance graciously. They say that if the monks had not been here they would have no pears or grapes. They recognize that hermits and monks established many of the plots the Bedouins work today, especially those in the highest and most remote places. These devout men grew crops where Bedouins would not want to, at windswept and bitter altitudes over 1,800 meters on mountains like Umm Shumar and Serbal.[9] Hermits were the first farmers to dwell in the large wind-eroded hollows of granite boulders the Bedouins call 'ariisha that serve as their orchard homes today. The Jabaliya still pay lip service to an ancient sharecropping arrangement with the monastery. Some remote orchards still belong nominally to the monks. The Bedouins work such gardens in Wadi Abu Juruus, Wadi Abu Tuwayta, and Wadi Itlaah. Monks today may be unaware that they own these gardens, but when I asked one of the Bedouins in Wadi Abu Juruus what he would do with his olive harvest, he grinned back, "We will pick all the fruit and give half to the monastery." Even living trees are the legacy of early Christian agriculture. The Jabaliya say that the sole walnut tree (*shawbak*) in the highest orchard of Wadi Tinya is the oldest tree in their territory, and that one of the first monks to live in this area planted it.

The Jabaliya today employ a surprising combination of ancient and up-to-date technologies to maintain their gardens. Where flat wadi bottomland is limited but soils are good, as in Wadi Tinya, people have terraced their orchards. Many gardens contain a *shaduf*, the ancient Egyptian weighted beam and bucket with which a man can move small quantities of water from source to irrigation channel. Most of these buckets and the millstones that serve as their counterweights, however, stand as idle relics of times past, replaced by roaring portable gasoline-powered pumps made in Japan. There is something odd about the sight of a camel carrying one of these metallic 20-kilogram devices, and the sound of their operation in even the remotest high mountain gardens. At sixteen hundred Egyptian pounds these pumps are expensive investments, and only gardeners who sell produce own them. Orchard owners in the Abu Jiifa area have cut costs by tapping into the electricity grid of nearby Katriin to run their less expensive electric pumps. There are other incongruities in Bedouin gardening. One afternoon I marveled at the labors of three Jabaliya men using a pick, hammer, and chisel to excavate a well in the solid rock of a dike in Wadi Abu Tuwayta. I walked off wondering how long their chore would take. An hour later I heard two large explosions. They had used illicitly obtained dynamite to finish the job. By conventional means they might have worked eight hours a day for three days to dig the 6-meter well.

The Jabaliya landscape is crisscrossed by tens of kilometers of 20-millimeter plastic irrigation pipes, obtained from Egypt at a cost of thirty Egyptian pounds per 100 meters. These pipes have overcome the traditional limitation of having to situate gardens at well sites. Some even span chasms to reach small soil-filled pockets high on red granite slopes. One pipeline runs 4 kilometers from a water source in Wadi at-Tbuuk to a garden just above Katriin. Plastic piping has all but replaced the cement-lined rock channels (*ganaa*), which required great effort and expense to build. Those channels which survive serve only as protective corridors for the plastic pipes. The Jabaliya acknowledge that the new system has diverted water away from and so destroyed some moist plant communities, but insist there is more water available overall because the pipes reduce evaporation.

The Jabaliya are masters of the art of grafting, which they say they have learned from their Christian neighbors and from hundreds of years of their

own experimentation with wild and domesticated trees. The gardener sometimes combines domestic varieties, for example grafting a pear onto quince root stock, but more commonly places a domestic fruit on a wild host. One of the native hosts is the wild fig, onto which the Bedouins graft the more succulent but less drought-tolerant domestic fig. The fruit produced is as large and sweet as that of the domestic fig but does not require irrigation. The Jabaliya also take advantage of the drought-resistant properties of the native Sinai hawthorn, grafting "shitawi," "kilaabi," and "injaas" pear varieties onto it. The "shitawi" pear is especially compatible with hawthorn, the Arab horticulturalist says, because both trees fruit in the same season. He usually does the graft in March. He saws off the young hawthorn about 12 centimeters above the ground, where its diameter is about 9 centimeters. With a scissor or knife he plies four to six openings between the bark and core of the hawthorn understock. Into each of these spaces he inserts a foliated pear sprig deep enough so that it can stand alone. He then ties a long strip of discarded clothing several times around the circumference of the hawthorn stump, to bind the bark against the core, compressing the pear sprigs. He applies a mud poultice to the top of the exposed hawthorn core, "so that wind will not get in," he explains, and finally covers the new organism with a dead shrub so that light but not cold will penetrate. The tree will bear fruit after two years. Ambitious and

Saalih 'Awaad grafting a domestic "kilaabi"-type pear onto native Sinai hawthorn rootstock, in his Wadi Abu Tuwayta orchard. September 16, 1989.

curious grafters achieve some unusual results. In Wadi Tinya, Saalih 'Awaad shows off an almond host onto which he grafted a second almond variety, a peach, and a prune, all of them now fruit-bearing.

Despite the symbols of common clan and tribal property in Bedouin society many valuable resources are privately owned. A few unwalled mulberries, pomegranates, and other fruit trees stand as the unselfish legacy of individuals who planted them for the enjoyment of all. Such people earn special places in the tribe's oral history. Those who dig wells and mark trails for the benefit of all people are likewise admired. But the great majority of wells and fruit-bearing trees in Jabaliya territory belong to particular families. Building a new orchard is expensive, equaling up to ten months' subsistence costs for a family.[10] Families defend these investments with their seasonal presence, their honor, and their legal code. The Bedouins conceptually liken damage to a tree to violation of a woman, because they draw a parallel between trees bearing fruit and women bearing children. Both trees and women are *hurma*, the "inviolable" property of men.[11] The tribal judge (*gaadhi*) therefore imposes what by Jabaliya standards are severe penalties on unlawful orchard intruders. One man explained:

If someone enters a garden and does wrong and is caught, he is prosecuted. Every step he took from the public trail to the garden wall would be counted. He might be fined one camel for this. For mounting the wall he would be fined another camel. Entering the garden would cost him another camel. Walking to the tree he robbed would be another camel. Reaching for the fruit would cost a camel. His steps out of the garden would cost another camel. The fine is decided by the gaadhi. There are many. Shaykh Abul-Haym is one of them. This crime does happen, fairly often. Today the fine is not paid in livestock but in a monetary equivalent between ten thousand and forty thousand pounds. A person who breaks orchard tree limbs is fined at a rate of five pounds per each finger length of the limbs he has broken. It does not matter how much fruit the violator took. It is the act of entering the garden with ill intent which is forbidden. However, it is permitted to enter a garden and go straight from the door to the well and drink and go straight out. That is not a problem. And there is another exception. If you are in need from hunger, you can enter a garden, eat fruit, and leave a message ('alaama) by placing a piece of green tree limb between two rocks. This means "I was hungry, I came here and ate, and I was not a thief."

Garden violations are the most common crime tried by traditional Jabaliya judges. The case is often resolved with the Bedouin trial by fire called *tilhas an-naar* ("licking the fire") or *al-bisha'*. A specialized judge called a *mubasha'* travels from his home in Ismailiya for the occasion. In a public ceremony he removes a spoon from hot coals and applies it to the tongue of the accused. If the spoon burns the tongue the defendant is guilty; if not he is innocent. Guilty parties often confess rather than undergo the ordeal.[12]

A man laughed when I asked him what would happen if an Egyptian broke the rules and ate someone's apricots. "We'd get a big stick and . . . no, he doesn't know the rules." Yet my experience suggests that outsiders must be unquestionably ignorant of the rules and Jabaliya tribesmen desperately hungry or thirsty if they are not to be accused. As we walked up Wadi Itlaah on a hot summer afternoon my Jabaliya companion and I became very thirsty. We passed one brimming pool after another but all were within walled orchards. No gardeners were in them to give us permission, so we would not drink. They so revere this code that Bedouins will not drink water or pick fruit from orchards whose protective walls have been lost, such as one in Farsh ar-Rumaana destroyed by a flash flood in 1979.

Male family members build the new garden. Plots pass from father to sons, and most have family histories of several generations. It is common for several brothers to tend a single garden and share its produce. They may sell the plot to a family outside the clan or even outside the tribe, but only with the consent of their wives, who are also responsible for dividing the garden produce.[13] Particular wadis are effectively in the possession of single clans. The Awlaad Jindi have a near-monopoly on gardens in Wadi Tinya, Wadi Abu Juruus, Wadi Abu Tuwayta, and Wadi Itlaah, while the Awlaad Saliim prevail in Wadi Jibaal and around Jebel Baab. Through purchases Awlaad Sa'iid tribesmen have acquired about 15 percent of the gardens within Jabaliya tribal territory, and Muzayna, Gararsha, and Suwalha tribesmen together own about 5 percent.[14] Their orchards tend to be neglected because their proprietors visit them from distant homes only to harvest almonds and other fruits requiring little maintenance. "But their claims are ancient and just," one Jabaliya man said of their plots.

Jabaliya affinities with their gardens contradict a popular perception of Bedouins as wandering, rootless people uninterested in the welfare of particular places. Orchards have a special place in the Jabaliya heart. A new garden must be established by "laying the hand" (wad' wad) on the right place. A man who thinks he has found a suitable site sleeps at the spot. If his dreams are sweet he will build there; nightmares mean he must find another locale. Just as entire gardens pass from father to son so do individual trees, and gardeners recall their lineages fondly. Saalim Farraj showed off a sixty-two-year-old apricot tree his father had planted which, he beamed, yields 200 kilograms of fruit annually. Old trees elicit strong emotions about Jabaliya roots. An elderly couple in a Wadi Tinya garden explained to me that the almond tree we sat under was first harvested by the man's ancestors 120 years ago. "We sit in its shade for a short time. We are nothing to the tree. It will stay on to shade other generations," the greybeard said. Anthropologist Iman El-Bastawisi witnessed an annual thanksgiving commemoration of those family members who have worked this ground before. It takes place on a moonlit summer night:

> *The celebration begins when one of the sons wears secretly the old clothes of his grandfather and sits under a tree. The members of the family soon arrive with a goat and pretend they were surprised seeing their dead grandfather again. The men slaughter the goat, take its blood and spray it all over the garden as a sacrifice to the trees to give them more of their fruits. The meat is cooked and everyone takes his share. After they eat they sing and dance to please themselves and the spirit of their ancestors.*[15]

In these special places families enjoy a tranquility they claim their permanently settled kinsmen in Katriin have forgotten. It is a setting for quiet industry on the part of the gardener and for low-key social interaction among men between short work periods. It is a splendid summer playground for children. Toddlers imitate and young boys assist the labors of their parents, for example by opening apricots to dry. Women and girls look after herd animals on the nearby mountain slopes by day, and return to garden encampments at nightfall to prepare meals. Garden shade is replaced by darkness and cricket song, and families stay up visiting and relaxing. They retire to stone houses, some of them simple rock circles without roofs, architectural testimony to the gentleness of summer's climate in the high mountains. Mosquitoes are the only nuisance, and the Jabaliya family often builds its stone home upslope and well away from the garden with its standing water sources. Summer is the best time, the Jabaliya say. Many men have told me how compellingly peaceful and pleasurable this environment is for them. They have a word for the sensation the garden retreat evokes: *kayf*, meaning "delight."

Mahmuud Mansuur gave me a very personal insight into the depth of feeling some Jabaliya men have for their gardens. In 1987 he began a loving restoration of an abandoned Byzantine-era garden site at 1450 meters in a place called Abu Dagash, above Wadi Itlaah. Single almond, apricot, and pomegranate trees had struggled to survive there, unattended by Mahmuud's grandfather who first acquired the site, and also neglected by his father. Mahmuud first built a rock wall around the plot and, to ensure that the nimble ibex would not enter it, surmounted the wall with a ring of barbed wire he carried all the way from the abandoned military post on the 2,665-meter summit of Jebel Katarina (an effort he described as a "son of a dog errand"). Water rarely occurs at hillside places like Abu Dagash,

but Mahmuud detected the remains of a telltale rock wall that had protected an early hermit's water supply. He dug and reached water. Upslope
from the garden and outside its wall, in an igneous intrusion under the
shade of a huge boulder, he excavated a second pool which serves as the
principal supply of irrigation for his crops below.

Mahmuud Mansuur
watering his Abu
Dagash garden.
September 11, 1989.

Mahmuud has come to terms with the wildlife of this place. He fertil-
izes his crops with dung from a nearby hyrax colony. In turn he has conceded his higher water source for hyrax and ibex to use. Several chukar
partridges took flight as we arrived at the garden one day. Mahmuud allows
them to feed on his figs, but he ties cloth sacks around his grapes to protect
these from the birds. He has introduced almonds, which he nurtured from
seed, tobacco, lemons, oranges, peaches, and a "shitawi"-type pear into
the garden. He explained his two ailing banana trees as "an experiment."
He transplanted several wild hollyhocks into the garden "just because they
are nice to look at," he said. At least once every six days in summer he
regularly walks the two-hour round trip from his home in Katriin for the
four-hour chore of watering the garden. Occasionally his wife Ghaaliya
and son Hussayn join him for several consecutive summer days camping
out at the site. Mahmuud in the garden is a man transformed. He is eu-
phoric as he explains how this is unlike any other garden: it is far away
from all the others, it has more shade and water, there are antiquities in it,

and the view is superb. For Mahmuud and his family the garden is more a retreat, a kind of summer resort, than it is an economic asset. "I don't care much for the village," Mahmuud complained of Katriin, "I come here just to enjoy the peace."

KNOWING THE DESERT

Wild plants and animals supplement Jabaliya diet, health, and income. The ways in which the Bedouins use these reveal much about the depth of their environmental knowledge, the antiquity of their relationship with the land, and their cultural perspectives. Religion in part prescribes what resources they may and may not use. Islamic taboos prevent them from eating mammals with canine teeth, birds with hooked beaks, and nonruminating herbivores, but they may eat the flesh of ruminating animals and animals such as hare and hyrax which they believe chew cud. The Jabaliya are amused by the custom of their Ma'aza Bedouin counterparts of not eating flesh of hyrax (*wabr, Procavia capensis*) because they regard the animal as a brother of humankind. A Jabaliya man told me hyrax flesh is delectable and has many textures and colors in different layers, like the *shawarma* meat prepared on braziers in Cairo cafes. I solemnly told a group of Jabaliya men the Ma'aza saying "Oh eater of the hyrax, oh eater of thy dear brother!" One of them chuckled, "I have eaten all my brothers then!" The Jabaliya do not observe the Ma'aza prohibition against eating *dhabb* lizards, which the Ma'aza believe are also akin to humanity. I told Jabaliya men the Ma'aza account of how *dhabb* meat quivers when cooked, a frightening clue that the animal might live on after death. "Yes, it does shake when cooking," one of the men said, "so what?"

Wild plants have always added flavor and variety to Bedouin diet. The Jabaliya today rarely enjoy Sinai's most famous wild food, the sticky substance they call *mann* which forms on tamarisk trees in the summer, and which many observers have identified as the Biblical manna. Shaykh Abul-Haym recalls gathering it from tamarisk needles and branches, or where it dripped onto rocks, but never from the soil. He described it as tasting "like honey." Now, he said, there are not enough tamarisk trees for people to enjoy this as a regular item of summer diet. Fruits of wild hawthorn (*za' ruur, Crataegus sinaica*), although not delicious, are edible. Another edible but infrequently eaten fruit grows on those few specimens of the burning bush (*'illayg, Rubus sanctus*) which grow in the backcountry. Although its seeds are spicy hot, fruits of caper (*laysuuf, Capparis aegyptiaca*) are edible. People eat the seeds of garliclike wild leek (*kurraat, Allium ampeloprasum*). They chew leaves of "ewe's nose" (*ikhnaanit an-na'ja, Phagnalon nitidum*) as a gum. Goat ghee may be spiced with the leaves of salty *muliih* (*Reau-*

muria hirtella), and a dehydrated person in need of salt may rub this plant's leaves between his fingers to extract the mineral. Fresh wild marjoram (*za'tar, Origanum syriacum*) enlivens the taste of many bland foods and creates a prized dish when mixed with sugar cane, sesame seed, and olive oil. The Jabaliya often add wild mint (*habbak, Mentha longifolia*) to their tea. "Mountain tea" (*shaay jabali, Pulicaria undulata*) prepared alone makes a delicious concoction. Freshly picked leaves of sorrel (*himaadh, Rumex vesicarius*) are a fine salad. Although sheep and goats eat *birkaan* (*Phaeopappus scoparius*), it is too bitter for human consumption; a Jabaliya maxim holds that "patience is bitter like *birkaan*." Bedouins use flowers of roquette (*shumaar, Foeniculum vulgare*) as a food spice and eat it directly as salad.

The Bedouins sometimes distill from roquette a potent liquor called *araki*. They occasionally produce both wines and vinegars from unripened dates (*tamar*) and "istambuuli"-type grapes. In 1822 naturalist Edward Rüppell described the main occupation of the Jabaliya as the distillation of date brandy for their own use, and sneered that if the Jabaliya died the world would lose little.[16] The Jabaliya, however, generally frown upon liquor. Saalih Musa told me three demons visited Noah's ark and stole away with two-thirds of that prophet's grape supply. They fermented wine from the grapes and indulged in it. The drunken demons became detestable creatures: a monkey, a peacock, and a pig. Saalih 'Awaad condemned insobriety in these terms: "Whoever drinks has a small world around him and forgets everything. He lives in a prison." He told me this parable: "A man told his son, 'If you are thinking you might like to drink alcohol, go to the bar about one or two o'clock in the morning, then decide if that's what you want to do.' The boy went and saw people throwing up and falling down and fighting with and stealing from one another. He saw a man who was a lion become a leopard and finally a pig, an animal that eats shit. And the boy was able to make up his mind." The Jabaliya know that henbane (*saykaraan, Hyoscyamus muticus*) in any form is a powerful and dangerous intoxicant. They claim to avoid it altogether but recount that at Nuweiba some Israelis smoked it recreationally, and that one of the smokers died while the others became seriously ill. The Bedouins say that a person who drinks milk of a goat which has eaten its purple flowers will experience unexpected and unpleasant intoxication.

Through experimentation and exchange of information with neighboring tribes the Jabaliya have learned an impressive array of medicinal uses for wild plants. The endemic wild thyme (*za'aytaraan, Thymus decussatus*) boiled up and consumed as a tea is an excellent remedy for nausea. I was able to verify this after eating the apricots that June day. The same remedy is effective against overeating of unripe pears, prunes, and grapes. A few sprigs of *hinayda* (*Jasonia montana*) in hot tea also soothes the stomach. In this dry climate constipation bothers man and beast. A constipated camel may be cured with the *guurdhi* bush (*Ochradenus baccatus*). The camel must breathe smoke of burning *guurdhi* charcoal, and the smoke must be allowed to permeate the animal's fur, for half an hour. "The camel does not like this," one man explained, "so he must be tied down." Human constipation is rather more easily and immediately relieved by swallowing just two tiny seeds of the colocynth gourd (*handhal, Citrullus colocynthis*). A gentler laxative is obtained from leaves and pods of Indian senna (*salla makki, Cassia senna*), which the Jabaliya acquire by trade from its habitat in the limestone country of central Sinai.

The Bedouins recognize infection-fighting properties in several plants. Jabaliya companions treated my severe ear infection with a hot poultice of wild mint leaves and stems boiled up, wrapped in a handkerchief, and tied around my head and ear. They apply the same treatment to infections of the eye, throat, and lymph glands. The principle is that in promoting perspiration the heat will "evaporate" the infection. They insist that the infection is something "wet" which must do combat with something "dry." A poultice of argel (*harjal, Gomphocarpus sinaicus*) leaves dried, ground, and applied to an open wound helps prevent infection. Boiled up as an infusion and applied as eyedrops, foliage of lavender cotton (*gaysuum, Achillea fragrantissima*) is useful against eye infections. For colds and flu the Jabaliya folk doctor recommends donkey dung. Although Islamic law renders the donkey's flesh inedible, the Bedouins do not hesitate to use its waste when illness strikes. They reason that because the animal eats so much *hinayda* its dung is highly effective. The patient boils the dung as a tea, drinks this infusion, covers himself with blankets, and perspires until the fever is broken. "In the morning you feel better," the Jabaliya say.

There are many analgesics in the Bedouin medicine chest. Boiled up as a mouthwash, leaves of camel thorn (*'aguul, Alhagi maurorum*) ease toothache. The best headache remedy is a poultice of leaves of freshly pounded wormwood (*shiih, Artemisia inculta*) leaves applied to the forehead. Rosemary (*zinzibiil, Rosmarinus officinalis*) steeped in goat ghee eases the pain and bleeding of a woman who has just given birth. Rheumatism and fatigue are among the most often complained-about ailments of people and livestock. Weary camels despise their handlers' prescription of pouring a hot broth of fox meat over and in the animal's muzzle and mouth. Although consuming fox is taboo according to Islamic tradition, weak children and arthritic elders of the Jabaliya are prescribed its meat. Perhaps as dispensation for its curative powers, the Jabaliya recognize the generally taboo hyena as an anomalous animal, its right side permissible (*shi'b muhallal*) and its left side forbidden (*shi'b muharram*). A person suffering from fatigue or rheumatism is prescribed the hyena sweating treatment known as *'ariiga*. The patient is enclosed in a tent or stone house in which a fire is built and the meat and bones of the permissible half of the hyena are boiled up. The patient drinks the broth and covers himself in blankets until he sweats profusely. This cooking, broth-drinking, and sweating should continue for about twenty-four hours or until the patient ceases to perspire. The fire is then extinguished but the patient should remain in the enclosed area overnight, only gradually allowing open air into the place. The patient leaves this treatment feeling so much better that he can reportedly "climb mountains with ease." Flesh of fox or hyrax may be substituted in this treatment if hyena is not available. In the case of the hyrax, the patient also eats the animal's stomach and some of its flesh. The decapitated corpse of a Burton's carpet viper, a snake bearing a potent neurotoxic venom, fried in olive oil and eaten, is also prescribed for fatigue and rheumatism. The Jabaliya say that immersion in the hot springs of Hammaam Fara'uun, the "Pharoah's Baths" north of Abu Rudeis on the Gulf of Suez, is also effective against rheumatism.

Plant and animal parts serve the Jabaliya with a number of other medicinal and hygienic uses. Rubbed across the face, foliage of horehound (*ghaasa, Ballota undulata*) leaves a powder which is an effective sunscreen. Dipped in water, root of wild rue (*haramlaan, Peganum harmala*) serves as a fine toothbrush. Wild rue roots may also be cooked up as a bitter toothpaste. Pituranthos (*zaguuh, Pituranthos tortuosus*) boiled and consumed as soup is good for the kidneys. Flowers and leaves of sage (*mardaguush, Salvia multicaulis*) boiled in tea or milk and then drunk is "good for the heart." Parts of venomous stinging animals help deter effects of those animals' stings. When a child is forty days old, a desert physician (*haawi*) who specializes in the treatment of snake bites and scorpion stings administers her or him an oral prophylaxis (*laguuna*) against scorpion sting. The potion is a mixture of the haawi's saliva, baked and pulverized yellow scorpion, and parts of a wasp. This dose renders a person relatively immune to scorpions throughout life, the Bedouins say: although the first sting will be painful, subsequent events will not be.

The traditional material culture of the Jabaliya has included a variety of devices created from local plants and animals. The Bedouin's canteen is a waterskin (*girba 'arabiyya*) fashioned from ibex or goat skin and tanned by the bark of pomegranate, ephedra (*'alda, Ephedra ciliata*), globularia (*handaguug, Globularia arabica*), or the ever-useful *hinayda*. Hyrax and goat skins are best for curdling-bags (*si'un*). Woods of domesticated almond, castor, and quince trees contribute different parts of a single camel saddle. Poplar trunks are best for the garden *shaduf* or weighted beam. Poplar, date palm, almond, apricot, willow, and wild fig provide roofing and other structural materials for mountain summer homes. Homeowners mix hyrax dung (*sunn*) with water and apply the solution to their wooden doors, creating a seal that deters termites. The substance doubles as a fertilizer in nearby gardens. It is often rich in fruits and leaves of wild fig, which the Bedouins believe the hyrax consumes to expel intestinal parasites. Lavender cotton foliage makes an excellent roofing thatch because it does not deteriorate quickly. Common reeds (*gasab, Phragmites australis*) provide good screens, allowing light but little heat to penetrate dwellings. Leaves of wild rue and Judean wormwood (*ba'aytharaan, Artemisia judaica*) protect the Bedouin goat-hair "wool home" against damage by beetles and moth larvae when it is in storage. Supple branches of the Moses stick (*yasar, Colutea istria*) are best for making the *salla* basket in which apricots and other fruits can be hauled to market on camelback. The *sa'af* basket in which people collect and store dates is made of palm fiber. Odd combinations of local and foreign materials comprise musical instruments. Jabaliya men use discarded Egyptian or Israeli oil cans, wire, and wood of palm, quince, or almond to fashion their lutes (*simsimiyya*). Girls make their flutes (*shabaaba* and *'ifaata*) from common reeds and iron pipes. Older men who still use flint-and-steel fire starters instead of or in addition to matches use the cocoon (*safuun*) of a butterfly spun on wormwood as their tinder. Sap of wild pistachio (*butm, Pistacia khinjuk*) makes a fine incense for weddings and other important occasions.

Before the introduction of the automobile, the rifle, and the daily wage into Sinai, the Jabaliya accommodated the natural world around them and worked to protect it. These Bedouins still generally respect wildlife and their folklore tends to elevate rather than vilify animals. They admire mourning wheatears (*bug'aa, Oenanthe lugens*) and white-crowned black wheatears (*umm suwwayd, Oenanthe leucopyga*) for calling loudly to warn people of the presence of vipers. I once saw a young man throw a rock at a mourning wheatear. An older Bedouin reprimanded him: "Don't hurt the *bug'aa*—he's better than Bani Aadam!" The scrub warbler (*ifsay, Scotocerca inquieta*) flits from place to place frenetically, they say, looking for the stick it will use to intervene in disputes between the wheatear and the lark. According to a Jabaliya parable which is a variant on a common tradition in the Muslim world, a spider protected Moses:

> *The prophet was being chased near Mecca by enemies who would kill him. He took shelter in a cave. A spider came and spun a web across the cave entrance. A mouse came and covered Moses' tracks. A rock dove came and quickly built her nest and laid eggs. Moses' pursuers arrived and said, "He can't be in there. If he were there would be no spider web or nesting bird, and there would be tracks."*
> *Only the gecko with its loud clicking would have given Moses away. The prophet was only lucky that the would-be killers did not recognize the lizard's alarm.*

The Jabaliya therefore regard the spider as an animal which should never be harmed, and the gecko as an evil and poisonous creature. A variant of this account is a Jabaliya story of the Prophet Muhammad fleeing would-be persecutors. After he took refuge in a cave the *guurdhi* plant grew to cover the entrance, making it appear that the cave had not been entered recently. The Bedouins say that in recognition of its service they never cut a *guurdhi* plant.

Traditions like these contribute to an overall respect for wild things as incumbent for the good Muslim. These Bedouins rarely kill or molest animals without cause. Despite their overall sense of responsibility for the welfare of wild things, however, the Jabaliya have always persecuted some species as agricultural pests. Hyrax are notorious for feeding on cultivated grapes and almonds. Certainly birds do harm to Jabaliya crops; particularly chukar (*shinaar, Alectoris chukar*), sand partridge (*hajal, Ammoperdix heyi*), Sinai rosefinch (*gazam, Carpodacus synoicus*), Tristram's grackle (*shahruur, Onychognathus tristramii*), and *abu fisaada* (several warbler species). Scores of Tristram's grackles and Sinai rosefinches indulge noisily in fruiting mulberry trees. Sinai rosefinches seem particularly fond of ripening figs. To deter these pests the Jabaliya sometimes place nets over fruiting trees, especially grape vines. They also employ scarecrows (*khayaal*), typically a dead falcon (either shot or found dead) staked with wings spread out, or plastic bags and rags hung from tree branches. Jabaliya gardeners told me that if they did not take sure measures birds would destroy all but their almond crops. Some cultivators concede to the animals. In mid-September brothers Subhi and Hassan Saalim retire for the winter from their garden at 1,900 meters in Wadi Abu Juruus, acknowledging that they leave many grapes to ripen on the vine and become food for partridges. They say it is not practical economically to remain vigilant against the birds in this remote place just to harvest some grapes.

With the exception of the burrow trap for leopards, traditional Jabaliya hunting technology did not decimate wildlife populations. The Bedouins fashioned crossbows (*nabla*) from hair and local pomegranate and quince wood. They hunted chukar, hyrax, and ibex with this weapon, often unsuccessfully. They used the *mirdaaha*, a stone basin-trap baited with grain, to capture sand partridges and chukar. Palmwood vegetable crates obtained from the market in Katriin now sometimes serve this purpose. The hunter turns the crate upside down and props up one side with a vertical stick. This supporting stick rests on two horizontal sticks which the game-bird disturbs when feeding on seeds left under the crate, thereby bringing the crate down over him. These edible birds and "pests" such as grackles may also be lured and captured by placing a few lentils in a wild cotton shrub (*wasbii-, Gomphocarpus fruticosus*). When the bird alights to eat the bait its feathers become glued to a sticky gum excreted by the bush. Chukar sometimes trap themselves without human inducement as they feed on ants stuck to the plant's adhesive. Traditionally the Jabaliya hunted ibex for food with rope snares, apparently with enough restraint to ensure that population levels would remain high. The snares were simple nooses placed around open water sources where ibex are compelled to drink in summertime. As it drank the animal's horns became ensnared in the noose. At the rope's other end was tied a tree limb blackened in fire. As the animal fled the blackened stick struck rocks and left easy-to-follow marks, and eventually lodged in boulders or vegetation to secure the quarry.

The Jabaliya had an ancient pasture conservation system known as "the alliance" (*al-hilf*) which forbade herds from entering high mountain pastures above 1,800 meters between February and May.[17] It was a deliberate means of protecting plants by allowing them to regenerate and flower before being besieged by livestock. Musa 'Awaad mused, "I remember the alliance. Oh peace, what a sight. Everyplace was like a garden, with flowers and greenery. There used to be a gate on the Abu Jiifa pass, between the well and the top of the pass. You can still see the remains. The upper mountain pastures above this gate were closed from February until the apricots." Mahmuud Mansuur recalled that the summer pasture was opened officially on a specified day in the year that was a great day of celebration, "like an 'Iyd festival," on which families would ascend in a festive mood to their mountain orchards and pastures.

The Jabaliya continue to praise the virtues of not overusing their natural resources. They extend special protection to living plants and especially to trees. Jabaliya tradition permits charcoal to be made from dead vegetation but never from living limbs or plants. "What would happen if a person charcoaled a green tree?" I asked. A Jabaliya man replied, "Then he would be a bad man," and explained the following:

> *There is a traditional law ('urfi) forbidding the making of charcoal from green plants. If it happens the violator is issued a fine (gharaama). But for the law to be applied someone must have claimed responsibility for protecting plants in the area where the violation took place. Otherwise the violator is just a "bad man" if he cuts in an area unclaimed by someone. But if he cut a* ratam *[white broom] claimed by someone, he might have to pay a fine of two hundred, three hundred, or four hundred pounds to the patron. Every tree is ancient and precious. We call them* sibha *["divine blessing"] because God blessed us with trees. The* butm *[wild pistachio] is such a blessing. No one cuts it—no one cuts or burns a live tree. It is the same with the* sayaal *[acacia]. It is a crime if you cut a whole living tree. If you do people will make trouble for you. We have a tradition. If a man*

goes through life doing bad deeds like cutting trees he lives badly and suffers misfortune, not only in this life but in the next.

195

•

The
Bedouin
Way of Life

The Jabaliya have a clear hierarchy in their taboo against cutting trees and shrubs. The most inviolable species are the ephedras (*'alda, Ephedra ciliata* and *E. sinaica*) followed by the the wild pistachio. I asked whether all trees were not worthy of protection. A man replied, "Yes, but some are very special; you would never cut or burn them. These also include any very old trees." Late in the nineteenth century Henry Palmer observed remnants of an ancient conservation system in the Sinai which had allowed some trees to become very old. Bedouins marked off specific valley floors, "the use of which was reserved to the sanctuaries. Inside this holy ground, the *hima*, no animal might be hunted and no tree might be cut down. Many valleys of Sinai today contain one tree of great age and often of prodigious size, which is accounted holy and therefore left untouched." [18] The Jabaliya still harvest edible and other useful plants on the principle of "sustainable yield." During the September harvest of wild thyme, for example, men carefully crop the shrubs to ensure the root stock is not damaged. They explain that such cutting will in fact stimulate regrowth the following spring.

It may seem ironic that a people of the wilderness like the Jabaliya should rely not only on carefully managed wild resources but on food staples produced by peoples settled in distant farming communities. In fact, dependence on settled folk for some of life's necessities is characteristic of all Bedouin societies, and has been an essential feature of the pastoral nomadic way of life since its inception some ten thousand years ago. Bread made from cereals grown by others is the staff of Jabaliya life. In the town of Katriin the Bedouins buy flour processed in the Nile Valley from American wheat. The government of Egypt subsidizes it heavily, and like all Egyptians the Jabaliya may purchase a monthly ration of 25 kilograms per person at a cost of .30 Egyptian pound per kilogram. Women and in some circumstances men prepare a tortilla-like bread (*fatiir*) by heating a thin disk of rolled flour on sheet metal. Men in all-male company more often prepare for themselves a thicker pizza-like bread baked directly between hot coals and sand. Exclusively male preparation of this *libba* or *gurs* is one of many manifestations of the strict gender segregation of roles in Jabaliya society. With few exceptions men tend the summer gardens and manage camels while women and children herd sheep and goats. Women are responsible for the preparation of all meals except those which men must prepare for themselves when they are alone or on the road in all-male company.

Among the imported staples of Jabaliya diet are lentils, which the Bedouins recognize as highly nutritious and call "the poor man's meat" (*lahmat al-fagiir*). A favorite dish called *fatta* consists of lentils mixed with bread and ghee. Rice is also a regular part of Jabaliya diet, especially in a dish called *ma'duush*, a delicious blend of rice and lentils seasoned with cumin, pepper, and onions. From their own goats' milk the Bedouins prepare yoghurt in a goatskin curdling bag (*girbat laban*). On outings away from the hearth they snack on *'afiig*, a soured, yellowish dried cheese they make from goat's milk. Meat contributes only a small portion of the Jabaliya diet because family herds are small and the animals are valued most for the cash they bring in. Sacrifice of a camel is reserved for very special occasions such as weddings, at which the groom's young male camel may be slaughtered. In more private settings a host honors guests by slaughtering a sheep or goat. From what is left over Jabaliya women prepare dried meats of camel, sheep, goat, and ibex by slicing them thin, dipping them in hot, salty water, and hanging them in a shaded, breezy place. The resulting jerky (*gadiid*) may keep for one or two years. People eat it as is or embellish it with rock salt and peppercorns, roast it on coals, and grind it into rice and soups.

Jabaliya plant and animal names are telling clues about Bedouin observations and perceptions of desert natural history. Bee-eaters, the "shining girls" (*banaat baarig*), are named for the radiance of these rainbow-colored migratory birds. "The mother of blackness" (*umm suwwayd*) is the white-crowned black wheatear. The common Adesmia or darkling beetle is the "girls' donkey" (*uwayr al-banaat*) because playful girls taunt the animal as they might a donkey. The "mother of avoidance" (*umm junayb*), the deadly Palestinian mole viper, should be avoided at all times. The "leopard of the flies" spider (*numayra adh-dhibaan*) stalks and jumps its prey like the great cat. "Hardhuun lizard's tomato" (*tamaatim al-hardhuun*) is a favorite item in that reptile's diet. Likewise "ibex candy" (*halaawat al-badan*) is the wild goat's favorite plant. Mushrooms are such unlikely and uncommon organisms that the Jabaliya have named them after another intangible substance, "hyena fart" (*faasit adh-dhab'a*).

Some place names also reveal Bedouin knowledge of plant and animal behavior, habitat, and distribution. Maayat ash-Shinaar, the Partridge Spring, is a favorite watering hole for these gamebirds. The birds also frequent Wadi ash-Shinaar. Kharazit as-Sayd is a water source which "game" (*sayd*), meaning "ibex," often visit. Farashaat al-Hamal, the "Basins of Bagging," are called that because they provided a setting where even unskilled hunters have a good chance of bringing down an ibex. Farsh al-Araanib, "Basin of the Hares," is ideal habitat for these animals. When they still inhabited the area leopards often came to Shuwiik an-Nimr, a drainage named after them. In Farsh Abu Liifa, the "Basin of Palm Fiber," a hunter camouflaged with palm fiber (*liif*) once pursued a leopard. Diista al-Fara'iyya is a stretch of Wadi Fara'iyya named for the many bulrushes (*diis*) occupying it. Wadis Za'atar and Za'aytaraan have high densities of their fragrant namesake plants, wild marjoram and wild thyme. Abu Hubbayk, "Father of Mint," is named for these water-loving plants that favor this drainage. Jebel Umm Shumar takes its name from its many roquette (*shumaar*) plants, and Farsh Hamamiidh from its saltwort (*haamdh*) plants.

Many place names attest to the Bedouins' agricultural occupation. Wadi Zawatiin, the "Valley of Olives," accurately depicts olives as the dominant orchard tree of this drainage. There is a single apple tree at 'Ayn at-Tufaaha, "Apple Spring." Nearby Nagub as-Skaykriyya in Wadi Tinya is named after the ancient, sole *skaykri* pear tree variety in Jabaliya territory and, if the Bedouins are correct, in all Sinai. Some Bedouins refer to Wadi Abu Juruus as Wadi Shawbaka because of the ancient walnut tree (*shawbak*) there, which they believe Byzantine monks planted. Farsh al-Kharayribba, "The Carob Basin," is named for the carob tree. Similarly Wadi Kalabiyya is named after the "dog" (*kilaabi*) pear variety Bedouins cultivate there. The tree takes its name from the fruit's long stem, which resembles a dog's tail. A large, lone mulberry (*tuut*) is the namesake of Wadi Abu Tuwayta. "The Rock of the Mulberry" (Hajar at-Tuwaytiyya) took its name from a tree which has long since vanished. Wadi Nakhala is likewise named for a lone palm which no longer occupies the site. Pomegranates (*rumaan*) lent their name to the wide upper stretch of Wadi Tala' known as Farsh ar-Rumaana. Wadi Tarkiiba has a population of fig trees produced by grafting (*tarkiib*) of wild and domesticated varieties.

Jabaliya place names also reflect creative interpretations of natural landscape. Jebel Na'ja, "Ewe Mountain," is named for the bright white aspect the mountain presents in a sea of red granite. Part of the drainage of Wadi at-Tbuuk or at-Tabag, "Defile Valley," is a narrow gorge. Nagub al-Haawa, "Pass of the Winds," is aptly named for the winds that prevail at all seasons there. Zibb Ruba'i, "Ruba'i's Penis," is a natural stone column above Nagub al-Haawa named long ago after a man of some stature. Baab ad-Dunya, "Door of the World," is an unusual squared-off cleft in Jebel Baab which opens onto a view of distant lowlands in southwestern Sinai. Jebel al-Galb, "Heart Mountain," is shaped like this muscle. Wadi Abu Jidda, "Father of the Dike," is a valley following the line traced by a great igneous intrusion. The "Flute Spring" of Ma'iin al-'Ifaata yields so little water that a person might drink it only by using a flute as a straw. Mahashuur, the "Tucked-Away Place" on the southern slope of Jebel 'Abbas Pasha, is an appropriate name for this secluded basin where at least one Jabaliya couple has courted in privacy. Farsh Abu Alwaan, "the Basin of

Colors," is splashed with numerous tints from rock intrusions. Wadi Tinya is named for the mud (*tiin*) associated with its abundant water supplies, which make this the most fertile of all high Sinai valleys. A stretch of Wadi Itlaah called "The Sweet" (al-Hilw) is named that because, the Jabaliya say, it is a nice place to camp.

Place names provide glimpses into local history and mythology. Wadi ash-Shrayj on Jebel Musa is named after the Shrayjiin, a prehistoric vegetarian people the Bedouins believe once inhabited the area. The Jabaliya say that King David visited this region and paused above Wadi Tala' at Sidd Da'uud, David's Dry Waterfall. They speculate that English soldiers may have rested on Jebel Farsh al-Jaysh, the "Basin of the Army," during colonial days. Monks use the shortcut of Nagub ar-Raahib, "the Monk's Route," between the Plain of ar-Raaha and their monastery in Wadi Tala'. A cross which monks installed long ago on Jebel as-Saliib, "Cross Mountain," still stands there. The Bedouins think that Wadi Abu Juruus, "Father of Bells," is called that either because Byzantine hermits once rang a bell near their cells there, or because the bells of the Monastery of St. Katherine are audible from there. A Jabaliya man told me that Wadi al-Bugiyya is named after the trumpet (*buug*) monks sounded in ancient times to announce they were ready to hand out bread to the Bedouins. When snow fell heavily over the area it was difficult for Bedouins to reach the monastery for their daily ration. Therefore, the monks baked bread once every few days and dispatched one of their own into Wadi ar-Raaha armed with a trumpet to make the "come and get it" call. The Jabaliya acknowledge that many of their place names are unintelligible borrowings from the monks' Greek toponomy, dating from times when ascetics lived all over these mountains. Al-Hakuura, ar-Ramziyya, Jarajniyya, Mugaffa, and Ibraan are some of these places. Other place names tell tales of early Bedouin occupation. Jebel Banaat, "The Girls' Mountain," marks the legend of two sisters whose father ordered them against their will to marry his choice of grooms. They tied their hair together and jumped to their deaths from one of the mountain's cliffs. The Cave of Muhammad and His Sister (Mughaarit Muhammad wa Khaytu) above Wadi ar-Rifaayidh is named after siblings who occupied the site long ago.

In their rocky environment the Jabaliya leave their mark and express themselves in stone. On the heavily traveled Nagub al-Haawa route is a large boulder onto which people throw wishing stones (*hajiir al-magariin*). If the stone comes to rest on the boulder, the supplicant's wish will be realized; if it rolls off, the wish will fail. Another boulder with an identical tradition is on the Abu Jiifa route. Farther down Nagub al-Haawa is the landmark of Hajar al-Maal, "Fortune Rock," which is decorated with an ancient and unintelligible script the Jabaliya call "Suuriyaani." They say

that the person who finally deciphers the writing will gain access to a treasure hidden within the rock. Another lithic tradition began in 1986 on
Farsh Umm Silla, a 1,900-meter-high basin between Wadi Tala' and Wadi
Abu Tuwayta. There Mahmuud Mansuur and some young Israeli hikers
built a single cairn to commemorate their visit. Soon the custom developed that every hiking party passing through the area should erect its own
monument. With the passage of time these cairns have become increasingly elaborate, some of them having peculiar shapes, great sizes, and especially delicate supports. This odd and compelling outdoor artwork suggests respect for the land.

   Jabaliya graffiti, rock drawings, and symbols in wood embellish the
landscape. Mulberries make the best paint. They leave a purplish stain
which may remain on sheltered red granite surfaces for many years. The
Bedouins depict trees as a love motif. Bare branches mean love lost or
unrequited. If one's amorous wishes are realized, he or she paints leaves on
the branches. A similar theme is the "mark of the notch" (*asar al-hazz*), an
outline of one or two human feet traced onto granite boulders, usually in
pass routes. The Jabaliya explain that in the old days a suitor would scrape
the outline of his foot on a rock. If the girl of his eye consented to marry
him, she traced her foot next to his. Finally, if the would-be bride's father
approved the union he drew a ring around both feet. On rocks throughout
the area there are single feet, pairs of uncircled feet, and circled pairs that

testify to all possible outcomes. A suitor may also propose marriage by offering a green tree limb and several gifts to his would-be father-in-law. If he keeps the gifts he is consenting to his daughter's marriage; if he returns them, the proposal has failed.[19] In modern times when a pastoral maiden is about to marry a man who will settle her in Katriin or another village and so remove her from the nomadic way of life, she ties a colored string on a tree branch on her last day in the mountains. About twenty-five of these decorate an ephedra bush in Wadi Nakhala. The Bedouins sometimes carve or paint dates onto rock. A boulder near the summit of Jebel Katarina is dated May 1967, the eve of a momentous time in the region's history. More rarely the Jabaliya express themselves in wood. One of the few circumstances in which a person will uproot a living plant is to indicate that he or she has just left a place and will return to it very soon. I once saw a man leave some personal belongings on a hillside. He dug up a green shrub and placed it on his baggage, notifying passersby they need not investigate these materials; they were his and he would be back for them shortly.

The Jabaliya are proud to create humble reminders of themselves for future generations. They disapprove of gaudy markers on the landscape. His kinsmen scorned Hassan Jabali for using white spray-paint to write his name in large letters on the most prominent rockfaces overlooking Wadi at-Tbuuk. The Jabaliya despise the blemish created by the Belgian artist Jean Verame, who in 1980 sprayed a large granitic area in Wadi Zaghra with 13 tons of unearthly cobalt blue paint. He called his work "Sinai Peace Junction."[20] "He was crazy," one Jabaliya man said of the artist, adding that the paint was already fading. I told this man about Christo, the Bulgarian artist who erects giant fences and wraps buildings and bridges in plastic just for a few hours or days. He thought Christo was crazy also.

THIS WORLD AND OTHERS

Social traditions are as important as knowledge of the environment in sustaining the desert way of life. Hospitality is a pervasive virtue among the Jabaliya. They say a person should be generous all the time rather than only occasionally sacrifice an animal for an honored guest. There is a sense of ceremony, ritual, and propriety at any meal where guests are present. First there are rounds of hot drinks: tea, coffee, or carob. Then everyone eats from a common bowl or dish, with the honored guest starting off the feast. If meat is served, host and lesser guests pass the biggest or best pieces to the guest's side, saying, "Eat, eat!" "No, thank you, I am full." "Eat, eat!" It is best to keep eating. Then come beverages again. With or without meals the round of hot tea is the most regular and incumbent ritual of hospitality

and group solidarity. The host prepares it with great care to achieve just
the right formula: it should be light and very sweet. Only once did I prepare tea. My companions threw it away politely.

Coffee is more expensive and appears only for the most special occasions. The Jabaliya expression "the coffeepot with cardamom followed by
bread!" translates roughly as "it doesn't get any better than this!" Likewise
the exclamation "bil-hayl!"—literally, "with cardamom!"—means "the
best there is." It is customary to accept no more than three cups, and to
"wag" the cup when you have had enough. On the Feast of the Sacrifice
(*'Iyd al-Adha*) Saalih 'Awaad related this account to emphasize the importance of not overindulging in hospitality:

*A stranger once entered a wool home without announcing his arrival with the cus-
tomary greeting of "peace be with you." This aroused the suspicion of the man
of the house. But rather than confront the intruder the host offered him coffee.
After the guest had accepted the second cup the host asked him, "Why did you
come here?" The visitor replied, "I smelled coffee and wanted some." The
guest accepted a third cup of coffee but when offered a fourth wagged his cup.
The host announced, "Ah, then I know that you have indeed come for coffee, and
not for my wife. If you had taken the fourth cup I would have cut your throat."
Instead the host slaughtered a sheep to honor his guest.*

Although tired after a late evening of socializing I was careful not to drink
too much of Uncle Saalih's coffee. I relaxed with his family in the shade
of their orchard in Wadi Tinya as Saalih read from the tales of David and
Solomon. He taught me that when the star known as the "star of the
guest" (*najmit adh-dhayf*) rises it is too late to call on a would-be host. If
that star rises while you are sitting at the host's fire it is time for you to
leave.

Mahmuud Mansuur has an idea of how the word "Badu" came to designate the desert nomads. When a person saw something in the distance,
he said that thing "bada-"—appeared—on the horizon. Settled people
would see nomads on the horizon but could not identify them. The nomads were the curious and indiscernible "apparent ones" of the distance.
The Jabaliya pride themselves as a people apart. They believe that as nomadic people they have known the world better than settled folk. They
view themselves as adventurous, outgoing, and physically fit. One of their
favorite sayings is, "Whoever lives sees; whoever walks about sees more."
They say that ranging over this land allows them to see all the world more
clearly. There is a sixty-year-old Awlaad Saliim clansman named 'Ayaada
who can tell by a young camel's tracks which animal was its mother. Such
refined senses and knowledge allow them a closer relationship with the

Creator, they insist. They recite this maxim: "The camel dung tells you about the camel, the track about the one who left it, and all this tells you about the Great One." In the early days of Islam, they say, some Muslims met a man who knew his country well but did not know God. The Muslims confronted him, saying, "How could you know all this without your knowledge leading you to God?" This challenge opened the man's heart.

Today the Bedouins say their ancestors knew more about the world and may have been closer still to their Maker. Oral history tells of unique individuals who were endowed with the ability to minister to the physical and spiritual health of their kinsmen. The *hakiim* or "wise one" was the chief physician. One of the most famous was Saalih Umbaarak, who died in 1983 at the reported age of 115. He reputedly was able to cure diseases which modern medicines cannot. The Jabaliya say an American woman afflicted with diabetes once sought his treatment. He diagnosed her illness by licking the palm of her hand. He prescribed her a potion of viper parts and other unknown ingredients and bled her scalp. All manner of horrible liquids issued from the incision and then the patient was cured. This hakiim also pulled teeth and tonsils. The Bedouins believe that tonsil removal alleviates thirst and suppose that Israelis must still have their tonsils because they "are always thirsty."

The Jabaliya emphasize that the hakiim was not a man who received formal training but who "knew the world" in all its dimensions— including its spiritual ones. One of the great hakiims was 'Awaad Musa, who had prophetic abilities and a wide range of healing powers. His descendants in the Diguuniyiin lineage of the Awlaad Jindi clan insist his power still lingers after four generations. They share a bead (*kharaza*) that once belonged to the old man. They say it has miraculous healing powers: a sick person who drinks from a cup in which the bead is placed becomes well. Kinsman Saalih 'Awaad once lost the bead somewhere on a 50-kilometer journey from at-Tur to Katriin. He discovered the loss after two days. Panicked and tired, he worried about how he would retrace his steps and find the tiny amulet. When he awoke the next morning the bead was under his headrest. On another occasion the bead was sitting on the window sill of a stone hut in Wadi Itlaah. A flash flood struck and destroyed all of the structure except for the area immediately around the window frame. The bead remained unmoved. Many people have tried unsuccessfully to purchase this miraculous charm from the Diguuniyiin.

Some women are accomplished shamans. At a reputed 110 years of age the "saint" (*waliyya*) Shaykha Salha of the Wuhaybaat clan is still performing miraculous deeds. This hermit travels through the mountains even in winter with her small goat herd. Each Friday night she goes into a trance and "speaks with God." A Bedouin with mental or emotional problems may approach her at this time and seek her cure. She will reportedly not treat "bad people" or "people who have done bad things," but from her trance will address suitable supplicants and rub her hands over their faces and bodies, imparting her power and curing them.

Exorcists (tahdiir) like Ibrahim Saalih perform another invaluable service. People complain to him of the spirits of the deceased who inhabit them. Ibrahim attempts to identify the 'afriit, asking it where it lived and when it died. He tries to find out what motivates the spirit, asking why it is bothering its host, and why it will not leave him or her be. This process of naming and challenging the spirit eventually drives it from the tortured host. The exorcist has no power over the jinn, a type of spirit which can assume corporeal form to taunt and even kill people. The most recent Jabaliya encounter with a jinn reportedly took place in 1980 when a man found a small and very old pair of pants in Wadi Abu Tuwayta. That cold night the man built a fire and lay close to it, using the pants as a headrest. In the firelight a three-year-old boy appeared wearing a shirt of animal skin but naked below the waist. The child cried and tried to reach for the pants. The man fled. He described the boy as someone from the "deep past" whose appearance was not Arab.

Jinn and other malevolent spirits serve to remind people how they should act in this life. "Maybe someone who was bad in his life becomes a jinn," Mahmuud Mansuur proposed. "If you do bad deeds in life, you go to hell. If you do good deeds, like fixing a bird's broken wing, helping a tired man, giving water to a thirsty beast, digging a well anyone may drink from, or planting a tree anyone may eat from, these things will earn you Paradise. There is no influence-buying (wasta) there, there are no government ministries and there are no nationalities." He predicted that mankind will behave in increasingly evil ways until the day comes when all people are bad, and that will be the Day of Judgment. Mahmuud's uncle Saalih 'Awaad supposes there is a basic struggle inside every person. The heart is always true but the tongue sometimes lies. Only if the tongue always tells what the heart feels is a person truly blessed. Saalih believes the Quran is a guide to the right things in life. Saalih grew somber and reflective as he spoke of these things, at one point uttering, "With the bitter marches the sweet, and with the sweet the bitter." Later his nephew told me Saalih was probably thinking of the untimely death of his son, who drowned in 1979 in a pool in Wadi Tala'. The boy's soul lingered on earth in the ranks of the martyrs (shuhaada), including all war dead and all who died accidentally or prematurely.

The Jabaliya landscape is decorated with monuments to holy men and women. These have become local pilgrimage shrines which help create bonds between past and present, living and dead, old and young, local people and neighbors. The imposing centerpiece of the Shaykh 'Awaad necropolis is the tomb of its namesake, the hakiim 'Awaad Musa. It is a simple rectangle of native granite surmounted by a whitewashed plaster dome and topped with the figure of a crescent moon. The holy man's cenotaph inside is wrapped in green cloth. A photograph of the Dome of the Rock hangs on the wall and nearby someone has scrawled "God is Great." A well-used Quran occupies a special niche and another recess is a place to burn incense. There is a milk can containing objects removed from the pockets of people who were laid to rest outside: a lock, some keys, a fossil, beads, a stove knob that was a child's toy. The individual visitor handles these reverently and recalls associations with the departed.

Once a year the Tomb of Shaykh 'Awaad is the focal point of a pilgrimage festival (*ziyaara*) which reunites great numbers of Jabaliya and neighboring tribespeople. Fifty meters from the tomb is a stone festival hall (*mag'ad*) designed to accommodate festival participants. Divided into male and female sections, it is equipped with braziers, coffee pots, tea trays and cups, and amphoras for storing and cooling water. The late summer feast begins on the morning of a full moon and concludes the following morning. Hundreds of people fill the surrounding plain. At the slaughtering-place (*madhbah*) as many as six camels and one hundred sheep and goats are killed for the feast. Like the Nabi Saalih festival, this gathering allows people to reestablish or create friendships, settle debts and disputes, and recite the aphorisms and legends that assert their distinctiveness as Bedouin people of the south Sinai. Lesser visitations take place at Shaykh 'Awaad on the Feast of the Sacrifice (*'Iyd al-Adha*) and the breaking of the Ramadan fast (*'Iyd al-Fitr*).

The only other large pilgrimage-feast which continues today in Jabaliya territory is the September festival of Afraynja. Members of the Jabaliya, 'Awarma, Suwalha, and Muzayna tribes attend it. Prior to the modern tourist age there was an annual feast to honor Shaykh Ahamad, whose tomb lies in the Jabaliya cemetery below Nabi Haruun at the mouth of Wadi ad-Dayr. Some Jabaliya men told me Ahamad was "al-Jindi," the soldier who was the progenitor of the Awlaad Jindi clan. He begat sons named Ja'ays and 'Afaali. Ja'ays begat the lineages of the Abu Alwaan, Daguuni, Abu Ja'ays, and Abu Krayshaan, while 'Afaali founded the Abu Mas'uud lineage. Near Ahamad's tomb are smaller mausolea of other local saints including Shaykh Saalih and Shaykh an-Nahama. Interspersed between these are recent burials and the graves of "the forgotten ones" (*al-mansiyya*) of ancient times. Awlaad Jindi clanspeople have their own yearly visitation to tombs in Wadi Abu Tuwayta of fellow clansman Shaykh Jumay'a and of a mysterious historical figure known as Shaykh Santa. There is uncertainty over Shaykh Santa's identity. People concur that he was a

wali or saint, but disagree about whether he was the father or the son of St. Katherine. Unaware of the Christian tradition that St. Katherine was a virgin, most Jabaliya favor the latter version. No one knows exactly where he came from or when he lived.

Ahmad Mansuur selling medicinal herbs to tourists and pilgrims at the traffic gate of the Monastery of St. Katherine. October 11, 1989.

ECONOMIC CHANGES

It is important to learn as much as possible, Mahmuud Mansuur said, but also to realize with humility that it is impossible to unravel all of the world's mysteries. "Suppose the tree is your object of study. You understand the trunk, then the branches, the leaves and fruits. You open the fruit, and within it are seeds. Within the seeds are fibers, and within the fibers . . ." He paused. Now in his late thirties, Mahmuud is extremely curious about his natural environment and its puzzles. Mahmuud's brother Ahmad Mansuur has learned some of the old ways. As the sole *hakiim* of the Jabaliya today he prescribes local wild plants for a wide variety of ailments. "People trust him," said his brother Mahmuud, "because his medicine works." Recently his clients have come to include Egyptian tourists visiting the monastery, where he works as a gatekeeper and does a brisk business selling herbal remedies for a wide range of ailments. In 1988 he received national media coverage in Egypt in a televised documentary about his practice. Such expertise and interests are becoming more rare among the Jabaliya.

The knowledge of the Mansuur brothers is a fragmentary, unsystematic remnant of a vast system once held by men like their great uncle the hakiim Shaykh 'Awaad. The Bedouin way of knowing is changing and along with it the Bedouin way of life. Pastoralism, gardening, and a simple material culture are giving way to wage labor and a more sedentary existence. There are more people and they have more things. Their relations with the wider world are more complicated and problematic.

Between 1930 and 1980 the Jabaliya population tripled from four hundred to twelve hundred.[21] Nineteenth-century visitors had described the Jabaliya as a "hungry, naked, thirsty horde," but antibiotics and other modern medicines that became readily available to the Bedouins by the mid-twentieth century improved health and reduced death rates.[22] The Bedouins say that two generations ago many children died; one or two boys might survive in a family. Middle-aged and elderly Jabaliya today recall losing siblings to epidemics of influenza and other diseases. Such occurrences are rare today. Now, say the Bedouins, six, eight, even ten offspring survive childhood. Mahmuud Mansuur used his genealogy as an example. His grandfather had three children, but each of those produced eight. Natural increase among the Jabaliya since 1980 has been especially pronounced, raising the population about 25 percent to fifteen hundred.[23]

Along with growing numbers of mouths to feed, the Bedouins have had growing means to feed them. Prior to Israeli occupation of the Sinai in 1967 few Jabaliya or other Sinai Bedouins worked for wages. In the 1950s and early 1960s a small number worked in oil fields, gypsum and manganese mines, and in the quarantine station of at-Tur.[24] Many more Jabaliya and other Bedouins began working for wages after 1967 as traditional means of livelihood waned and new ones arose. Israeli surveillance of the peninsula made smuggling too risky. The Egyptian market for Jabaliya orchard crops and livestock products vanished, and with Israeli demand for these goods negligible the Bedouins scaled back on their gardening and pastoralism. Israeli enterprises offered jobs to the Bedouins which Egyptians from the Nile Valley had filled previously.[25] Jabaliya men began to work as drivers, mechanics, and manual laborers. A growing tourist industry created many new niches. Bedouins guided and provided camels to parties of backcountry hikers and daywalkers on Jebel Musa. They worked in the cafeterias, grocery stores, small hotels, campgrounds, and trailside cafes that grew to service the tourist industry. Some men left their homeland to work in the distant towns, tourist resorts, and mining communities of Sinai and Israel, often for years. They sent infusions of cash home, eventually returning as wealthier men.

By becoming wage laborers the Jabaliya were compelled to give up nomadic pastoralism almost completely. Previously, reliance upon a herd

of sixty sheep and goats for much of its income required the family to be
mobile, living in "wool home" tents or stone dwellings in the high mountains during the summer and at lower elevations wherever pasture was
available in winter. With cash wages coming in most Bedouins did not
need the income which livestock provided, and by scaling back their herds
they could live wherever they wanted to.[26] They began building permanent homes in the basin on the southwestern edge of the Plain of ar-Raaha
at the small market center of al-Milgaa. They situated their cinder block
and stone homes there over the small crypts where they had traditionally
stored summer fruits for later use and sale.[27] Some families initially tried to
keep their livestock. The animals quickly overgrazed the pasture around
al-Milgaa. Families then tried to purchase supplemental feed for the animals. They discovered, however, that by becoming more sedentary they
had become more vulnerable to the vagaries of a worldwide economy.
Until 1980 subsidized Israeli flour was so cheap that the family could afford
to feed it to as many as fourteen sheep and goats in backyard enclosures
attached to their homes.[28] When the Sinai returned to Egyptian control
Egypt's government continued to provide subsidized goods at low cost. As
the International Monetary Fund pressured Egypt to reduce its debts,
however, the government had to cut subsidies and raise prices. By the late
1980s a settled Jabaliya family could afford to feed only eight to ten goats.
In July 1989 the price of 100 kilograms of wheat jumped from seventeen
to thirty Egyptian pounds, and by August 1993 had reached fifty-four
pounds. The Jabaliya could not successfully incorporate pastoralism into
their more settled way of life.

The Jabaliya have adapted themselves to the new life. Some have relocated permanently outside their traditional homeland, especially to Suez,
where about 30 families live on al-Ma'aamil Street. Local settlements have
grown. The former market center of al-Milgaa has become the residential
community of Katriin. By 1980, 80 Jabaliya families had settled in Katriin,
and by 1989, 120 families.[29] In living space and amenities some Jabaliya
homes in Katriin and Abu Sayla rival middle class homes in Cairo or
Alexandria. They typically contain one or two bedrooms which are the
hariim or women's domain, a kitchen, an enclosed indoor public area
where male visitors are entertained, and an outdoor reception area. The
television is the centerpiece of the indoor sitting-room, and the electric
washing machine has found a place in the outdoor enclosure. Although
from a distance the village of Abu Sayla blends in with the surrounding
landscape, closer inspection reveals alien influences. Pickup trucks and
motorcycles are parked smartly by homes, and television antennae bristle
incongruously from roofs. The most popular shows are the same "soaps"
Egyptians favor in the Nile Valley. Such media and contact with visitors

from all corners of the world have introduced unlikely knowledge into the Jabaliya world. At a summer campfire in a remote mountain garden one man asked me whether it were true that camels came originally from America. Another told me he had heard of the bombing of Hiroshima. I told him one of the bomb's creators had predicted that the fourth world war would be fought with sticks and stones. He responded that the Jabaliya say that after the great nuclear war no one will live except "he who walks in the mountains and rides on the camel."

The Jabaliya may be giving up the wilderness option. By taking wage labor jobs and settling down the Bedouins are forsaking their unique system of high mountain agriculture. The few new gardens they are building are close to Katriin, where a plot may sell for two thousand Egyptian pounds. In the backcountry more gardens are up for sale than ever before, and at lower prices, around two hundred pounds. Many owners are neglecting completely or barely using their high mountain plots. Prior to 1967 as many as 100 families worked nearly 300 orchards. By the mid-1970s only 30 to 40 families continued to cultivate, and in only about 120 plots.[30] Through the 1980s only about 20 families continued to migrate from lowland settlements to mountain orchards.[31] Mahmuud Mansuur had this perspective on the changes:

> *Look, right now in Wadi Tinya and Wadi Abu Tuwayta are my uncle's household, his sister's household, and perhaps two others. But in the old days there were 30 to 40 households in Tinya and Abu Tuwayta in the summer. Now, though, people aren't interested in the mountains and gardens the way they used to be. Instead they have coffee shops and are mechanics. In the old days there were perhaps 100 households in the high mountains, even ten years ago. And now there are only about 20 to 25 altogether in the mountains in the summer. As for the gardens, the same gardens are present, but people worked them harder and better in the old days. You would see them all green. Now a lot are scraggly and "tired."*

Their permanently settled peers regard mountain gardeners as relics of a fast-retreating way of life. "In the past there was no 'center,'" one man recalled. "Every place was the same. Now there is the village and the country. In the past those who dwelled in the mountains were like those who dwelled in the village. Now there is a difference between them." Most of those who do take to the mountains are spending less time there, only about three months instead of six months as they did before. A more common pattern is for the entire family to remain at home in Katriin or Abu Sayla throughout the year, with the father both working for wages and briefly attending to the orchard during the summer. Saalim Farraj hikes up to his deceased father's neglected garden in Wadi Jibaal in mid-

June just to harvest apricots for sale in Katriin, where he works as a carpenter. He explains that the rising cost of living has made it more difficult to rely upon gardening, and woodsmithing is his mainstay. This trend toward less time spent gardening is evident in the types of crops the Bedouins grow. Vegetables, which require regular irrigation, are declining in relative importance to almonds and other orchard trees that may be neglected for long periods. The almond is best, seasonal gardeners explain, because birds do not eat it, but camels, sheep, and goats can eat its shells; it may be harvested over a period of several weeks, unlike the apricot, which if unpicked will rot; it requires little watering; and it can be stored for up to four years after the harvest.

The Jabaliya are giving up gardening because wage labor is more profitable, paying 120 to 150 Egyptian pounds per month for full-time jobs and 12 pounds per day for occasional work. Saalih 'Awaad estimated that in 1989 after working for six months in two orchards he earned 300 pounds by selling his harvest from thirty apricot and almond trees. If he were any younger than his sixty years he might have earned 720 to 900 pounds as a salaried wage laborer in the same period. The value of agricultural produce has not kept pace with general inflation. The Jabaliya family's expenditures rose five to ten times between the mid-1960s and 1977. Before 1967 an average orchard could provide enough income to sustain a family for at least six months. By the mid-1970s it would not support them for a month.[32] With continued inflation and growing family sizes, gardening is becoming even more unprofitable.

The culture of Jabaliya gardening persists only because with their families' support some old-timers and able-bodied young men make measured sacrifices to enjoy the delights of Sinai summers. Sexagenarian Saalih 'Awaad is well-paid for his service of grafting orchard trees for Gararsha, Sawalha, and Awlaad Sa'iid tribesmen in the Feiran Oasis, but insists, "I do not garden for money but because I love it." Of his tomatoes in Wadi Abu Tuwayta he said, "I grow them for my pleasure, not for money, just to see how they progress." He added happily that he grew them without chemicals. His nephew Mahmuud Mansuur is struggling to indulge in some of the traditional pleasures, recognizing that in order to garden at all he is giving up potential income. "I would live up here in Abu Dagash year around with my wife and son if I could," he lamented, "but the garden cannot support people as it used to. I must work with Abdul Fataah at the vegetable market in Katriin, for two, three days at a time, to get the money I need." His wife looks after two sheep in the backyard enclosure of the home he built in Katriin in 1983. "In the old days life came from the goats," he said. "Look, I have only two sheep and no goats. The camel I use does not belong to me but to my lineage." He feels caught between two worlds: "The Bedu do not like having a steady job . . . but there is good money working in town," he said. He is one of the few young Jabaliya men trying to bridge those worlds.

ENVIRONMENTAL CHANGES

With the increasing sedentarization of these Bedouins pressures on wilderness resources have ironically increased. Automobiles, firearms, and the need to provide sustenance to growing numbers of settled families have led to unprecedented uses of native flora and fauna. Outside a Jabaliya home I spotted a palm wheel-trap which a young woman had found deep in a granite cleft. She did not know what its purpose was. Even Jabaliya elders today cannot remember this technology for catching ibex. Young men sneered when I told them how their Ma'aza counterparts in the Eastern Desert hunted ibex with stones, snares, and dogs. "They must have guns but didn't show them to you," they retorted. Firearms made their way into Sinai Bedouin material culture during World War I, rendering such technologies—some of them as old as Neolithic times—obsolete instantly.[33] The effects on wildlife have been devastating. The most esteemed trophy, the five-handspan-horned male ibex (Arabic, *khamaasi*) is already extremely rare. Saalim Farraj, who visits a high mountain orchard each summer, estimates that only "about ten" ibex remain in the Jabaliya homeland. This figure is certainly lower than the true number but is representative of the Jabaliya perception of the animal's status. Noting that people now only infrequently see the animal, Mahmuud Mansuur predicted that the ibex will become extinct locally within a few years. He asked me if the Jabaliya might obtain new stock from Ma'aza Bedouins on the other side of the Gulf of Suez. Most Jabaliya admit that they are responsible for decimating ibex populations although some men, uncertain of how I would react to their illegal possession of firearms, had other explanations. Perhaps with tongue in cheek, one man blamed tourist hikers for scaring away the animals. Another attributed the dearth of ibex to a succession of cold winters which might have killed them off. Bird populations suffer from boys armed with air rifles (*nabaala*), which reportedly can be obtained in Cairo without a permit. A boy may be seen carrying as many as twenty slain Sinai rosefinches at the conclusion of a day's sport. With less success younger boys use slingshots they fashion from inner tubes and tree branches. The finches are edible and permissible by Islamic law, but the Bedouins rarely eat them, complaining they are too fatty. The Bedouins often shoot chukar and other larger game for food from stone blinds (*mihraas*) located at water sources.

There is a long history of deforestation in the Sinai, and in some areas

An armed Jabaliya
man with his
daughter in Wadi
al-Arba'iin.
August 27, 1993.

trees continue to disappear. Nineteenth-century sources suggest that this area was much richer in acacia woodland at locales like Shaykh 'Awaad until the Egyptian government in 1873 imposed a tax, payable exclusively in charcoal, on the local Bedouins. The resulting deforestation was dramatically evident by 1882.[34] The process of deforestation continues. Within living memory there were more large trees around Jebel Musa than exist today. Father Good Angel recalled that as recently as 1940 to heat monastery water he collected fuelwood from trees and shrubs located close to the monastery. No such sources of firewood exist within reasonable walking distance from the monastery today. The monks themselves have contributed to this problem, but growing sedentarization of the Bedouins is the main force behind deforestation. Their permanent and semipermanent settlements such as Katriin and Abu Sayla have created permanent fuelwood supply problems, particularly in the winter when demand rises sharply. The striking shortage of large trees near these settlements testifies to the Bedouins' inability to continue their traditional resolution not to harm trees. The Jabaliya deal with the shortage in part by importing truckloads of dead articulated anabasis and white broom wood from al-'Ilu, near at-Tarfa. In larger wadis such as Wadi Itlaah where it is impossible to truck in fuel, and where locals have long since used the available dead vegetation, gas stoves and camel dung fires are the commonest fuel sources. One incident underscored for me the severity of the fuelwood situation in the high mountains. In Wadi Tinya my hosts cooked our evening meal with the dung of a donkey, an animal the Jabaliya nominally despise as unclean. When I pointed out this anomaly they apologized that *this* donkey was clean, because it ate only plants, "not like a city donkey."

The Jabaliya grudgingly acknowledge the growing impact of their domestic livestock on the environment, and recognize the irony that although families own smaller herds the animals are doing more damage. They say shepherds have the responsibility of preventing herd animals from eating more than a small portion of a living plant, and should constantly move the animals on to prevent overgrazing. They admit that in practice this is often impossible. They point out that the areas around the permanent settlements of Katriin and Abu Sayla are severely overgrazed.[35] Jabaliya men even do some grazing for their animals, climbing mountainsides near Katriin to cut roquette (*silla, Zilla spinosa*) and germander (*ja-'ada, Teucrium leucocladum*) for their camels. The Bedouins regard the large population of feral donkeys in remote areas as particularly destructive of the high mountain floral communities.

Permanent grazing and the impacts associated with it are anathema to the traditional seasonal migration of the Jabaliya and their herds from low winter to high summer pastures. The Bedouins blame the problem not on the animals themselves but on changes in society and economy that accompanied increasing sedentarization of the Jabaliya after 1967. "The Bedouins have an ancient conservation system but they have forgotten it," Mahmuud Mansuur lamented. "They are not interested in protection like they were in the old days. The old people who were the keepers of the law have all died." Musa 'Awaad continued, "Back then every donkey had a family brand. If your donkey was caught violating the alliance, you were fined. Today there are [feral] donkeys everywhere unmarked. If they cause problems, as they do, destroying vegetation or gardens, people say, 'That's not my donkey.' " I asked why people do not shoot the donkeys if they are so destructive; Musa answered, "Because people would then say, 'You killed my donkey!' " The alliance system began to unravel after 1967 because Israel's occupation of the Sinai introduced a cash economy that increasingly replaced the traditional pastoral economy and imposed fewer constraints on uses of local environment. Tribal laws against resource abuse faded, apparently because tribespeople felt they were no longer needed. Largely forgotten, the rules now are largely unenforceable.

THE SETTLED PEOPLE

The Jabaliya worldview has changed markedly in the past few decades. Many Bedouins say that the gradual process of sedentarization is detrimental to their culture, especially to their prized senses of freedom, knowledge, and self-reliance. Traditionally the Bedouins looked after their own health with prescriptions requiring intimate knowledge of the local environment. Today a clinic in Katriin, staffed by an Egyptian physician and stocked with Western pharmaceuticals, caters to the medical needs of the Jabaliya. Memories of the hakiim who "knew the world in all its dimensions" are fading. The village of Katriin boasts primary and secondary schools which are attended by an estimated 70 percent of Jabaliya boys and 20 percent of the girls. These schools are staffed by teachers trained in the Nile Valley. Jabaliya parents perceive opportunities for their boys to gain employment or other advancement as a result of schooling. They are often disappointed. Many young men do not realize their post-educational ambitions, and in the process they have learned about the alien and irrelevant environment of the Nile Valley. Traditional knowledge is inevitably being lost in Jabaliya exposure to Egyptian textbook education. The Bedouins acknowledge, for example, that good trackers these days are few and elderly. The process of education which might have enabled the Bedouins to record their own traditional knowledge is instead robbing them of it.

"For the Egyptians have a horror of all shepherds" (Genesis 46:34). The settled people of the good "black land" of Egypt's Nile Valley throughout history have been ignorant and disdainful of those who roam the "red land" of the desert. Ancient Egyptians called the Bedouins "sand fleas."[36] Sedentarization and the education process, which help erase Bedouin ways, serve the interests of the Egyptian government today. It is official policy to promote settlement of Bedouins throughout Egypt's deserts, in part by building new villages that officials reason nomads cannot resist occupying. Once settled, the Bedouins can be counted, taxed, conscripted, and trusted.

Egypt's push to sedentarize the Jabaliya and other Sinai Bedouin has a strategic rationale. Before 1967 Egyptian authorities and institutions neglected Sinai's Bedouin communities, contributing to a political vacuum that Israel filled easily.[37] Israeli administrators waged a largely successful public relations campaign with the Bedouins by creating jobs for them, allowing them to enter Israel proper to work, not restricting their migrations, and not pressing them into military service.[38] Many Egyptians fear that Sinai's Bedouins may retain loyalty to Israel. A travel agent in Cairo who had visited Jebel Musa many times told me, "I don't like the Bedouins. I don't trust them." I asked why. "I don't know whether they are Egyptians or Israelis." He added, "The most important thing to them is money." The older generations of Jabaliya Bedouins, many of whom were educated in Hebrew schools and employed by Israelis during the occupation, are very sensitive about being perceived as Israeli sympathizers. Some are fluent in Hebrew but do not want Egyptians to know this. One of the Jabaliya employees at the monastery does an excellent Moshe Dayan imitation. He had seen the Israeli military commander at the monastery. He will not do his act for anyone he does not know well.

The Bedouins are uncomfortable when Egyptians question them about their perceptions of Israel. I witnessed this exchange between a government official and a Jabaliya man. The official began, "What frankly is your opinion of the Israeli occupation?" adding emphatically, "We are a long way from the Ministry of Interior" (meaning that no one from state security would hear the reply). The Bedouin responded with nervous diplomacy, "There was a lot of work under Israeli occupation. But work isn't everything. There was also a lot of uncertainty and apprehension. There is more freedom of movement and opinion under the Egyptians. The Israelis inspired fear and restricted movement. It was a military system, not civilian, affecting all aspects of our lives. We were treated like animals."

Compulsory military service is one means by which the government hopes to Egyptianize Sinai Bedouins. Zaayid Saani' did the mandatory three-year term including six months in at-Tur and two-and-a-half years in Cairo. He summed up his feeling about army service: "I hated it." The Bedouins are now subject to Egyptian law and legal procedure affecting even their guarded concepts of women and land. Policemen once took some Jabaliya wives to the Katriin police station and held them there as a means of making their husbands confess to an alleged crime. The incident shamed the women.[39] Bedouin claims to the land also must now answer to state interests. No matter how long he has owned it, the orchard owner must purchase his land from the state at a cost of three pounds per square meter. He must pay a fee of fifty Egyptian pounds to register his property title with the Katriin City Council and must register new construction of any kind. In theory these laws apply to even the most remote properties, but in fact apply only to holdings near roads. The Bedouins say roadside plots are the only ones Egyptians are aware of. "So who would build near a road?" a Jabaliya man scoffed. The Bedouins insist their sedentary habits prevent Egyptians from venturing into the mountains. "Do Egyptians come up here?" I asked. "No," said one man, "they eat fuul beans and sleep." I told him Ma'aza Bedouins had remarked to me that Egyptians are like goats, always living together in large groups. "At least you can eat goats," he replied.

The cultural gulf separating these groups is enormous. Bedouins mock the discomfort which Egyptians experience in the outdoors. Saalih 'Awaad laughed heartily as he imitated the motions of an obese Egyptian sitting at an office desk and struggling to raise a tea glass to his lips. "That is not living!" Saalih said of that lifestyle. At a backcountry campfire a group of Jabaliya men exchanged jokes about Egyptians and condemned their habits. "It takes them forever to do anything," one man said. They recalled that only two parties of Egyptian hikers had ever visited the backcountry. One of these stayed out only two days and the hikers were very afraid, one man related. He said the other party visited al-Galt al-Azraq and disfigured the site with trash, leaving fuul bean cans on the ground and writing their names with charcoal on nearby rocks. The place had been pristine before their visit, he claimed. These men complained that Egyptians prohibit "everything nice; if it's good, it's forbidden (*mamnuu'a*)." "For example," one said, "it is forbidden for us to speak with foreigners. Even in Katriin there are problems. They ask us, 'Why are you meeting with foreigners?' "

Through most Egyptian lenses the Bedouins appear to be savage, ignorant, and indolent. Bedouin knowledge is inaccurate superstition. "Don't ask the Bedouins about plants and animals," an Egyptian veterinarian in Katriin advised me, "They don't know anything. Talk to Mr. Nuur, the man in charge of environmental affairs at the Sinai governorate office in at-Tur." The Egyptian proprietor of the restaurant in the Katriin shopping center which is the only rival to a nearby Bedouin cafe boasted to me, "This is not like the Bedouin restaurant. I am trained in a restaurant school." I spoke with Husni, the affable director of the central telephone office in Katriin. He had been stationed in Katriin since the office was established in 1981, living apart from his wife and child in the Nile Valley. His family had visited only once. "The climate here is too harsh for them," he insisted. I thought there might be other reasons they had not moved here. I asked whether there weren't schools here for his children. "Yes," he said, "primary and secondary, but only Bedouins attend them." Some of his telephone employees were Bedouins, he said. "They are clever people," I said. "Yes," he replied, "but they are lazy."

From an outsider's perspective it may appear that the Bedouins know more and have a better way of life than they did a generation ago. Many and perhaps most of the Jabaliya do not share this view. As Mahmuud Mansuur and I rested on an overlook of the Nagub al-Haawa Pass, he spoke of the changes wrought on his people:

My grandfather Saalih once counted seventy ibex standing together at Jebel Abu Tarbuush. In those days there were leopards and plenty of game. And there was enough wheat for everyone. People would grow a wheat called kirmaniyya, *which they first found in pottery jugs in the ruins of Wadi Feiran. People found it, planted it, and discovered that it was more productive and grew better here than any other wheat variety. People would make bread from it, adding a little salt and wild marjoram and by itself it was a substantial meal. You didn't need other food. Wheat today is nothing in comparison. Long ago people were mostly self-sufficient in growing crops and raising animals, especially because of this wheat. Now they are not. They were more free before because they did not have or need all of the things they have now: sandals, sugar, tea, and clothing. Instead they made these of local materials. There may have been more rainfall, or at least the wheat that could be grown with the water available went further because there were fewer people. Now we are fifteen hundred people. Life has become harder.*

Eight

♦

THE
PILGRIM

In about 400 A.D. the abbot of a monastery in Spain wrote of a nun named Etheria who "with a bold heart undertook a journey across the world." The climax of her three-year pilgrimage to the Holy Land was a visit to Mount Sinai.[1] From the time people first identified Jebel Musa as Mount Sinai it has been a magnet. Pilgrims, travelers, and tourists have come. Pilgrims have sought spiritual reward and redemption. Travelers and scholars have wanted to satisfy aesthetic and intellectual curiosity about this remote, wild place. Tourists have added it to their lists of "must" places to visit. Outwardly the differences between these types of visitors are not always clear. Some pilgrims have been scoundrels and some tourists have experienced miraculous conversions. Nevertheless as guardians of Mount Sinai the monks of St. Katherine have decisive opinions about visitors. First, they agree they have too many: fifty thousand each year are overwhelming their ability to fulfill their principal spiritual duties. They also perceive fundamental differences between pilgrims and tourists. "Vast numbers of people come here today," Father Makarios said. "They do not come for religious reasons. They are tourists and visitors as distinct from pilgrims." I asked whether there had not been other times when large numbers of visitors descended upon this tiny institution. In the old days of medieval pilgrimage there were groups of forty, fifty, sixty, I said. "Or hundreds," he responded:

There was an ordination in the sixth century in the monastery and six hundred people were there—in the sixth century A.D.! But these people were pilgrims, they were not tourists, you see; this is something else. And the tradition of hospitality that the monastery still tries to maintain as much as possible under very difficult circumstances these days has to do not with tourists but with pilgrims, that is, members of the Christian community who were Orthodox, who were coming to the monastery for pilgrimage purposes. And it was not for a day or two, it was for months. These people stayed around for a long time. Pilgrimages generally lasted months or years sometimes. You would leave your hometown and spend a year or two on a pilgrimage going to all the shrines in Europe and the Middle East.

Whether labeled as pilgrim, traveler, or tourist, the visitor has responded to the same appeal: visit Mount Sinai and you will leave the place somehow changed.

''A LONG LIFE'S DREAM''

Those who have traveled to Mount Sinai as pilgrims have walked, sailed, driven, and flown there under different flags and faiths, and for different reasons. The majority have been Christians, particularly of the Orthodox faith. No Jewish tradition of pilgrimage to Jebel Musa has ever existed.[2] Pre-Islamic Semitic peoples other than Jews probably traveled as pilgrims to sacred sites that later acquired Biblical associations. On rocks around Jebel Musa and Jebel Serbal there are numerous Aramaic inscriptions reading "so-and-so came to this place." Their writers may have been subjects of the Nabataean Kingdom based in Petra who came to these places after landing in ships on Sinai's west coast, roughly at the time of Christ.[3]

There have also been Muslim pilgrims to Jebel Musa, but it is difficult to discern from historical records whether significant numbers of Muslims other than local Bedouins ever visited holy places around the mountain. The Arab chroniclers Ibn Zobeir and al-Idrisi (c. 1153 A.D.) mention the monastery and mountain only in general terms.[4] Late in the fifteenth century Felix Fabri wrote, "Indeed, Arabs, Egyptians, Saracens, and Turks make pilgrimages hither from distant parts of the world out of reverence for Moses. With the exception of Jews, men of all religions and sects flock together to this place from all parts of the world."[5] Muslim pilgrims to Jebel Musa "must have been quite numerous right down to the fifteenth century," Heinz Skrobucha proposed without examples.[6] John Lewis Burckhardt reported that "foreign Moslem pilgrims often repair to the spot" and that early in the nineteenth century Egypt's Mameluke strongman Muhammad Ali had intended to make the pilgrimage with his son to the mosque on Jebel Musa's summit, but failed to do so.[7] However, just twenty-two years after Burckhardt's visit Edward Robinson reported that "only now and then a Mussulman" makes the pilgrimage.[8] In the early 1920s Augusta Dobson related that "there are always also a certain number of Mohammedans who visit Jebel Musa," but she did not indicate whether these were local Bedouins or others.[9] Modern monks recall visits by former Saudi Minister of Petroleum Shaykh Ahmad Zaki Yamani and Sultan Qaboos of Oman, but insist that other Muslim pilgrimage is negligible. One monk said that most Egyptian Muslims who do come are "too lazy" to climb Mount Sinai, but many want to visit the Chapel of the Burning Bush. Gordon Brubacher, a leader of Biblical tour groups, told me that he had seen hundreds of Shi'ite pilgrims "from all over the world, judging by their dress," camped on Jebel Musa on the last night of Ramadan of several years of the 1980s. Jebel Musa was the third most sacred pilgrimage destination for Shi'ite pilgrims after Mecca and Karbala, he said. I have not been able to verify his claims. Burckhardt, and a half-century later Edward Palmer, reported that Muslim pilgrims of unidentified origins left inscriptions and graffiti on rocks around Jebel Musa.[10]

Christians have always been the majority of pilgrims to Mount Sinai. They came even before the monastery was built. After Rome adopted Christianity in the fourth century, devout European and western Asian pilgrims began to travel to the Holy Land, especially to visit Jerusalem and the Coptic monasteries of Egypt's Eastern and Western deserts. Like the Spanish pilgrim Etheria some continued on to Mount Sinai. In about 500 A.D. the monk Anastasius saw six hundred Armenian pilgrims at the Bush. He related that thirty years earlier as many as eight hundred had climbed Mount Sinai, where they saw a vision of God and the miracle of the summit enveloped in flame.[11] Many of the early pilgrims to Jebel Musa from whom written records survive were themselves monks from other Near Eastern deserts. Ammonius traveled from his monastery near Alexandria in about 372 A.D. Moschus (c. 550–620 A.D.) walked from his Judaean monastery to Mount Sinai, Egypt, Syria, and Rome.[12] In about 530 A.D., on the eve of the monastery's construction, the monk Antoninus Martyr ("the Piacenza Pilgrim") traveled for eight days from Gaza to reach Mount Sinai, where he stayed for a few days. Some of his pilgrim companions continued on to Egypt and he returned to Jerusalem.[13]

Like most pilgrims through the centuries which followed, Etheria visited Mount Sinai as an adjunct to her principal pilgrimage destination of Jerusalem, 380 kilometers away. Pilgrims were most anxious to see the places where Christ was born, lived, and most especially died, and was buried, and was resurrected—although these lay 3,500 kilometers from Madrid, 3,250 kilometers from Paris, and 2,800 kilometers from Moscow. The places of Exodus were of lesser importance, yet pilgrims confronted

Доп. Москов:Е. Духовн. Цеин 14 Сент 1872 г.

Лит. А.Орлова въ Москвѣ.

ИЗОБРАЖЕНІЕ СВ. ГОРЫ СИНАЙСКОЙ И МОНАСТЫРЯ СВ. ВЕЛИКОМУЧЕНИЦЫ ЕКАТЕРИНЫ

Russian pilgrims at the Monastery of St. Katherine. Mountains from left to right are Jebel ad-Dayr, Jebel Musa, and Jebel Katarina. By L. Orlov, 1872. Courtesy of the Monastery of St. Katherine.

great difficulty to reach them. Political upheavals deterred pilgrims only temporarily. After Islam swept through the Levant and Egypt in the mid-seventh century, Rome became their chief destination until they perceived it was safe to travel east again. Early in the eleventh century, before Turkish warriors began encroaching on the eastern Byzantine empire, increasingly large numbers of ordinary people traveled, sometimes in "mass-pilgrim-ages," from Europe to the Holy Land. One of the largest pilgrimages oc-curred in 1033 on the thousandth anniversary of Christ's death.[14] The great era of pilgrimage to Jerusalem and Sinai was the twelfth through four-teenth centuries, prior to the Reformation and discovery of new sea routes to the east, when people typically traveled in groups of thirty to forty.[15] The Plague interrupted pilgrimage for a while after 1348. After rebound-ing, pilgrimage tapered off again in the early 1400s as the Ottomans ad-vanced upon Byzantium, then increased again between 1460 and 1497.[16]

After Martin Luther posted his ninety-five theses on the Wittenberg church door in 1517 the great age of the Western European pilgrimage came to an end. The discovery of new sea routes to India and the Far East and the accompanying decline of seaborne commerce eroded ready means for pilgrims to get to their destinations, even if the goal remained in their hearts.[17] Christian inhabitants of the Near East continued to visit Mount Sinai. One left an Arabic inscription in marble on the east wall of the monastery: "Nicola Wahba Moise Suleiman Wahba Ibrahim Gorgos, who came from Jerusalem to visit this holy place in 1675."[18] By the late eigh-teenth century most pilgrims came from Egypt, including a single party of five hundred Copts, and from Armenia, including a band of eight hundred believers. By the time Burckhardt visited the monastery in 1816, only sixty to eighty pilgrims came there each year, most of them residents of nearby at-Tur.[19] After 1820 pilgrimage picked up again with a flow from the realm of Orthodoxy's "Third Rome."[20] Russian pilgrimage was still consider-able in 1909, when Hoskins observed, "The accommodations of the mon-astery are sorely taxed by the bands of Russian pilgrims, sometimes 100 in number, which come from Suez once or twice a year."[21] Some English, Dutch, and other Western Europeans came, but Russian pilgrims were the most prevalent and apparently the most pious:

With many of them this pilgrimage is the realisation of a long life's dream, and to accomplish it they undergo unheard-of toils and privations. Aided by small contributions from a public fund, they set off, frequently from the remotest parts of Russia, and proceed on foot to Odessa, stopping for rest and food at the various convents which line the road. Thence long weary journeys by ship, rail and camels bring them to Sinai; and after being trotted up and down the mountain, and taken

round to all the sacred spots, they are sent back to Alexandria, to be again
shipped to Jaffa, en route *for Jerusalem.*[22]

Russian pilgrimage traffic dried up after World War I and the Revolution.[23]

Pilgrims still come. Most are Greek-Egyptians who trickle in throughout the year but flood the monastery during feast days and school holidays. On such occasions a group of 150 or more garrulous, enthusiastic Greeks from Cairo nestle in the monastery's hostel for three days. Hostel-keeper Father George complained to me about his guests: "It is easy to handle 150 Germans. They're disciplined. But just 10 or 15 Greeks can really wear you out." Late that night his words came back to me as the pilgrims below my room broke bottles and played Michael Jackson at maximum volume on a "boombox." Other pilgrims try the monks' patience. Women who linger are particularly suspect. Monks commented sarcastically on the Canadian who stayed for a week and "called herself an icon painter," and the "odd little Chinese woman" who came to all the church services. The Jabaliya also recall some unusual pilgrims. One Bedouin told me of members of a Christian sect who burn money on Jebel Musa's summit. He supposed that friends at home give money to Sinai-bound pilgrims to burn there as a symbol of disavowal of material things.

German pilgrims
singing hymns at
sunrise on the
summit of Jebel
Musa, with the peak
of Jebel Katarina
behind.
October 12, 1989.

                                                    •

                                                    The

                                                    Pilgrim

Pilgrimage historically was an arduous undertaking. Aware of the time, expense, difficulty, and danger involved, what kind of person would make a pilgrimage, and for what reason? Most pilgrims were men, but it is difficult otherwise to depict a "typical" pilgrim. Some were complex personalities with varied motivations for pilgrimage:

> *A knight or merchant or priest; almost all are on pilgrimage; but the knight may combine with this a military reconnaissance of an enemy country, or a new Renaissance interest in travel for its own sake; the merchant may be a passing visitor who eyes with interest the commodities of a strange land or one who, having been resident there for years, is as friendly with its Moslem as with its Christian inhabitants; the priest may be a Venetian patrician by birth, a sea-captain turned Friar, a man who had first known Alexandria when he and other gay sparks from the ships had gone about with sticks at the ready, to beat the devil out of an aggressive Moslem.*[24]

Some pilgrims wanted simply to expand their spiritual horizons beyond those achievable through ordinary ritual. Others sought to escape the parish priest's monopoly on their spiritual lives. For some penitent pilgrims monasticism was the model: just as monks had rejected the earthly city for their "new and special land," the pilgrim could forsake at least temporarily the pleasures of sedentary life for the uncertainty and discomfort of spiritual journeying. Many monasteries in Syria, Palestine, and Egypt— including the Monastery of St. Katherine—became destinations for pilgrims who emulated monks.[25]

One of the strongest motivations of pilgrimage was the passion to experience firsthand the places where holy people had walked and miraculous events had occurred. "One may only truly understand the Holy Scriptures after looking upon Judaea with one's own eyes," wrote St. Jerome.[26] In their written accounts most Sinai pilgrims described the pleasure of being able to read aloud the passages of Exodus at the exact spots where Biblical events occurred. They reveled in the geographical realities that confirmed their faith. This conjunction of belief and place elicited powerful emotions in believers. Augusta Dobson watched pilgrims on Mount Sinai:

> *The Russian pilgrim has the simplicity of a child. He believes not only what he cannot prove, but also what has been proved to be absolutely untrue; if he is told that some spot was ever visited by a saint, he will with a tearful reverence fall on his knees and kiss everything that could have known a holy contact, and travellers*

who have seen them at Sinai toiling up the steep ascent to Jebel Musa singing
Psalm XXIV, or prostrate in adoration in the Church of the Transfiguration,
have been deeply impressed with the sight.[27]

Still today a group of French, German, or English pilgrims may be seen on
the summit reading from Exodus and in the nearby Basin of Elijah from 1
Kings, exactly where Etheria's party had performed the same rite sixteen
hundred years earlier: "There, too, we made the oblation, with very ear-
nest prayer, and also read the passage from the book of Kings, for it was
our special custom that, when we had arrived at those places which I had
desired to visit, the appropriate passage from the book should always be
read."[28]

Some people became pilgrims to better acquaint themselves with the
origins of saints whose relics they venerated in Europe, especially after the
eighth century.[29] By medieval times the relics of St. Katherine were ac-
complishing miracles in Europe, and as the fame of this martyr spread, so
did the desire to visit her final resting place and honor her other remains.[30]
Veneration of St. Katherine became the chief attraction for pilgrimage to
Sinai.[31] Dressed as a Georgian monk, in 1216 Magister Thietmar set out
from Jerusalem to "carry out his fervent wish to visit the body of the
blessed St. Katherine which exuded the sacred oil."[32] However dubious
their value in some theological circles, relics were highly prized in others.
There were three reasons why people should revere relics, Thomas Aqui-
nas said: "to create a personal relationship with the saints by establishing
contact with their physical reminders; to venerate the spirits of the saints,
which are now in heaven but which once inhabited earthly bodies; and to
acknowledge that God wishes them to be venerated because he works
miracles through them."[33] Jonathan Sumption supposed that heresy and
the challenge of Islam created a mood of gloomy pessimism in medieval
Christianity. In this uncertain spiritual atmosphere people venerated relics
of the saints who might intercede on their behalf, curing them miraculously in soul or body.[34]

Some people undertook pilgrimage as voluntary penance or mandatory
sentence for sins and crimes such as adultery, incest, bestiality, murder,
arson, and sacrilege. In the sixth century pilgrimage as a form of public
penance began to be imposed, especially in Ireland. Minor or venial sins
could be redeemed automatically by pilgrimage to specified shrines; this
practice was especially common after the tenth century. The more heinous
or scandalous the offense, the farther afield was the penitent pilgrim sentenced to travel. Rome, Cyprus, and by the twelfth century Jerusalem represented the worst deeds.[35] A Norman Knight of the Eagle named Fro-

mont, reportedly with the aid of his brother, killed his uncle in about the year 855. The bishops of King Lothar had the brothers chained together and sentenced to a penitential pilgrimage to Rome, Jerusalem, and India. They traveled by sea to the Levant and visited Jerusalem and Upper Egypt before spending three years in Sinai. Still chained together they returned to Rennes, where one of the brothers died. Some version of this legend apparently became the monks' explanation of the "king's two sons from India," whose still-chained skeletons they showed to visitors earlier this century. The monks say they ended their lives as hermits in adjoining cells. Their chains were designed so that as one of them lay down the other was pulled upright; by this means one was able to pray while the other slept.[36] In 1738 monks showed their cells near Jebel Musa's Chapel of St. John the Baptist to Bishop Pococke.[37]

The Crusades introduced a pattern of movement which resembled earlier pilgrimages of piety but was fundamentally different. Pope Urban II proclaimed his holy war in 1095 at the Council of Clermont in France, promising there was salvation in a sinful world for those who journeyed to the Holy Land to fight infidelity. Over the next two hundred years knights and lords who received the consent of their territorial sovereign, and commoners who were granted spiritual permission, undertook the crusade as a new kind of pilgrimage.[38] Many performed the crusade-pilgrimage as an indulgence. In the Latin church truly penitent persons who confessed and were absolved of sin could obtain "indulgences" from their confessors which would shorten their sentences in purgatory.[39] A "donation" could secure an indulgence. So could a pilgrimage or a pilgrimage combined with military service in the crusade.[40] A papal bull granted a one-year indulgence to pilgrims who visited the Monastery of St. Katherine, for example.[41] There was an alternative: rather than assume the expense and life-threatening risks of a real pilgrimage or pilgrimage-crusade, the would-be voyager could purchase an indulgence for a price equal to the projected cost of the pilgrimage.[42]

Those who did travel as crusaders to fight Islam in the Holy Land portrayed themselves as pilgrims.[43] Most, however, were of a different cloth than those who had come before them on more strictly personal and spiritual quests. From France and England came pilgrims who were really spies to reconnoiter the strengths and weaknesses of the Muslim kingdoms.[44] Some undertook pilgrimage for material aggrandizement and enhanced social status. After crusaders took Jerusalem on July 15, 1099, nobles aspired for military successes that would have them knighted in the Church of the Holy Sepulchre and enrolled in its Order.[45] This would qualify them for the additional honor of admission into the Order of St. Katherine.[46]

Parties of eager Frankish knights toiled across the Sinai to reach the monastery and obtain this distinction.[47] Association with these enemies of Islam made the monks uneasy. The Crusader King Baldwin of Jerusalem wanted to make the pilgrimage to Mount Sinai in 1116, but the monks dissuaded him, arguing that his trip would arouse Muslim hostility and endanger the monastery.[48]

Yet another style of pilgrimage developed in the wake of the Crusades. In 1187 the brilliant Muslim leader Salah ad-Din Yusif Ibn Ayyub took Jerusalem. He granted its people clemency and allowed freedom of movement to Christian pilgrims throughout his domain.[49] European knowledge of the East grew. Jerusalem changed hands again in 1229 during the Fourth Crusade, and veterans continued to return home with accounts that stirred Europeans' imaginations. Jerusalem fell finally to the Turks in 1244 and the Crusades came to an end. In the ensuing peace Sultan Malik an-Naasir (1293–1341) established good relations with Europe and protected pilgrims in the Holy Land. Europeans' fascination with the sacred and exotic East now manifested itself in a kind of early package tour industry, the "Long Pilgrimage" which brought pilgrims to Jerusalem and Mount Sinai.[50] Compelled by curiosity about new places, many were unabashedly travelers first and pilgrims second. They used special guidebooks such as *The Way from Venice to the Holy Sepulchre and Mount Sinai*, kept travel diaries, bought gaudy souvenirs, and carved their names and insignia in the places they visited, including the refectory of the Monastery of St. Katherine.[51]

There were pilgrims who traveled for the "wrong" reasons and pilgrims who did not travel at all. Mass flagellation became one substitute for pilgrimage. Even fantasy pilgrimage was popular in the fifteenth century; a handbook instructed the armchair pilgrim how to undertake all stages of pilgrimage without ever leaving home.[52] Tourists who travel today for the "four S's" of surf, sand, sun, and sex had early counterparts in some pilgrims.[53] A relaxation of moral restrictions has been a feature of pilgrimage throughout the ages and across cultures.[54] Pilgrimage for some was "a license to sin."[55] Bawdy pilgrimage was commonplace when it became possible for would-be pilgrims to dispatch deputies in their place. Often of doubtful character, these agents obtained spiritual mileage for their sponsors but also behaved in a manner that might have sullied their reputations.[56] I asked one of St. Katherine's monks if there were traditionally a festive atmosphere associated with pilgrimage. "The Arabs have an axiom," he replied, "which says, 'Beware of anyone going to Jerusalem.' There is another axiom associated with Western Europe that says, 'Go a pilgrim, come back a whore.' And don't forget the *Canterbury Tales!*"

Before the Swiss-born Dominican brother Felix Fabri set out from Ulm
for Jerusalem and Mount Sinai in 1480, veteran pilgrim Prince Count
Eberhard of Württemberg counseled him: "There are three acts in a man's
life which no one ought either to advise another to do or not to do. The
first is to contract matrimony, the second is to go to wars, the third is to
visit the Holy Sepulchre. I say that these three acts are good in themselves,
but they may easily turn out ill; and when this is so, he who gave the advice
comes to be blamed as if he were the cause of its turning out ill."[57] Sacrifice would be demanded at every turn of the journey. The trip would be
long: in the fourteenth century, ten months for the Tuscans who visited
both Mount Sinai and Jerusalem. The financial cost was taxing. The trip
to Jerusalem called for "good intentions, stout heart, ready tongue, and fat
purse."[58] French noblemen financed their pilgrimages by taxing their vas-
sals.[59] The commoner could expect to pay at least one year's income for
the Jerusalem pilgrimage. In 1450 that was about 175 ducats, with 50 allot-
ted for a round-trip sea voyage between Venice and Jaffa or Alexandria, 50
for medical needs, and 75 for general expenses including entrance fees, poll
taxes, and departure taxes.[60] An escorted round-trip extension between
Cairo or Jerusalem and Mount Sinai, covering meals and transportation by
camel, cost an additional 25 ducats.[61] To raise funds some pilgrims sold land
to monasteries. Some became beggars. Others found wealthy patrons who
expected spiritual returns by financing a pilgrimage. Alms and hospitality
defrayed some of the poorest pilgrims' expenses. Others were able to re-
coup some of their expenses after the pilgrimage by selling spices and cloth
they had obtained in the East.[62]

In the eleventh century most European pilgrims preferred the least expensive means of travel, the route overland through the Balkans and Asia
Minor to the Holy Land.[63] There were laws against molesting the pilgrims,
but with their quaint deportment and forgiving demeanor they were inviting targets for bandits. They were unmistakable figures. In the eleventh
century they wore a pilgrim's uniform of a coarse tunic often emblazoned
with a red cross and, following the tradition of fourth-century Egyptian
monks, a staff and a leather waist-pouch containing food and other necessities.[64] In the thirteenth century the pilgrim's fashion was to wear a large,
broad-brimmed hat with a turned-up front and a scarf trailing from the
back and wound around the body until it reached the waist. It was considered most virtuous but also most foolhardy to travel alone. Large numbers
of pilgrims traveled together for their safety. Unfortunately, some who
signed on as "companions" were professional robbers who would gain the

trust of and then plunder their unsuspecting wayfellows. Deteriorating security in Europe made the sea voyage almost mandatory for the twelfth-
century pilgrim. Venetian shipowners offered all-inclusive package tours
from Venice, Genoa, and Marseilles.[65] It was good business. By sailing
their galleys in the autumn they could transport pilgrims in a cooler time
of the year and return with holds filled by spices and other exotic goods
arriving in Alexandria and Jaffa from points farther east.[66] Shipowner and
pilgrim signed a detailed contract. The traveler paid half the fare at the
point of departure and half upon arriving in Jaffa or Alexandria. The terms
stipulated that if the pilgrim decided in Jerusalem to continue on to Mount
Sinai rather than return home on the ship, the shipowner had to refund
ten ducats, or about half the return fare. Safe, comfortable, and expensive
passage was guaranteed on the larger oared galleys. Owners of smaller ships
did not promise their poorer clients a comfortable cruise. For six weeks or
more people were crammed into close quarters with stale food, rats, bore-
dom, sickness, and the threat of piracy.[67]

There were special attractions and problems in Egypt for those who
began their Mount Sinai pilgrimage in Alexandria rather than Jaffa. Arriving from Venice in a merchant galley on October 20, 1392, after forty-
eight days at sea, a party of English and German knights and squires toured
Alexandria for ten days. They sailed on to Cairo for a five-day visit and
toured the Balsam Garden of al-Matariya in the northeastern Delta before
setting out for Mount Sinai and Jerusalem.[68] Eight years earlier a party of
six Tuscans traced a similar path, arriving in Alexandria on September 4
after a twenty-three day voyage. In Cairo they noted that monks of
St. Katherine fed and housed poorer pilgrims in a hostel, perhaps at the
site of the monastery's property on today's Midan adh-Dhaahir. Only after
reaching Cairo did they make arrangements for the journey to Sinai, paying ninety-six gold ducats to hire a party of five cameleers, fourteen camels, and three riding donkeys. These rather wealthy travelers also hired an
Italian-speaking Egyptian escort. For less affluent pilgrims who could not
communicate with their guides the trip must have had a strong element of
culture shock. The Tuscans' provisions included two bushels of biscuits,
vinegar, sugar, and cheese. Some of the biscuits were extras "to give them
to the caloyers of Mount Sinai and to the Arabs, that they should not treat
us roughly, because we were advised by those who had done the journey."
They also carried a special firman they obtained from the sultan's office in
Cairo which would inform Sinai Bedouins of their peaceful intentions.[69]
On October 19 they left Cairo, visited al-Matariya briefly, and on the 22nd
set out for Mount Sinai.[70]

Many pilgrims who arrived in the Holy Land at the port of Jaffa visited
Jerusalem and continued on to Jebel Musa. In 1452 Felix Fabri had become

a friar "out of love for St. Katherine, His spouse," so his pilgrimage to
Mount Sinai thirty-one years later was especially meaningful.[71] For two
weeks in Jerusalem he had been in the company of about two hundred
pilgrims of several nationalities. Late in the summer all but twenty boarded
Venetian galleys in Jaffa to return home. Those who remained to make the
pilgrimage to Mount Sinai included strangers and neighbors, friends and
kinsmen, noblemen and knights, cooks and servants, laymen and clergymen, German, Hungarian, and Pole. Their guide was a Muslim, apparently a Palestinian, who had already escorted pilgrims to the monastery at
least forty-eight times. On August 24 the party traveled south from Jerusalem, pausing to visit holy sites in Bethlehem. In Gaza they chose the
donkeys which would be their mounts all the way to the monastery. They
obtained provisions: sacks of bread and biscuits, jars of wine, waterskins,
cheese, butter, oil, rice, almonds, medicines, eggs, live chickens, lanterns,
boots, tableware, and baskets. Now doubled in size to forty, Fabri's party
left Gaza on September 9 in a caravan of 25 camels, 30 donkeys, and "7
camel-men, 6 donkey-men, two head guides, Arabs, the Lesser *Calinus*
[guide], Elphahallo, and a young Ethiopian." The cameleers were Jordan-
ian Muslims, and the donkey handlers were Christians from the Caspian
region.[72]

It was a twelve-day ride on camel or donkey from Gaza to Mount Sinai.
From Cairo it was ten days by camel—and in summer 1336, for an extraordinary pilgrim named Wilhelm de Baldensel, by horse.[73] Even in the
best circumstances this was not an easy journey. As late as 1739 Richard
Pococke declared it "is to be look'd on as the most difficult of all the
eastern voyages."[74] Fortunately security was not a problem. St. Katherine's
monks and Sinai Bedouins had cooperated to secure the safety of pilgrim
routes through the peninsula. In 1063 knights banded together in a semi-
religious order to guarantee safe passage of pilgrims to Mount Sinai.[75] By
the late fifteenth century pilgrim parties like Fabri's were routinely well-
armed. Such measures helped ensure that Bedouins would not become a
threat to pilgrims. While most pilgrims disliked the Sinai Bedouins—Fabri
called them "most miserable and beast-like men" and "those hateful
dogs"—a rare few admired their loyalty, honesty, and hospitality.[76] In their
journey south along the Gulf of Suez shore in 1384 the Tuscan party encountered a caravan carrying Indian spices and later "running down the
dunes at us . . . were people almost nude and without arms, save some
carrying javelins." The Tuscans shared their biscuits with these Arabs, who
"departed without doing anything novel." Caravans were sometimes
plundered, but usually by their own guides and cameleers rather than by
local Bedouins.[77]

Nature was the greatest adversary. Water was sometimes foul. In the north Sinai desert Brother Fabri and companions drank water which was "disgusting to us, because it took the colour, a blood-red, of the skins, and caught the salt taste of the leather. But all the same, we often got so thirsty we would put our mouths to the empty skins, and think it delicious to suck the tainted water from the stinking leather."[78] The party's meat putrified. Longing for fresh food they were deceived by colocynth gourds, which resemble watermelons. Their escorts laughed as the foolish foreigners bit into the fruits which the Arabs know as the epitomy of bitterness; Fabri's mouth kept the taste for hours.[79] The Tuscan party suffered from heat and aridity in late October: "You must all day stay in the rays of the sun, which appears to have the spasms; and if you drink water which is in the goat skins, it is more than tepid, and there is not a body so constipated that it would not move."[80] "The country is very hot," one of the men wrote. "When the wind blows, it carries the said sand from one place to another and who there finds himself is in danger of death."[81] A ferocious sandstorm in 1497 claimed the lives of fifty men and six hundred camels from a single caravan.[82] Sickness took its toll. The Tuscans met nine survivors of a party of twenty French pilgrims to the monastery; the rest had died of dysentery and other diseases.[83] In 1483 an epidemic in Gaza prevented many of Fabri's peers from making the pilgrimage to Mount Sinai.[84] Large groups of pilgrims enforced a draconian rule that if a man sickened he must be left to die.[85]

There were bright moments, too. As the men entered central Sinai, Felix Fabri's chief guide pointed out a feature which enchanted the pilgrim: "He now turned towards the southern quarter of the wilderness, and showed me an exceeding bright star which had but just risen, which he said was St. Catharine's star; 'and lo,' said he, 'beneath this star is the Mount Sinai, toward which we are journeying, and when we have to travel by night, we shall go no other way than straight towards that star until we come quite underneath it upon Mount Sinai.' " Fabri grew attached to the holy star. "After we left Mount Sinai, I often used to look back at this star, and I saw it while I was in Egypt, and at Alexandria, and for a long way as we sailed over the sea; but at last, after we passed Cyprus and came upon the Cyclades Islands, I could no longer see it."[86] Initially repelled by the desert, describing it as "a region itself of immense desolation, in which certainly no man lived nor could live," the Dominican friar grew sensible of its charms:

Among all the other things which enliven a pilgrimage through the wilderness, the chief is that every day, almost every hour, one comes into new countries of a fresh soil and climate, and among mountains of fresh shape and colour, which things cause a man to admire what is present, and look eagerly forward to seeing what is to come. Something new is always happening to fill a man with admiration, either of the strange aspect of the mountains, the colour of the earth and rocks, the numberless kinds of pebbles, or the exceeding rugged, barren, and waste nature of the country, all of which things delight the inquiring mind. I confess that, for my own part, I felt more pleasure in the barren wilderness than I ever did in the rich and fertile land of Egypt, with all its attractive beauty.[87]

For most pilgrims the journey was one of hardship, privation, and danger with few delights. It was supposed to be that way: the most physically difficult means of reaching sacred places brought the greatest spiritual rewards to the truly pious pilgrim. Walking was the most rewarding means of all.[88] Buddhist, Jain, Hindu, and Bonpo pilgrims still toil across the Himalaya to reach sacred Mount Kailas.[89] Lama Anagarika Govinda described their ordeal of crossing the roof of the world as a kind of chastening preparation for the ultimate experience of the mountain itself, a "grinding down" of the pilgrim's ego followed by the "joyful tension" of reaching a sacred mountain with "the indescribable beauty of a gigantic domed temple of perfect symmetry and breathtaking splendour."[90] Sinai pilgrims had these sensations. When they first caught sight of Mount Sinai the pilgrims in Felix Fabri's party went down on their knees just as they had when they first saw Jerusalem.[91] In the final approach to the holy place the pilgrim felt rapture and enchantment but also anxiety. Would the experience be all the pilgrim had hoped for? How would the monks of St. Katherine, the guardians of this holy place, receive strangers from a faraway land?

IN SACRED SPACE

On October 28, 1384, the pilgrims Frescobaldi, Gucci, Sigoli, and their companions reached the "plateau of the Holy Mounts . . ."

where we arrived very weary, and outside the place we unloaded our baggage. And immediately the servants of the house helped to put it inside and assigned us a good and beautiful room. We were led to the archbishop of the place and the monks and made the procession to all the altars of the church. Then each one was given half a glass of wine and bread, and salty fish in plenty of that of the Red Sea, and they gave us as guide Friar John of Candia, and a companion monk of the said place, to bring us to the mount and on other visits. . . . They do great honour to the pilgrims in the way of reception and food, and help to keep the animals and in every material service . . . They honour the guests with all they have; and first, they see them with pleasure and smiles.[92]

As the two-hundred-strong band of monks greeted the Tuscans, the archbishop stepped forward to offer his visitors a vial of "white manna" which he said had issued from the ears of St. Katherine. This gesture awed the humble pilgrims.[93]

Nearly four hundred years later the monks still welcomed pilgrims with food, shelter, and special blessings. With the great Christian ritual of humility and hospitality they washed their guests' feet. Bishop Richard Pococke enjoyed this reception in 1739:

> *When pilgrims arrive at the convent, a caloyer or lay-brother is appointed to attend*
> *on them, to prepare their provisions in a place apart, which is served in their*
> *chamber. They are shewn all the chapels and offices of the convent, the library,*
> *where there are a few manuscripts . . . The pilgrims commonly attend the service of*
> *the church twice a day, and on some certain days they dine in the refectory with the*
> *monks; and soon after they arrive, being conducted from the church to the refectory,*
> *they perform the ceremony of washing the feet, as they do at Jerusalem. If the*
> *pilgrim is in orders, a priest performs the ceremony; I had that honour*
> *done me by the superior.*[94]

Throughout most of its history the Monastery of St. Katherine has been famous as a welcoming refuge for the weary and hopeful pilgrim. Accommodations have been predictably spartan but adequate. In the sixth century a monk named Isaurus built a hostel for pilgrims within the newfound monastery's walls. There monks provided the visitor with a cell and some reading materials and, in exchange for menial chores around the place, a seat at the daily meal.[95] Late in the sixth century Pope Gregory the Great sent resources to improve the facility: woollen coverings and bedding for 15 beds and money for purchasing feather beds.[96] Facilities had to keep pace with growing numbers of pilgrims, and the monastery in effect became a caravansary. Visitors in excess of the hospice capacity camped outside the monastery wall.[97] In the 1940s the southern wall of the monastery was enlarged to incorporate the library and an expanded hostel of 150 beds. Greatly increased visitation after 1967 required the construction of new facilities. In 1978 Jabaliya Bedouins built a two-story, 200-bed hostel 100 meters west of the monastery.[98] It, too, is rudimentary.

Some visitors have observed cynically that it is in the monks' best interest financially to be gracious hosts to pilgrims. In the heyday of pilgrimage prior to the fifteenth century, visitors noted ungrudgingly their own important contributions to the monastery's welfare. Admiring the monks' asceticism, one of the Tuscans wrote, "They live on alms which are given them; because the pilgrims who come here do them great favours and make them great gifts of their own money, and of money given them to carry there from persons who have great devotion for the place, chiefly great lords, barons and knights and rich men of Germany, Flanders, England, France and Gascogne and from very many places, who go there." [99] A century later Friar Fabri had a different view of the monks: "Whatever they do for us, they do for money." [100] As he viewed the remains of St. Katherine, Fabri noticed that each of the lords and knights of his party left two to four ducats in her reliquary, and poorer visitors left up to a ducat. Fabri related that the monks also charged the pilgrim for every additional service possible: to enter the church, to hire a staff as an aid in climbing the mountain, to fill a waterskin from the monastery's well. Parochial differences certainly colored Fabri's view of the monks. The Dominican friar was angry that these practitioners of the Greek rite would not allow Latin priests to celebrate mass in their church, or permit Latin pilgrims to be buried in their graveyard. He was too indignant to report a kindness noted by one of his companions, that the monks presented the party with a lamb and a kid when they left the monastery. [101] Years later when one of St. Katherine's monks called on his German parishioners for donations, Fabri instructed them to give him nothing, and ordered the monk to leave Ulm immediately. [102] On his 1844 visit Tischendorf observed, "The monastery has an indisputable liking for the gratitude of pilgrims entertained therein." He wrote that he was advised to pay the monks 100 piastres per day for his accommodation, while the fare for the ten-day return trip to Cairo was only 120 piastres. "Upon this I took counsel with myself," the German scholar wrote. "Besides, the monastery is considered to be, and is really, very rich; for, in addition to the benefices it enjoys at a distance, and the costly presents of pilgrims, especially of the Greek Christians, it has other sources of revenue, in productive gardens, olive plantations, and date groves, in Feiran, in Tor, and elsewhere, which it confides to the charge of its serfs." [103] Such grumblings are rare in pilgrims' accounts. Most pious visitors stayed happily at the monastery for a week, enjoying the monks' hospitality and visiting the holy places associated with St. Katherine and Mount Sinai.

Climbing the God-Trodden Mountain was the punishing and rewarding climax of pilgrimage to Mount Sinai. This final effort was a microcosm of the greater struggle the Christian had undertaken by pilgrimage. In a final physical sacrifice the pilgrim would escape the bounds of the ordinary world and come closer to God. Such approaches to high holy places occur in many faiths: to Tibet's Mount Kailas for Buddhists, Jains, Hindus, and Bonpos; to Sri Lanka's Adam's Peak for Buddhists, Hindus, and Muslims; to China's T'ai Shan for Buddhists; and to Ireland's Croagh Patrick for Catholics. [104] Across cultures a theme of final obstacles to overcome repeats itself. At Mecca's Ka'aba men armed with sticks once stood between the fervent pilgrim and the black stone at the center of the Islamic world; a few light symbolic blows made the final sensation of touching or kissing the stone a more intense spiritual experience. On Mount Sinai for some years old St. Stephen stood in the way at his Shrive Gate on the Stairway of Repentance, challenging climbers with the question of Psalm 24: "Who shall ascend into the hill of the Lord? Or who shall stand in his holy place?" The pilgrim who answered correctly could continue the ascent: "He that hath clean hands, and a pure heart; who hath not lifted up his soul unto vanity, nor sworn deceitfully. He shall receive the blessing from the Lord, and righteousness from the God of his salvation." [105] Monks continued to challenge pilgrims at the gates through at least the 1880s, even offering communion there.[106] During the 1650s, when monks apparently were absent, entrepreneurial Bedouins manned the gates to demand a toll from all walkers returning to the monastery.[107] By 1697 monks attended the gates again. At the first a monk administered the holy wafer to the pilgrims, and at the second absolved the pilgrims and presented them with a certificate of pilgrimage. In the 1700s a Byzantine bureaucracy accompanied the procedure. Pilgrims who confessed at the monastery received a certificate which they displayed at the first gate. A monk exchanged that document for another which the pilgrim surrendered to a second monk at the next gate.[108] Until very recently monks continued to act as guides on the sacred landscape and thereby controlled visitors' behavior on the mountain. As late as 1943 it was customary for a monk to accompany the traveler or pilgrim all the way to the summit, explaining points of interest and holy associations along the route. Monks and guests often spent the night in the small dormitory of the summit church, where there is a kitchen and sitting room.[109]

Even without St. Stephen's examination the physical challenge of climbing the Holy Mountain represented a serious final obstacle to the pilgrim's goal. The 3,750 steps of Mount Sinai's Stairway of Repentance punished many. A fifteenth-century pilgrim found his shins "so heavy that they seemed like beams of wood, and several times I said to myself,—'Turn back! You see! You can't keep up with the other pilgrims!' "[110] Guided by two monks the Tuscan pilgrims climbed to the summit to "gain the indulgence."[111] They reckoned there were "fourteen thousand very steep steps, which were made by Moses and his friends" for the ascent, which "is very steep and difficult to climb." They passed through the arches of St. Stephen, visited the chapels of the Basin of Elijah, and finally reached the summit where, "from whatever side you look, you appear to be in the air, and you see much farther by reason of the height and from the fact that the air is much clearer in these parts than with us."[112]

Reaching the peak, the pilgrim was exhausted and ecstatic. "We ar-

rived, at the fourth hour, at the summit of Sinai, the holy mountain of
God, where the law was given, that is, at the place where the Glory of the
Lord descended on the day when the mountain smoked," Etheria recalled.[113] Throughout many centuries the monks of St. Katherine practiced modest rites which embellished the pilgrims' climax experience. Etheria described the scene late in the fourth century:

> *When, therefore, at God's bidding, we had arrived at the summit, and had*
> *reached the door of the church, lo, the priest who was appointed to the church came*
> *from his cell and met us, a hale old man, a monk from early life, and an ascetic, as*
> *they say here, in short one worthy to be in that place; the other priests also met us,*
> *together with all the monks who dwelt on the mountain, that is, such as were not*
> *hindered by age or infirmity. When the whole passage from the book of Moses had*
> *been read in that place, and when the oblation had been duly made, at which we*
> *communicated, and as we were coming out the church, the priests of the place gave*
> *us eulogiae, that is, of fruits which grow on the mountain.*[114]

On Jebel Musa's summit each member of Felix Fabri's party squeezed part-
way into the little cave their monk-guide explained was Moses' "cleft in
the rock." In the adjoining church they read relevant passages from their
processionals, the little prayer books compiled for pilgrimage. They were
moved with "enormous joy and devotion."[115] Pilgrims still sing and pray
with joy here. Physical contact with the holy places of the Exodus, along
with the exhilaration of having finished the difficult climb and the stunning view of the roof of Sinai, combine to overwhelm the pilgrim's senses.
What Lama Govinda wrote of the pilgrim's perceptions of sacred Mount
Kailas fits the pilgrim's experience on Mount Sinai, too: "It certainly is
one of the most inspiring views of this earth, a view, indeed, which makes
the beholder wonder whether it is of this world or a dreamlike vision of
the next. An immense peace lies over this divine landscape and fills the
heart of the pilgrim, making him immune to all personal concerns, because, as in a dream, he feels one with his vision. He has gained the equa-
nimity of one who knows nothing can happen to him other than what
belongs to him already from eternity."[116]

After visiting the summit of Mount Sinai the pilgrim traditionally descended south into Wadi al-Arba'iin. The Tuscans found the descent "very
disagreeable and rough and dangerous so that in many places one has to
go on all fours."[117] They met eight monks at the Church of St. Mary of
Mercy, set in Wadi al-Arba'iin amidst what one pilgrim called "the thick-
est olive trees I have ever seen."[118] This monastery served then as in subsequent centuries as a convenient overnighting place between the ascents
of Mount Sinai and Mount Katherine. Those who chose a three-day

rather than two-day excursion also slept there after descending from Mount Katherine.[119] For the Tuscans the climb of Jebel Katarina was "from seven to eight miles of the steepest in the world." On the summit they detected "a scent of the best in the world, and for the great height there is great wind and one cannot stay long." During a brief rest there they saw ships in the distant Red Sea which they presumed were carrying spices from India. After they arrived safely back at the Church of St. Mary, monks there honored them "as they do to each one who ascends the said mount."[120] In 1739 Bishop Pococke traced the same route: "We after begun to ascend the mountain of St. Catharine, which was a fatigue that lasted four hours. From the top I had a fine view all around, and descended to the convent of the martyrs, where we reposed that night, after a day of great labour."[121] Fabri's party descended euphorically: "When we had done all that there was to be done on the holy mount, we kissed the holy place, and went down with exceeding great joy, not walking, but running and tumbling down, because we were now beginning our return home."[122] On the final day out from the monastery the pilgrim usually visited the sites associated with the Israelite camp and golden calf on the Plain of ar-Raaha and at the mouth of Wadi ad-Dayr. Some, like Bishop Pococke, visited the refuge of St. John Klimakos in Wadi Itlaah.[123]

The pilgrim's experience was not complete until he or she venerated the relics of St. Katherine. Before Magister Thietmar set out for his journey home to Germany in 1216, monks gave him some of the precious oil from the reliquary of St. Katherine. Monks continued to dispense the oil to pilgrims in the 1330s, but less generously and only in small vials.[124] Here there was great temptation to carry away a memento. Devout thieves depleted her limited remains and even parts of their container. In 1483 the abbot himself watched Fabri and his companions carefully as they viewed the saint's relics. He failed to notice that one member of the party had broken off a piece of the reliquary as a souvenir, but successfully held up the departure of the pilgrims' caravan until the guilty pilgrim, without having to identify himself, returned the object.[125] By this time the flow of oil from her relics had ceased. In 1489 the flow resumed at a snail's pace of three drops per week, then ceased again and has never recurred. Many Christians blamed Muslim desecration of the shrine for the final cessation of the holy oil.[126] Thereafter monks gave the pilgrim a piece of cotton, wool, or silk taken out of the reliquary of St. Katherine and steeped in lamp oil. Today the monks display the saint's relics when very honored pilgrims and guests call, and at the climax of the all-night service in her honor on the Feast of St. Katherine on November 25. The monks say that in a never-ending miracle her remains still exude a sweet fragrance.

Pilgrimage throughout the world has a transformative effect on the pilgrim. Francis Younghusband wrote of meeting Hindu pilgrims returning from Mount Kailas: "They have attained to such a degree of sanctity that holiness positively radiates from them." [127] Lama Anagarika Govinda wrote of the Kailas veteran: "No evil powers can have any more influence; the vision he has seen, nobody can ever take from him. He is suddenly filled with such perfect confidence and inner security that he feels as if he were surrounded by a magic armour which no outer force can break or destroy." [128] Moses' venture on the Mountain of God transformed the man: "When Moses came down from Mount Sinai with the two tablets of the Testimony in his hands, as he was coming down the mountain, Moses did not know that the skin of his face was radiant because he had been talking to him. And when Aaron and all the Israelites saw Moses, the skin on his face was so radiant that they were afraid to go near him" (Exodus 34: 29,30). The basilica of the Monastery of St. Katherine commemorates a similar transfiguration of Christ on the holy mountain of Tabor, flanked by the great prophets of Mount Sinai: "Jesus took with him Peter and James and his brother John and led them up a high mountain by themselves. There in their presence he was transfigured: his face shone like the sun and his clothes became as dazzling as light" (Matthew 17:1–2).

In the footsteps of God and His prophets, pilgrims have sought to transform themselves on the mountain. Some have come with specific goals. In 592 a Roman patrician woman named Rusticiana traveled from Constantinople with her ill daughter and her son-in-law to Sinai, in hope of curing the young woman. [129] More often the pilgrim has experienced the unexpected. Pilgrims' accounts through the centuries repeat the odd, apparently miraculous sensation of not feeling pain from the grueling climb of Mount Sinai. In the fourth century Etheria marveled, "These mountains are ascended with infinite toil, for you cannot go up gently by a spiral track, as we say snail-shell wise, but you climb straight up the whole way, as if up a wall. Thus the toil was great, for I had to go up on foot, the ascent being impossible in the saddle, and yet I did not feel the toil, on the side of the ascent, I say, I did not feel the toil, because I realized that the desire which I had was being fulfilled at God's blessing." [130] The Tuscan pilgrim Gucci wrote, "[W]e came beside Mount Sinai, that is, at the foot of this mount. And all these visits were made on Sunday, the 30 day of October, and though the said visits are long and the way very hard to ascend and descend, and though we were very weak from the discomfort of the desert, and some of us felt ill, nevertheless all, as said, by the grace of God did these visits. And it is said that by a miracle nobody has ever come to this place of St. Katherine, no matter how low or weak, to whom God has not promised that the said visits would be made." [131] During seven months in the area I recorded several accounts of people feeling better, or not feeling as bad as they thought they should have, after climbing the mountain. One visitor remarked that she had not become sore after climbing the mountain, although her muscles had ached after just a short walk in Cornwall the previous week. I spoke to another woman who sprained her ankle climbing Jebel Musa, but came away the next morning from the vigil of the Feast of St. Katherine without pain. I wrote in my own journal, "Somehow, these two mountains [Musa and ad-Dayr] have an energizing effect on me in a way other mountains do not."

On the mountain many devout visitors have recorded a sense of euphoria, manifested as a perception of "belonging" in place, or of being near a place where time or creation began, or where the past and present meet. Augusta Dobson related:

> *Any pilgrim who at length visits a place he has long desired to see, and who, in that place, meditates long on the events which are in his own soul connected therewith, comes, at last, to the point where he feels as if he belonged to that spot in a special manner, and as if that part of the globe were an intrinsic part of him. He even comes to instinctive conclusions, the reasons for which he cannot give fully to the world, but which are often perfectly right; and these things happened to some of us during our stay in Sinai, as we roamed the mountain-sides and heard great sounds, and saw great sights, which only those who go to Sinai can ever hear and see.* [132]

Pilgrims in sacred space describe sensations of serendipity and unexpected insight. Rudolf Otto supposed such sensations are universal reactions to the "wholly other" landscape of the sacred: "The truly 'mysterious' object is beyond our apprehension and comprehension, not only because our knowledge has certain irremovable limits, but because in it we come upon something inherently 'wholly other,' whose kind and character are incommensurable with our own, and before which we therefore recoil in a wonder that strikes us chill and numb." [133] The sacred place is a portal where the pilgrim peers into the other kingdom, according to Michael Sallnow "a spot on the spiritually animated landscape where divine power has suddenly burst forth":

> *Forces that are usually submerged have here broken the surface, in an epiphany that has become fixed in the perceptual territory of human beings. And not just in*

space: the shrine marks an irruption into history, the entry of the divine into the temporal as well as the spatial order of reality. By approaching it, pilgrims seek to tap its still active power, to draw this into their lives and thereby to induce existential change.[134]

239

•

The

Pilgrim

Pilgrimage centers generate a "field," according to anthropologist Victor Turner. "It is as though such shrines exerted a magnetic effect on the whole communications system, charging with sacredness many of its geographical features."[135] Pilgrimage centers like Mount Sinai are unique landscapes on earth, transformed physically by the shrines that mark holy places and perceptually by the beliefs and emotions of the pilgrims who visit them.

Many pilgrims have wanted to carry a piece of the holy place away, perhaps hoping its power was not confined to a particular locale. Since the sixth century European pilgrims returned home with soil from the Holy Land.[136] At Mount Sinai they pruned and even stripped the burning bush. De Laborde reported that monks allowed pilgrims to take away little twigs of the cypress tree growing in the Basin of Elijah.[137] Near the summit the Tuscan pilgrim Gucci and his companions picked up pieces of the dendritic pyrolusite they believe God's blinding manifestation on the mountain had created: "And on that mount are found the stones, which bear the impression of a palm, which is a miracle to see in very great stones with the palm sculptured inside: and we took of these little stones with the palm."[138] On the summit of nearby Mount Katherine the men chipped away at a rock near where they believed the body of the namesake saint had lain for five hundred years: "We went there armed with chisels with which we broke off some of those stones, which they say is a good cure for fever. And there is none who for his life would dare take from that place wherein is the form of the holy body." They noted that in Jerusalem the guardians of Mount Zion had strict orders not to allow pilgrims to take souvenirs in this fashion.[139] Before they entered Jerusalem in 1483, a priest preached to the pilgrims in Felix Fabri's party the twenty-seven articles of appropriate behavior in the holy city. Article five specified excommunication as the penalty for chipping off fragments from the Holy Sepulchre.[140]

Rather than feel a compulsion to carry away physical reminders of sacred place, some pilgrims have experienced at the pilgrimage site a revelation that would make such souvenirs meaningless: the sacred is everywhere.[141] Louis Golding explained, "I found I had got to the top of Gebel Musa, a grand mountain commanding grand views, but not to the top of Mount Sinai. For the Holy Mountain is a spiritual, not a physical experience. Few men have ever reached the summit, and few will get there

again. Perhaps it is only when the Mountain is veiled round with impene-
trable cloud, that the Mountain begins to be visible at all." [142] Such a revelation must be a humbling insight for the pilgrim who has been obsessed
for a lifetime with the thought of visiting the holy place. Beginning the
journey in a familiar place, the pilgrim has gone to a far place and returned,
changed forever, to a familiar place. [143]

Nine

◆

THE
TRAVELER

Long after the great age of pilgrimage concluded, the tide of visitors to Sinai began anew. An age of travel began late in the eighteenth century. Explorers, scholars, and artists led the way, depicting landscapes of romance and adventure. Western Europeans grew entranced by their descriptions and images of the "gorgeous East."[1] Many were not satisfied just to read about the Orient. The spirit of the age of the nineteenth century was a spirit of revolution and change, of all things being possible, of a heightened sense of personal energy, of experimentation, of creativity, of mobility.[2] The Industrial Revolution offered growing leisure time and affluence for a few to take to the road, and efficient means to transport them to their destinations. They traveled.

The distinction between travelers and the pilgrims who preceded them is not complete. Many travelers and researchers perceived themselves or were viewed by others as pilgrims, wayfarers to the Holy Land who would return home with new spiritual or aesthetic insights. "From one end of the nineteenth century to the other the Orient was a place of pilgrimage," wrote Edward Said, "and every major work belonging to a genuine if not always to an academic Orientalism took its form, style and intention from the idea of pilgrimage there."[3] While metaphorically there were similarities between medieval pilgrimage and nineteenth-century travel, the motivations were quite different. Pilgrimage for most was necessity, penance, exile, suffering in unpleasant lands; travel for most was choice, leisure, participation, and acceptable discomfort in enchanting places.[4] The latter description fits some styles of tourism today; again the distinction between travel and tourism is not complete. There is a difference in scale: tourism is a mass phenomenon while nineteenth- and early twentieth-century travel involved movements of small numbers of people.[5] Others' perceptions of the visitor and the visitor's notion of self also distinguish traveler from tourist today. "Tourism is a pejorative term the world over," E. Eliot observed. "Tourists are sought for their money and despised for their ignorance. It is not a noble role. Travel implies for me something deeper: a sincere attempt to know and understand an alien world, a wish to learn its history and culture and language, to become in some small way a part of it."[6] Even visitors on package tours to the Middle East today hope to assume some of the traveler's dignity through personal encounter with romantic and historic places like Mount Sinai.

SCHOLARS, SPIES, AND SCOUNDRELS

Mass tourism to Mount Sinai was more than 150 years away when Napoleon Bonaparte's 150 savants conducted their extraordinary survey of Egypt from 1798 to 1801. The publication of their twenty-four-volume *Description de l'Egypte* opened the way for the European "rediscovery" of the Middle East.[7] In the following years while the great powers of the day carved up the Middle East, European merchants, missionaries, explorers, scholars, and spies investigated every corner of the region. Whatever their ultimate objective, all had the confidence of can-do scientific rationalism that the eighteenth-century Enlightenment bestowed on them. They enjoyed relative security of movement because of the growing control their governments exerted over the region. At home in Europe a fast-growing reading public anticipated their publications eagerly. The educated middle class wanted to be informed of progress and discovery on all fronts. They wanted voyagers into strange lands to write in a style interesting and clear, witty and with a light touch.[8] Explorers and scholars did write engagingly of their freedoms and insights in these exotic lands, creating an extraordinary genre of Orientalist literature and setting paths for travelers and tourists.

European interest in Egypt, Sinai, and the Holy Land was intensified by the scholarly trends of "higher criticism" and "historical criticism" of the Bible which began in Germany and spread throughout Europe in the eighteenth and nineteenth centuries. These were rationalistic approaches to religion, based on the assumption that the Bible should be treated like any historical document and analyzed for authorship and authenticity.[9] Scholarly compulsion to prove and retrace the events of Exodus emerged in this intellectual climate. Theologians and Biblical scholars became explorers, for their bona fides were not established until they had walked in the pathways of the patriarchs and helped verify the foundations of the faith. In 1636 the Lutheran scholar Georg Neitzschitz came to the Sinai to find the "inscriptions of the children of Israel." [10] Bishop Richard Pococke tracked the route of the Israelites in 1738, accepting as truth the Biblical sites which monks and Bedouins pointed out to him. In 1743 the publication of his report, *Description of the East and Some Other Countries*, aroused deep interest in Britain about determining with certainty the geography of the Exodus. Bishop Clayton established a fund to assist in a five-year exploration of Mount Sinai.[11] In 1883–1884 Professor Edward Gordon Hull, Director of the Geological Survey of Ireland, undertook a geological and surveying expedition under the auspices of the Palestine Exploration Society.[12] One of the principal aims of this survey was to prove Mount Sinai's location. American Biblical historians also took up the quest. Edward Robinson, professor of Biblical literature at Union Theological Seminary in New York, traveled with colleague Reverend Eli Smith on the Israelites' path in 1838 and 1852.[13] Germans came, too. Prussian King Friedrich Wilhelm IV fielded a team to copy and publish the hieroglyphic inscriptions at Serabit al-Khadim, a site which subsequently became one of the Mount Sinai contenders. With the publication of his *Discoveries in Egypt, Ethiopia and the Peninsula of Sinai in the Years 1842–1845*, Karl Richard Lepsius, a member of that expedition, became a prominent voice in the debate over the places of Exodus.[14]

Some scholars came to Sinai to increase geographical knowledge, with only marginal concern for Biblical associations. Carsten Niebuhr commanded a Danish expedition which included engineers, a mathematician, and surveyor. The men spent a year in Egypt beginning in September 1761, studying many aspects of Sinai including its botany and archaeological inscriptions.[15] Other eighteenth- and nineteenth-century students of the Sinaitic inscriptions included Egmont von der Nyenburg (1721), Edward Montague (1761), L. de Laval (1855), and Heinrich Brugsch (1883).[16] The extraordinary Swiss explorer John Lewis (or Johann Ludwig) Burckhardt traveled in Sinai disguised as a Bedouin in 1816 and 1822, documenting all aspects of land and life. German naturalist Wilhelm Peter Edward Simon Rüppell observed and collected Sinai wildlife in 1817, 1822, 1826, and 1831.[17] William Henry Bartlett studied the region's geology on a short visit in 1845.[18] Classical scholar and naturalist John Hogg published his 1849 field data in an account of the geography and geology of Mount Sinai.

Botanists found fertile ground in the high Sinai. Under Russian orders, botanist and Arabist Ulrich Jaspar Seetzen visited the monastery and collected plants in the nearby mountains in 1807. He described the route across Sinai to the monastery as dangerous. An even more hazardous path took his life in Syria.[19] One of the most accomplished botanists of the Sinai was American missionary and professor George Edward Post, who collected in 1884 with fellow-countryman Henry Field.[20] Two years later the Swiss naturalist Alfred Kaiser began several years of field work on Sinai's flora, fauna, paleontology, and geology. He lost his first wife and a newborn son to a cholera epidemic there in 1893. The great Swedish botanist Vivi Täckholm, who studied his botanical collection, called it "the finest collection ever made on Sinai."[21] Even the most rigorous naturalists pursued the Israelites through Sinai. Christian Ehrenberg identified manna as a product of shield-louse infestations of tamarisk trees, and other botanists described the ecology of the burning bush.[22]

There were darker unstated motives for travel and research in Sinai. The peninsula's global crossroads location made it a focus of strategic, commercial, and ideological interests. Already by the mid-fifteenth century the Franciscans hoped to establish the monastery as a stepping stone for missionary work in India.[23] Merchants from Milan stopped at the monastery en route to the coral and pearl fisheries of the Persian Gulf. Portuguese and German explorers in search of Prester John, the spices of Malabar, and information on Madagascar and the Mountains of the Moon came to the monastery.[24] Egyptian botanist K. H. Batanouny questions the intentions of many early "travelers" and "scholars." Citing the archaeological expedition of T. E. Lawrence ("of Arabia") and Sir Leonard Woolley to Sinai in 1914, he asserts that "spying was an ulterior motive for trekking into Sinai."[25] British commercial and strategic interests were behind the general ordnance survey of Sinai undertaken between 1868 and 1870 under the leadership of General C. W. Wilson. The team members included the Reverend Frederick Whitmore Holland, who had already studied the peninsula's geography and geology in 1861 and 1865, engineer Henry Palmer, and the Arabic scholar Professor Edward Palmer, whose growing interest in Bedouin affairs on this expedition would lead eventually to his death.[26] Edward Said labeled Edward Palmer one of many "Orientalists–*cum*–imperial agents" whose scholarship was a thin disguise of colonial ambitions. In August 1882 the British government, knowing of Palmer's contacts with Sinai tribes, enlisted him to raise ten thousand Bedouin troops to oppose the rebellion of military officer Arabi Bey against British intervention in Egypt. Unidentified Bedouins sympathetic to Arabi ambushed and killed Palmer and his companions in Wadi Sudr.[27] In Said's view the entire genre of nineteenth- and early twentieth-century travel and description of the region is suspect: "Orientalism, which is the system of European or Western knowledge about the Orient, thus becomes synonymous with European domination of the Orient."[28]

The damaging legacy of Western leisure, exploration, and scientific re-

search has been long-lived, according to some Egyptian observers. Batanouny attributes the dearth of early Egyptian research in the Sinai on British
colonial administrators like Alfred Parker and Claude Jarvis. These gover-
nors tried to isolate Sinai from Egypt and make it difficult for Egyptians to
obtain the necessary permissions to visit the peninsula.[29] Batanouny also
blames the bureaucratic inefficiency of the Desert Institute of Egypt for
hampering scientific progress in the Sinai until 1967. Then came the Israeli
occupation when, Batanouny relates, only poor science was done: "In the
last three decades, hundreds of books have been written about Sinai. Almost all offer no scientific contribution, instead are about politics and contain insinuating remarks. Some however have well produced photographs."[30] Suspicion toward foreign researchers in Sinai and Egypt's other
deserts persists today. Egyptian security agencies rarely grant desert research permits to non-Egyptians. Authorities are not required to explain
why they deny permissions, but the unstated reason is phrased well in a
magazine article published in another country where foreigners are suspect; it was entitled "Research is the Name. Espionage the Game."[31]

Many imposters have traveled in the Sinai and some have done irrepa-
rable damage to the cultural heritage of Egypt and the Monastery of
St. Katherine. Burckhardt posed as a Syrian merchant, drawing derision
and abuse from his Arab traveling companions but gaining unprecedented
insights into their society. Incredibly, he was able to steal away from their
company long enough each day to keep exhaustive field notes. A favorite
scholar's ruse was to pose as pilgrim. French nobleman Léon Emmanuel
Simon Joseph de Laborde assumed this status to draw the antiquities and
natural history of the Holy Land in 1828. He wrote:

> Even at the present day the best introduction for any person travelling in the
> East is to announce himself as a pilgrim. During the whole of our journey from
> Constantinople to Egypt, to the questions which were repeatedly addressed
> to us as to the object of our travels by the pachas and Musselims, in presence of
> their assembled courts, our answer was always the same, that we were on a
> pilgrimage to the tomb of our Lord. It would be difficult to describe the
> respect with which this answer was universally received, and the extent to which it
> facilitated all our arrangements.[32]

German theologian—and according to some, master thief—
Constantin von Tischendorf described himself as "a pilgrim." He first visited the monastery in 1844 but unlike most pilgrims returned again—in
1853—and again—in 1854—and again—in 1859. He did not return after
1859, when he finally wrested the Codex Sinaiticus from the monastery,
vowing to "return it, undamaged and in a good state of preservation, to

the Holy Confraternity of Mount Sinai at its first request."[33] Written in Greek in the fourth century, this priceless Septuagint manuscript subsequently became the basis for revision of much of the Old and New Testaments.[34] Tischendorf presented it as a gift to Russian Tsar Alexander II, and it remained in the Imperial Library in St. Petersburg until the people and government of the United Kingdom purchased it for 100,000 pounds sterling in 1933.[35] It now rests in a glass case in Room 30 of the British Museum. Its label reads misleadingly in passive voice: "The MS was discovered in 1859 by the German biblical scholar Constantine Tischendorf in the Greek Monastery of St. Katherine on Mount Sinai, and was subsequently presented by the monks to the Emperor of Russia."

Writers and artists did their share to promote European interest in the East, particularly during the Romantic period of 1798–1832. "I met a traveller from an antique land . . ." begins Percy Bysshe Shelley's sonnet "Ozymandius."[36] Some writers undertook journeys to the Middle East while others stayed home to invent or embellish images of the region. The visions they created, even if not rooted in reality, had marked impacts on Europeans' imaginations and behaviors. A "Grand Oriental Fête," an Irish rendition of a Middle Eastern bazaar, was held in Dublin in May 1894. It was the setting for James Joyce's story *Araby*. The youthful protagonist muses, "The syllables of the word *Araby* were called to me through the silence in which my soul luxuriated and cast an Eastern enchantment over me."[37] The faraway East and things romantic and sensual became inseparable in the European imagination. "A damsel with a dulcimer, an Abyssinian maid" appears in Samuel Taylor Coleridge's vision of the stately pleasure dome in Xanadu.[38] Even some scholars perpetuated the fiction of a licentious East. In 1836 Edward William Lane published *Manners and Customs of the Modern Egyptians*, an instant classic which piqued European appetites. Lane was the first to "Orientalize" the Orient, according to Edward Said, depicting exotic lands of sensuality and natural wonder: "In most cases, the Orient seemed to have offended sexual propriety; everything about the Orient exuded dangerous sex, threatened hygiene and domestic seemliness with an excessive 'freedom of intercourse' . . . In the Orient one suddenly confronted unimaginable antiquity, inhuman beauty, boundless distance."[39]

In the age of European industrialization, while the West became blemished by Blake's "dark Satanic mills," the countryside of the East grew wildly attractive.[40] Europeans had viewed wilderness in general and mountains in particular as abodes of demons and bandits and as obstructions to travel, but the Romantic poets changed those perceptions.[41] A few miles above Tintern Abbey on July 13, 1798, William Wordsworth wrote of being a lover of meadows and woods and mountains.[42] "I traveled among

Adventure, nature, mountain, Biblical association, and exoticism converged at Mount Sinai and other places in the Middle East. English clergyman and poet John Keble (1792–1866) wrote these lines:

> *On Horeb, with Elijah, let us lie,*
> *Where all around, on mountain, sand and sky,*
> *God's chariot-wheels have left distinctest trace.*[44]

Almost every explorer struggled to capture the mountain grandeur of
Sinai. "This peninsula, naked of the gentler beauties of natural scenery,
foliage, lake, running waters, does combine nature's three grander features—the sea, the desert, the mountains," wrote Reverend C. Pickering
Clarke in 1880. "But notice-worthy beyond everything is the desolation
and mountain confusion. Most desolate, most barren—these hills of Sinai
are the 'Alps unclothed.' A naked Switzerland, even though its glaciers
and snows should remain, seems inconceivable; but Sinai is naked . . .
Then the confusion—the intricate complication of peak and ridge!"[45] Edward Palmer expressed his awe of the high country:

> *The very nakedness of the rocks imparts to the scene a grandeur and beauty pecu-*
> *liarly its own. For, as there is no vegetation to soften down the rugged outlines of*
> *the mountains or conceal the nature of their formation, each rock stands out with*
> *its own distinctive shape and colour as clearly as in some giant geological map. In*
> *some wadies the mountain sides are striped with innumerable veins of the most*
> *brilliant hue, thus producing an effect of colour and fantastic design which it is*
> *impossible to describe. These effects are heightened by the peculiar clearness of the*
> *atmosphere and the dazzling brightness of the sunlight; one part of a mountain*
> *will glow with a golden or ruddy hue, while the rest is plunged in deepest shade.*
> *Sometimes a distant peak will seem to blend with the liquid azure of the sky,*
> *while another stands out in all the beauty of purple or violet tints; and, with what*
> *would seem the mere skeleton of a landscape, as beautiful effects are produced as if*
> *the bare rocks were clothed with forests and vineyards or capped with perpetual*
> *snows. Nature, in short, seems here to shew that in her most barren and*
> *uninviting moods she can be exquisitely beautiful still.*[46]

A passion for mountain landscapes also converged with interest in the
exotic and Biblical in artistic renditions of the Near East. Scotsman David
Roberts depicted Mount Sinai and the Monastery of St. Katherine in
1839. He portrayed the monastery with painstaking accuracy, but provided
as its backdrop an impossibly steep and symmetrical Mount Sinai (frontis-

piece). This was the forbidding Mountain of God the Westerner would want to see. Other artists, and Roberts in other drawings, perceived Sinai's true landscapes as too dramatic to warrant embellishment. The monastery and mountain of de Laborde in 1828 are almost photographic in their accuracy, yet no less visually stunning than Roberts'. These men and others including I. Taylor (1830), F. Arundale (1833), E. Finden (1836), J. M. Bernatz (1837), W. H. Bartlett (1845), L. de Laval (1850), C. Tobin (1854), and C. W. Wilson (1880) created graphic images that added to the mystique of Sinai and made it an irresistible destination for travelers.

VOYAGERS

In the late eighteenth century travel was simply a means of getting from one place to another, a necessary evil. Guidebooks for Western European travelers described the shortest possible routes, listed schedules and accommodations, and compared prices, but told little about attractions along the way. Social changes accompanying the Industrial Revolution made travel an attractive opportunity for recreation, leisure, and education. The Industrial Revolution also provided relatively safe and convenient means for people to reach their destinations. Railways and steam locomotives shrank time and distance across the face of Europe and North America. The steamship opened doors to distant lands. In 1846 Thomas Cook founded the world's first travel agency.[47]

Travelers to the East were generally well-to-do English and other Europeans. Following the landmark 1844 publication of Alexander Kinglake's *Eothen, or Traces of Travel Brought Home from the East*, many travelers published letters and books about their journeys. These offer a wealth of information about personal attitudes and regional conditions in the colonial Middle East. Their writers traveled for various reasons. Like scholars, adventurers, and pilgrims who preceded them, some wanted to set foot on the actual places of the Exodus. In 1909 Franklin Hoskins, John Goucher, and S. Earl Taylor retraced what they believed was the Israelites' route from mainland Egypt to Jericho. Their thousand-mile journey by camel and horse took them forty days. "We camped literally within the Old Testament . . . It was a physical review of some of the greatest events and characters in human history."[48] Hoskins was not disappointed with the experience of matching real places with Biblical narrative:

Critics seated thousands of miles away in distance and three thousand years later in time have formulated doubts and queries, have raised imaginary difficulties which vanish into thin air when the observant traveler enters the almost changeless Peninsula of Sinai with the Bible in his hand. Some have gone so far as to deny

that the inspired writers had the Sinai region in mind at all. Nothing could be
more gratuitous and farther from the truth. The Bible writers plainly knew that
country as well as George Washington ever knew the country between Boston and
Yorktown, and the writer, after 26 years in Bible lands and many journeys into
these more remote portions, would record his conviction that the geography of
the Bible fits the land as the key fits the lock, and each succeeding generation
of men will realize this more clearly.[49]

In 1912 the Cook office in Cairo arranged a camel trip to Mount Sinai
for Arthur Sutton. The agency had proposed that he begin and end the
journey at at-Tur. He declined, arguing that this would detract from the
opportunity to retrace the entire route of the Exodus. Noting that "any
desert tour is costly, and especially the Sinai tour," he spent the extra
money and sixteen days to do the trip properly, and found the experience
extremely satisfying. Like avowed pilgrims before them, Sutton and his
companions reveled in being at Biblical places. They camped at the foot
of the Nagub al-Haawa pass, below the Plain of ar-Raaha. "After dinner
we read together in Exodus xx of the giving of the law, and also in Exodus
xxxii of the idolatry of the Children of Israel in the worship of the golden
calf, and of the breaking of the tables of the law as Moses came down and
saw the wickedness of the people, and we knew that to-morrow we were

Arthur Sutton at
'Ayun Musa
"mounted, and
ready to start
for Sinai."
March 8, 1912.

to see the place where this occurred."[50] Sutton joined the swollen ranks of commentators on the geography of the Exodus, attaching to the publication of his journey an appendix entitled "Some Notes on the Exodus of the Israelites and the Problem of Their Numbers." Oddly, Sutton did not climb Jebel Musa. "The ascent of this mountain is the first aim and object of the Sinai traveller," Edward Palmer noted.[51]

Other visitors enjoyed a more vague but no less rewarding sensation of traveling in an antique land. As Europe industrialized there was growing nostalgia for the innocence and achievement of pre-industrial civilization. Travelers wanted to experience the past before it grew more distant. "I seemed to have stepped back in time to a more primitive life and more primitive beliefs," J. C. Hawksley wrote of his journey into Sinai. "There was still something in the wilderness that mattered to the prophets, perhaps there is still something there; perhaps the monks at St. Katherine's monastery still value that something."[52] "Geographically its position is peculiar," wrote C. Pickering Clarke of the Sinai desert:

> *Palestine, Egypt, and Arabia each have an interest in it, while from each it is kept distinct. Historically its interests embosomed herein are stupendous. From Sinai the very life of the human race takes a fresh departure. If, as great writers have suggested, Egypt with its prodigality of antiquarian information is yet a tomb whose occupants excite no interest, in the Desert—and the farther and farther we advance into it will the impression become more real—we feel that we are on the stream of continuous history. It will flow on and on through the Desert.[53]*

Some travelers were motivated by a sense of adventure in the "terrible and waste-howling wilderness" of Sinai. To conquer the desert! English travelers in particular wanted to shape personal relationships with the desert that would distinguish them from ordinary men. Alexander Kinglake wrote that the people of Cairo

> *could not understand, and they wanted to know, by what strange privilege it is that an Englishman with a brace of pistols and a couple of servants rides safely across the Desert, whilst they, the natives of the neighboring cities, are forced to travel in troops, or rather in herds. One of them . . . ventured to ask . . . whether the English did not travel under the protection of evil demons, [a notion that] owes its origin partly to the strong wilfulness of the English gentleman (a quality which, not being backed by any visible authority, either civil or military, seems perfectly superhuman to the soft Asiatic). . . . The theory is that the English traveller has committed some sin against God and his conscience, and that for this the evil spirit has hold of him, and drives him from his home like a victim of the old Grecian furies, and forces him to travel over countries far and strange, and most chiefly over*

deserts and desolate places, and to stand upon the sites of cities that once were, and
are now no more, and to grope among the tombs of dead men. Often enough there
is something of truth in this notion; often enough the wandering Englishman
is guilty (if guilt it be) of some pride or ambition, big or small, imperial or
parochial, which being offended has made the lone places more tolerable than
ball-rooms to him a sinner.[54]

The march through Sinai would be difficult, perhaps dangerous, and certainly invigorating. Preparations for the trip were colorful, involving haggling over arrangements and fares with Sinai Bedouins. Travelers who did not negotiate round-trip transport from Cairo often had to repeat the process at the monastery. The overland journey continued to be treacherous through the early twentieth century. As recently as 1909 the principal means of reaching the monastery from Suez was still a nine-day walk with camels. Four hours out of Suez most parties camped at the palms of 'Uyun Musa, the Biblical Elim for some. Three days later they reached the mouth of Wadi Gharandal, also Elim for some.[55] The weather on that stretch was often dreadful. Tischendorf dealt with it on the way to and from the monastery. On May 16, 1844, he wrote, "The heat towards midday became almost insupportable. I never experienced it so intense."[56] Dean Stanley and his companions endured Egypt's annual *khamsiin* sandstorm in this region in 1853:

But soon Red Sea and all were lost in a sand-storm, which lasted the whole day.
Imagine all distant objects entirely lost to view,—the sheets of sand fleeing along
the surface of the Desert like streams of water; the whole air filled, though invis-
ibly, with a tempest of sand, driving in your face like sleet. Imagine the caravan
toiling against this,—the Bedouins each with his shawl thrown completely over
his head, half of the riders sitting backwards,—the camels, meantime, thus virtu-
ally left without guidance, though, from time to time, throwing their long necks
sideways to avoid the blast, yet moving straight onwards with a painful sense of
duty truly edifying to behold. . . . Through the tempest, this roaring and driving
tempest, which sometimes made me think that this must be the real meaning of
"a howling wilderness," *we rode the whole day.*[57]

For those who bypassed the hardship of the coastal plain and instead arrived by sea at at-Tur, a scenic but also challenging ride of three-and-a-half days lay ahead. By whatever route they came, all who traveled overland to Mount Sinai emphasized the hazards along the way. From the early nineteenth century such obstacles became an attraction in themselves, a reason to travel. It was encounter with nature.

On the journey travelers were forced to reconcile reality with the images that had drawn them to remote places. Some travelers were displeased by Near Eastern landscapes and must have felt deceived by artists and essayists. Travelers expected "if not the world of the Arabian Nights, then at least that of Byron's poems and Chateaubriand's romances," wrote geographer J. Malcolm Wagstaff; "The mundane, faded reality which they found was often a big disappointment . . . that provoked appropriately melancholy feelings and stimulated thoughts of death and decay."[58] Travel to the East was supposed to be a romantic, potentially sexual adventure that according to Kinglake was vital to the "moulding of your character—that is, your very identity."[59] In the real, very conservative climate of Muslim society the traveler struggled to perceive sensuality. Kinglake's contact with Bedouin women was hardly passionate, but he boasted that he controlled their emotions: "The feint which they made of concealing their faces from me was always slight: when they first saw me, they used to hold up a part of their drapery with one hand across their faces, but they seldom persevered very steadily in subjecting me to this privation. . . . I had the complete command of their affections, for at any moment I could make their young hearts bound and their old hearts jump by offering a handful of tobacco."[60]

Although they left a rich literature the number of travelers to Jebel Musa was not large. When Nikos Kazantzakis visited the monastery in 1927 then-Archbishop Porphyrios III showed him the guest book and recounted the number of visitors who had called between 1897 and 1925: 145 English, 69 French, 58 Americans, 60 Germans, and 35 Greeks.[61] The arrival of the automobile did not change the nature of travel or travelers immediately. Through the 1920s vehicular access to Jebel Musa via Wadi Feiran was extremely difficult, and most visitors continued to use camels belonging to the monastery or to Sinai Bedouins.[62] In January 1926 Ahmed Shefik, Egypt's Director-General of the Frontiers Administration, arrived in a caravan of Ford cars after a fourteen-and-one-half hour drive from Heliopolis, an eastern suburb of Cairo. His purpose was to examine the motor road that had just been completed between Suez and at-Tur, and between that road and the monastery. He was important enough and visitors of any cloth were still sufficiently novel that all twenty-one priests and monks stood in their vestments at the monastery gate to receive the party. Shefik and companions saluted the monks, who answered by firing their cannon and ringing the monastery bells.[63] Archbishop Porphyrios II even supplied his guest with a monk, Pere Polycarpos, to serve as personal escort. In April 1927 Ralph Bagnold with five companions traveled in three cars to the monastery. Bagnold recorded that the only automobile route in all Sinai ran down the west coast of the peninsula for 260 kilometers to at-Tur, with a branch leading up Wadi Feiran to the monastery.

No gasoline was then available in the entire Sinai Peninsula.[64] Maynard Williams and four companions made the trip in luxury in 1927, beginning with a steamer passage from Suez to at-Tur. Their thirty-two baggage camels carried four patchwork embroidered tents which their servants erected nightly. They slept in "comfortable iron beds with spotless linen" and enjoyed numerous other comforts: "bottled water from beside the Lake of Geneva; tea from Darjeeling; coffee from Mocha; shortbread from Scotland; as we saw the greatness of our possessions we felt sorry for the children of Israel."[65] Williams noted that "automobiles have recently scurried in flocks" to the monastery, carrying "frock-coated officials to this far retreat."[66] In November 1943 J. C. Hawksley nevertheless found automobile travel difficult: "Beyond Abu Senima, which is about halfway, the coastal road is left and the journey is continued through sandy and rocky valleys with a good prospect of disaster to tyres, springs and axles. The journey from Abu Senima by camel is more direct and takes three days, but as camels have no tyres, springs or axles the Bedouins still prefer camels. I am of one mind with the Bedouin."[67]

Barring disaster, by Hawksley's time the driving time from Suez to the monastery was only six hours. The tourist age was at hand. The first airplane landed in the vicinity in 1956. This Israeli aircraft touched down during the brief invasion that accompanied the Suez Crisis.[68] In the 1950s the Egyptian administration paved roads to service the oil fields and mines along the western Sinai coast, and maintained the dirt track to the mon-

Monk Pere Polycarpos with the Ford caravan party of Ahmed Shefik, preparing to depart from Shatt. January 1926.

astery via Wadi Feiran.[69] Increasing numbers of European tourists traveled this route on five-seat taxis from Cairo, but monks recall that in the mid-1960s only about thirty visitors called on the monastery each year. Despite the increasing traffic, virtually no physical development took place in the area between 1956 and 1967, and Egyptian authority was limited to a small contingent of camel-mounted police and an army encampment.[70] The traveler still had obstacles to overcome. One was bureaucratic. The hopeful visitor to the monastery had first to apply for a permit from the monastery's office in Cairo, then present that form to the Frontiers Office in Cairo together with another form from that office and three passport photographs. "That is all," William Bassili wrote cheerfully in his 1964 guidebook to the monastery, "and within an hour you will have back your passport together with the official permit which allows you to travel through Sinai."[71]

EAST MEETS WEST

Travelers' accounts provide some insight into how monks and Bedouins received visitors. These are particularly useful in understanding how the nature of visitation to Mount Sinai changed when it acquired mass proportions. These sources contain some information about Bedouin and monastic cultures, but reveal much more about the attitudes and milieu of travelers themselves. Many travelers and eventually tourists to Mount Sinai came without humility. Perhaps Sir Richard Burton established a precedent by writing, "The more haughty and offensive [the traveler] is to the people, the more they respect him."[72]

The unlettered Bedouins of Sinai were unable to record their impressions of visitors, but outsiders wrote copious judgments of these nomads. The Tuscan pilgrims who visited Mount Sinai in 1384 were impressed by the material poverty of the Jabaliya, who "have no abode but they have caves in the rocks, and they have no utensils. Their house is a piece of woollen cloth."[73] These visitors withheld condemnation of Bedouin character and society, unlike Western European scholars and travelers during the colonial era. Those who perceived the monks as protagonists on the Sinai landscape depicted Bedouins as their unkindly foils. Carl Ritter, for example, saw the monastery "situated at the very heart of the wilderness, surrounded by hordes of hostile Mohammedan Arabs."[74] The unschooled sons of the desert were a perfect contrast with erudite scholars like this German geographer: "Those who have visited the region . . . have had to follow the caprice of ignorant Bedouins."[75] Ignorance was the least perilous attribute of Ritter's Bedouins, whose presence added a special element to the alluring danger of travel in Sinai:

The difficulties of climbing these shattered granite peaks, and the perfect worthlessness of the region in an agricultural point of view, are not the only obstacles which have stood in the way of travelers; but the extortion, the greed, the robberies, the cheating, the faithlessness of the Beduins, without whose assistance the journey cannot be attempted, have paralyzed all enterprise in this direction. The attempt is a bold one in face of all these difficulties, and it would not be too much to call it a dangerous one.[76]

Some travelers depicted the Bedouins as not only cheaters but murderers. In his account of a journey through northern Arabia in 1862, William Palgrave wrote that "Deeds of the most cold-blooded perfidy are by no means uncommon among these nomades, and strangers under their guidance and protection, nay, even their own kindred and brethren of the desert, are but too often the victims of such conduct. To lead travellers astray in the wilderness till they fall exhausted by thirst and weariness, and then to plunder and leave them to die, is no unfrequent Bedawin procedure."[77] English contempt for Bedouins was heightened after the 1882 killings of Edward Palmer and two English officers. Edward Hull blamed a nasty bite by an insect he identified as a specimen of "Arab lice" near Jebel Musa on a "vagabond Arab" who had slept under the Englishman's camel saddle, undoubtedly infesting it with vermin.[78] Major Kitchener, who accompanied Hull on this trip, was skeptical about one Bedouin's version of Palmer's murder: "Arabs, as everybody knows who has had to do with them, have a remarkable facility for making up a story to meet a supposed occasion."[79] The perception of Bedouin as brigand lingered as late as 1922, when the sixteen-member party of scholar Rendel Harris was delighted by the unexpected honesty, gentleness, and cleanliness of their Bedouin escorts. Before their journey one of the members had proclaimed, "As to the Bedawin, I have had experience of them; they are miserable, half-starved creatures, without sufficient [sic] to keep body and soul together; they steal everything on which they can lay hands, so we must never leave boxes unlocked in our tents, or our things will disappear; and we must be most careful never to let our camelmen ride our camels if we are not on them, for the Arabs are perfectly filthy."[80]

Some travelers had ambivalent attitudes toward the Bedouin, depicting both darkness and light in the Arab character and adding to the mystique of cultural encounter in the Sinai. The Bedouin is a volatile, deceptive, but essentially harmless and good soul, according to observers like C. Pickering Clarke:

Very charming is the sound of Arab laughter, and, though one does not understand a word of it, the never-ending song, which seems capable of any amount of "gag," and not to be injured by constant interludes, does not really weary any one. Their demeanour is noticeably courteous . . . When they dispute, which is not infrequently in the day, and especially on the subject of adjusting the loads on the camels each morning, or on the question of agreeing to terms of apportioning the money, they are as violent, demonstrative and abusive as the frequenters of Billingsgate. In the bargaining the Arab will lie right and left and overreach you, but the bargain being made, his word is his bond.[81]

Even those Westerners who admired Bedouin hospitality, dignity, and piety often explained these as unintentional traits or as unfathomable counterparts of violence in a primitive society. "But their open-handedness often springs more from the childish levity of the savage than from true and praiseworthy liberality of character," William Palgrave wrote. "He is at best an ill-educated child, whose natural good qualities have remained underdeveloped or half stifled by bad treatment and extreme neglect."[82] Scottish geographer George W. Murray was a lifelong chronicler of Bedouin cultures in Egypt, but summarized the south Sinai Bedouin in no more sympathetic terms than the brief visitor of his colonial age: "They may be called shy, shifty and suspicious—especially of one another . . . They are all conservative to a degree, incurably greedy, incurably generous, incurably romantic, and incurably lazy. Their contempt for the accumulation of worldly possessions and their chivalry are their best points, their love of litigation their most tiresome."[83]

Distrustful or ignorant of the monastic purpose and colored by their notions of civility, travelers also commented on the lowly character of monks and monasticism at Mount Sinai. "Being of the lower orders of society, and educated only in convents, they are extremely ignorant," Burckhardt complained of the monks.[84] "They were, for the most part, mere drones and sluggards," the American traveler John Lloyd Stephens wrote a few years later. "I do not mean to say that they were bad men. Most of them were too simple to be bad."[85] On his 1844 visit Tischendorf was escorted throughout his stay at the monastery by a Signor Pietro whom the German described as a "half-witted fellow: the first question he asked me was, if I had already travelled in the sun and moon. Notwithstanding his mad *capriccios*, he is doubtlessly one of the most witty and intellectual individuals of the monastery."[86] Henry Palmer wrote caustically of the monastery's inhabitants: "Now the interior presents a scene of hopeless confusion and dirt, well befitting the character of the present inmates."[87] Monks were obstructions of his companion Edward Palmer's vision of the authentic sacred landscape of Mount Sinai: "But the interesting and solemn associations of the place were marred by the mingled indifference and superstition of the monkish crew; and it was only in the solitude of the mountains, or in the retirement of our own camp, that we really felt that we were at Sinai."[88] Edward Palmer was one of many visitors who had built up unrealistic expectations of what the holy men of Sinai must be like, and were disappointed bitterly by their gruff worldliness. "I had hoped that in such a place as Sinai there might still linger some trace of that devotion which seems to have characterized the recluses of old; some religious enthusiasm which should atone for their having fled from the duties of that state of life to which it has pleased God to call them. But no! I found in them no enthusiasm, no hopes, no aspirations—no care for anything but indolence and rum."[89] "A dismal spirit of wearied indolence and ignorance lies like a heavy cloud on their discontented countenances," Richard Lepsius wrote of mid-nineteenth-century monks.[90] Arthur Stanley was even more harsh:

Yet looking from an external point of view at the singular advantages enjoyed by the convent, it is hard to recall another institution with such opportunities so singly wasted. It is a colony of Christian pastors planted amongst heathens and hardly a spark of civilisation or of Christianity, so far as history records, has been imparted to a single tribe or family in that wide wilderness. It is a colony of Greeks, of Europeans, of ecclesiastics, in one of the most interesting and most sacred regions of the earth, and hardly a fact, from the time of their first foundation to the present time, has been contributed by them to the geography, the geology, or the history of a country, which in all its aspects has been submitted to their investigation for thirteen centuries.[91]

Some visitors assumed credit for what merit they did see in the monastery. Arthur Sutton claimed the monks told him that "up till the English rule in Egypt their lives were in danger, one of the monks having been shot through the chapel window while celebrating Mass. Now, thanks to the English, all the country was peaceful and quiet, but yet they had not dared to mention Christianity to their Moslem dependents for fear of raising antagonism."[92]

Whatever judgments they made of the monks' mental and moral properties, travelers were surprised and often deeply touched by their generosity and hospitality. "Notwithstanding the ignorance of these monks," Burckhardt wrote, "they are fond of seeing strangers in their wilderness; and I met with a more cordial reception among them than I did in the convents of Libanus, which are in possession of all the luxuries of life. The monks of Sinai are even more generous: three years ago they furnished a Servian adventurer, who styled himself a Knes, and pretended to be well known to the Russian government, with sixty dollars to pay his journey back to Alexandria, on his informing them of his destitute circumstances." [93] In 1836 John Lloyd Stephens found his welcome at the top of the monastery's windlass too warm: "Nearly all the monks had assembled, and all pressed forward to welcome me. They shook my hand, took me in their arms, kissed my face; and if I had been their dearest friend just escaped from the jaws of death, they could not have received me with a more cordial greeting. Glad as I was, after a ten days' journey, to be received with such warmth by these recluses of the mountains, I could have spared the kissing. The custom is one of the detestable things of the East." [94] Regarding him as a pilgrim, the archbishop was exceedingly kind to the American traveler: "The superior renewed his welcome, telling me that the convent was the pilgrim's home, and that everything it contained was mine for a week, a month, or for the rest of my days." [95] Arthur Sutton and his party reached the monastery in March 1912 after a nine-day trip by camel from Ismailiya. The twenty-five resident monks received the men with coffee and date liqueur, and allowed them to pitch their tents in the monastery garden. [96] "I can only report they treated us with the utmost kindness," Golding wrote of his party's reception by the monks. [97] In 1922 the monks accommodated Rendel Harris' sixteen-member group, which included several women, inside the monastery enclosure, although hosting women overnight was by then against monastery regulations. [98] On his 1924 visit with a patrol of the Frontiers District Administration, A. S. Merton was astonished at the clerics' generosity. They insisted that Merton take all his meals with them. He declined but stayed for a lunch which "started with sardines, followed by rich vermicelli soup, roast turkey, fresh beans and fried potatoes, cucumber salad, stewed pears, cheese, fruit, and wine with coffee and liqueurs. A banquet in the midst of the wilderness." [99] The monks saw Merton off with equal zeal: "The good monks came down to the gate to bid us farewell as our caravan passed out. At the last moment they added to the great debt we already owed them by sending over to our camp three baskets crammed full of eggs, melons, tomatoes, plums, grapes, nuts and bread, with three bottles of wine and two legs of veal. They had indeed killed the fatted calf for us." [100] "One cannot dismiss the monks of Mount Sinai without a testimony to their wondrous hospitality and kindliness," Claude Jarvis wrote in the 1930s. "One of the chief charms of a visit to this remote spot is the opportunity of meeting and being entertained by a community whose old-time courtesy and dignity savour of the past and are not to be met with in the outside world . . . There is no place in the world where one is made so thoroughly welcome as in this old-world monastery in the wilderness." [101]

Hospitality has cost the monastery dearly. Constantin von Tischendorf inflicted an insufferable loss that has caused the monks to deal more cautiously with visitors ever since. Ironically the monastery had already been on guard against all kinds of vandalism. Monks required all would-be visitors to obtain a letter of recommendation from the office of the Sinai Archbishop in Cairo. Many travelers described how monks examined this document carefully before lifting them into the monastery.[102] Recalling that Niebuhr had not been admitted to the monastery because he lacked the necessary permission, Tischendorf took extra precautions, securing letters from both the Cairo office and the monastery's office in Suez.[103] Apparently the Cairo official was suspicious and wrote a note that according to Tischendorf had "a trait of a Uriah's letter," in reference to a Biblical instruction to a message-reader to kill the message-bearer (2 Samuel 11: 14). After Bedouins shouted loudly and discharged their rifles to signal Tischendorf's arrival, a monk appeared atop the monastery wall. Tischendorf passed up to him the letter from the Suez monastery, hiding the document he had obtained in Cairo. To his delight the monk accepted the lesser document and cranked the windlass to haul him in. The archbishop also must have been suspicious of Tischendorf, as the German observed ironically: "The present superior of this monastery, who, notwithstanding the delicacy of his features, bears the strongest expression of duplicity in his glance."[104] Searching in vain for the manuscript he would later obtain, he cursed his hosts for deceiving him about its whereabouts: "The prior is a native of Crete; St. Paul's notorious character of the Cretes (the Cretes are always liars) he seems to verify, even in the present day."[105]

There is still some disagreement over how Tischendorf secured the Codex Sinaiticus, but none about the monks' sense of violation and their subsequent views of scholars and lingering travelers. In the 1920s monks told visitors about "Tischendorf the Thief."[106] "Tears formed in the eyes of the Prior when I told of seeing the departed Codex in Leningrad," Maynard Williams wrote.[107] Heinz Skrobucha defended Tischendorf as the man who "saved it from destruction" but "received no gratitude from the monks for his action."[108] Father Makarios believes the archbishop at the time must bear some blame: "Most of the monks would say that Tischendorf had stolen the Codex Sinaiticus," he told me, "but the issue is a bit more complex than that since the abbot released the material to him." He added that the monastery had recently and unsuccessfully petitioned to purchase back the Codex Sinaiticus from the British Museum. Furthermore, he insisted, a pattern of scholarly deception has continued to the present day. An American university expedition had microfilmed all of the monastery's vast library holdings, promising to provide a complete set of the microfilms to the monastery, but failed to keep this promise. When U.S. Congressman Les Aspin visited the monastery in 1988 the monks asked him to resolve the problem. According to the monks, Aspin pursued the matter with the Library of Congress, which informed him that the monastery could purchase a microfilm set for $30,000. The monks also complain that a scholar who has the only photographic record of documents destroyed by a fire at the monastery in 1971 will not publish or release his photographs of that collection.

Today photography in the monastery library is strictly prohibited. A wrought-iron grill protects the priceless manuscripts. Few visitors are allowed even to see the collection, and none is left alone with it. While acknowledging the importance of scholarship, the monks still bristle at any suggestion that scholars should have access to the collection. Father Makarios stated the monks' position: "There is a tremendous amount of interest on the part of scholars in the world to dig into libraries like St. Katherine's, because everybody wants to find something that has never been known before. And believe me, there are a lot of not very nice people who know that if they get access to our facility, they may not do any research and they may not benefit the monastery, but they certainly can benefit themselves. We've been burned in the past by these kinds of people, so the monastery is very, very cautious."

Scholars are not the greatest threat to the monastery today. There is a new Trojan horse.

Ten

♦

THE
TOURIST

"The world was coming to an end." That is what one monk thought in
1956 when Israeli paratroopers scaled the monastery wall and dropped inside during Israel's brief occupation of the Sinai. The monastery weathered
that invasion as it has all threats to its existence. Today, however, the monks
are not sanguine about their future. They fear another force may end their
world. For three hours on five days of each week the monastery opens its
doors to all who want to enter. Tourists pour in. They come in greater
numbers and for different reasons than the visitors preceding them through
the centuries. Their presence threatens to ruin the monastic tradition at
Mount Sinai, and structures to accommodate them have already scarred
the face of the sacred land (Map 3).

Like traditional peoples everywhere the monks of St. Katherine are
finding it difficult to resist the force of modern tourism. Tourists want to
see unique places and the tourism industry is eager to accommodate them.
The financial stakes are high. Tourism is the largest business in the world,
with annual receipts exceeding two trillion dollars and representing about
12 percent of the world's economy.[1] For an impoverished, debt-ridden,
overpopulated nation like Egypt, income from tourism represents a hedge
against financial ruin and a resource for economic development. In 1991
Egypt's tourism-related revenue totaled three billion dollars. In an effort
to bring down the Mubarak regime, in 1992 and 1993 Muslim extremists
attacked tourist buses and restaurants, killing and wounding several foreign
tourists. Tourist arrivals declined by 70 percent, tourism-generated revenue fell by 30 percent, and the nation's economy worsened.[2]

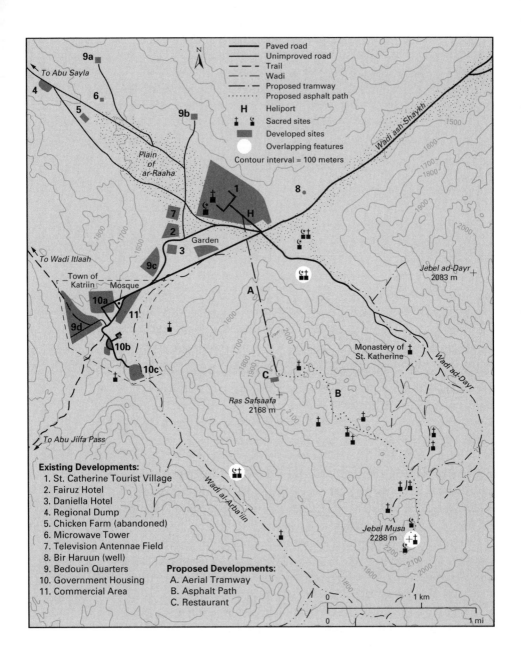

Legend:
- Paved road
- Unimproved road
- Trail
- Wadi
- Proposed tramway
- Proposed asphalt path
- H Heliport
- ‡ c Sacred sites
- Developed sites
- ○ Overlapping features
- Contour interval = 100 meters

9a
To Abu Sayla
4
6
5
9b

Plain of ar-Raaha

1
H
8

7
2
Garden
3
9c

To Wadi Itlaah
Town of Katriin
Mosque
10a
11
9d
10b
10c

A

C

Jebel ad-Dayr
2083 m

Monastery of St. Katherine

Wadi ash-Shaykh

1500
1600
1700
1800
1900
2000

Ras Safsaafa
2168 m

B

2100

Wadi ad-Dayr

To Abu Jiffa Pass

Existing Developments:
1. St. Catherine Tourist Village
2. Fairuz Hotel
3. Daniella Hotel
4. Regional Dump
5. Chicken Farm (abandoned)
6. Microwave Tower
7. Television Antennae Field
8. Bir Haruun (well)
9. Bedouin Quarters
10. Government Housing
11. Commercial Area

Wadi al-Arba'iin

Proposed Developments:
A. Aerial Tramway
B. Asphalt Path
C. Restaurant

Jebel Musa
2288 m

1900
2000
2100

0   1 km
0   1 mi

MAP 3
Modern
developments around
Jebel Musa.

Tourism is a vulnerable industry not only because unrest deters visitors but because tourism carries the seeds of its own ruin. Too many people visiting attractive destinations make those destinations unattractive. Reckless tourist development at Mount Sinai may be spoiling the places and the cultures that tourists come to see.

Modern tourism to Mount Sinai began with Israel's occupation of the
Sinai in 1967. Numbers of visitors rose modestly in the first few years of
the occupation when security issues were prominent. Israel's confidence
in its ability to hold its new borders and public fascination with the Sinai
as a place of great natural and cultural interest led to an explosion in tourism in the 1970s. For such a remote place the traffic was remarkable. During the Israeli occupation of 1967–1979 an average of fifty thousand
people visited the Jebel Musa area each year.[3] On many peak days in the
1970s there were as many as three thousand visitors within a 5-mile radius
of Jebel Musa. On one day in April 1979, seventy forty-seat buses and fifty
private cars arrived in the area.[4] On such days aircraft arrivals from Tel Aviv
and Eilat included up to five one-hundred-seat Viscount airplanes and ten
six-seat planes. The monks recall a day when twenty-eight planes carrying
sixty persons each arrived from Tel Aviv. In deference to the monks Israeli
tourist authorities allowed no more than four hundred persons to enter the
monastery on a given day, so perhaps less than half of the fifty thousand
yearly visitors to the area actually entered the monastery.[5] The others
climbed Jebel Musa and neighboring mountains and camped in the backcountry. After the region reverted to Egyptian control in November 1979
no ceiling was placed on the number of visitors allowed into the monas-

A view
northwestward from
Ras Safsaafa to
Katriin (left half)
and the Plain of ar-
Raaha (right half),
with the St.
Catherine Tourist
Village (right
quarter). Two hotels,
the Daniella and,
above it, the
Fayruuz, are on
opposite sides of the
road, right of center.
August 26, 1993.

tery. Fifty thousand entered in 1987, according to monastery records. The Palestinian uprising or Intifada which began in December 1987 frightened away many North American and European tourists, so that by 1989 only thirty thousand visited the monastery. Even with overall visitation down, some days saw high numbers; on November 4, 1989, six hundred visitors came through the gate. The Gulf War of 1990–1991 and attacks on tourists in 1992 and 1993 continued to keep tourist numbers below earlier levels.

Large numbers of people were able to visit Jebel Musa after 1967 because of a dramatic transformation of the Sinai's infrastructure. Israeli forces constructed a military airfield 24 kilometers northeast of the monastery. In 1976 a passenger terminal was added there to accommodate growing tourist needs. A paved road from Eilat to Sharm ash-Shaykh opened in 1971. A dirt track from this route to the monastery was developed in 1977.[6] This road opened the door for the spectacular tourist boom at Jebel Musa. After regaining the Sinai, Egypt continued to improve the peninsula's links. A road paved through Wadi Feiran reduced the traveling time from the Gulf of Suez to the monastery by three hours. The monastery is now only a four-hour drive from the Ahmad Hamdi tunnel beneath the Suez Canal (300 kilometers away) and six hours from Cairo (430 kilometers away). Bus service to and from Cairo four times weekly began in 1982 and by 1986 ran on a daily basis. In the late 1980s Air Sinai began to carry passengers between the St. Katherine and Cairo airports twice weekly.

The growth of Katriin from a handful of residents in 1967 to 6,300 in 1993 reflects the general boom in Sinai's development.[7] The town's name is an Egyptian creation dating to 1979, when the returning power broke ground on a new administrative headquarters. The Jabaliya had always known the settlement as al-Milgaa, "the meeting place," after the numerous drainages from surrounding mountain blocks that join there. Before 1967 the Jabaliya marketed their produce and obtained provisions in Feiran and at-Tur, and al-Milgaa became a market center only because of Israeli development. In al-Milgaa the Israeli administration built a medical clinic, a primary school offering instruction in Arabic and Hebrew, and an agricultural extension office to provide Bedouins with improved orchard tree varieties. Israeli authorities initiated similar development projects in the Sinai villages of Nuweiba, Dahab, and Sharm ash-Shaykh. All of them included tourist facilities.[8]

Much of Katriin's growth has been tourism-related. In 1975 Israeli developers built a touristic commercial center there and in 1978 added an ethnographic museum to the complex. Today this facility includes two souvenir shops, two groceries, a post office, a tourist police office, a bank, and a restaurant. A bakery and several shops have grown nearby. Expanding Bedouin, Israeli, and later Egyptian residences were linked to a diesel-powered electric generating plant in the village center. The Egyptian-built mosque at the village edge is armed with loudspeakers to broadcast the call to prayer, audible from 3 kilometers away on the summit of Jebel 'Abbas Pasha and at Mahmuud Mansuur's Abu Dagash garden in Wadi Itlaah. An Egyptian-built microwave tower on the Plain of ar-Raaha permits international telephone calls to be made from the central telephone exchange in Katriin. Above-ground telephone lines built in 1987 link Katriin with the airport, 24 kilometers distant. The monks complain that these lines are unsightly but use them and other available amenities. When Archbishop Damianos is in residence he and several monks visit Katriin at least once a week in the archbishop's white Peugeot wagon. They attend to monastery banking business and buy a few luxuries like 2-liter bottles of Pepsi Cola. News of emergencies such as the death of one of the monks' mothers in 1989 reaches the community from the central telephone exchange in Katriin.

Tourist accommodations around Jebel Musa have grown steadily since 1967. In 1968 a 250-bed tented camp opened 1 kilometer east of al-Milgaa. Egyptian builders modified this facility into the two-star, 135-bed Fayruuz Hotel. At the airport in 1977 Israeli developers built a 130-bed hotel, now the Egyptian-run Salama Hotel. A tented camp of 350 beds opened in the mid-1970s at Abu Zaytuuna, between the monastery and airport. Egyptians continue to run that facility and have added the 120-bed "Green Lodge Campground" adjacent to the service station at the Nabi Saalih junction, 10 kilometers from the monastery. An additional 120 beds are available at the field study center on the southern edge of the al-Milgaa basin. Created in 1974 as the Zukey David center of the Society for the Protection of Nature in Israel, this is now the Suez Canal University Field Center. The monastery joined in the growth, building a 200-bed hostel outside its walls in 1978. All these facilities have made growing demands on water, met until now by pumping from the 40-meter-deep well of Bir Haruun, near Nabi Haruun.[9] Israeli engineers drilled that source in the 1970s, along with the well of Abu Zaytuuna, which is the source for truck deliveries of water to the Fayruuz Hotel and the airport and its hotel.

There are seasonal variations in the numbers and origins of people who use these facilities. Greek-Egyptians and Copts, representing about 10 percent of the annual visitor total, crowd the monastery hostel from early summer until school and university classes begin in the second week of September. Then European and North American tourists begin arriving. Most are on package tours which include the major sites of Egypt or Israel or both countries. Day trips to Mount Sinai are also available from the

Hilton and other tourist hotels at Sharm ash-Shaykh and Eilat. According to monastery estimates 60 percent of all visitors to the monastery are German. Other European and North American visitors and smaller numbers of Israelis and Muslim Egyptians comprise most of the remaining 30 percent. Israelis may visit the Jebel Musa area and eastern Sinai for up to fourteen days on a "Sinai Visa" without having to obtain an Egyptian visa. Many come on organized guided tours in minivans. Those who arrive in private vehicles speak of the pleasure and sense of freedom of being able to drive out of their tiny nation—excluding the occupied territories, just one third the size of the Sinai Peninsula—into a neighboring country. Israelis are especially fond of visiting over the Passover holiday, ironically recalling the Exodus from Egypt by returning there.[10]

THE BACKCOUNTRY EXPERIENCE

Nature-loving Israelis began a distinct "sleeping-bag" style of tourism which endures in the Jebel Musa area today. During the Israeli occupation individuals and small parties hired Bedouin guides and camels for one-day to two-week trips in the high Sinai backcountry. Israelis continue to be the vast majority of backcountry users, typically on trips organized by the Society for the Protection of Nature in Israel and companies such as Neot Hakikar and Geographical Tours. The Society for the Protection of Nature in Israel alone fields fifteen hundred to two thousand hikers in the Jebel Musa area each year, escorted by capable Israeli naturalists including Moshe Ma'oz and Jehudit Blauschild. The Egyptian company Isis Tours began operating similar trips in 1988. Four-day "safaris" from Egypt or Israel which begin and end with an overnight at the Abu Zaytuuna tented camp and include a climb of Jebel Musa cost $225 per person. Six-day trips by special off-road vehicle into the south Sinai with Jebel Musa as an overnight stop sell for $370. The more rugged six-day trek into the high country around Jebel Musa costs $295.

The Jabaliya have established a fair but inflexible system for assigning guides and cameleers to these hiking parties. One guide is assigned to every fifteen to twenty clients, and on average one camel and one camel handler to every three clients. The Jabaliya shaykh assigns these escorts on a rotation through a pool of about thirty individuals and sixty camels from the four clans. The Bedouins patterned this system after their ancient rotational hiring of workmen at the monastery. If the guide is from the Awlaad Jindi clan, for example, the first cameleer must be from a second clan and the second from yet another clan. If no more camel men or guides are needed for that outing, a man from the fourth clan would be offered the next available duty. The number of camels is determined by baggage

weight, with no animal allowed to carry more than 60 kilograms. Very large camping parties of up to sixty clients, two guides, twenty camels, and their handlers resemble caravans. Hiking parties must pay a fixed rate for Jabaliya backcountry services: twenty Egyptian pounds per day for each camel hired, twenty pounds per day for each guide, and twenty pounds per day "for the shaykh's services," Abul-Haym's duty of contacting the next person on the rotation and supplying local officials with passport numbers and names of hikers. The Bedouins complain of the shaykh's greed, an issue that has contributed much to Abul-Haym's unpopularity and caused many guides to drop out of the rotation. The system and price structure have local government approval, and Abul-Haym is quick to display the official document to clients who protest the cost. In this uncompromising system it is impossible to secure the services of a particular guide unless the rotation assigns him. Some of the men in this pool seem unschooled or uninterested in their landscapes and wildlife, or at least not keen to share their knowledge with outsiders. Hikers sometimes complain about "lazy" guides who attend their clients as little as possible, preferring to point in the direction they should walk, saying, "I'll see you at the end of the day." The inability of the most capable guides to command any competitive edge over other tribesmen has caused many of the best to give up their places in the rotation.

Many Jabaliya men are frustrated by the unreliability of this supplemen-

Musa, a Jabaliya guide, preparing bread for Israeli hikers in the shade of the willow tree below Ras Safsaafa. August 26, 1993.

tal source of income. During the hiking season a guide usually comes up in the rotation only once in two or three weeks. Guiding work is at best seasonal, with August the busiest month. A typical August day finds about thirty hikers in the backcountry, but on peak days there are as many as three hundred. On one day in mid-October 1989 during the Jewish holiday of Succoth, the entire rotation of available Jabaliya guides and camelmen was employed. Two hundred fifty Israelis were participating in thirty separate trips into the mountains. Aware of the frigid temperatures in the high country, Israelis avoid camping from November through March. By early November backcountry hikers fall to about fifteen daily, most of them from France and other Western nations.

Some men who do not participate in the guide rotation system have found creative ways to benefit from the tourist trade. Saalih Musa, for example, is an aggressive entrepreneur who has set up a "rest house" with a tea service and shaded shelter by one of the finest pools in the high Sinai, the Kharazit ash-Shi'g of Wadi Shi'g. He spray-painted advertisements announcing his "Baghdad Cafe" on rocks above and below the pool, and at a nearby water source enlisted a tourist to spray-paint the plea "Drink Water. Do Not Wash Hands or Body." Families tending livestock in the mountains can count on selling a few goats to passing tour groups, whose Jabaliya guides slaughter and cook the animals as special end-of-trip meals. Hikers pay fifty Egyptian pounds for a kid goat. Jabaliya businessmen also derive modest income from tourists and pilgrims climbing Jebel Musa. Working through the four-clan rotation system, Jabaliya camel-owners charge tourists twenty pounds for a one-hour camel ride from the monastery to the Basin of Elijah. During peak season each of the proprietors of the five refreshment stands on the camel path between the monastery and Jebel Musa's summit earns ten to twenty pounds per day—or the equivalent in pounds sterling, marks, francs, dollars, and shekels—from sales of drinks and biscuits. The first stand above the monastery is the most elaborate. It is one of the last wool homes to be seen in the area. Recognizing the appealing novelty of Bedouin life for foreign tourists, proprietor 'Awaad Mansuur displays many artifacts of Jabaliya material culture under the tent. He offers for sale a variety of rocks, gems, and "fossils"—Jebel Musa's trademark dendritic pyrolusite. Inspired by the example of his brother Ahmad at the monastery gate, 'Awaad also sells bags of Jasonia, mint, and other herbal medicines. Prices of tea, bottled water, and biscuits rise from each stall to the next, so that a bottle of water selling for one Egyptian pound at 'Awaad's shop fetches two-and-a-quarter at the fourth shop, Sulimaan ad-Daguuni's stand located just below the Basin of Elijah. The most expensive and briskest business is conducted in the shop on Jebel Musa's summit, where the bottle of water sells for three pounds.

Jabaliya perceptions of hikers are generally favorable because of the in-

269
•
The
Tourist

'Awaad Mansuur's refreshment stand, a traditional Bedouin wool home, is the closest stand to the Monastery of St. Katherine. November 7, 1989.

come these visitors generate and because they do little direct harm to the landscape. There are some problems. Shaykh Musa complained that when they travel in large groups of thirty to forty, hikers uproot living vegetation to build bonfires. This must stop, he insisted. Near many of the most popular camping sites visitors have burned all available dead vegetation for fuel. Jabaliya guides are hard-pressed to provide a quick campfire for their clients and inevitably turn to green vegetation. Campers who trample crops in Jabaliya gardens are also a nuisance. There are few incentives or mechanisms for hikers to dispose of trash and bodily waste. Some orchard owners who maintain unofficial but heavily used campsites in Wadi Zawatiin, Farsh ar-Rumaana, Wadi Abu Tuwayta, and Wadi Tinya ask groups to pay five to ten Egyptian pounds for their service of burying the visitors' trash. Whether paid or not these gardeners eventually bury the waste. Some of the most beautiful and therefore heavily visited natural sites have become open garbage dumps. Just yards from the swimming hole of al-Galt al-Azraq in Wadi Tala' is a cool and moist grotto whose entrance is flanked by profuse growth of maidenhair fern and a superb summer-flowering specimen of *Rubus sanctus*, the rare shrub revered in the monastery as the burning bush. The grotto is filled with a deep deposit of toilet paper, human feces, bottles, and cans; one of Sinai's best "dripping-place" habitats is a dump.

Hikers of questionable virtue sometimes offend the conservative Jabaliya. Saalih 'Awaad warned me not to make friends with a single Israeli woman who belonged to a backcountry hiking party camped near his Wadi Tinya garden. Such women are promiscuous, he said, and he had seen unmarried Israeli couples making love where all could see them, even on sacred Jebel Musa. "Would these women become the men's wives?" another man asked me innocently. "You know that sort of thing is forbidden for Muslims." Egyptian anthropologist Iman El-Bastawisi learned from Jabaliya women that some young Jabaliya men have succumbed to the charms of foreign women. One eloped with a Swiss woman and another with an Israeli woman. The Bedouin women telling this account would not even mention the men's names, so much shame had they brought on the tribe.[11]

St. Katherine's monks take a similar dim view of the largest contingent of overnighters on Jebel Musa, young budget travelers who make their way here on a route that includes highlights of Egypt or Israel, and sometimes both. While they give Mount Sinai one night, their mecca and place of most lengthy stay is Dahab, on the Gulf of Aqaba coast. A small Muzayna Bedouin fishing village and market center until about 1984, Dahab is now a shoestring-budget Waikiki lined with open-air cafes and nightspots. Several of these are managed by expatriate women who have married Egyptians and local Bedouins. One of these is Renée, a Frenchwoman reputed to be Dahab's best cook. At one end of the beach are several concrete block hotels with tiny rooms and few windows. For three Egyptian pounds per night a youngster may rent a mattress and key to one of these cells and join the unstructured, often barely clothed, comings and goings of counterparts from all over the world. The norms and standards of tourism in mainland Egypt do not apply here. Some women ignore the "no topless" sign posted on the beach, even as local Muzayna men parade back and forth offering camel rides and Muzayna children carrying satchels offer pants for sale, calling out "trousers, trousers." The odor of hashish is pervasive. Theft is common, with many of the incidents attributable to the poverty of young tourists stranded here. Dahab is a limbo between Egypt and Israel. Travelers may enter Sinai from Israel with the "Sinai Visa" that allows them to go no farther west than Sharm ash-Shaykh. When they exhaust their funds at Dahab they are unable to reach Cairo and cannot reenter Israel because of a requirement to change money for the reentry visa. Young people trapped in this way at Dahab work at miserable wages in the local cafes. Some of the women move in with local Muzayna men who have abandoned their society to take up with the foreigners. Other women become prostitutes. Having heard such reports, the monks of St. Katherine call the place "a bordello."

THE PEAK EXPERIENCE

Young budget tourists account for most of those who elect to sleep on Jebel Musa's summit rather than in the monastery's hostel or one of the area hotels. From April through October forty to eighty persons camp on the summit each night. They literally step on each other as they negotiate the darkness in the tiny summit area. Hard-pressed to find any flat space on which to sleep, few can. Most pass the night talking and shivering; this high place is cold. Those who do fall asleep are awakened in the predawn darkness by hikers celebrating their arrival at the summit with loud hurrahs. The newcomers pick their way through unexpected stirring bodies to reach the church and mosque. By the climactic moment of dawn two hundred to three hundred people are standing at the summit. Many take to the flat roof of the mosque for a better view. It is an odd mix of people. German and French pilgrims sing hymns in friendly competition. One October morning some Bedouins saw a man take off on a hang glider from the church, followed all the way to the monastery by curious ravens. Young Egyptian men listen to Sony Walkmen and stare at scantily clad

Belgian girls. Everyone is exhausted. At the instant of sunrise shutters whirr. Colors shift quickly from delicate pink to the harsh whiteness that dominates the landscape until late afternoon. Everyone leaves.

Both pilgrim and tourist hope to experience on the summit an encounter with the sacred or at least some moments of peaceful reflection in a lovely natural setting. This is difficult. Too many people are thrown together in a small area. Jebel Musa's summit is the most crowded place in the Sinai wilderness. Reality bursts the visitor's vision of this place, creating resentment and even anger. "How dare they come up onto *my* mountain?" was Lesley Hazleton's reaction to the tourists who awakened her from her rest on the summit.[12] I spoke with two Dutchmen who had passed a May night with about twenty-five other persons on the summit. "They were really noisy, and then around 6:00 A.M. many damned Moslems arrived," one said. "It was terrible," his companion added. Australian engineer Ian White told me he arrived at the summit just before dawn and overheard two Germans who had spent the night there complaining of the "sleep-disturbing conversation" of two English-speaking persons. They were discussing the events of the Exodus. "I can see the Germans complaining if the others had been talking about the Top 20 music releases," White said, "but they were quietly discussing religion, and what after all is Sinai about?"

The daily tide of visitors to Jebel Musa's summit creates a huge volume of trash: bottles, cans, papers, wrappers, bags, cigarette butts, and the most troublesome, human waste. There are no facilities to dispose of any of this refuse. The Bedouin who runs the tea shop on the summit picks up trash around his immediate area, but outside this cordon the trash accumulates. The stench of human waste is overwhelming. No one is willing to do anything about the excrement problem. Thanks to the efforts of foreign soldiers there is a mechanism to deal with the larger trash problem on Jebel Musa. Since the Camp David Treaty the monks of St. Katherine have befriended officers of the eleven-nation, 3,500-member Multinational Force and Observers (MFO) detachment which monitors the peace between Egypt and Israel in the Sinai. In 1983 the MFO commander asked the monks if there were anything his troops could do for the monastery. Mount Sinai was a trash-heap, the monks replied: would the MFO be willing to clean up the mountain? Twice-yearly since then Jebel Musa has seen the extraordinary gathering known in MFO parlance as the "Sinai Sweep."

The cleanup is conducted as a military operation. A reconnaissance precedes the mission by ten days. Troops arrive before dawn on the specified day. I participated in the event one November morning, donning rubber gloves and carrying plastic trash bags with 150 young soldiers under the command of British colonel Charlie Knaggs. One party worked the

Sunrise on the eastern wall of the Church of the Holy Trinity. October 12, 1989.

*Members of the
Multinational Force
and Observers
(MFO) delivering
lunches and picking
up trash at the
Basin of Elijah in
the biannual
"Sinai Sweep."
November 4, 1989.*

Stairway of Repentance and a second the camel path, while a third made
straight to the summit to pick its way down. The three detachments met
with bags filled at the Basin of Elijah precisely on schedule at 10:30 A.M.
Their job done, many of the men removed their shirts to sunbathe there
on the rocks. Women soldiers kept their tops on but sprawled out, too. A
few meters away at the Well of Our Lord Moses several Jabaliya shepherd
girls sat watching. More than a hundred goats bleated. A soldier's "boombox" played a Tracy Chapman song. Just outside the Chapel of Elijah a

group of French pilgrims sang hymns. At 11:00 the roar of helicopter blades overwhelmed this unlikely cacophony. A duststorm filled the basin as the red and white military aircraft set down. Before the blades stopped turning, soldiers reached the helicopter to remove a cargo of lunches boxed that morning in Sharm ash-Shaykh. Fijians, Finns, and Colombians consumed ham sandwiches, cookies, and Israeli tomato juice with their counterparts from Western Europe and North America. After lunch they loaded their trash bags on the helicopter. The aircraft lifted off in another dust event followed by the cheering of soldiers. As the engine noise subsided the French pilgrims resumed their hymns. Descending the Stairway of Repentance, the troops were drenched by a great thunderstorm.

Sinai is home to another international organization whose members frequent Jebel Musa and who have made friendships with St. Katherine's monks. It is the United Nations Truce Supervision Organization, which has the same mission today as when it was founded in 1956: "to show the flag," as one member phrased it, and to supervise the disengagement of potentially hostile Egyptian and Israeli forces. Eighteen nations are represented, with Russians and Americans making up most of UNTSO's fifty-five officers. As I dined in a mobile patrol building near the Gulf of Suez with an extraordinary trio of UNTSO men—a Russian from Kiev named Victor, a Jamaican named Oliver, and Rob Monroe, an American from Seattle—they spoke of one of their favorite activities on their bleak mission: to race up Jebel Musa. Rob had set a personal best and, until a Russian undercut it by six minutes, a record of running from the monastery's southeast corner to the summit in 39 minutes, 34 seconds. He had not seen the Russian run and said, "I just can't see how he did it," but nevertheless conceded to him.

The many unlikely and unwelcome things that happen on Mount Sinai have compelled Bedouins and monks to abandon their ritual activities on the mountain. The Jabaliya became living tourist attractions after 1967. The most sacred occasion of their calendar, the annual visitation to Jebel Musa on the Feast of the Sacrifice, fell a casualty to tourism in 1973. Tourists knew in advance when it would be held and flooded the summit to witness the traditional festival. They jostled and vied for positions to photograph and participate in the celebrations. Some photographed Jabaliya women. The offended Bedouins finally decided to halt the pilgrimage altogether. Now only a few Bedouin families commemorate the Feast of the Sacrifice on Jebel Musa, and then only by feasting quietly far from the crowded summit. Individuals sometimes leave herbs as blessings on the nearby holy spot of Matabb an-Naaga in a much scaled-back version of the herd blessings and other rituals the Jabaliya practiced there previously.

The Bedouins now keep the summit's mosque closed and locked because tourists were sleeping in it and using it as a toilet. The Jabaliya regret having to take this step, because their tradition insists that mosques and shrines should be open for prayer and visitation at all times. The Jabaliya proprietor of the summit's tea stall keeps the key to the mosque and to the cave beneath it, in which Moses is said to have passed his forty nights. He opens these shrines to the faithful.

I asked Father George whether he objected to tourists visiting the summit of Mount Sinai. "It's a free world," he replied, but grew more critical as he recalled specific incidents on the mountain. "It's like being in a zoo. They want to talk to me and take my photo. They ask why I have short hair. But we still go there to pray sometimes." Another monk told me he climbs to pray at the church only on the coldest days, when tourists are likely to be absent. He asks a Bedouin to guard the church against intruders as he prays inside. He was bitter about these secular visitors and the "ungodly" things they do: "The big thing is the sunrise. I mean how blasphemous can you be? You go up that mountain only to see the sunrise and to listen to your music? It's ridiculous. They leave their own bodily waste around, not to mention the contraceptives and empty syringes and all the rest of it. There's no control. There's no control."

Tourism has altered completely the unusual social and ritual balance maintained for centuries between the monks and the Jabaliya Bedouins. These communities have curtailed and eliminated their joint ritual activities. Their most important joint annual occasion, the Nabi Haruun festival, was halted after 1967 because like the Feast of the Sacrifice it became a tourist spectacle. One Bedouin told me that with tourists attending, it was so confused and crowded that "you could not tell where your place was, and with whom you were supposed to share your food. There were too many people for you to be hospitable." The monastery tried unsuccessfully to reinstitute this event in 1982.[13] The Jabaliya suggest that even the weather may have changed because of the deteriorating relations between Bedouins and monks which accompanied the rise of tourism.

"Do the monks have power over the weather?" I asked Mahmuud Mansuur.

"Long ago, if the rains were late, the monks would sit with the Bedouins and read and pray, and the clouds and rain would come. The monks were good in the past, not like those today."

I asked why they were better in the past.

"Because now all of them have become 'advanced' a bit, so there is disintegration."

"And has their progress changed the weather?" I asked.

"Well, the monks who prayed for rain are not these monks. The rain was much, much more abundant in the past. Maybe our Lord brings goodness from one direction and closes it off from another."

I asked when the weather changed.

"When the Israelis came. Before they came there were just the monks and the Bedouins."

"Then maybe the Israelis were responsible for the weather change."

"No, they opened the region, and built things, and brought tourists, and the Egyptians followed them. Then the change was unstoppable."

"Why did the weather change then?"

"Only God knows."

I found unexpected corroboration of a link between deteriorating spiritual conditions at the monastery and the decline of rainfall. "The Bedouins can name the monks in the old days who went up the mountain and prayed for rain, and came back down, and it rained," Father Makarios explained:

The Bedouins still encourage us. They still say, "Why don't you do something about this lack of rainfall? Why don't you climb the mountain like the monks used to do in the old days and say a few prayers? You know what the prayers are." All they know is that the monks would climb Mount Sinai from time to time and say some prayers up there, and it would rain afterwards. We did it. We had prayer services, the monastic rain dance as it were. The whole service involved it.

The priest added that although all the monks prayed, only one held the keys to the rain. "Not just any monk, one monk in particular. Someone worthy." No monk of this caliber resides in the monastery now. It is not difficult to understand why such spiritual talent would not be drawn to Mount Sinai today.

THE CURSE OF HOSPITALITY

Centuries have passed since St. Stephen examined the souls of pilgrims who toiled to reach the peak of Mount Sinai. Only learning about Stephen, I asked Father Makarios, "So you mean pilgrims had to justify themselves before they went on?" He snapped back, "Would you rather put up with that or the boomboxes and the drugs and the sex? Take your pick." The monks maintain two gates today, one closing vehicular access to the monastery between 10:00 P.M. and 6:00 A.M. and the other limiting tourist entry into the monastery to three hours in the morning on five days of the week. Neither of these gates affords the monks the solitude they treasure or controls foot traffic on Mount Sinai. Monks have no means of guiding visitors on the right path through sacred space as was their historical cus-

The visiting hours posted by the Monastery of St. Katherine distress many would-be visitors. Supplies from Cairo are being delivered at the western entrance. August 25, 1993.

tom. Today even the hermit Father Adrianos must contend with tourists, chasing away youngsters who bathe and cavort in the pool which is his water supply.

Having paid much money and traveled great distances in large buses on short time budgets to reach the site, tourists and their guides are not inclined to respect the strict visiting times the monastery imposes. Many tour itineraries do not consider the many feast days the monks observe. Tourists do not understand why the place should be closed to them for such an obscure reason as the Feast of St. Dimitrios, patron saint of faraway Salonika. The tourist lacks the traditional deference of the pilgrim, and disputes with monks occur frequently. "They all know when the monastery is closed," Father George said, "but they come anyway and insist on getting in after hours and on Friday and Sunday. They complain 'the monks won't let us in.' All the tour operators care about is profit." Many tourists perceive the monks as gruff and hostile, he said: "Tourists sometimes write to the monastery complaining about the monks' behavior, saying we are not friendly or helpful, or we are rude." Father George admitted that he and other monks sometimes lose their tempers with visitors, adding, "I go back to my cell feeling guilty about this. But we're only human. Tourists are not bad people. They want to see the monks and visit the church. They're demanding. They're right. If I were in their situation I would be the same."

The scale of modern tourism has caught the monks of St. Katherine off guard. Early pilgrims' and travelers' accounts depict a monk being assigned to each group, and sometimes to individuals, visiting the monastery. That special attention is impossible now. The herd or siege behavior that is the trademark of mass tourism everywhere is the prevailing pattern of visitation at the monastery today. Father Makarios recalled the change:

Before 1967, visitation to the monastery was not a problem, not a problem, that is, for the monks, because there wasn't any. After 1967, that's when we started seeing more and more people coming to visit the monastery. Until about the end of the '70s, early '80s, when it was just totally out of hand: no control, no way of adequately providing for these people when they came and went from the monastery.

The monks perceive modern tourism as incompatible with their spiritual mission. "There is no way any of us can avoid on a daily basis having contact with visitors, one way or the other, absolutely no way at all," Father Makarios complained. "It's unending. Really, it's awful. It places an unnecessary burden on the monks, because taking time to deal with hundreds of thousands of people on a weekly basis, on a daily basis, takes us away from the whole purpose of our being here, which has to do with spiritual things rather than being hospitable or, as I like to put it, baby-

Tourists and pilgrims visiting the Monastery of St. Katherine. August 25, 1993.

sitting and being a tour guide." The practical issues of handling large numbers of visitors bother Father George:

We really have only eight to ten monks at this monastery. We have many duties for so few people. It's too much. We take something from the place, but it's the daily routine that is killing us. People come and say "what dramatic mountains you have," but I've lost this sense. With such heavy visitation it is hard to pray. When I go to pray I'm almost exhausted. All the fathers are very tired. On Friday Brother George was weeping with fatigue. We are sometimes given a week's retreat to the Monastery of Forty Martyrs to meditate in silence. But after you have five, six, seven years here you need a clinic in Switzerland. We are going to lose our balance. We are going to lose our balance. You can't live the monastic life with these visitors. The monastery is already destroyed as an institution.

As keeper of the hostel Father George is the monk most in contact with visitors. I asked him when the high season was. "All seasons are high season," he said with dismay:

In summer it's Egyptians and Greeks, and beginning now [November] the international tourists. Egyptians can be very unreasonable. Once 150 members of the Police Academy with their major showed up at the hostel and took accommodation. Their leader asked me, "When do we eat?" I told him "whenever you want" before I realized they were demanding me to feed them. So I went to the archbishop. He said, "Go ahead and fix them something." So I made them rice. The Egyptians complained, "Is that all?" Just last Friday a major of the Tourist Police forced open the door of the monastery to let in 200 passengers from a Swan Hellenic ship that came to Sharm ash-Shaykh. His argument was the same as always. "They have come all this way, you're going to let them in."

I asked the obvious question. Why doesn't the monastery close its doors to all tourists? It is cynical and incorrect to suppose that money is the answer. There is no admission fee to the monastery, but when 30,000 visitors called in 1989 they spent 300,000 Egyptian pounds on books and postcards at the monastery bookshop, according to monks' estimates. But this revenue is not worth the real danger of the monastery's demise. The monks insist that their uninterrupted history of hospitality keeps them from turning away visitors. "Why would you have to treat tourists as you do pilgrims?" I asked. "The only reason we could not close the monastery is because of the tradition of hospitality here," Father Makarios explained. "You cannot turn these people away." I responded that there must be limits to that tradition, saying, "They are secular visitors—there is nothing religious about them." The monk said, "That does not matter. Where would the monastery be today if it had turned Muhammad away when he came?"

As I spoke with other monks I learned that they were not hospitable just out of kindness. There is a spiritual motivation for their graciousness. "Mount Sinai is sacred to many religions," Father George said:

Even when the Japanese come they respect it as a holy place. Also the Indians.
They have a strange feeling. It's another place, a sacred place. Everybody takes
with them something of the holiness of this place, even if they come as atheists. A
Russian was overcome with the place. He asked and was given permission to stay
a week, and left a changed man. Who knows what will happen even when
the most secular visitors come? You don't know what can happen to a soul,
even if it's an atheist soul. They must be allowed to enter. When we don't
allow people to enter, we worry.

Periodically something happens to reassure the monks that this premise for opening their doors is correct. Father Makarios told me more about the Russian. He was an officer in the United Nations Truce Supervision Organization who visited the monastery with his wife and daughter in the mid-1980s. His time with the monks at the Holy Mountain transformed him. He asked for and received the sacrament of baptism from the monks. "It was enough to bring tears to your eyes," Father Makarios said. "It is really the first time such people ever experience freedom, and this is what they do with it."

Instead of serving as cornerstone of the institution, hospitality may be leading toward its collapse. Tourism is weakening many pillars of the Monastery of St. Katherine. Historically some of the monks at Mount Sinai attained such spiritual perfection that they went out into the world to change and improve it. Not any more. I had this exchange with Father Makarios:

"Are there so few monks here now because of the pressure of tourism and the outside world coming in?"

"Those factors have a negative impact on the life of all the monks. If you polled the monks and asked them how they felt the first thing they would say is there is too much visitation. And this is a monastery that was developed in an area purposely—the site of St. Katherine's is where it is located geographically—because of its isolation, because it was so far, so hard for people to get to."

"So St. Katherine's has lost its qualities as a place of isolation and prayer and solitude?"

"Of course. Definitely. Without a doubt. But there are other areas around, as you well know because you visited them yourself, where there is this element. It still exists. The cave of John Klimakos, for example. The monastery of Wadi al-Arba'iin. The little mountain where the hermit lives by himself that you visited. These places still exist, so that you can go to places still in the Sinai and be by yourself completely, and never see another person. Father Adrianos is the only one doing this, and we cannot even afford to have him away from the monastery because we are so few people now inside the monastery. The requirements on our time are enormous, from outside pressures, not from inside. If we were speaking idealistically about all of our lives, we all wish to do what he is doing, we all desire that isolation and that peace and quiet that he has been able to achieve. The Monastery of St. Katherine obviously would be much better off with no visitors whatsoever. Tourism is a major disruption to our spiritual life here. The monastery is a difficult place these days to become spiritual, the way the fathers did in the past. We spend so much time doing other things that we ignore for the most part the reasons for our being here from the spiritual point of view. We lack the time to devote our lives to the spiritual aspect of monasticism—in this monastery. In other words we are living on our laurels here. My perception is, and this may not be proper even to suggest, but because of the conditions that exist around the monastery these days, it is difficult to produce another St. John. The monastery will *not* produce another St. John, or another Nilus, or another Gregory, because everything else is happening here: the modern situation, the transportation and society and the encroachments and all that. It would take a very special situation, a special gift on the part of an individual, to break through that mould."

"What is the main purpose of the monastery right now?"

"Right now the purpose is protection and preservation, nothing else. Spiritual life here these days is secondary to the rest of it."

"Is yours a precarious situation?"

"Extremely precarious, because there are so few people in the monastery. That many people are not going to stop a bureaucracy of a government as powerful as the Egyptian government."

THE EGYPTIAN LANDSCAPE

The government of Egypt does have special plans for the Jebel Musa area. The region fits into a development vision for the entire Sinai. The plan makes sense. Ninty-five percent of Egypt is desert, and Egyptians and their government have done little yet to redistribute populations and economic activities out of the overcrowded Nile Valley, where 96 percent of Egypt's 59 million people live.[14] Now the government is intent on creating what one development study describes as "a bold new style and pattern—'a new map of Egypt.' "[15] The face of Sinai is to be transformed.

One of the strongest but most understated motives for Egypt's development of the Sinai is strategic. The Israeli occupation was a lesson that land unattended and undeveloped is vulnerable. A foreign diplomat in Cairo told me that Egyptian development of Sinai is a deliberate strategy to preclude any reoccupation. The sheer weight of Egyptian infrastructure and population would become the main deterrent, parallel to the Israeli strategy of "creating facts on the ground" in the occupied West Bank. Egyptian planners hoped to see Sinai's population grow from 172,000 at the close of the 1980s to one million by the year 2000. Migration was expected to provide about 600,000 of that number, with natural increase supplying the balance.[16]

Sinai's most tangible assets to Egypt are economic, and the government recognizes tourism as the peninsula's greatest potential resource. Tourism is sacred to Egypt. By 1991 it had become the country's leading source of hard currency revenue. The government hopes that tourism will rebound from the present crisis of Islamic militancy as it did after previous incidents including the *Achille Lauro* hijacking in 1985. Tourism officials believe that even in the best years Egypt's tourist potential is far from realized. Egypt commands only 0.5 percent of the world's tourist market. Too many are budget travelers, and the government would like to increase the number of wealthy tourists, especially Americans. In 1984 a record 192,000 Americans visited Egypt, but due to instability in the region in 1988 only 117,000 Americans came.[17] The numbers declined further with the Gulf War and the Islamist campaign. Tourist authorities want the Sinai to be ready for record levels of upscale tourism when the political situation stabilizes. That requires construction of world-class facilities to accommodate visitors. At Na'ama Bay, close to southeastern Sinai's great dive sites, developers in the late 1980s built a string of five-star hotels that set the pace for growth. With hotels now three-deep on Na'ama Bay the tourism potential in that area may be saturated, and developers are building in new areas. Hotels are emerging all along the Gulf of Aqaba shoreline. In 1988 there were 1,080 beds in hotels between Sharm ash-Shaykh and Taba. By 1995 there were to be 11,384 beds, and the projected "final" capacity is 25,000 beds.[18]

The Jebel Musa area is the frontier for touristic development in the Sinai. Egyptian authorities recognized in the early 1980s that no more than 50,000 visitors might come to Mount Sinai each year. Not enough of them would stay overnight to spend money; instead they would visit for a few hours from good hotels in Cairo, Sharm ash-Shaykh, and Eilat. Those

who would stay the night—on the mountaintop, in a tented camp, or in one of the two-star hotels—would spend little money. Developers reasoned that by providing better accommodations they could transform Mount Sinai into a destination rather than detour, where people would spend longer time and more money. The potential could be at least doubled to 100,000 visitors annually.[19]

So it was that in 1984 President Hosni Mubarak presided at the ceremony opening the St. Catherine Tourist Village, a five-star, 164-bed hotel built by the Misr Sinai Tourist Company, a public corporation operated by the Egyptian Ministry of Tourism. It is a handsome facility of forty-one duplexes, each faced with native granite and separated from its neighbor. Even the local monks and Bedouins admit that it blends in rather well with the surrounding landscape. What they object to is its location. The St. Catherine Tourist Village sprawls across the Plain of ar-Raaha, the holy place where believers say the Israelites were camped when God gave the Law to Moses, a place where secular construction is taboo. A century ago Edward Wilson was viewing this place from Ras Safsaafa when he wrote, "The Sinai mountains and their wild surroundings seem to be just as the Book describes them—as the Great Architect constructed them. No change appears to have taken place since the followers of Moses made their departure for the Promised Land."[20] The scene was virtually the same in 1979.

In recognition of its sacred status Israeli administrators had prohibited any development on the Plain of ar-Raaha.[21] Unblemished since the time of the monastery's construction, the plain experienced its first alteration as soon as Egypt repossessed the Sinai in 1980. President Anwar el-Sadat chose it as the site of his Sinai rest house, one of a complex he maintained throughout Egypt. Critics complained that it was not built of native stone.[22] Egyptian anthropologist Iman El-Bastawisi condemned it boldly in 1982 when she wrote of future touristic development in the area: "My hope is that these projects will not destroy the beautiful and unique landscape of the holy mountains and valleys of St. Katherine, as in the case of Sadat's rest house in the holy Wadi El Raha. People come from all over the world to see by themselves the sandy Wadi through which Musa passed. No one has the right to disturb this place by building any kind of buildings for any reason."[23] When the monks learned where the St. Catherine Tourist Village would be built, they protested to local authorities and, through the monastery's lawyer, to the Misr Sinai Tourist Company and the Ministry of Tourism in Cairo. This was a holy and historic site, the monks insisted. A monk told me the reply was, "Who are you?" Dismayed by its construction and perceiving great irony in its location where the Israelites had erred, the monks dubbed the hotel "the Golden Calf."

The harshest critics of the new development may be the tourists it was

A view southward across the Plain of ar-Raaha to the northwest flank of Jebel Musa, with Ras Safsaafa just right of upper center and the Monastery of St. Katherine at left center. The stone bungalows are guest facilities of the St. Catherine Tourist Village. August 24, 1993.

An advertisement in Wadi ash-Shaykh listing the facilities of the nearby St. Catherine Tourist Village. August 28, 1993.

designed to serve. The St. Catherine Tourist Village has a reputation for inadequate and poorly planned facilities. An Egyptian tour guide told me that at least half of her clients who overnight there complain about the hotel, particularly that its heating and plumbing systems do not work properly. Sinks, for example, are installed so that water stands where they are joined to walls. She said it was not the five-star hotel it rated itself. In an article promoting tourism to the Sinai, *New York Times* journalist C. L. Sulzberger wrote about cold food and a freezing room at the hotel.[24] Development has nevertheless continued to consume the Plain of ar-Raaha. Amenities added to the St. Catherine Tourist Village include a helicopter pad, a restaurant, an administrative building, a power plant, and an enormous stone gateway. Contractors have built a web of asphalt roads radiating from a central roundabout at the plain's southern end to the hotel, the town of Katriin, and the Monastery of St. Katherine. An eight-meter-high stone tower with no apparent utility rises from the middle of the roundabout. A few meters north of it the al-Monaga Restaurant opened in 1991. The microwave transmission tower of Katriin's telephone exchange stands on the northern end of the plain. Nearby is the large chicken farm building, constructed in 1985 and abandoned three years later as unprofitable. Farther north on the plain is the dump for the entire Jebel Musa region. All trash remains unburied on the surface. The incinerator is broken. Jabaliya men say they have complained several times to the Katriin City

Council about the dump, especially because the next flash flood will certainly drop waste into their village of Abu Sayla below. They complained
in 1991 and 1993 when St. Catherine Tourist Village staff poisoned the
dump, apparently to eliminate stray dogs. The toxins killed scores of
pigeons and three camels, and Bedouins feared they would pass up the
food chain to foxes and other wild animals. Such protests have gone
unanswered.

The Jabaliya add several practical objections to their spiritual reasons for
resenting the new developments. They say Egyptian construction in Katriin is unsightly and helter-skelter. "Five years ago," a Jabaliya man told
me, "there were only Bedouin homes here, and they all blended in with
the mountains. The Egyptian buildings do not." We were sitting on Ras
Safsaafa enjoying a bird's-eye view of the settlements below. He pointed
out the place on the Plain of ar-Raaha where construction of the new
Daniella Hotel was about to begin. It was on a rise the Jabaliya call "the
Banana" because of its distinctive shape. They believe the site is occupied
by antiquities which date from "before the flood" and so, he said, it was
"a crime" to build here. He discussed a feature of Egyptian construction
that seemed foolhardy: most of the new Egyptian buildings were erected
well below the flash-flood line. From this perspective the floodplain of
Katriin's chief drainage is demarcated clearly by the height to which black
stones washed down from distant Jebel Katarina have been deposited. The

*A view westward
from Jebel ad-Dayr
of the hub of
development in the
Jebel Musa area. The
Wadi ash-Shaykh
road in the lower
right quadrant brings
in all outside traffic.
Clockwise, the other
roads lead out to the
Monastery of
St. Katherine, the
town of Katriin, the
Fayruuz Hotel, and
the St. Catherine
Tourist Village.
Nabi Haruun is just
below center.
September 6, 1989.*

rocks tell how high water will rise in a heavy rainfall event. "Look," the Bedouin said, "when the flash flood comes the mosque, the city council building, and most of the government housing will be destroyed." In the adjoining drainage of the Plain of ar-Raaha he pointed out another hazard: much of the complex of the St. Catherine Tourist Village lies in the drainage bed. The lowest and most vulnerable unit of the hotel complex is the diesel-powered electric generating plant. Rainfall in April 1989 had already flooded the power plant and several guest bungalows. My companion noted that on either side of the al-Monaga Restaurant are solid rock walls, about 1 meter high and angled upslope, which will funnel any surface water directly into the building. He predicted with undisguised glee that the next flash flood will devastate the restaurant and much of the Tourist Village complex. He pointed out that the newly paved road leading from the roundabout to the monastery blocked the mouth of Wadi ad-Dayr completely, and would also be destroyed by a large rainfall. He was angry about developers' attitudes toward seeking advice from local inhabitants. "The Egyptians never ask. They just know everything." He cited a Bedouin aphorism that would underscore the benefit of consulting local experts: "Ask a man of experience or ask the man with the certificate?"

The monks of St. Katherine felt that tourism already imposed a burden too great for them to bear. They and their Bedouin neighbors believed that tourist developments were desecrating sacred places. The situation was out of control. They were unprepared for a scheme that would dwarf their existing woes.

Eleven

◆

THE NEW
GOLDEN CALF

The aerial tramway would transport sightseers on two fifteen-passenger cars hung on 972-meter-long cables between the St. Catherine Tourist Village and Ras Safsaafa at the western end of Jebel Musa. A cafeteria and "casino"—in Egypt, an outdoor restaurant and lounge—would stand near the Ras Safsaafa terminal, offering superb views of the Plain of ar-Raaha below. An asphalt pathway about 2,000 meters long would be laid to connect Ras Safsaafa with the Basin of Elijah. Streetlights would illuminate this route throughout the night. I read these details from a cost-benefit study of the project loaned to me by a concerned official of the Egyptian Environmental Affairs Agency. The report projected that the tramway and its associated amenities would draw 565,000 visitors annually, an 1,100% increase over the record level of 50,000. Sixty percent of the visitors—339,000 people—would actually use the tramway. That would put an average of more than 900 people on the mountain each day of the year, or about four times the number there now on the busiest days. Since few tourists climb the mountain during cold months, on some days of the peak tourist season thousands of people would be on the mountain.

"DON'T TOUCH THAT MOUNTAIN"

I read the project details to the monks of St. Katherine on July 4, 1989. They exploded in anger and fear. Father Makarios was furious:

God Himself told Moses to tell the people not even to touch this mountain because they would die. And what, are they going to do this, here, now? The Bedouins

*themselves do not build on the mountain, any buildings whatsoever. They graze
their sheep on it and that is it. If God would strike anyone dead who even touched
that mountain, in terms of Moses' Ten Commandments experience, and the
Bedouins themselves have such a reverence for the mountain that they would not
even build a house on it, how can there be such total disregard for that sanctity?*

Later I asked him how he thought the project might affect the monastery.

*This is not Giza, this is not Alexandria, this is not Luxor. I don't know what
these people think this area of the world is, but it is not an area that is conducive to
that kind of tourist pressure. The impact of tourism, the secular attitude, the
mentality of the tourist is going to destroy this monastery today, and anything that
adds to that like this cable car and other things that do not relate at all to the
spiritual aspect of this monastery—how can that contribute to the welfare, our
welfare? It cannot. What is the government looking at? Are they looking at what
our attitude is here? This project will destroy the monastery within two years.*

As a controversy unfolded a foreign diplomat suggested to the monks
that they should not be upset about the project, because the cable car
would not even be visible from the monastery. One monk protested,
"Whether you can or cannot see that object from the monastery is not the
relevant question. The relevant question is what is going to be done to
that mountain and also the monasteries that are going to be in the way of
the path of that structure [the chapels on Safsaafa]—these things are part
of the reality of this institution—not to mention the spiritual damage that
is going to be done. How can they even consider such a thing?"

As we looked east from Ras Safsaafa, the Bedouin Mahmuud Mansuur
told me Jebel Musa was a "special place." It would be "forbidden" (*haraam*) in a religious sense to build a cable car on it, he said. When I told
another Jabaliya man that the project would include street lighting on the
mountain he shook his head and also uttered "*haraam!*" The prospect of
crowds in the gentle basins of Safsaafa saddened Mahmuud Mansuur. This
was a nice area, he said, because so few people come here. The land existed
because of the goodness of God; it was "a blessing" (*sibha*). "We say there
are two bad things you can do in life," he explained. "One is to be athe-
istic. The other is to mistreat the Earth (*faasid fil-ard*)." To build a cable
car on Mount Sinai would be to mistreat the Earth. He seemed resigned
to what might happen, saying later, "People come here to climb the
mountain, to get the reward and satisfaction of doing that. If you put in a
lift you destroy that effect. And it is bad for nature. People come here to
enjoy nature, not amenities. But look, everything changes. Twenty or

thirty years ago it was just us and the monastery here." I suggested that because of the work opportunities it would create, the project should please the Jabaliya. Mahmuud shook his head. Ominously, he supposed that harm would come to those who harmed the mountain: "What goes around, comes around," he cited a Jabaliya saying.

Curious about the views of the people the cable car would be built to serve, I interviewed about forty tourists and pilgrims on the trails of Jebel Musa. One fatigued woman from New Zealand who was climbing up the mountain admitted she would rather ride. All other opinions were negative. Her male companion snapped, "It's a terrible idea." She proposed that people could be given the option of hiking or taking the cable car. He challenged her sarcastically, "I think you should have a revolving restaurant on top, and helicopter rides." Australian Ian White called the cable car "a ghastly idea." Another Australian man who had spent the night on the summit described the plan as "bloody awful." A Belgian woman walking up the mountain commented on the tramway, "No, no. It's true? No, it can't be. Don't do it. Because it will destroy the natural scene." I asked if it would not be convenient to have more rapid access to the summit. "No, I think if they want to see the top, they have to do something for it. If you want to take a picture and there's a cable car . . ." Her friend broke in, "But after a few years, it will be normal. I don't like it. It's touristy. I think if you want to go to the top and you want to see a special view, you have to do something special for it. Of course you will say at first how you are tired and you are hungry but we know why we did it. I think a lot of views in Europe are destroyed just because of things like that." A man from Toronto called it "ridiculous . . . I think it just would ruin the whole atmosphere of the place, for a cable car to whisk you up there." His wife added, "You've got to work for it. That's the point of it." I asked the man if the cable car were available whether he would ride it or walk up. "It depends on when my bus is leaving," he replied. His wife commented, "I wouldn't like the choice. I like to be forced to walk. If the cable car goes in and I come back I'll say I remember the good old days." I proposed that those who did not know the difference might not care. She remarked, "It will change the whole experience." Her husband had the last word: "That's progress for you." An Englishman said, "I think it would ruin it. If you're too lazy to walk it, don't come. I think it defeats the object. I think it makes it a lot better if you sweat it and really work hard to get up to the top and it makes the whole thing worthwhile. If you just took the cable car up there you ain't sweated it, you ain't done nothin' to get to the top. I think it's better this way. With the cable car you get to the top, lay there and look at the scenery and it don't seem so nice. When you've worked for it, you see the scenery very early in the morning." His Australian companion remarked, "It'd be too commercialized. I think the majority of people come up here to walk it."

Modern pilgrims opposed the cable car project. When I asked Gordon Brubacher, who for two years had been leading groups of pilgrims to the mountain for the organization Biblical Resources, whether his clients would use the tramway, he replied: "They would have no interest in it. The tradition is the mystique of climbing the mountain. There would be a lot of objection about it, and outrage. You've got to climb it. I know that leaves out the old people. Nonetheless. Let's put in helicopter rides while we're at it! I think their objection would be a combination of spiritual, aesthetic, and ascetic. You should have to walk it or it's no damn good." Two of his clients on this special tour to several possible Mount Sinais in Egypt and Israel were a man from New York and his Australian wife who made their home in Geneva, Switzerland. Aged in their fifties, they were struggling to keep up with their group on the steep camel path up Jebel Musa as I spoke with them. She ventured, "I think it would be dreadful. It would just detract so much from what it's all about. It would spoil the countryside as well. I think it should take a lot of effort to get there." She paused and concluded, "They will come for the cable car. I'm glad I've come here now." Her husband added, "It's this old and this sacred. I don't think it should be commercialized. You'd have all these German and Dutch and Scandinavian tour buses piling in at the bottom for a cable car ride and a restaurant on the top and then it'd lose a lot of its religious significance. You'd have hordes of people up there, like going to a ski resort: you know it's like going to the top of peaks in Switzerland. Then it attracts all the vendors and the tacky little shops, and the hot dog stands. I'm not sure that's what this place is all about, for me anyway." He felt Jebel Musa was already very close to civilization in comparison with Har Karkom and other possible Mount Sinais he had visited on this tour. I introduced the cable car idea to an Australian man, an Australian woman, and a South African woman who had just climbed the mountain. They objected: it would destroy the purpose of pilgrimage, and would turn the site into a "Disneyland."

"IT'S JUST A MOUNTAIN"

Few Muslim Egyptians climb Jebel Musa and I did not sample their opinions on the mountain. Those I did question in Cairo and in Upper Egypt had contrasting views. "This is desecration of a sacred site, sacred even to Muslims," said Sayyed Gamei, an employee of the Egyptian Wildlife Ser-

vice. "From a touristic standpoint I think it's marvelous," said Iman El-
Bastawisi, the Egyptian anthropologist who had opposed construction on
the Plain of ar-Raaha. Gamaal Sharif, a Muslim peasant from Luxor, recalling that God had spoken with Moses on the mountain, predicted about
the cable car that "God will not permit it." I asked Mohamed Ibrahim, an
official of the Egyptian Environmental Affairs Agency (EEAA), whether
Muslims would object to the cable car because of Jebel Musa's religious
significance. "No. Jebel Musa is important to Muslims because Moses was
there. It is different than for Christians." The opinion that mattered most
in shaping the mountain's future was that of Ibrahim's boss, EEAA Vice-
Chairman Dr. Muhammadi 'Iyd. The project would afford visitors "a fantastic panorama," he said, adding "that is a mountain, and you can climb
it. Or instead of climbing it you can establish this project to make facilities
for pilgrims."

Arguments in favor of the cable car development are persuasive. Have
Egyptians not been criticized for neglecting the development potential of
their deserts? Here was an opportunity for progress outside the Nile Valley.
And what rights have outsiders to question how Egyptians use their resources? The Swiss have their cable cars, the Americans their Disneylands.
A veteran British archaeologist in Egypt who followed the cable car controversy saw the Egyptian resolve to develop Mount Sinai as consistent
with a long-standing cultural pattern. "Egyptians have no sense of propor-
tion," he said. "They can't leave anything alone." He added, "Of course,
no one else can either." He compared the proposed development to the
electrification of the Karnak Temple in Luxor for the nightly sound and
light show. Previously, he said, the visitor could wander through the
temple in the evening and enjoy a rare charm that evoked David Roberts'
romantic lithographs. Now there was only commercial pomp.

Egyptians wince at such criticisms. Having achieved freedom from colonial domination, Egypt is experiencing a new and humiliating dependence upon the United States and other outside powers for economic
survival. Many Egyptians resent what they perceive as the patronizing
expertise of foreigners. U.S. Fish and Wildlife official David Ferguson, not
writing specifically of the Egyptian case but describing the problem as it
exists there, observed that "Regardless of intent to further scientific and
technological progress in the host country, foreign projects often get sub-
verted by local feelings of nationalism that claim there is a conspiracy to
assure the country's dependence on foreign sources for progress."[1] That
position may explain rejection of foreign studies which have recommended conservation in the Sinai. In the 1980s the American consulting
firm Dames and Moore undertook for the U.S. Agency for International

Development an expensive master development plan for the Sinai Peninsula. Among its recommendations was that the Jebel Musa area become an "intensive management area" to protect "the natural landscape, the monastery, the wildlife and the plants in the surrounding mountains and wadis."[2] I asked Egypt's leading conservationist Dr. Mohamed Kassas about the status of the massive Dames and Moore report. "It is dead—dead!"

The economic rationale for the cable car project seemed sound. The St. Catherine Tourist Village had been built to draw tourists who would spend money, but the results were disappointing; in the late 1980s tourism at Jebel Musa was still far short of its perceived potential. The Ministry of Housing, Utilities and New Communities conducted a study which concluded that most visitors were young people on a budget. An older, wealthier clientele should be targeted. The study found that those wealthier tourists who did come did not stay long enough because there was little for them to do or spend money on after they visited the mountain and monastery. The hotel's billiard tables and library had not proved to be sufficient attractions. Those who were not fit enough to climb the mountain might not come at all.[3]

They would come for the cable car on Mount Sinai. The concept was not new. The Dames and Moore study had recommended that for the area to become a greater tourist magnet an aerial tramway should be built, but not on Jebel Musa: "Additional developments could increase the attractiveness of the St. Catherine area. For example, a telepherique on Mt. St. Catherine would make the spectacular mountain views available to tourists who are physically incapable of a strenuous climb, while not disturbing the religious significance and historical character of Mount Sinai."[4] The report also cautioned that "Much of the appeal of Sinai's Central Mountains area, in the vicinity of St. Catherine's Monastery, is dependent on the uncluttered desert and mountain vistas. Careless development caused by short-term expediency could ruin the area's long-term appeal."[5] Egypt's Ministry of Housing, Utilities and New Communities concluded that only on Mount Sinai itself would the cable car be attractive financially. The Ministry's cost-benefit analysis estimated construction costs at 5,545,000 Egyptian pounds (2,132,700 U.S. dollars) for the government's subcontractor Moharram Bakoum and 3,030,000 Swiss francs (1,870,370 U.S. dollars) for the foreign contractor to be identified by tender bids. Annual revenue from the dollars charged to foreigners and Egyptian pounds to Egyptians for the round-trip cable car ride would equal 812,000 Egyptian pounds (312,317 U.S. dollars). The study did not consider the expenses and revenues of the infrastructure that would be added to accommodate the anticipated explosion in visitor numbers. It did specify that a new two-star hotel would be built "between Nabi Haruun and the foot of Jebel

Safsaafa," an area currently occupied by the large Jabaliya cemetery of Shaykh an-Nahama.

In the 1980s the Egyptian government passed legislation protecting natural environments and requiring environmental impact assessments before development of specified areas. In 1983 Egypt's Parliament and Senate ratified and President Hosni Mubarak signed the Egyptian Conservation Law (Law 102) establishing the legal framework for the creation, protection, and management of natural protectorates within Egypt. Its preamble declared that "It is forbidden to commit actions which will lead to the destruction or deterioration of the natural environment or harm the biota, or which will detract from the esthetic (beauty) standards within protected areas."[6] It tentatively designated areas including St. Katherine which should be protected, specifying that future Prime Ministerial Decrees appended to Law 102 would formally establish the reserves. The Council of Ministers on authority of Egyptian Prime Minister Dr. Atef Sidki issued the relevant decree, No. 613 of 1988, establishing the St. Katherine region as a protected area.[7] Citing text from Law 102, this decree charged that "It is forbidden to erect buildings and establishments, pave roads, drive vehicles, or undertake any agricultural, industrial or commercial activities in the protected area except with the permission of the concerned Administrative Body and restrictions specified by the Prime Ministerial decree." Decree 613 prescribed the same penalties for violations established in Law 102: a fine of not less than five hundred or more than five thousand Egyptian pounds and/or imprisonment for no more than one year.[8] Decree 613 also cited a maze of less prominent Egyptian conservation laws which would apply to the St. Catherine Natural Protectorate.

If the cable car were to be built it would have to receive the approval of the Egyptian Environmental Affairs Agency, the "concerned Administrative Body" cited in Law 102. Then the Minister of Cabinet Affairs for the Environment and finally Egyptian President Hosni Mubarak would have to approve the project.

An EEAA official addressed a report to EEAA Vice-Chairman Dr. Muhammadi 'Iyd in which he raised numerous objections to the project. He cited the environmental costs: impacts on plants and animals, trash, waste disposal, sewage, and especially limitations of water. Where would the water for all the new hotels come from? The existing wells of Abu Zaytuuna and Haruun were already taxed. He complained to me that Dr. 'Iyd had never visited the area, and being trained as a chemist and geologist saw no obstacles to development because the area is "just the monastery and Mount Moses." "Dr. 'Iyd sees prospects of fantastic sightseeing from Jebel Safsaafa, but did not put in his mind about the deterioration of natural resources which will occur in that area," the official said. "He didn't know about any flora or fauna which will occur on top of the mountain. He can push his point only on geological structures: that is a mountain." There was no integrated, comprehensive plan for the developments that would follow the construction of the tramway, the official complained. He recounted the costs of building and the estimated 800,000 pounds per year the project would generate and asked rhetorically, "So where are the benefits?" I asked him whether in the end the project would be implemented. "Yes," he said grimly, "it's a hopeless case. It's a hopeless case."

Egypt's leading environmentalist and titular director of the EEAA, Dr. Mohamed Kassas of Cairo University's Faculty of Science, decided to weigh in against the project in the summer of 1989. He expressed his environmental objections directly to Minister Hasibullah Kafrawi of the Ministry of Housing, Utilities and New Communities, the agency which would oversee the cable car project. Kassas traveled to the site with Dr. Ibrahim Moharram, an official of the subcontracting company Moharram Bakoum which would build the tramway. Mamduuh 'Abdulla, manager of the St. Catherine Tourist Village, joined the two men in a stroll across the Plain of ar-Raaha. They came to the spot that would be the cable car's lower terminus. Kassas told me about their conversation there. "I told them, instead of talking about the telepherique, you should look at options, for example improving existing paths, using hot air balloons, or picking another site. If you decide the telepherique is the best choice, don't put it at Safsaafa. That is the worst possible option because it would destroy the grandeur of the mountain." He recommended an alternative route from Wadi al-Arba'iin to a point near the Basin of Elijah, arguing that this would not create an eyesore. As an alternative to the asphalt walkway that would be built across the Safsaafa portion of Jebel Musa, the footpath from Wadi al-Arba'iin to the summit could be improved, he suggested. Kassas told the men that the "carrying capacity" of Jebel Musa's summit is very limited, that the site was already polluted, and that toilet and other facilities would have to be provided there. He warned them that Jebel Musa was a habitat for several rare and endemic plant species. He reminded them that the site was sacred not only to Christians but to Muslims, because the Prophet Muhammad had visited it. Hotel manager Mamduuh 'Abdulla was very enthusiastic about the cable car project until hearing Kassas' sobering assessment that the cable car might actually diminish the hotel's business. "Look," Kassas told him, "now tourists stay two nights, visit the monastery, and climb the mountain. If you speed their ascent they'll stay one or even two nights less." Kassas spoke privately with several Egyptian and foreign tourists at Jebel Musa and found a uniform split in opinion about the cable car project: Egyptians favored it and foreigners opposed it. Kassas was worried about how Christians in Egypt and around the world would react to the proposed project. "The Pope would object," he was certain. He condemned the lack of any comprehensive plan—in fact of any plan at all—for development in the St. Katherine region.

The Ministry of Housing, Utilities and New Communities and its contractor Moharram Bakoum studied these concerns and responded with a compromise. Three provisions would make the project acceptable from an environmental standpoint: no pavement would be employed on the walkway between Ras Safsaafa and the Basin of Elijah; no explosives would be used in the construction; and the new facilities would employ solar energy to the maximum extent possible. With these assurances, on July 20, 1989, Dr. 'Iyd gave the approval of the Egyptian Environmental Affairs Agency to the project and forwarded his recommendation to Dr. Atef Ebeid, Minister of Cabinet Affairs for the Environment. On September 20, 1989, Ebeid reportedly approved the plan. Neither approval was made public but news spread quickly among Egypt's environmentalists. Kassas described his reaction to the approvals given the project: "I was astounded."

A DIPLOMATIC SOLUTION?

Opponents of the cable car scheme had few cards to play. Some hoped for divine intervention. Archbishop Damianos said that St. Katherine herself would prevent the abomination from happening.[9] "The hand of God is protecting the monastery," Father Makarios told me, "but humans are able to help God." He believed the monks themselves would have to act. "If the monastery is interested in preserving itself," he said, "it must deal with this problem one way or the other, for the good or for the bad of the situation." But by taking a stand the monastery would invite risks, he said: "It is a delicate situation. You don't know who to pull into this situation. The more we show our weakness, the worse it gets for us." A member of a group of international religious scholars conferring with the monks proposed that the shaykhs of al-Azhar might be persuaded to issue a decree or *fatwa* invoking the sanctity of Mount Sinai that would promote public reaction against the project among Egyptian Muslims. Another responded that this act might provoke a political backlash because of broad government sentiment against Islamic fundamentalism in the country. The monks and visiting scholars discussed the possibility of involving the Ministry of

Antiquities, but concluded that this might invite more government intervention and erode the monastery's sovereignty over its remaining possessions even further.

The monks were also not in a position to act decisively against the cable
car plan because their presence in Egypt depends upon the good will of
Egyptian authorities. All but two of the monks are Greek nationals and
none holds Egyptian citizenship. Each is required to renew his residency
work visa every ten months. "We are all guests of the Egyptian government," a monk told me. "There is genuine fear among many of us in the
monastery that we will be expelled. They could throw a few of us out.
Our visas will simply not be renewed. The monastery would be turned
into a museum. Its antiquities would be removed to other museums. We
argue that the greatest appeal of the monastery is the fact that it has been
continuously occupied since its founding. This place would not be the
place it is without the monks, so how can they change that issue? It seems
like they are looking for excuses for something to happen that would give
them an excuse to do something negative to the monastery." The monks
worried that with the growing Islamist movement in Egypt there might be
a move to occupy the monastery because of the mosque within it. "Built
to save the monastery, it may in the end destroy it," one monk described
the mosque's ironic status.

There had already been incidents that the monks perceived as provoca-
tive. In October 1989 a lieutenant colonel of the Egyptian army and seven
attendants burst their way into the basilica after hours and demanded to
have a guided tour of the sanctuary. An angry monk ordered them to leave
the place. The officer grabbed the monk by the collar, shook him, and
shouted, "Who are you to tell me what to do?" The monk shouted back
the same words. The incident ended for the moment when the officer and
his retinue withdrew, but within days security officials confiscated the
monk's passport and questioned him at length about his origins, travels,
and recent activities before finally returning it. State security plainclothes-
men, some posing as tour guides, maintain constant vigil at the Monastery
of St. Katherine. "There are people here whose only business is to watch
what we do," a monk cautioned me. "We are under a microscope here."
I had traveled with him by car to at-Tur that morning. "Our trip today has
been reported in Cairo already," he said.

The monks would have to depend upon others' opposition to the cable
car project. They reasoned that diplomacy might be the answer. On July 4,
1989, the day I informed him of the project, Father Makarios initiated a
diplomatic offensive that might succeed if the environmental opposition
were to fail. He stayed up through the night writing letters describing the
cable car project and appealing for intervention. A courier posted them

the next morning to U.S. Senator Larry Pressler, who had visited the monastery; U.S. Ambassador to Egypt Frank Wisner; the Duke and Duchess of Kent, known as friends of the monastery; John Taulorites, Dean of the Greek Orthodox community in New York; Lydia Carras, co-director of the Alexander S. Onassis Public Benefit Foundation; Jack Covey of the U.S. State Department in Washington, who had been stationed in the U.S. Embassy in Cairo and had become a friend of the monastery; Paul Sarbanes, Maryland senator and member of the Orthodox faith; and Wisconsin Congressman Les Aspin, who at the time was Chairman of the House Armed Services Committee and who would become a U.S. Defense Secretary for the Clinton administration. The monk's letter raised two objections to the funicular: it would be built on the sacred God-Walking Mountain and it would harm a delicate environment. He asked his correspondents to do whatever they could to prevent the project's implementation. Aspin, who had visited the monastery in 1988, replied on August 29, 1989. Describing the cable car problem as a matter of sensitivity that would require deft handling, he wrote that it would be counterproductive and damaging to the monastery's interests if he "barged in" on his own, and recommended that all initiatives be directed by Ambassador Wisner. Father Makarios' similar appeal to the U.S. Ambassador to the United Nations Thomas Pickering also failed to produce intervention; he replied he could "not do much" about the situation. A mood of pessimism settled over the monastery. "I don't think we have a chance," one monk said. "I think it's a *fait accompli*."

The monks now pinned their hopes on the American ambassador to Egypt. On September 12 Ambassador Frank Wisner's son Oliver visited the monastery and received a note written by Father Makarios to his father, asking for his assistance. Noting that Ambassador Wisner would fly with President Mubarak later in the month to Washington, pursuing a hope for regional dialogue that had been growing with Secretary of State James Baker's Middle East peace plan, Father Makarios told me hopefully, "Wisner could take it right to the top." At the same time the monks worried that the American diplomatic community might not take the monastery's side, because the U.S. Agency for International Development was undertaking a feasibility study on future touristic development in the Sinai. They feared the cable car project was the type of development the study would recommend. The monks said that AID had funded Egyptian development of the "Bath of Moses" near at-Tur, which leveled gardens belonging to the Monastery of St. Katherine. They believed Ambassador Wisner was ultimately responsible for approving all AID projects in Egypt, and wondered what he would do, knowing what he knew. On September 23 Ambassador Wisner informed the monastery that he hated the idea of the cable car but felt "totally helpless" to do anything about it. He insisted it was a matter for the Swiss to resolve, since the cost-benefit analysis named a Swiss consultant and specified an investment in Swiss francs, but he would look further into the matter.

Plans for the cable car project were being conducted so discreetly that concerned parties had difficulty verifying their existence. At the end of July the monks had asked Barbara Brillioth, wife of Swedish Ambassador to Egypt Lars-Olaf Brillioth and a member of the Orthodox faith, to learn what she could in Cairo's diplomatic community about the status of the cable car project. She met with Minister of Cabinet Affairs for the Environment Dr. Atef Ebeid on November 10. Ebeid admitted to her that the cable car plan existed and defended it vigorously. "Yes, yes," the project was planned, he said, "but it is only to help the aged and disabled to get up on Moses Mountain." Mrs. Brillioth expressed her concern for the mountain's environment and rare herbs. The minister assured her that the builders would be so careful "they wouldn't harm anything." "At that point I had in any case obtained my goal: I knew I was not fighting windmills," she told the monks. "I had the fact from the horse's mouth. Until now we couldn't well take any action before one was sure the idea of the project really exists—it was no fantasy."

With their hopes for diplomatic progress against the cable car dimmed, opponents of the project had few remaining options. In early November Archbishop Damianos appeared bewildered and desperate about the impending implementation of the scheme. The monks now favored a new approach. The issue should be made public in the Egyptian and foreign media, particularly in countries such as the United States, United Kingdom, France, and Japan which have large commercial and touristic interests in Egypt. Surely the world public would condemn the project and force its cancellation. The details of the project should be released to the Associated Press, *The Times* of London, and *Time* Magazine. I prepared to make the details of the cost-benefit study public in an interview in Cairo on November 30. Late in the evening on November 29 I received a phone call from Father Makarios. Do not speak with anyone, he insisted: there has been a breakthrough.

I met with a jubilant Father Makarios the next day. He explained that on November 13 Barbara Brillioth had met with Suzanne Mubarak and informed Egypt's first lady of the project. "Here was finally a person who reacted against the idea," she wrote him of Mrs. Mubarak. "She said it was horrible and should be stopped 'quickly before it was too late.' One can only hope she'll discuss it with her husband. I'm aware this may be in vain. Prayer may move mountains." Within a week Mrs. Brillioth contacted the monks again to inform them of an apparent shift in Egyptian commitment to the project. She had learned from a diplomat friend who attended a party in Sweden in celebration of Naguib Mahfouz' Nobel Prize for Literature that an Egyptian diplomat at the event snapped in response to an inquiry about the cable car, "The Americans have stopped this project and don't even mention it again!"

Father Makarios carried with him what the monks viewed as the surest indication the cable car was dead. It was a letter from Ambassador Wisner reading: "The Egyptian government in the person of the Minister of Reconstruction Hasibullah Kafrawi is unaware of any plans for the construction of an aerial tramway in the Jebel Musa area. My colleagues from Switzerland are unaware of commercial interests from their country in such an endeavor. I count on you to inform the Archbishop of my inquiries and make sure that those you have contacted are similarly brought up to date." On November 14, four days after Dr. Atef Ebeid told Mrs. Brillioth the project would not harm anything, Ambassador Wisner had also phoned Ebeid. "No such project exists," he told Wisner. "If it did it would be rejected on account of the sensitivities involved." One of Wisner's officials told Father Makarios that there had indeed been a plan to build the cable car but it had been "foiled." The priest was delighted. By pushing his inquiries the American ambassador had apparently given Egyptian officials "cold feet" about the project. "They can't possibly do it now," Father Makarios speculated, "otherwise they'll be caught lying. Wisner knows what he's doing. The man is a saint." But he worried that when the ambassador retired from his post in six months the project would be resurrected. "I am ready to pop the champagne corks," he said, "but I am not celebrating."

"TELL EVERYONE YOU KNOW"

Any celebration would have been premature. On January 10, 1990, Father Makarios contacted me in Columbia, Missouri, to tell me that "The Cable Car situation has once again reared its ugly head." A relative of an official in the Ministry of Housing, Utilities and New Communities had just informed the monks that the cable car project would be implemented within the year. Reporters began investigating the story and found it still unfolding. On January 21, 1990, the London *Observer* ran an article by Shyam Bhatia:

One of the world's most sacred sites for Christians and Muslims is under threat from a secret Egyptian government plan to boost tourism. . . . Details, which include building an alpine-type cable car four kilometers long in an area of outstanding natural beauty, have been leaked to the Greek Orthodox monks at the monastery, foreign diplomats in Cairo and conservationists. Despite their protests, Housing Minister Hasballah Kafrawy has refused to back down and ordered a new feasibility study for the project. His argument that improved access to the area will generate more hard currency by bringing in more tourists has won qualified cabinet approval. The Egyptian authorities will not discuss the issue, but a Swiss engineer commissioned by the Ministry of Tourism has confirmed the project is about to be put out to tender. Paul Glassey, a project engineer [of the Swiss firm Sionin Valais], said: "I have made a plan for a cable car to go to the tourist village from a nearby mountain. As the plan stands, the car will not be visible from the monastery, but the monastery will be visible from the top of the car. International tenders should be going out soon." [10]

On February 16, 1990, I received a phone call from Anthony Rudkin, the monastery's book purchaser in London. He had met with the monks on February 4, when they asked him to pass a message on to me: despite all promises to the contrary, work on the cable car would soon be under-way. A few days later I received a letter Father Makarios had written at the monastery on February 7: "A nightmare project planned by the Misr Sinai Tourist Company in Abbasia is to be constructed in the Zeituna area, 6 kilos north of the monastery near two already existing tourist camps. [Delfa Land] is boldly advertised on a huge billboard: 500 bungalows; two hotels capacity 400 beds; shopping center; hospital; school. And we were worried about a silly cable car! This area is about to be hacked and gouged into rubble." The priest appealed for help, asking me to go ahead with the interview I had aborted in November. He turned even to tourists at the monastery, instructing them: "Go home and tell everyone you know about it. It should not happen. It will happen unless you take the message back and cause worldwide pressure."

I related the details of the project's cost-benefit analysis to essayist Lance Morrow of *Time* Magazine. He relayed the information to the magazine's Cairo bureau for verification. On March 4 bureau researchers spoke with officials from the Ministry of Housing, Utilities and New Communities who affirmed that a plan had been in the works to install a cable car from the Tourist Village up the mountain, but that due to opposition from en-vironmentalists and the monastery the project had been "shelved." The officials also stated that they were concerned that a tripling of hotel accom-modations would harm the environment. On March 7 Morrow received a cable from the magazine's Cairo bureau. Reporters had contacted an engineer consulting for the project. He confirmed that the plan would be implemented, adding that it had been conceived in 1988 and approved in

February 1990 by Mohammad al-Kotari of the Authority of Sinai Development. Construction was to cost about 1.5 million dollars and would take no more than one year, although no starting date had been announced and the investment group had not been chosen. "The cable car will save tourists from going up 150 steps to the top of Mt. Safsaafa," al-Kotari said, "and then they will have only 80 steps to walk to the top of Jebel Musa." He denied that there were any plans to build a restaurant and casino on the mountain. He confirmed Misr Sinai's plans to build Delfa Land but refused further comment on the subject. Inquiries by Associated Press reporter Mimi Mann revealed that a new power plant would be built north of Sharm ash-Shaykh to provide power to the cable car, and that the government of Kuwait had pledged two million dollars to install a water pipeline from the Nile Valley to the developments at Jebel Musa.[11] Misr Sinai's chairman Abdel Azim A. Bassiouni, convinced that the uproar about the cable car would fade away just as the controversy about his hotel project on the Plain of ar-Raaha had, told her, "You can propose a road and people will object, but in the end everybody will use it."[12] He perceived no contradiction between the sanctity and development of Mount Sinai, telling Mann, "We Egyptians are very religious. It's unrealistic to think that technology has no place in sacred places. We cannot bring it here if it would destroy the sanctity or the solitude."[13] This was also the reasoning behind a pre-1967 Egyptian proposal to run a cable car from the foot of Jerusalem's Mount of Olives to the Temple Mount, and to build a restaurant for tourists on the Temple Mount.[14]

On March 7 Morrow told me he had written a "nuclear" editorial against the project, which because of its significance would replace an editorial which had been scheduled for the next issue of *Time*.

Elvis Presley's Graceland in Memphis has become a shrine, a sort of tackiness made sacred. Mount Sinai, where God came to earth, is about to become a sacred place made tacky. . . . "Whosoever toucheth the mount shall surely be put to death," said the Lord. For over 3,000 years, the occupiers of the Sinai Peninsula, from Justinian to the Prophet Muhammed to Abdel Nasser and Golda Meir, took the site under their protection. Mount Sinai is enclosed in a convective dignity that is primitive and powerful. The mountain seems to gather thousands of years into a prismatic clarity. The Egyptian Ministry of Housing and Reconstruction, however, is not awed. . . . Somewhere this bulldozing desanctification for money must end. If the attraction of Mount Sinai is its holy wilderness, and even the physical effort required to approach it, tourist development threatens to destroy the uniqueness and transcendence of the pilgrimage. The Egyptians are often haphazard about protecting their dead treasures. Now they seem ready to sacrifice a powerful, living

mountain that is in their care. Perhaps they will make the cable cars in the
shape of calves and gild them. The golden calves can slide up and down
Mount Sinai and show God who won.[15]

"Lance Morrow's article hit like a nuclear explosion," Father Makarios wrote to me from the monastery on March 22. "Everybody I've talked to is pleased." On March 29 Morrow called me to report that the magazine's editor had received about fifty letters divided almost evenly between those approving and condemning the development. Several letters of indignation came from people who had been to the site and for whom news of the development "brought tears to their eyes." The thesis of most of the approving letters was, "What is wrong with doing that in a country that is short on cash?" *Time* published three letters to the editor in its April 9 issue. James Atwater of Rochester wrote, "Morrow's essay reminded me of a Mark Twain anecdote. A Boston businessman known for his ruthlessness disclosed to Twain his ambition to travel to Mount Sinai, climb to the top and there read the Ten Commandments aloud. Twain replied, 'I have a better idea. You could stay home in Boston and keep them.' "[16]

Another letter to *Time's* editor was one of several official assurances that the cable car project would not be implemented. Egyptian Minister of Tourism Fouad Sultan wrote:

The Egyptian Ministry of Tourism appreciates the concerns expressed in the article
about the sanctity of Mount Sinai, believed to be threatened by plans for
development. We would like to make it clear that the ministry is committed to and
concerned with the preservation of Mount Sinai and considers the monastery and
the mountain a sacred site for the three great monotheisms (Judaism, Christianity
and Islam). Mount Sinai is an important part of the world's cultural patrimony.
The projects mentioned by Morrow are merely developers' ideas that have not
gained and will not receive approval from the ministry, as they do not conform to
the ministry's development objectives. Such projects would not pass the requisite
review process, which includes a comprehensive environmental-impact assessment.[17]

Following the publication of this letter Morrow received a letter from Egyptian Ambassador to the United States El Sayed Abdel Raouf El Reedy, dated May 8, reaffirming that the cable car project was not an issue. He wrote that Morrow's concerns were legitimate, but that fortunately they were untrue. He explained that the preservation of Egypt's heritage was a national duty and an international obligation which exceeded the country's need for hard currency. It would be a short-sighted policy to create massive development projects which would attract more tourists, but in the long run endanger important sites, the ambassador concluded.

Governor of South Sinai Nureddin Afify told a reporter, "Mount Sinai was declared a conservation area because it is a holy area. We do not want to change the environment of this holy place." He said of the cable car, "Forget it. Nothing like this will happen." [18]

Despite these assurances the apparent conclusion of the cable car controversy was once again premature. On May 7 an article published in the semiofficial Egyptian daily newspaper *Al-Ahram* argued that the project was environmentally sound because all construction would be hidden from view in a deep gully on the mountain. In early June the Ministry of Housing, Utilities and New Communities applied to the office of President Hosni Mubarak for the unquestionable authorization to go ahead with construction of the cable car project. President Mubarak rejected the application. [19] On June 9, 1990, he relayed a personal promise to the monks of St. Katherine that a cable car would not be built on Mount Sinai. On June 12 the monks sent me a message: they were "100 percent sure" that the project was "dead and buried."

◆

CONCLUSION

I returned to Mount Sinai last week. I spent the first afternoon walking across the Plain of ar-Raaha, taking stock of the growth that has occurred there since my last visit in 1989. There are twenty new bungalows in the St. Catherine Tourist Village complex, and the desk manager told me several increments of thirty bungalows each would be added in the future. A cinema is under construction there. More television channels reach Katriin, thanks to two satellite dishes and an antenna installed in a fenced enclosure on the western end of the plain. I spent the night in a two-year-old, one-hundred-bed hotel called Daniella Village. It reportedly sits directly atop a Neolithic period settlement on the banana-shaped rise at the southern end of the plain. Across the road the Ministry of Housing, Utilities and New Communities is building a three-story residential complex.

I spent the next night under the willow tree by the Chapel of the Holy Girdle of the Virgin Mary, the Bedouins' Kaniisat as-Safsaafa. This is just below where the upper terminus of the cable car would have stood. A very different type of construction is underway there now. Mahmuud Mansuur and several Jabaliya companions working for the monastery are rehabilitating this ancient Byzantine site. Around the perimeter of a garden where hermits grew almonds, apricots, and grapes—Mahmuud had found remains of the fruits and nuts—the Bedouins have built a sturdy rock wall, topped by a wire to keep out goats and ibex. Inside, the men are raising young almonds, apricots, and grapevines. They have planted several of the willows which are the namesake of this part of Jebel Musa. They have dug a new well below the old one, reaching sweet water at a depth of 4 meters.

They have built a new hermitage next to the church. Father Michael is moving in. It will be more difficult now to erect a restaurant and nightspot at this place.

After the workmen left to spend the night at the nearby Chapel of St. Panteleimon, where they are also restoring and planting, I was alone in the silence. That morning Father Nicholas had encouraged me to "try to find one quiet place there, where you can listen with your heart. There is a special quality there on the mountain, and that is why here the God came. And many saintly men lived there. They had no barrier between them and the God." As we sat by the willow in the afternoon Mahmuud had also reflected on what he called "the stillness" (*al-huduu*). "I think God is always present in the stillness, in the desert. That is why Moses saw God here." He told me again about the monastery, the night, and the mountain. "That is all that was here. The view of the mountain and the monastery by night was beautiful. At the sight you would say, 'God is present here.'" In the moonlight I paced the garden enclosure, listening. I could not hear the generators and cars on the plain below. I heard bats, and in the morning the clucking of chukar partridges. The boundary around the sacred space of the Mountain of God is holding, for now.

On the eve of the twenty-first century, people still believe in Mount Sinai. I passed my third night in Wadi al-Arba'iin behind the Rock of Moses (Hajar Musa), where tradition says the prophet brought water forth from the rock. In the morning I watched Bedouin women in reverence to Moses touching and kissing the rock, and placing fragrant sprigs of *hinayda* and *ja'ada* in the fissures representing the twelve tribes of Israel. I spent that night in the monastery hostel, which was crowded with Greek pilgrims who had come to attend an all-night mass celebrating the Feast of the Virgin. After dawn a long line of Ethiopian pilgrims filed their way down the Stairway of Repentance. Arriving to find the monastery closed, they prayed outside its walls.

Despite the troubles in Egypt there were surprising numbers of tourists at the mountain. In the basilica Father Nicholas spoke to each group at length and answered individual questions with patience. When the monastery closed at noon I asked what he thought about tourism here. I heard what I expected. "Suffering purifies our souls. And so we have the tourism here. Maybe it is here to bring us to repentance." But I also heard something new. "Maybe tourism is protecting the monastery somehow." He used the analogy of another historical irony to suggest that as long as tourists visit the monastery, the authorities will not transform it into something else: the Monastery of St. Katherine and others located in lands controlled by Muslims were spared the ravages of the Christian Iconoclasm.

In fact tourism at Jebel Musa today does create unexpected benefits, even enhancing some aspects of the natural environment. In principle the Bedouins would not hunt ibex and birds on sacred Jebel Musa; in practice they perhaps do not because the ever-present tourists might report gunfire. The Jabaliya admire the consequences of their not hunting here. Ibex pass regularly, unafraid, between Jebel Musa and adjacent Jebel ad-Dayr. An old solitary male often approaches the perimeter of the new garden at Kaniisat as-Safsaafa, and last week he breached a gap in the fencing and ate several grapevines to the nub. The usually skittish chukar displays little fear of walkers on Jebel Musa. Rosefinches, bulbuls, and grackles may be seen at close quarters on Jebel Musa and at the monastery. This would be impossible in the backcountry. Scrub warblers take handouts from Bedouin proprietors of rest stops on the mountain. There is a healthy population of hyrax in Wadi Shu'ayb on Jebel Musa's northern flank. The animals water at the spring which the Jabaliya say the herd of Jethro drank from.

In 1991 Dr. Muhammadi 'Iyd lost his job as Vice-Chairman of the Egyptian Environmental Affairs Agency. His successor, Dr. Salah Hafez, and the organization's Director of Natural Protectorates, Dr. Essam al-Badry, seem sincerely committed to the preservation of Egypt's dwindling wilderness jewels. With the Ras Mohammed National Park already established at Sinai's southern tip, the agency's top priority is now the St. Catherine Natural Protectorate. This week the agency convened a conference in nearby Sharm ash-Shaykh to formulate a strategy for the management of wildlife at St. Katherine and in other protected areas. Archbishop Damianos, notified of but not invited officially to the conference, strolled boldly into the opening session a few moments after it began. Dr. al-Badry kindly invited him to the podium. The archbishop pleaded for mercy for Mount Sinai. "The first environmentalists were the monks," he said, "by their spiritual modality, seeking and keeping the quietness that is there."

Dr. al-Badry told me there was now a need to identify places within the larger St. Catherine Natural Protectorate that were in most urgent need of protection. I suggested that his agency begin with Jebel Musa, and also impose an immediate moratorium on building on the adjacent Plain of ar-Raaha. I had heard that such a moratorium had already been imposed. Regrettably it had not, al-Badry said. I had heard that the Monastery of St. Katherine and Jebel Musa had been nominated as a UNESCO World Heritage Site, to join the list of such places as the Pyramids of Giza and the antiquities of Luxor, a status which would do much to help protect the area. This turned out to be untrue. For complex political reasons both in Egypt and at UNESCO's Paris office there would be no nomination for St. Katherine.

This week I heard many rumors, wishes, and prophecies about Mount

Sinai. The monastery's book purchaser told me he had been informed that all existing hotels and other buildings on the sacred Plain of ar-Raaha would be dismantled and relocated. Archbishop Damianos told me that fundamental changes in the spirit of the human race might bring an end to tourism at the God-Trodden Mountain. "Now tourism is the modality," he said. "Maybe it will fade. Now is the modality of the exterior. Maybe later they will feel the need to turn inside, to the heart. This may solve the problem. Maybe they will not travel just to see and see and see and see." The hermit Father Adrianos received a more vivid revelation that "soon" there would be no more tourists at the Monastery of St. Katherine. Associated ominously with that prophecy was another that all of the Sinai monks would be martyred. Father Nicholas shared a brighter prediction that "as the world deteriorates, the Monastery of St. Katherine will play some kind of very important role. There is a prophecy that there will be a great miracle at the monastery, and it will become a great spiritual center again."

It may be that in the end only Providence will protect Mount Sinai and other of the world's wild and sacred places. However, the recent history of this mountain suggests that faith alone, or passivity, or indifference, might have allowed a very different landscape to emerge. The threat is still there. In the town of Katriin today I met with the same official of the Egyptian Environmental Affairs Agency who told me four years ago about the cable car scheme. He had just come from a meeting with Mr. Rifa'it Helmy, Chief of the Katriin City Council, who told him, "I want to have a cable car built on Mount Sinai."

"This mountain has a special grace," Archbishop Damianos said. God warned Moses and his people to "mark out the limits of the mountain and declare it sacred." We have inherited that admonition.

MONASTERY OF ST. KATHERINE
September 9, 1993

NOTES

◆

EPIGRAPH

Stewart 1897, vol. 4:560.

INTRODUCTION

1. Dewing 1940:355.
2. Lane 1988:11.

1. "A TERRIBLE AND WASTE-HOWLING WILDERNESS"

1. Dobson 1925:18.
2. Danin 1978:84.
3. Perevolotsky 1981:335.
4. Bellorini and Hoade 1948:108.
5. Except for this quote from Kitto 1872:190, all Bible translations in the book are from Henry Wansbrough, ed., *New Jerusalem Bible*, 1985.
6. Dobson 1925:35.
7. Perevolotsky 1981:333.
8. Ibid.
9. Where possible common English names, Jabaliya Bedouin Arabic names, and Latin scientific names of plants and animals are listed in sequence. Not all species have common names. For plants, common names are from Bedevian 1936 and Latin names from staff at the Cairo Herbarium and Täckholm 1974; for birds, common and Latin names are from Goodman et al. 1989; for mammals, common and

Latin names are from Osborn and Helmy 1980; for reptiles, common and Latin names are from Marx 1968 and Werner 1973.

10. Ritter 1866:173.

11. Hoskins 1909:1016.

12. Petrie 1906:231.

13. Perevolotsky 1981:333.

14. Shefik 1926:11,23.

15. Dames and Moore 1985, vol. 7:EN-3.

16. Bellorini and Hoade 1948:108.

17. Hoskins 1909:1016.

18. Robertson 1936:17.

19. In Eckenstein 1921:6; in Hoskins 1912:253.

20. Har-El 1983:410.

21. Perevolotsky 1981:348.

22. Michael Jones, personal communication.

23. Dick Doughty, personal communication.

24. Danin 1978:84; El-Hadidi n.d.:4; Egyptian Environmental Affairs Agency 1992:10.

25. Danin 1983:71.

26. Perevolotsky et al. 1989:153.

27. Danin 1978:83.

28. Zahran and Willis 1992:xiii.

29. Danin 1983:11.

30. Shmida 1977:41.

31. Ibid.: 39.

32. Danin 1983:71,104.

33. Ibid.: 71.

34. M. N. El-Hadidi, personal communication.

35. Danin 1983:26.

36. Perevolotsky et al. 1989:162.

37. Perevolotsky and Finkelstein 1985:35,34.

38. Rabinowitz 1982:87.

39. Perevolotsky 1981:338.

40. Jarvis 1932:240.

41. Rabinowitz 1982:87.

42. Inbar 1979:20.

43. Heinzel et al. 1984:302.

44. Ibid.: 217.

45. Eckenstein 1921:158.

46. Ibid.

47. Egyptian Environmental Affairs Agency 1992:11.

48. Ibid.

49. In Werner 1982:154.

50. Baha El-Din 1991.

51. Haim and Tchernov 1974:203.

52. Ibid.: 207,210,217,219; Osborn and Helmy 1980:155,191,286,181,321.
53. Baharav 1981.
54. Eckenstein 1921:112.
55. See also Elliot 1987:163–167.
56. Levi 1977:158.
57. Ibid.: 156.
58. Tischendorf 1851:85.
59. Kazantzakis 1975:116.
60. Ilany 1990:20.
61. Dani Barkai, personal communication.
62. Palmer 1872:45.
63. Eckenstein 1921:113.
64. Mendelssohn 1983:279.
65. Osborn and Helmy 1980:368.
66. Alon 1978:249.
67. Gasperetti et al. 1985:400.
68. Ibid.: 402.
69. Osborn and Helmy 1980:370; Ferguson 1981:464.
70. Ferguson 1981:464.
71. Ibid.: 460,461.
72. Ibid.:460.
73. Gasperetti et al. 1985:414.
74. Hobbs 1989:88,98,141.
75. Musil 1928:122.
76. Dobson 1925:30.
77. Ilany 1990:17.
78. Prescott 1958:72.
79. Ibid.: 99

2. "YOU WILL WORSHIP GOD ON THIS MOUNTAIN"

1. Baly 1976:22.
2. Newman 1962:30.
3. In Anati 1985:57.
4. E.g., Aharoni 1962:178.
5. Reik 1959:34,82.
6. Orlinsky 1974:29.
7. See also Romans 7:1–25; Galatians 3:1–4:31; Wansbrough 1985:1877, footnote d; Lockyer 1961:71.
8. Silver 1982:165.
9. Clements 1972:19; Lockyer 1961:70; Shefik 1926:4; Clifford 1972: 115,119; Anati 1986:180; Stewart 1897, vol. 4:550.
10. Pococke 1743:145.
11. Dobson 1925:29; Pococke 1743:145.

12. Lockyer 1961:70.

13. Dobson 1925:29; Shefik 1926:3.

14. Clifford 1972:108.

15. The quail may provide a clue about the timing of the Exodus. Orlinsky supports the conclusion that abundant quail indicate a fall migration (Orlinsky 1974:23). However, quail are more abundant on the Red Sea coast in the spring than in the fall (Goodman et al. 1989:215). Gaubert (1969:91) and Robertson (1936:57) propose that the presence of quail indicates that the Exodus took place in early spring.

16. Day 1938:115.

17. Meinertzhagen 1954:569; Parmelee 1959:76.

18. Personal communication.

19. Bodenheimer 1947:4.

20. Tischendorf 1851:87,88.

21. Prescott 1958:74.

22. Dobson 1925:27.

23. Beitzel 1985:85.

24. Orlinsky 1974:15; Aharoni 1962:178; Eller 1858:54; Rothenberg 1979:29.

25. Gaubert 1969:52; Finkelstein 1988:46; Lepsius 1852.

26. Personal communication.

27. E.g., Palmer 1871:177; Robinson 1841.

28. E.g., Tullock 1981:76; Aharoni 1962:179.

29. E.g., Jarvis 1932.

30. E.g., Beit-Arieh 1988:36; Hull 1899:47.

31. E.g., Haynes 1896.

32. Finkelstein 1988:46.

33. Dobson 1925:19.

34. Baly 1976:36; Bimson 1981:32; Gaubert 1969.

35. Baly 1976:36; Aharoni 1962:178; Arden 1976:9.

36. Jarvis 1931:189; Orlinsky 1974:24.

37. Gaubert 1969; Prentice 1912:1282.

38. Jarvis 1931:189; Gaubert 1969; Robertson 1936; Har-El 1983:357.

39. Tullock 1981:77; Sarna 1986; Gaubert 1969; Orlinsky 1974:24; Prentice 1912:1282.

40. Tullock 1981:77; Sarna 1986; Har-El 1983:357; Gaubert 1969; Robertson 1936.

41. Jarvis 1931:189; Williams 1927:713.

42. Jarvis 1931:189; Har-El 1983:357; Hull 1899:42; Gaubert 1969; Arden 1976:8.

43. Daiches 1975:84; Jarvis 1931:189; Beitzel 1985:90; Arden 1976:9; Gaubert 1969; Robertson 1936; Phythian-Adams 1930; Williams 1990.

44. Frank 1990:10; Gaubert 1969.

45. Jarvis 1931:189; Gaubert 1969; Frank 1990:10.

46. Har-El 1983:357; Williams 1927:713; Lepsius 1852:369; Gaubert 1969; Beitzel 1985; Robertson 1936.

47. Tullock 1981:77; Arden 1976:8.

48. Frank 1990:10; Lepsius 1852:357; Arden 1976:8; Williams 1927:713; Beitzel 1985; Gaubert 1969.

49. Robertson 1936; Tullock 1981:77; Sarna 1986.

50. Tullock 1981:77; Prentice 1912:1282; Robertson 1936; Frank 1990:10.

51. Whiston 1987:71.

52. Sotah 5a, in Robertson 1936:100.

53. Chapter 13, in Robertson 1936:100.

54. See Galey 1985:49; Anati 1986:161; Cassuto 1951:225; Levenson 1985: 21; Rothenberg 1961:126; Kleiman 1990:13.

55. See Sarna 1986:203,205.

56. Clements 1972:117.

57. Eckenstein 1921:74.

58. Anati 1985:47.

59. Stiebing 1985.

60. Beke 1878:415; Lucas 1938:71,79.

61. In Har-El 1983:283.

62. Williams 1990.

63. Robertson 1936:87,98.

64. Eckenstein 1921:81; see also Musil 1926:298.

65. Jarvis 1931.

66. Har-El 1983:421.

67. Beitzel 1985.

68. See, for example, Hoskins 1912:195, and a similar sketch of criteria by Palmer 1872:166.

69. In Lepsius 1852:422.

70. Lepsius 1852:350.

71. Har-El 1983:178,209; Ritter 1866:208.

72. In Lepsius 1852:359.

73. Beitzel 1985:92.

74. In Ritter 1866:221.

75. Hull 1899:30.

76. Ibid.: 43.

77. Robinson 1841:141.

78. Hull 1899:46.

79. Ritter 1866:216,218.

80. Hull 1899:54.

81. Ibid.

82. Ibid.: 47.

83. Velikovsky 1950:134,36,381; Velikovsky 1952:29,53; Anati 1985:60.

84. Peacock 1992.

85. Shewell-Cooper 1977:133; Hareuveni 1984:39.

86. Hareuveni 1984:39.

87. Wilford 1992:A-9.

88. Jarvis 1931:200.

89. Orlinsky 1974:23.

90. Jarvis 1931:197.

91. In Ritter 1866:187.

92. Har-El 1983:421.

93. Robertson 1936:99.

94. In Ritter 1866:208.

95. Har-El 1983:425.

96. Anati 1985:245.

97. Phythian-Adams 1930:206.

98. Musil 1926:215.

99. In Daiches 1975:115.

3. THE HEAVENLY CITIZENSHIP

1. Ali 1983:9.

2. Brueggemann 1977:40.

3. Wansbrough 1985:1499.

4. See Vivian 1993:18–26.

5. Rothenberg 1979:202.

6. Chitty 1966:2.

7. Schaff and Wace 1953:209.

8. Chitty 1966:2; Florovsky 1987:118.

9. Chitty 1966:13.

10. Schaff and Wace 1953:209.

11. Ibid.: 210.

12. Chitty 1966:4.

13. Sumption 1975:16.

14. Chitty 1966:5.

15. Florovsky 1987:106.

16. Hirschfield 1992:69.

17. Schaff and Wace 1953:208.

18. Hirschfield 1992:11,18; Hussey 1986:337.

19. Hirschfield 1992:33,72,235.

20. Eckenstein 1921:114; Chitty 1966:38.

21. In Skrobucha 1966:20.

22. Florovsky 1987:104.

23. Ware 1963:45,48.

24. Hussey 1986:348.

25. Hirschfield 1992:1.

26. Ibid.

27. For the life of St. Mary the Egyptian, see also Elliot 1987:68.

28. Sumption 1975:129.

29. Dobson 1925:48; Weitzmann 1985:11.

30. Har-El 1983:393.

31. Skrobucha 1966:19; Eckenstein 1921:95.

32. Har-El 1983:243.

33. See Stanley 1911:340; Har-El 1983:244; Palmer 1872:137.

34. Chitty 1966:168; Skrobucha 1966:27; Eckenstein 1921:98; Har-El 1983: 379; Weitzmann 1985:11.

35. McClure and Feltoe 1920:1.

36. Eckenstein 1921:119.

37. Lepsius 1852:429.

38. Skrobucha 1966:35.

39. Burckhardt 1822:609.

40. Har-El 1983:381.

41. Silver 1982:159.

42. Dobson 1925:48.

43. Chitty 1966:168.

44. Eckenstein 1921:99.

45. Papaioannou 1980:7; Skrobucha 1966:19.

46. Dobson 1925:48.

47. McClure and Feltoe 1920:8.

48. Ibid.: 5.

49. Perevolotsky 1981:353.

50. Stewart 1897, vol. 4:587.

51. Perevolotsky and Finkelstein 1985:41.

52. In Skrobucha 1966:31.

53. Hirschfield 1992:244.

54. Skrobucha 1966:43; Moore 1991:203; Louth 1991:2.

4. THE MONASTERY OF SAINT KATHERINE

1. Eckenstein 1921:122.

2. Ibid.

3. Stanley 1911:342; Browning 1974:57.

4. Fortescue 1907:354.

5. In Lepsius 1852:437.

6. Galey 1985:plate 4.

7. Ibid.

8. Williams 1927:725.

9. Har-El 1983:397; Hoskins 1909:1025; Eckenstein 1921:177; Dobson 1925:58.

10. Wilson 1888:333.

11. Papaioannou 1980:8.

12. Skrobucha 1966:109.

13. Liphschitz and Waisel 1976:40.

14. Dewing 1940:357.

15. Eckenstein 1921:124.

16. Forsyth 1985:51.

17. Bellorini and Hoade 1948:62.

18. Pococke 1743:151.

19. Shefik 1926:24.

20. Lewis 1971:2.

21. Bellorini and Hoade 1948:58,113.

22. Tischendorf 1851:106; Burckhardt 1822:550.

23. Burckhardt 1822:550.

24. Tischendorf 1851:97.

25. De Laborde 1836:232.

26. Burckhardt 1822:550.

27. Hirschfield 1992:215.

28. Burckhardt 1822:570.

29. This account of the life of St. Katherine is from Papadopulos and Lizardos 1985:4–8.

30. Skrobucha 1966:74.

31. Papadopulos and Lizardos 1985:23.

32. In Eckenstein 1921:152.

33. Skrobucha 1966:74.

34. Eckenstein 1921:140.

35. Ibid.: 141.

36. Skrobucha 1966:68.

37. Ibid.; Eckenstein 1921:142.

38. Eckenstein 1921:142.

39. Papadopulos and Lizardos 1985:25; Weitzmann 1985:88.

40. Galey 1985:14.

41. Fortescue 1907:31.

42. Eckenstein 1921:166,168.

43. Ibid.:146.

44. Manafis 1990:380.

45. Eckenstein 1921:148.

46. Frangouli 1985:15; Weitzmann 1985:14.

47. Skrobucha 1966:74.

48. Weitzmann 1985:96.

49. Eckenstein 1921:175.

50. Golding 1937:129; Skrobucha 1966:91.

51. Manafis 1990:380.

52. Eckenstein 1921:143–144,162,173.

53. Shefik 1926:26; Merton 1924:890.

54. Burckhardt 1822:556.

55. Jarvis 1932:229; Shefik 1926:14.

56. Shefik 1926:22.

57. Ritter 1866:239.

58. Stewart 1897, vol. 4:576.

59. Rabinowitz 1983:10; Robinson 1841:167; Meistermann 1909:156,161.

60. Skrobucha 1966:104.

61. De Laborde 1836:281.

62. Monks of St. Katherine, personal communication; Rabino 1938:31; Dobson 1925:49.

63. Sources for Table 1: Skrobucha 1966:93; Har-El 1983:183,391; Michael Jones, personal communication; Dobson 1925:52,62; Eckenstein 1921:176,184; Tischendorf 1851:97; Robinson 1841:142; Wilson 1888:333; Hoskins 1912:211; Prentice 1912:145; Shefik 1926:15; Father Good Angel, personal communication; Williams 1927:727; Rothenberg 1961:146; Marx 1977:33; Rabinowitz 1983:10; Bellorini and Hoade 1948:113; Bassili 1964:66.

64. Michael Jones, personal communication.

65. Bellorini and Hoade 1948:58.

66. Abu-Lughod 1971:39.

67. Prescott 1958:80.

68. Eckenstein 1921:177.

69. Burckhardt 1822:550.

70. Prentice 1912:1245.

71. Kazantzakis 1975:111.

72. Eckenstein 1921:111.

73. Hirschfield 1992:214.

74. Ritter 1866:243.

75. Dobson 1925:77.

76. Ritter 1866:243.

77. Dobson 1925:97.

78. Williams 1927:733.

79. In Robinson 1841:193.

80. Bellorini and Hoade 1948:113.

81. Pococke 1743:151.

82. Florovsky 1987:241,247.

83. Moore 1991:92.

84. Florovsky 1987:121; Moore 1991:xxv.

85. Skrobucha 1966:43,47.

5. THE CHRISTIAN LANDSCAPE

1. Hoskins 1912:200.

2. Robinson 1841:129.

3. McClure and Feltoe 1920:1.

4. Palmer 1871:148.

5. Stanley 1860:74–75.

6. Robinson 1841:131.

7. Dewing 1940:355.

8. Hoskins 1909:1023.

9. Palmer 1871:148.

10. Wilson 1888:331.

11. Dobson 1925:34.

12. McClure and Feltoe 1920:1–11.

13. Pococke 1743:147; McClure and Feltoe 1920:11.

14. Pococke 1743:145; Robinson 1841:168; Tischendorf 1851:109; Ritter 1866:230; Stephens 1991:194.

15. See McClure and Feltoe 1920:9; Dobson 1925:128; Eckenstein 1921:172.

16. Bellorini and Hoade 1948:120.

17. McClure and Feltoe 1920:9; Eckenstein 1921:172; Robinson 1841:168; Stephens 1991:194; Stewart 1897, vol. 4:596.

18. Tischendorf 1851:109.

19. Bellorini and Hoade 1948:64.

20. Dobson 1925:36.

21. Jarvis 1932:240.

22. Robinson 1841:134.

23. McClure and Feltoe 1920:8.

24. Forsyth 1985:51. The ancient tradition of removing one's shoes before entering this chapel is still observed by the few visitors the monastery permits into it today. There is a legend that once a year on March 23 sunlight pierces through a cleft on nearby Jebel ad-Dayr to shine through the chapel's window and illuminate its sacred floor. This scene is depicted on some nineteenth-century travelers' lithographs. See Dobson 1925:131; Kamil 1991:50.

25. Forsyth 1985:51.

26. Official monastery literature makes the same claim: "It is the only bush of its kind in the entire Sinai Peninsula, and every attempt to transplant a branch of it to another place has been unsuccessful" (Papaioannou 1980:24).

27. The literature contains many mistaken identifications of the burning bush in the monastery: as *Colutea istria* (Har-El 1983:405); *Fraxinella* (Peacock 1992; Skrobucha 1966:100); *Zizyphus spina christi, Acacia* species, *Loranthus acaciae,* and *Cassia obovata* (Daiches 1975:46); and flowering shoots of acacia mistletoe (Skrobucha 1966:100). In 1926 Shefik noted and photographed another bush growing just above the burning bush, which monks said was of the same kind as the one from which Moses and Jethro took their staffs (Shefik 1926:17). In the 1920s monks also told pilgrims this was the original stock of Aaron's rod (Dobson 1925: 54). This was probably a specimen of *Colutea istria*, an Irano-Turanian relict known to Dr. Nabil El-Hadidi of the Cairo University Herbarium as "Moses' stick." He saw and photographed the shrub in 1955, but does not know what happened to it after that.

28. Govinda 1966:200.

29. Ibid.:199.

30. Lane 1988:15.

31. Wilson 1888:331.

32. Govinda 1966:197,198,215.

33. Lev 1989:99.

34. See Skrobucha 1966:55.

35. Bellorini and Hoade 1948:118.

36. Eckenstein 1921:151.

37. Dobson 1925:49.

38. Skrobucha 1966:27.

39. Ibid.:14.

40. Tuan 1978:89,98.

41. Eckenstein 1921:128.

42. Ibid.

43. De Laborde 1836:243.

44. Bellorini and Hoade 1948:61.

45. Skrobucha 1966:80.

46. Stewart 1897, vol. 4:553.

47. Wilson 1888:131.

48. De Laborde 1836:240.

49. Golding 1937:136.

50. Palmer 1872:77; Dobson 1925:125; Tischendorf 1851:99.

51. Stephens 1991:194. This water source is an intermittent spring, and was dry through most of the 1980s and early 1990s. Hirschfield reports that on this path there are twelve east-facing semicircular prayer niches, each marking a spot associated with the giving of the Law (Hirschfield 1992:223). Somewhere on this route a monk showed Kazantzakis the spot where he said the Israelites took their stand against the Amalekites (Kazantzakis 1975:123). I could not verify either tradition.

52. Bellorini and Hoade 1948:142.

53. Ibid.:60.

54. Ibid.:142.

55. In Skrobucha 1966:78.

56. Pococke 1743:144.

57. Eckenstein 1921:98; Skrobucha 1966:19.

58. Papaioannou 1980:38.

59. Stewart 1897, vol. 4:597.

60. Williams 1927:735.

61. Har-El 1983:415; Hoskins 1912:241.

62. Father Makarios, personal communication.

63. Pococke 1743:145.

64. Prentice 1912:237.

65. E.g., Stewart 1897, vol. 4:550; Pococke 1743:143; de Laborde 1836:249; Palmer 1871:118; Ritter 1866:184.

66. In Ritter 1866:206.

67. Dobson 1925:126.

68. Ritter 1866:206.

69. Stewart 1897, vol. 4:556.

70. Hull 1899:45.

71. Skrobucha 1966:117; Bellorini and Hoade 1948:61; Pococke 1743:146.

72. Elliott 1987:119; Stewart 1897, vol. 4:555.

73. Meistermann 1909:145.

74. McClure and Feltoe 1920:7.

75. Perevolotsky and Finkelstein 1985:36.

76. Pococke 1743:146.

77. Ibid.:145,154.

78. Father Michael, personal communication; Wilson 1880:115.

79. Wilson 1888:340.

80. Robinson 1841:158.

81. Palmer 1871:108.

82. Sutton 1913:92.

83. Wilson 1880:111; Pococke 1743:146.

84. Hoskins 1909:1027.

85. Hull 1885:52.

86. In de Laborde 1836:243.

87. De Laborde 1836:242.

88. Wilson 1880:113.

89. In Ritter 1866:212.

90. Ibid.:213.

91. Robinson 1841:154.

92. Hazleton 1980:27.

93. McClure and Feltoe 1920:4.

94. Papaioannou 1980:40.

95. Skrobucha 1966:80.

96. Pococke 1743:146.

97. Stewart 1897, vol. 4:559.

98. Bellorini and Hoade 1948:114.

99. Ibid.:118.

100. Pococke 1743:146–147.

101. Palmer 1871:111.

102. Palmer 1872:77.

103. Tischendorf 1851:102.

104. McClure and Feltoe 1920:4.

105. Bellorini and Hoade 1948:114,61.

106. Tischendorf 1851:101.

107. Shefik 1926:21.

108. Pococke 1743:147.

109. Robinson 1841:167; Stephens 1991:195.

110. Dobson 1925:130.

111. Palmer 1871:120.

112. Archbishop Damianos, personal communication.

113. Pococke 1743:143; Ritter 1866:227.

114. In Ritter 1866:230.

115. Palmer 1871:119.

116. Pococke 1743:143.

117. Ibid.:149; Eckenstein 1921:95,99.

118. Bellorini and Hoade 1948:119.

119. Fourteenth-century Tuscan pilgrims attributed construction of this garden and its water sources to Moses (Ibid.).

120. Ibid.: 196.
121. Prescott 1958: 89.
122. Bellorini and Hoade 1948: 197.
123. Prescott 1958: 89.
124. Skrobucha 1966: 74.
125. Papaioannou 1980: 38; Rabinowitz 1982: 13.
126. Dobson 1925: 124; see also Hoskins 1912: 208.
127. Michael Jones, personal communication.
128. Skrobucha 1966: 73.
129. Bernbaum 1990: 229.
130. In Skrobucha 1966: 82.
131. Engel 1992: 87.
132. Palmer 1871: 148.
133. Hoskins 1909: 1022.
134. Tischendorf 1851: 101.
135. Whiston 1987: 71.
136. Palmer 1872: 128.
137. Tischendorf 1851: 109.
138. Bagnold 1935: 60.
139. Ritter 1866: 203.
140. Palmer 1871: 105.
141. Lane 1988: 25.
142. Palmer 1871: 55,85.
143. Ibid.: 76.
144. Jarvis 1932: 235.

6. THE PEOPLE OF THE MOUNTAIN

1. Marx 1977: 351; Eckenstein 1921: 188.
2. El-Bastawisi 1982: 29; Murray 1950: 259.
3. Rabinowitz 1982: 9.
4. Papaioannou 1980: 44.
5. Glassner 1974: 34; Rabinowitz 1983: 3; Bailey 1984: 33,34; Ritter 1866: 241.
6. Bailey 1984: 34.
7. Ibid.: 35.
8. Marx 1977: 38.
9. In Rabinowitz 1983: 13.
10. Bailey 1984: 38.
11. E.g., Burckhardt 1822: 563; Field 1952: 78,106.
12. Field 1952: 78.
13. Ibid.: 129; also Glassner 1974: 34.
14. Iman El-Bastawisi, personal communication; Murray 1950: 268.
15. Marx 1977: 38.
16. Palmer 1872: 70.

17. Rabinowitz 1982:15.

18. Rabinowitz 1983:16.

19. Ibid.:15,4.

20. Ibid.:16.

21. Papaioannou 1980:44.

22. Rabinowitz 1983:7.

23. Marx 1980:114.

24. Palmer 1871:72.

25. Skrobucha 1966:94.

26. Eckenstein 1921:163.

27. Bellorini and Hoade 1948:113.

28. Prescott 1958:79.

29. In Ritter 1866:173.

30. Eckenstein 1921:178.

31. Shefik 1926:14; Jarvis 1932:230; Golding 1937:131.

32. Golding 1937:129.

33. Ibid.:131.

34. Tischendorf 1851:112.

35. Palmer 1871:61.

36. Dobson 1925:107.

37. Field 1952:92; Murray 1950:266.

38. Rabinowitz 1983:22.

39. Ibid.:4.

40. Ibid.:6.

41. Depending on their origins in Europe and Egypt the ancestors of the Jabaliya spoke dialects of Greek, Latin, and Coptic and became predominantly Arabic speakers after the seventh century (Nishio 1992:x).

42. Rabinowitz 1983:24; Marx 1980:114.

43. Ritter 1866:238.

44. Rabinowitz 1983:18,24.

45. Eckenstein 1921:95.

46. Dobson 1925:49; Har-El 1983:181.

47. Lewis 1971:2.

48. Mayerson 1976:376.

49. Lewis 1971:7.

50. Ibid.:8,9.

51. Ibid.:11,12.

52. Eckenstein 1921:106.

53. Skrobucha 1966:27; Har-El 1983:181,243,390; Eckenstein 1921:108.

54. Papaioannou 1980:8.

55. Mayerson 1976:376; Lepsius 1852:441.

56. Eckenstein 1921:95.

57. Skrobucha 1966:26.

58. Eckenstein 1921:105.

59. Perevolotsky and Finkelstein 1985:32.

60. Skrobucha 1966:26.

61. Forsyth 1985:50.

62. Dobson 1925:49.

63. Weitzmann 1985:155.

64. Skrobucha 1966:60.

65. In Prescott 1958:78.

66. Eckenstein 1921:130,167.

67. In de Laborde 1836:233.

68. In Ritter 1866:74.

69. Ibid.:232.

70. Eckenstein 1921:183.

71. Burckhardt 1822:491.

72. Ibid.:556.

73. In Ritter 1866:243.

74. Palmer 1871:58.

75. Ritter 1866:243.

76. In ibid.:209.

77. Ritter 1866:248.

78. Bailey 1984:28.

79. Monks today say the Jabaliya have never troubled the monastery. However, Clinton Bailey relates that manuscripts at the monastery indicate "the periodic if not continual displeasure of the Jebeliya with their obligations, and of their numerous attempts from the late fourteenth to the late nineteenth century to end and amend them, sometimes by actually pillaging the monastery" (Bailey 1984:33,34).

80. Rabinowitz 1983:7,10,30; Murray 1950:258.

81. Palmer 1871:66; see also Prescott 1958:84.

82. Stewart 1991:102.

83. Eckenstein 1921:190; Tischendorf 1851:94; Pococke 1743:137; Stewart 1991:99; Bailey 1984:28; Father Good Angel, personal communication.

84. See Murray 1950:260 for the account of how Gararsha tribesmen forfeited eligibility for this special status. Monks and allied Bedouins reportedly killed six of them in the monastery when they demanded this right.

85. Eckenstein 1921:190; Pococke 1743:137; Rabinowitz 1983:9; Ritter 1866:243.

86. Rabinowitz 1983:30.

87. Eckenstein 1921:137.

88. Bailey 1984:33,34.

89. Dobson 1925:105; Burckhardt 1822:564.

90. In Ritter 1866:241.

91. Papaioannou 1980:10.

92. Stanley 1911:344.

93. Skrobucha 1966:58.

94. Ibid.

95. Ritter 1866:236.

96. Prescott 1958:78.

97. Skrobucha 1966:58.

98. Lev 1989:108.

99. Skrobucha 1966:14; Eckenstein 1921:144.

100. Galey 1985:13.

101. Har-El 1983:405.

102. Forsyth 1985:51.

103. Ritter 1866:236.

104. Golding 1937:133.

105. Forsyth 1985:51.

106. Jarvis 1932:229.

107. Palmer 1871:76.

108. Williams 1927:725.

109. Tischendorf 1851:112.

110. Rabinowitz 1983:20,31.

111. In 1739 Richard Pococke reported that the monk Sergius, who resided at the monastery, had helped Muhammad write the Quran (Pococke 1743:151).

112. Palmer 1871:66.

113. Burckhardt 1822:568.

114. All cited passages from the Quran are from the translation by Ali 1983.

115. E.g., Ali 1983:806, footnote 2601 and Ali 1983:778, footnote 2504; Iman El-Bastawisi, personal communication; Michael Jones, personal communication.

116. See Nebenzahl 1986:153.

117. In Ritter 1866:176.

118. Palmer 1872:77.

119. Pococke 1743:146–147.

120. In Eckenstein 1921:128.

121. Eckenstein 1921:128.

122. Shefik 1926:20.

123. Burckhardt 1822:567.

124. E.g., Dobson 1925:126; Ritter 1866:211.

125. Bellorini and Hoade 1948:58.

126. Prentice 1912:1258.

127. Wilson 1880:11; Pococke 1743:146; Shefik 1926:21; Dobson 1925:57; Stewart 1897, vol. 4:559.

128. Palmer 1871:11.

129. Prentice 1912:1258.

130. Jarvis 1932:235; Meistermann 1909:148.

131. In Ritter 1866:175.

132. Stanley 1860:46.

133. Tischendorf 1851:105.

134. Marx 1977:41.

135. Mahmuud Mansuur, personal communication.

136. There is considerable confusion about the identity of Nabi Saalih. The Jabaliya are uncertain, saying his real identity might be known if they knew what was in his shrine. If he is buried there, he probably was the patriarch of the Bani

Saalih tribe. If it is merely a place he visited (a *magaam*, literally, "standing place"), then "we will never know who he was." Edward Palmer identified Nabi Saalih as Moses himself (related in Hoskins 1909: 1027). Eckenstein used the Banu Saalih as a synonym for the Jabaliya, while Richard Burton equated the Bani Saalih with the Suwalha (in Eckenstein 1921: 188,124). Some sources contend that he was a prophet of the Arabs of Tammud in Arabia, where he tried to influence them through miracles to worship God instead of idols. When they did not heed him the people were killed and their city destroyed. Nabi Saalih then went to Palestine to become a hermit, and was buried in the White Mosque of Ramleh (Har-El 1983:38).

137. Dobson 1925: 108; Wilson 1880: 123; Eckenstein 1921: 190.
138. Eckenstein 1921: 127.
139. Skrobucha 1966: 80.
140. Palmer 1871: 118.
141. Pococke 1743: 146–147.
142. In Eckenstein 1921: 125.
143. Dobson 1925: 128; Meistermann 1909: 155; Stephens 1991: 177.
144. Palmer 1871: 118.
145. Rabinowitz 1983: 19.
146. Marx 1977: 43.
147. Rabinowitz 1983: 19,20.

7. THE BEDOUIN WAY OF LIFE

1. Sinai Conservation Group n.d.:15; Perevolotsky et al. 1989: 163.
2. Hobbs 1989: 42.
3. Perevolotsky et al. 1989: 162,158.
4. Perevolotsky and Finkelstein 1985: 38.
5. Perevolotsky 1981: 343.
6. Marx 1980: 114.
7. Perevolotsky 1981: 353.
8. See Rabinowitz 1983: 8.
9. Perevolotsky and Finkelstein 1985: 38.
10. Perevolotsky 1981: 341.
11. El-Bastawisi 1982: 63.
12. Ibid.: 64; Roeder 1989: 231.
13. El-Bastawisi 1982: 65.
14. Perevolotsky 1981: 339.
15. El-Bastawisi 1982: 62.
16. In Ritter 1866: 243.
17. Perevolotsky et al. 1989: 156 reported that this system was called *anwa*.
18. In Eckenstein 1921: 6.
19. El-Bastawisi 1982: 65.
20. See Ebensten 1987: 84; Kamil 1991: 38.
21. Jarvis 1932: 229; Golding 1937: 131; Marx 1980: 114.

22. Ritter 1866:241.

23. Dames and Moore 1985, vol 7:PO-1. Sinai's entire Bedouin population is approximately 200,000.

24. Marx 1980:114.

25. Ibid.:115.

26. Rabinowitz 1982:12.

27. Ibid.

28. Perevolotsky et al. 1989:163.

29. Rabinowitz 1982:20; Perevolotsky et al. 1989:155; Perevolotsky 1981:337.

30. Perevolotsky 1981:347.

31. Rabinowitz 1982:20.

32. Perevolotsky 1981:349–351.

33. Baharav 1981:9.

34. Robertson 1936:16; see also Rabinowitz 1985:218.

35. An experiment Egyptian botanists conducted on the Plain of ar-Raaha in the 1980s demonstrated the vegetation potential of heavily grazed areas. They fenced a plot there for five years against all herbivores. Within the enclosure a mature community dominated by wormwood (*Artemisia inculta*) developed rapidly as an island surrounded by overgrazed range (Ramadan 1988:148).

36. Roeder 1989:230.

37. Dames and Moore 1981b:3–1.

38. Marx 1980:116.

39. El-Bastawisi 1982:86.

8. THE PILGRIM

1. Eckenstein 1921:114.

2. Silver 1982:161.

3. Skrobucha 1966:15.

4. Eckenstein 1921:146.

5. Stewart 1897, vol. 4:559.

6. Skrobucha 1966:62.

7. Burckhardt 1822:567.

8. Robinson 1841:194.

9. Dobson 1925:122.

10. Ritter 1866:205; Palmer 1871:107.

11. In Eckenstein 1921:126.

12. Hirschfield 1992:215.

13. Eckenstein 1921:125.

14. Sumption 1975:89,95,114,133.

15. Jarvis 1932:238; Skrobucha 1966:100.

16. Eckenstein 1921:156,165.

17. Skrobucha 1966:100.

18. Har-El 1983:397.

19. Burckhardt 1822:552.
20. Galey 1985:15.
21. Hoskins 1909:1025.
22. Palmer 1871:67.
23. Dobson 1925:83.
24. Prescott 1958:18.
25. Sumption 1975:13,95,98.
26. In ibid.:90.
27. Dobson 1925:123.
28. McClure and Feltoe 1920:7.
29. Sumption 1975:51.
30. Skrobucha 1966:74.
31. Eckenstein 1921:139.
32. In ibid.:151.
33. In Sumption 1975:23.
34. Sumption 1975:21,59.
35. Ibid.:98,104.
36. Skrobucha 1966:68.
37. Pococke 1743:130.
38. Skrobucha 1966:78.
39. Palmer and Colton 1971:52.
40. Sumption 1975:141.
41. Eckenstein 1921:153.
42. Sumption 1975:289.
43. Ibid.:137,138.
44. Skrobucha 1966:77.
45. Sumption 1975:266.
46. Skrobucha 1966:91.
47. Jarvis 1932:238.
48. Ritter 1866:236.
49. Fisher 1969:136; Jarvis 1932:238.
50. Eckenstein 1921:153,155.
51. Ibid.:169; Sumption 1975:13,257; Jarvis 1932:207; Galey 1985:15.
52. Sumption 1975:299,300.
53. Lea 1988:28.
54. Turner 1973:193.
55. Sumption 1975:289.
56. Skrobucha 1966:77.
57. Stewart 1897, vol. 1:3.
58. In Sumption 1975:204.
59. Sumption 1975:263.
60. Eckenstein 1921:169,170.
61. Prescott 1958:28.
62. Sumption 1975:182,263,206,207,209,182.
63. Ibid.:119.

64. Skrobucha 1966:78.

65. Sumption 1975:171,196,184,188.

66. Eckenstein 1921:156.

67. Sumption 1975:189,185,187.

68. Labarge 1982:76.

69. Eckenstein 1921:156.

70. Bellorini and Hoade 1948:55–58; Sumption 1975:194.

71. Labarge 1982:79; Eckenstein 1921:168.

72. Prescott 1958:20,21,25,35,39,40.

73. Eckenstein 1921:157.

74. Pococke 1743:130.

75. Eckenstein 1921:139.

76. In Skrobucha 1966:78; Stewart 1897, vol. 4:477; and see Prescott 1958:49.

77. Prescott 1958:46.

78. Ibid.:52.

79. Ibid.:54.

80. Bellorini and Hoade 1948:58.

81. Ibid.:55.

82. Eckenstein 1921:170.

83. Bellorini and Hoade 1948:57.

84. Eckenstein 1921:170.

85. Prescott 1958:50.

86. Stewart 1897, vol. 4:491.

87. Prescott 1958:61; Stewart 1897, vol. 4:512.

88. Sumption 1975:127.

89. Johnson and Moran 1989:9.

90. Govinda 1966:214,215; Snelling 1983:198.

91. Prescott 1958:69.

92. Bellorini and Hoade 1948:60,113.

93. Ibid.:58.

94. Pococke 1743:153–154.

95. Hirschfield 1992:196.

96. Eckenstein 1921:130.

97. Skrobucha 1966:78; Palmer 1871:67; Forsyth 1985:51.

98. Rabinowitz 1982:13,18.

99. Bellorini and Hoade 1948:114.

100. Stewart 1897, vol. 4:619.

101. Prescott 1958:79,81,82.

102. Stewart 1897, vol. 4:623.

103. Tischendorf 1851:111.

104. Bernbaum 1990:211.

105. Psalm 24:3–5; Wilson 1880:131.

106. Wilson 1888:335.

107. In Ritter 1866:175.

108. Pococke 1743:145.

109. Golding 1937:134; Hawksley 1944:410. In some cultures portions of pilgrimage shrines are so holy that even the purest pilgrim may not enter them. While pilgrims circumambulate Mount Kailas, for example, they do not climb it, because that would be an act of desecration (Snelling 1983:85). Recalling God's admonition to Moses to "mark out the limits of the mountain and say 'Take care not to go up the mountain,' " in 1697, 1828, and perhaps other times the monks of St. Katherine assigned forbidden status to the summit of Mount Sinai. They allowed confessed pilgrims to pass no farther than the Basin of Elijah (in Ritter 1866:205).

110. Prescott 1958:86.

111. Bellorini and Hoade 1948:60.

112. Ibid.:61.

113. McClure and Feltoe 1920:4.

114. Ibid.

115. Prescott 1958:87.

116. Govinda 1966:208; Snelling 1983:15,199.

117. Bellorini and Hoade 1948:62.

118. Ibid.:60.

119. Mayerson 1976:376; Palmer 1871:119.

120. Bellorini and Hoade 1948:65.

121. Pococke 1743:153.

122. Stewart 1897, vol. 4:581.

123. Pococke 1743:154.

124. Eckenstein 1921:152,157.

125. Prescott 1958:95.

126. Eckenstein 1921:172.

127. In Johnson and Moran 1989:24.

128. Govinda 1966:207.

129. Eckenstein 1921:131.

130. McClure and Feltoe 1920:4.

131. Bellorini and Hoade 1948:120.

132. Dobson 1925:133; see also Tuan 1977:184; Govinda 1966:197.

133. Otto 1923:28; see also Acquaviva 1979:28.

134. Sallnow 1987:3.

135. Turner 1973:228.

136. Sumption 1975:91.

137. In Ritter 1866:205.

138. Bellorini and Hoade 1948:118.

139. Ibid.:63.

140. Stewart 1897, vol. 1:249.

141. See Lane 1988:15.

142. Golding 1937:138.

143. Turner 1973:213.

1. Milton, in Wagstaff 1985:214.
2. Abrams 1979:5.
3. Said 1979:168.
4. See Mieczkowski 1990:53.
5. Mieczkowski 1990:43.
6. In ibid.:31.
7. Eickelman 1981:26.
8. Palmer and Colton 1971:325.
9. Eickelman 1981:25,34.
10. Eckenstein 1921:178.
11. Ibid.:181,180.
12. Batanouny 1985:197.
13. Ibid.:194.
14. Eckenstein 1921:185; Batanouny 1985:195.
15. Batanouny 1985:190; Skrobucha 1966:100.
16. Skrobucha 1966:100.
17. Eckenstein 1921:185; Batanouny 1985:191.
18. Eckenstein 1921:185.
19. Ibid.; Batanouny 1985:190.
20. Batanouny 1985:198.
21. In ibid.:199.
22. Skrobucha 1966:100.
23. Eckenstein 1921:165.
24. Ibid.:168.
25. Batanouny 1985:204.
26. Ibid.:196.
27. Eckenstein 1921:191; Hull 1885:200.
28. Said 1979:196.
29. Batanouny 1985:205.
30. Ibid.
31. Ferguson 1991:491.
32. De Laborde 1836:317.
33. In Bentley 1986:98.
34. Eckenstein 1921:132.
35. Bentley 1986:111.
36. In Abrams 1979:690.
37. Ibid.:2058.
38. Ibid.:355.
39. Said 1979:167.
40. Oxford University Press 1955:75.
41. Tobias 1986:184,187; Mieczkowski 1990:53.
42. Abrams 1979:157.
43. In ibid.:177.

44. In Clarke 1880:95.

45. Clarke 1880:13,17.

46. Palmer 1871:27.

47. Mieczkowski 1990:43,53,59,62.

48. Hoskins 1909:1012; Hoskins 1912:17.

49. Hoskins 1909:1019.

50. Sutton 1913:89.

51. Palmer 1871:104.

52. Hawksley 1944:412.

53. Clarke 1880:13.

54. Kinglake 1908:147.

55. Hoskins 1909:1022.

56. Tischendorf 1851:81.

57. Stanley 1860:68,69.

58. Wagstaff 1985:214.

59. In Said 1979:193.

60. Kinglake 1908:139.

61. Kazantzakis 1975:110.

62. Rabinowitz 1982:12.

63. Shefik 1926:11.

64. Bagnold 1935:59.

65. Williams 1927:709.

66. Ibid.:719.

67. Hawksley 1944:409.

68. Rabinowitz 1982:15.

69. Glassner 1974:47.

70. Rabinowitz 1982:12.

71. Bassili 1964:62.

72. Burton 1856:27; Eickelman 1981:27.

73. Bellorini and Hoade 1948:55–58.

74. Ritter 1866:231.

75. Ibid.:171.

76. Ibid.:191.

77. Palgrave 1865, vol. 1:4.

78. Hull 1885:54.

79. Ibid.:200.

80. Dobson 1925:98.

81. Clarke 1880:6.

82. Palgrave 1865, vol. 1:37.

83. Murray 1950:256,243.

84. Burckhardt 1822:551.

85. Stephens 1991:198.

86. Tischendorf 1851:96.

87. Palmer 1872:124.

88. Palmer 1871:121.

89. Ibid.:651.

90. Lepsius 1852:335.

91. Stanley 1860:56.

92. Sutton 1913:94.

93. Burckhardt 1822:551.

94. Stephens 1991:179.

95. Ibid.:180.

96. Sutton 1913:93.

97. Golding 1937:129.

98. Dobson 1925:42.

99. Merton 1924:894.

100. Ibid.:898.

101. Jarvis 1932:230; Jarvis 1930:54.

102. See de Laborde 1836:242; Rothenberg 1961:146.

103. Tischendorf 1851:95.

104. Ibid.:95.

105. Ibid.:107.

106. Dobson 1925:69.

107. Williams 1927:733.

108. Skrobucha 1966:102.

10. THE TOURIST

1. Mieczkowski 1990:1.

2. Gauch 1993:6; Hedges 1993:3.

3. Dames and Moore 1981a:2-8.

4. Rabinowitz 1982:89,17.

5. Ibid.:89.

6. Ibid.:19.

7. Mohamed Ibrahim, personal communication.

8. Rabinowitz 1982:15.

9. Ibid.

10. Haberman 1993:9.

11. El-Bastawisi 1982:79.

12. Hazleton 1980:40.

13. Rabinowitz 1983:19.

14. Haas 1990:45.

15. Dames and Moore 1985, vol. 1:5-4.

16. Dames and Moore 1985, vol. 6:2-13.

17. Middle East Times n.d.:3.

18. Michael Pearson, personal communication.

19. Dames and Moore 1981a:2-8.

20. Wilson 1888:340.

21. E.g., Society for the Protection of Nature in Israel 1979, Appendix 1:1.

22. E.g., Rabinowitz 1982:25.

23. El-Bastawisi 1982:90.
24. Sulzberger 1987:9.

11. THE NEW GOLDEN CALF

1. Ferguson 1991:491.
2. Dames and Moore 1985, vol. 4:5-10.
3. Bouverie 1990:61.
4. Dames and Moore 1981a:2-8.
5. Ibid.:3-6.
6. Arab Republic of Egypt, National Commission for UNESCO 1983:39.
7. Arab Republic of Egypt, Council of Ministers 1988:1.
8. Arab Republic of Egypt, National Commission for UNESCO 1983:39.
9. Mimi Mann, personal communication.
10. Bhatia 1990:13.
11. Mimi Mann, personal communication.
12. Mann 1990:10.
13. Ibid.
14. Rabinovich 1994:48.
15. Morrow 1990:26.
16. Atwater 1990:13.
17. Sultan 1990:13.
18. Bouverie 1990:61.
19. Ibid.

♦

REFERENCES CITED

Abrams, M. H., ed. 1979. *The Norton Anthology of English Literature*, vol. 2. New York: W. W. Norton.

Abu Lughod, Janet. 1971. *Cairo: 1001 Years of the City Victorious*. Princeton, N.J.: Princeton University Press.

Acquaviva, S. S. 1979. *The Decline of the Sacred in Industrial Society*. London: Basil Blackwell.

Aharoni, Yohanan. 1962. *The Land of the Bible: A Historical Geography*. Philadelphia: Westminster Press.

Ali, A. Yusuf, ed. 1983. *The Holy Qur'an*. Brentwood, Md.: Amana.

Alon, Azaria. 1978. *The Natural History of the Land of the Bible*. Garden City, N.Y.: Doubleday and Company.

Anati, Emmanuel. 1985. "Has Mt. Sinai Been Found?" *Biblical Archaeology Review* 11(4):42–57.

———. 1986. *The Mountain of God*. New York: Rizzoli.

Arab Republic of Egypt, Council of Ministers. 1988. *Prime Ministerial Decree No. 613 of 1988 for the Establishment of a Protected Area in the Region of St. Catherine in the Governorate of South Sinai* (in Arabic). Cairo.

Arab Republic of Egypt, National Commission for UNESCO. 1983. *Egyptian National Committee for Man and the Biosphere Periodical Bulletin 3–4*. Cairo.

Arden, Harvey. 1976. "In Search of Moses." *National Geographic* 149(1):2–37.

Atwater, James. 1990. "Letter to the Editor." *Time* 135(15):13.

Bagnold, Ralph A. 1935. *Libyan Sands: Travel in a Dead World*. London: Michael Haag (reprinted 1987).

Baha El-Din, Mindy. 1991. "Towards Developing a Biological Resources Strategy for Egypt." Unpublished manuscript.

Baharav, Dan. 1981. "The Status of the Nubian Ibex *Capra ibex nubiana* in the Sinai Desert." *Biological Conservation* 20:91–97.

Bailey, Clinton. 1984. "Dating the Arrival of the Bedouin Tribes in Sinai and the Negev." *Journal of the Economic and Social History of the Orient* 28:20–49.

Baly, Denis. 1976. *God and History in the Old Testament.* New York: Harper and Row.

Bassili, William Farid. 1964. *Sinai: The Monastery of St. Catherine; A Practical Guide for Travellers.* Cairo: Costa Tsoumas Printing House.

Batanouny, K. H. 1985. "Botanical Exploration of Sinai." *Qatar University Science Bulletin* 5:187–211.

Bedevian, Armenag K. 1936. *Illustrated Polyglottic Dictionary of Plant Names.* Cairo: Argus and Papazian.

Beit-Arieh, Itzhaq. 1988. "The Route through Sinai: Why the Israelites Fleeing Egypt Went South." *Biblical Archaeology Review* 14(3):28–37.

Beitzel, Barry J. 1985. *The Moody Atlas of Bible Lands.* Chicago: Moody Press.

Beke, Emily. 1878. *The Late Dr. Charles Beke's Discoveries in Arabia and of Midian.* London: Trubner and Company.

Bellorini, Theophilus, and Eugene Hoade, trans. 1948. *Visit to the Holy Places of Egypt, Sinai, Palestine and Syria in 1384 by Frescobaldi, Gucci and Sigoli.* Jerusalem: Franciscan Press, Publications of the Studium Biblicum Franciscanum No. 6.

Bentley, James. 1986. *Secrets of Mount Sinai: The Story of the World's Oldest Bible—Codex Sinaiticus.* Garden City, N.Y.: Doubleday.

Bernbaum, Edwin. 1990. *Sacred Mountains of the World.* San Francisco: Sierra Club Books.

Bhatia, Shyam. January, 21 1990. "Resort Developers Prey on Mt. Sinai." *Observer*: 13.

Bimson, John J. 1981. *Redating the Exodus and Conquest.* Sheffield, England: Almond Press.

Bodenheimer, Fritz S. 1947. "The Manna of Sinai." *Biblical Archaeologist* 10(1): 2–6.

Bouverie, Jasper P. 1990. "On the Beaten Track." *Cairo Today* 11(7):58–63.

Browning, Iain. 1974. *Petra.* London: Chatto and Windus.

Brueggeman, W. 1977. *The Land: Place as Gift, Promise and Challenge.* Philadelphia: Fortress Press.

Burckhardt, John Lewis. 1822. *Travels in Syria and the Holy Land.* London: John Murray.

Burton, Richard F. 1856. *Personal Narrative of a Pilgrimage to El-Medinah and Meccah.* New York: G. P. Putnam and Co.

Cassuto, U. 1951. *A Commentary on the Book of Exodus.* Jerusalem: Magnes Press.

Chitty, Derwas J. 1966. *The Desert a City: An Introduction to the Study of Egyptian and Palestinian Monasticism under the Christian Empire.* Oxford: Basil Blackwell.

Clarke, C. Pickering. 1880. "Sinai." In Wilson, Charles W., ed. 1880. *Sinai and the South.* Jerusalem: Ariel (reprinted 1976), pp. 1–120.

Clements, Ronald E. 1972. *Exodus.* Cambridge: Cambridge University Press.

Clifford, Richard J. 1972. *The Cosmic Mountain in Canaan and the Old Testament.* Cambridge: Cambridge University Press.

Daiches, David. 1975. *Moses: Man in the Wilderness.* London: Weidenfeld and Nicolson.

Dames and Moore. 1981a. *Sinai Development Study. Early Tourism Action Recommendation.* Los Angeles.

———. 1981b. *Sinai Development Study. Phase 1. Preliminary Summary of Findings on Population in Sinai.* Los Angeles.

———. 1985. *Sinai Development Study. Phase 1. Final Report. Volume 1: A Strategy for the Settlement of Sinai.* Los Angeles.

———. 1985. *Sinai Development Study. Phase 1. Final Report. Volume 4: The Land and Environment of Sinai.* Los Angeles.

———. 1985. *Sinai Development Study. Phase 1. Final Report. Volume 6: Settlement and Social Development.* Los Angeles.

———. 1985. *Sinai Development Study. Phase 1. Final Report. Volume 7: Sinai Data Book.* Los Angeles.

Danin, Avinoam. 1978. "Plant Species Diversity and Ecological Districts of the Sinai Desert." *Vegetatio* 36(2):83–93.

———. 1983. *Desert Vegetation of Israel and Sinai.* Jerusalem: Cana.

Day, J. Wentworth. 1938. *Sport in Egypt.* London: Country Life Limited.

De Laborde, M. Léon. 1836. *Journey through Arabia Petraea to Mount Sinai and the Excavated City of Petra, The Edom of the Prophecies.* London: John Murray.

Dewing, H. B., trans. 1940. *Procopius. Volume VII. Buildings.* Cambridge, Mass.: Harvard University Press.

Dobson, Augusta Mary R. 1925. *Mount Sinai: A Modern Pilgrimage.* London: Methuen.

Ebensten, Hanns. 1987. "Blasphemy in Blue." *Archaeology* 40(2):84.

Eckenstein, Lina. 1921. *A History of Sinai.* New York: Macmillan.

Egyptian Environmental Affairs Agency. 1992. "Saint Catherine Natural Protectorate Project Baseline Study." Unpublished document.

Eickelman, Dale F. 1981. *The Middle East: An Anthropological Approach.* Englewood Cliffs, N.J.: Prentice-Hall.

El-Bastawisi, Iman Youssef. 1982. "Adaptation to a Unique Environment: El Jebelya of Saint Catherine." Master's thesis, Department of Sociology-Anthropology-Psychology, The American University in Cairo.

El-Hadidi, M. Nabil. n.d. "Flora of Sinai." In *International Training Course on Wildlife, Sharm el Sheikh, Background Paper No. 4.* Cairo: Al-Ahram.

Eller, Meredith. 1958. *The Beginnings of the Christian Religion: A Guide to the History and Literature of Judaism and Christianity.* New York: Bookman Associates.

Elliot, Alison Goddard. 1987. *Roads to Paradise: Reading the Lives of the Early Saints.* Hanover, N.H.: University Press of New England.

Engel, J. Ronald. 1992. "Renewing the Bond of Mankind and Nature: Biosphere Reserves as Sacred Space." In Peter Sauer, ed. *Finding Home: Writing on Nature and Culture from Orion Magazine.* Boston: Beacon Press.

Ferguson, David A. 1991. "The International Politics of Field Projects." *Applied Animal Behaviour Science* 29:489–499.

Ferguson, Walter W. 1981. "The Systematic Position of *Canis aureus lupaster* (Carnivora: Canidae) and the Occurrence of *Canis lupus* in North Africa, Egypt and Sinai." *Mammalia* 45(4):459–465.

Field, Henry. 1952. *Contributions to the Anthropology of the Faiyum, Sinai, Sudan and Kenya.* Berkeley: University of California Press.

Finkelstein, Israel. 1988. "Raider of the Lost Mountain—An Israeli Archaeologist Looks at the Most Recent Attempt to Locate Mt. Sinai." *Biblical Archaeology Review* 14(4):46–50.

Fisher, Sydney Nettleton. 1969. *The Middle East: A History.* New York: Alfred A. Knopf.

Florovsky, Georges. 1987. *The Byzantine Ascetic and Spiritual Fathers.* Vaduz, Liechtenstein: Büchervertriebsanstalt.

Forsyth, George H. 1985. "The Monastery of St. Catherine at Mount Sinai: The Church and Fortress of Justinian." In John Galey, ed. *Sinai and the Monastery of St. Catherine*: 49–64. Cairo: American University in Cairo Press.

Fortescue, Adrian. 1907. *The Eastern Orthodox Church.* New York: Burt Franklin.

Frangouli, Argine G. 1985. *The Sinaia School of St. Catherine at Khandaka.* Athens: H(Omega)E.

Frank, Harry Thomas, ed. 1990. *Atlas of the Bible Lands.* Maplewood, N.J.: Hammond Inc.

Galey, John. 1985. *Sinai and the Monastery of St. Catherine.* Cairo: American University in Cairo Press.

Gasperetti, J., D. L. Harrison, and W. Büttiker. 1985. "The Carnivora of Arabia." *Fauna of Saudi Arabia* 7:397–461.

Gaubert, Henri. 1969. *Moses and Joshua: Founders of the Nation.* London: Darton, Longman and Todd.

Gauch, Sarah. May 20, 1993. "The Risky Existence of an Egyptian Extremist." *Christian Science Monitor:* 6.

Glassner, Martin Ira. 1974. "The Bedouin of Southern Sinai under Israeli Administration." *Geographical Review* 64: 31–60.

Golding, Louis. 1937. "I Stood upon Sinai." *Geographical Magazine* 6:129–140.

Goodman, Steven M., Peter L. Meininger, Sherif M. Baha El Din, Joseph J. Hobbs, and Wim C. Mullié. 1989. *The Birds of Egypt.* Oxford: Oxford University Press.

Govinda, Lama Anagarika. 1966. *The Way of the White Clouds: A Buddhist Pilgrim in Tibet.* London: Hutchinson.

Haas, Peter M. 1990. "Towards Management of Environmental Problems in Egypt." *Environmental Conservation* 17(1):45–50.

Haberman, Clyde. August 8, 1993. "For Israelis, Getting Away Is a Necessity." *New York Times:* 9.

Haim, A., and E. Tchernov. 1974. "The Distribution of the Myomorph Rodents in the Sinai Peninsula." *Mammalia* 38(2):201–223.

Har-El, Menashe. 1983. *The Sinai Journeys: The Route of the Exodus.* San Diego: Ridgefield.

Hareuveni, Nogah. 1984. *Tree and Shrub in Our Biblical Heritage.* Kiryat Ono, Israel: Neot Kedumim.

Hawksley, J. C. 1944. "A Short Holiday in the Mountains of Sinai." *Alpine Journal* 54:408–412.

Haynes, A. E. 1896. "The Route of the Exodus." *Palestine Exploration Fund Quarterly Statement* 27:175–185.

Hazleton, Lesley. 1980. *Where Mountains Roar: A Personal Report from the Sinai and Negev Desert.* New York: Penguin.

Hedges, Chris. March 14, 1993. "Cairo Security Is Tightened after Blast." *New York Times*, Travel Section p. 3.

Heinzel, Hermann, Richard Fitter, and John Parslow. 1984. *The Birds of Britain and Europe, with North Africa and the Middle East.* London: Collins.

Hirschfield, Yizhar. 1992. *The Judean Desert Monasteries in the Byzantine Period.* New Haven, Conn.: Yale University Press.

Hobbs, Joseph J. 1989. *Bedouin Life in the Egyptian Wilderness.* Austin: University of Texas Press.

————. 1992. "Sacred Space and Touristic Development at Jebel Musa (Mt. Sinai), Egypt." *Journal of Cultural Geography* 12(2):99–113.

Hoskins, Franklin E. 1909. "The Route over which Moses Led the Children of Israel out of Egypt." *National Geographic Magazine* 20 (12):1011–1038.

————. 1912. *From the Nile to Nebo: A Discussion of the Problem and the Route of the Exodus.* Philadelphia: Sunday School Times Company.

Hull, Edward. 1885. *Mount Seir, Sinai and Western Palestine: Being a Narrative of a Scientific Expedition.* London: Richard Bentley and Son.

————. 1899. "Where Is Mount Sinai?" *Journal of the Victorian Institute* 31:39–55.

Hussey, J. M. 1986. *The Orthodox Church in the Byzantine Empire.* Oxford: Clarendon.

Ilany, Giora. May-June 1990. "The Spotted Ambassadors of a Vanishing World." *Israela*:15–24.

Inbar, Reuven. 1979. "The Secret Life of the Sinai Rose Finch." *Israel—Land and Nature* 5(1):20–22.

Jarvis, Claude Scudamore. 1930. "A Sinai Wandering." *Blackwood's Magazine* 228:41–55.

————. 1931. "The Forty Years' Wanderings." *Blackwood's Magazine* 229:187–203.

————. 1932. *Yesterday and Today in Sinai.* Boston: Houghton Mifflin.

Johnson, Russell, and Kerry Moran. 1989. *The Sacred Mountain of Tibet: On Pilgrimage to Kailas.* Rochester, Vt.: Park St. Press.

Kamil, Jill. 1991. *The Monastery of Saint Catherine in Sinai: History and Guide.* Cairo: American University in Cairo Press.

Kazantzakis, Nikos. 1975. *Journeying: Travels in Italy, Egypt, Sinai, Jerusalem and Cyprus.* Translated by Themi Vasils and Theodora Vasils. Boston: Little, Brown and Company.

Kinglake, Alexander William. 1908. *Eothen*. London: J. M. Dent and Sons.

Kitto, John. 1872. *An Illustrated History of the Holy Bible*. Norwich, Conn.: Henry Bill.

Kleiman, Seymour. 1990. "Letter to the Editor." *Time* 135(15):13

Labarge, Margaret Wade. 1982. *Medieval Travellers*. New York: W. W. Norton.

Lane, Beldon C. 1988. *Landscapes of the Sacred: Geography and Narrative in American Spirituality*. New York: Paulist Press.

Lea, John. 1988. *Tourism and Development in the Third World*. London: Routledge.

Lepsius, Richard. 1852. *Discoveries in Egypt, Ethiopia and the Peninsula of Sinai in the Years 1842–1845*. London: Richard Bentley.

Lev, Martin. 1989. *The Traveler's Key to Jerusalem: A Guide to the Sacred Places of Jerusalem*. New York: Alfred A. Knopf.

Levenson, Jon D. 1985. *Sinai and Zion: An Entry into the Jewish Bible*. Minneapolis: Seabury Books.

Levi, Shabtai. 1977. "The Sinai Leopards: A Tale of Extinction." *Israel: Land and Nature* 2(4):156–163.

Lewis, Agnes Smith, trans. 1971. "The Forty Martyrs in the Sinai Desert and the Story of the Eulogios." *Horae Semiticae* 9. Jerusalem: Raritas.

Liphschitz, Nili, and Yoav Waisel. 1976. "Dendroarchaeological Investigations in Israel: St. Catherine's Monastery in Southern Sinai." *Israel Exploration Journal* 26:39–44.

Lockyer, Herbert. 1961. *All the Miracles of the Bible*. Grand Rapids, Mich.: Zondervan.

Louth, Andrew. 1991. *The Wilderness of God*. London: Darton, Longman and Todd.

Lucas, A. 1938. *The Route of the Exodus of the Israelites from Egypt*. London: Edward Arnold and Co.

McClure, M. L., and C. L. Feltoe, trans. 1920. *The Pilgrimage of Etheria*. New York: Macmillan.

Manafis, Konstantinos A., ed. 1990. *Sinai: Treasures of the Monastery of Saint Catherine*. Athens: Ekdotike Athenon.

Mann, Mimi. April 1, 1990. "Plans Afoot to Run a Cable Car up Mount Sinai." *Honolulu Sunday Star-Bulletin and Advertiser*: F-10.

Marx, Emanuel. 1977. "Communal and Individual Pilgrimage: The Region of Saints' Tombs in South Sinai." In R. P. Werbner, ed. *Regional Cults*: 29–51. London: Academic Press.

———. 1980. "Wage Labor and Tribal Economy of the Bedouin in South Sinai." In Philip Salzman, ed. *When Nomads Settle*: 111–123. New York: J. F. Bergin.

Marx, Hymen. 1968. *Checklist of the Reptiles and Amphibians of Egypt*. Cairo: Special Publication, United States Naval Medical Research Unit Number Three.

Mayerson, Philip. 1976. "An Inscription in the Monastery of St. Catherine and the Martyr Tradition in Sinai." *Dumbarton Oaks Papers* 30:375–383.

Meinertzhagen, Richard. 1954. *Birds of Arabia*. Edinburgh: Oliver and Boyd.

Meistermann, P. Barnabé. 1909. *Guide du Nil au Jourdain par le Sinai et Pétra sur les Traces d'Israel*. Paris: Alphonse Picard et Fils.

Mendelssohn, H. 1983. "Status of the Wolf in the Middle East." *Acta Zool. Fennica*
174:279–280.

Merton, A. S. 1924. "Mount Sinai and Its Monastery." *Nineteenth Century and After*
95:889–898.

Middle East Times n.d. "How the U.S. Tourist Trickle Could Become a Flood."
Middle East Times.

Mieczkowski, Zbigniew. 1990. *World Trends in Tourism and Recreation.* New York:
Peter Lang.

Moore, Lazarus, trans. 1991. *The Ladder of Divine Ascent by Saint John Climacus.*
Boston: Holy Transfiguration Monastery.

Morrow, Lance. 1990. "Trashing Mount Sinai." *Time* 135(12):92.

Murray, George W. 1950. *Sons of Ishmael: A Study of the Egyptian Bedouin.* New
York: Humanities Press.

Musil, Alois. 1926. *The Northern Hegaz: A Topographical Itinerary.* New York:
American Geographical Society.

———. 1928. *The Manners and Customs of the Rwala Bedouins.* New York: American Geographical Society Oriental Explorations and Studies No. 6.

Nebenzahl, Kenneth. 1986. *Maps of the Holy Land: Images of Terra Sancta through
Two Millennia.* New York: Abbeville Press.

Newman, Murray Lee. 1962. *The People of the Covenant: A Study of Israel from Moses
to the Monarchy.* New York: Abingdon.

Nishio, Tetsuo. 1992. "A Basic Vocabulary of the Bedouin Arabic Dialect of
the Jbali Tribe (Southern Sinai)." Studia Sinaitica I. Tokyo: Institute for the
Study of Languages and Cultures of Asia and Africa, *Studia Culturae Islamicae*
No. 43.

Orlinsky, Harry M. 1974. *Essays in Biblical Culture and Bible Translation.* New York:
Ktav Publishing House.

Osborn, Dale J., and Ibrahim Helmy. 1980. *The Contemporary Land Mammals of
Egypt (Including Sinai).* Chicago: Field Museum of Natural History Fieldiana
Zoology New Series, No. 5.

Otto, Rudolf. 1923. *The Idea of the Holy: An Inquiry into the Non-Rational Factor in
the Idea of the Divine and Its Relation to the Rational.* London: Oxford University
Press.

Oxford University Press. 1955. *The Oxford Dictionary of Quotations.* London: Oxford University Press.

Palgrave, William Gifford. 1865. *Narrative of a Year's Journey through Central and
Eastern Arabia.* 2 vols. London: MacMillan and Co.

Palmer, Edward Henry. 1871. *The Desert of the Exodus: Journeys on Foot in the Wilderness of the Forty Years' Wanderings, Undertaken in Connexion with the Ordnance
Survey of Sinai and the Palestine Exploration Fund.* Volume 1. Cambridge, England: Deighton Bell.

Palmer, Henry Spencer. 1872. *Sinai from the Fourth Egyptian Dynasty to the Present
Day.* London: Society for Promoting Christian Knowledge.

Palmer, R. R., and Joel Colton. 1971. *A History of the Modern World.* New York:
Alfred A. Knopf.

Papadopulos, Leonidas J., and Georgia Lizardos, trans. 1985. *The Life and Sufferings of Saint Catherine the Great Martyr.* Seattle: St. Nectarios Press.

Papaioannou, Evangelos. 1980. *The Monastery of St. Catherine.* Cairo: Isis Press.

Parmelee, Alice. 1959. *All the Birds of the Bible.* New York: Harper.

Peacock, Kelly, ed. 1992. *Ancient Secrets of the Bible.* New York: CBS Television.

Perevolotsky, Avi[ram]. 1981. "Orchard Agriculture in the High Mountain Region of Southern Sinai." *Human Ecology* 9(3):331–357.

———, and Israel Finkelstein. 1985. "The Southern Sinai Exodus Route in Ecological Perspective." *Biblical Archaeology Review* 11(4):26–41.

———, Ayelet Perevolotsky, and Immanuel Noy-Meir. 1989. "Environmental Adaptation and Economic Change in a Pastoral Mountain Society: The Case of the Jabaliyah Bedouin of the Mt. Sinai Region." *Mountain Research and Development* 9(2):153–164.

Petrie, William M. Flinders. 1906. *Researches in Sinai.* London: John Murray.

Phythian-Adams, W. J. 1930. "The Mount of God." *Palestine Exploration Fund Quarterly Statement* (January 1930): 135–149, 192–209.

Pococke, Richard. 1743. *Description of the East and Some Other Countries.* London: W. Bowyer.

Prentice, Sartell. 1912. "Sunrise and Sunset from Mount Sinai." *National Geographic* 23 : 1242-1282.

Prescott, Hilda Frances Margaret. 1958. *Once to Sinai: The Further Pilgrimage of Friar Felix Fabri.* New York: Macmillan.

Rabino, M. H. L. 1938. *Le Monastère de Sainte-Catherine du Mont Sinaï.* Cairo: Royal Automobile Club of Egypt.

Rabinovich, Abraham. 1994. "Gilt Complex." *Eretz* 34 : 46–73.

Rabinowitz, Dan. 1982. "Environmental Planning in the Santa Caterina Area, Sinai, Egypt." Unpublished B. Sc. Final Year Project, School of Human Environmental Studies, King's College, University of London.

———. 1983. "Tribal Politics in the Jebaliya Bedouins of the Sinai Desert, with Reference to the Community of Monks in the Monastery of Saint Catharine." Master's thesis, Department of Social Anthropology, Pembroke College, University of Cambridge.

———. 1985. "Themes in the Economy of the Bedouin of the South Sinai in the Nineteenth and Twentieth Centuries." *International Journal of Middle East Studies* 17(2):211–228.

Ramadan, Adel al-Ashwami Ahmad. 1988. "Ecological Studies in Wadi Feiran, Its Tributaries and Adjacent Mountains." Ph.D. thesis. Department of Botany, Faculty of Science, Suez Canal University, Ismailiya.

Reik, Theodor. 1959. *Mystery on the Mountain: The Drama of the Sinai Revelation.* New York: Harper and Brothers.

Ritter, Carl. 1866. *The Comparative Geography of Palestine and the Sinaitic Peninsula.* Translated by William L. Gage. Edinburgh: T. and T. Clark.

Robertson, C. C. 1936. *On the Track of the Exodus.* London: Gale and Polden.

Robinson, Edward. 1841. *Biblical Researches in Palestine, Mount Sinai and Arabia*

Petraea. A Journal of Travels in the Year 1838 by E. Robinson and E. Smith. Vol. 1. Boston: Crocker and Brewster.

Roeder, Larry W. 1989. "Trial Law and Tribal Solidarity in Sinai Bedouin Culture." *Anthropos* 84:230–234.

Rothenberg, Beno. 1961. *God's Wilderness: Discoveries in Sinai.* London: Thames and Hudson.

———, ed. 1979. *Sinai: Pharaohs, Miners, Pilgrims and Soldiers.* Bern, Switzerland: Kummerly and Frey, 1979.

Said, Edward. 1979. *Orientalism.* New York: Vintage Books.

Sallnow, Michael J. 1987. *Pilgrims of the Andes: Regional Cults in Cusco.* Washington D.C.: Smithsonian Institution Press.

Sarna, Nahum M. 1986. *Exploring Exodus: The Heritage of Biblical Israel.* New York: Schocken Books.

Schaff, P., and H. Wace, eds. 1953. *A Select Library of Nicene and Post-Nicene Fathers of the Christian Church, Vol. IV: St. Athanasius: Selected Works and Letters.* Grand Rapids, Mich.: Eerdmans.

Shefik, El Lewa Ahmed. 1926. *Notes on a Visit to Sinai Monastery and a Motor Car Tour in Sinai Peninsula in January, 1926.* Cairo: Government Press.

Shewell-Cooper, W. E. 1977. *Plants, Flowers and Herbs of the Bible.* New Canaan, Conn.: Keats Publishing.

Shmida, A. 1977. "Remarks on the Palaeo-Climates of Sinai Based on the Distribution Patterns of Relict Plants." *Qedem* 7:36–41.

Silver, Daniel Jeremy. 1982. *Images of Moses.* New York: Basic Books.

Sinai Conservation Group, U.K. n.d. "The Santa Caterina Area, South Sinai, United Arab Republic of Egypt: A Summary of Environmental Characteristics." Unpublished manuscript.

Skrobucha, Heinz. 1966. *Sinai.* London: Oxford University Press.

Snelling, John. 1983. *The Sacred Mountain.* London: East West Publications.

Society for the Protection of Nature in Israel. 1979. *Proposed Nature Conservation Plan in Sinai.* Tel Aviv.

Stanley, Arthur Penrhyn. 1860. *Sinai and Palestine in Connection with Their History.* London: John Murray.

Stanley, Dean. 1911. "The Convent of St. Catherine." In Esther Singleton, ed. *Egypt as Described by Great Writers*: 339–346. New York: Dodd, Mead and Co.

Stephens, John Lloyd. 1991. *Incidents of Travel in Egypt, Arabia Petraea, and the Holy Land.* San Francisco: Chronicle Books.

Stewart, Aubrey, trans. 1897. *The Wanderings of Felix Fabri.* 4 vols. London: Committee of the Palestine Exploration Fund.

Stewart, Frank H. 1991. "Notes on the Arrival of the Bedouin Tribes in Sinai." *Journal of the Economic and Social History of the Orient* 34:97–110.

Stiebing, William H., Jr. 1985. "Should the Exodus and the Israelite Settlement be Redated?" *Biblical Archaeology Review* 11(4):58–69.

Sultan, Fouad. 1990. "Letter to the Editor." *Time* 135(15):13.

Sulzberger, C. L. March 29, 1987. "In the Sands of Sinai, an Ancient Monastery." *New York Times*: 9–10.

Sumption, Jonathan. 1975. *Pilgrimage: An Image of Mediaeval Religion*. Totowa, N.J.: Rowman and Littlefield.

Sutton, Arthur W. 1913. *My Camel Ride from Suez to Mount Sinai: A Diary*. London: J. and J. Bennett.

Täckholm, Vivi. 1974. *Students' Flora of Egypt*. Beirut: Cooperative Printing Company.

Tischendorf, Constantin von. 1851. *Travels in the East by a Pilgrim*. London: Longman, Brown, Green and Longmans.

Tobias, Michael. 1986. "Dialectical Dreaming: The Western Perception of Mountain People." In Tobias, Michael, ed. *Mountain People*: 183–200. Norman: University of Oklahoma Press.

Tuan, Yi-Fu. 1977. *Space and Place*. Minneapolis: Minnesota University Press.

———. 1978. "Sacred Space: Explorations of an Idea." In Karl W. Butzer, ed. *Dimensions of Human Geography: Essays on Some Familiar and Neglected Themes*: 84–99. University of Chicago Department of Geography Research Paper 186.

Tullock, John. 1981. *The Old Testament Story*. Englewood Cliffs, N.J.: Prentice Hall.

Turner, Victor. 1973. "The Center Out There: Pilgrim's Goal." *History of Religions* 12(3):191–230.

Velikovsky, Immanuel. 1950. *Worlds in Collision*. New York: Macmillan.

———. 1952. *Ages in Chaos, Volume I: From the Exodus to King Akhnaton*. Garden City, N.Y.: Doubleday.

Vivian, Tim, trans. 1993. *Histories of the Monks of Upper Egypt and the Life of Onnophrius by Paphnutius*. Kalamazoo, Mich.: Cistercian Publications.

Wagstaff, J. M. 1985. *The Evolution of Middle Eastern Landscapes: An Outline to A.D. 1840*. Totowa, N.J.: Barnes and Noble.

Wansbrough, Henry, ed. 1985. *New Jerusalem Bible*. Garden City, N.Y.: Doubleday.

Ware, Timothy. 1963. *The Orthodox Church*. Harmondsworth, Middlesex, England: Penguin Books.

Weitzmann, Kurt. 1985. " 'The History' and 'The Art.' " In John Galey, ed. *Sinai and the Monastery of St. Catherine*: 11–16, 81–159. Cairo: American University in Cairo Press.

Werner, Yehudah L. 1973. *The Reptiles of the Sinai Peninsula*. Jerusalem: Hebrew University of Jerusalem, Department of Zoology.

———. 1982. "Herpetofaunal Survey of the Sinai Peninsula (1967–77), with Emphasis on the Saharan Sand Community." In N. J. Scott, Jr., ed. *Herpetological Communities: A Symposium of the Society for the Study of Amphibians and Reptiles and the Herpetologists' League, August 1977*. U.S. Fish and Wildlife Service, Wildl. Res. Rep. 13.

Whiston, William, trans. 1987. *The Works of Josephus*. Peabody, Mass.: Hendrickson Publishers.

Wilford, John Noble. 1992. "Oceanographers Say Winds May Have Parted the Waters." *New York Times*, March 15:A-9.

Williams, Larry. 1990. *The Mountain of Moses: The Discovery of Mount Sinai.* New York: Wynwood Press.

Williams, Maynard Owen. 1927. "East of Suez to the Mount of the Decalogue." *National Geographic* 52:709–743.

Wilson, Charles W., ed. 1880. *Sinai and the South.* Jerusalem: Ariel (reprinted 1976).

Wilson, Edward L. 1888. "Sinai and the Wilderness." *Century Magazine* 36(3): 323–340.

Zahran, M. A., and A. J. Willis. 1992. *The Vegetation of Egypt.* London: Chapman and Hall.

♦

INDEX

Jaffa, 228

Jarvis, Claude: as British administrator, 245; and Exodus, 52; herbal scents, 20; and Jabaliya Bedouins, 162; and manifestations of God, 55–56; and Monastery of St. Katherine, 103; and monks, 258

Jebel 'Abbas Pasha, 18, 20

Jebel Abu Sumayl, 8

Jebel Abu Tarbuush, 8, 18–19

Jebel ad-Dayr, 12, 23–24, 65, 78, 113, 145

Jebel al-Huwayt, 8

Jebel Fray'a, 150

Jebel Halaal, 52

Jebel Ideid, 52

Jebel Jiraab ar-Riih, 8

Jebel Katarina: animals of, 24, 30; and cable cars, 294; chapel of St. Katherine on, 81, 130–131, **131**; and Jebel Musa summit, 124; land of, 6, 8; monks of, 78; as Mount Sinai, 53; and pilgrims, 236; plants of, 18; and Saint Katherine's remains, 81–82, 130–131; souvenirs from, 239; weather on, 9, 12

Jebel Kharif, 52

Jebel Madsuus, 8

Jebel Maghara, 52

Jebel Mizna, 24

Jebel Mugassim, 8

Jebel Munayja, 56, 114, 137, 159

Jebel Musa: animals of, 21–31; and backcountry hikers, 144, 206, 266–270, **267**; and burning bush, 69, 105; and cable cars, 289; churches on, 124–125, 135; conservation studies of, 294; and deforestation, 211; and desert, 60, 72; and Egyptians, 282–284; and events of Exodus, 106; gardens on, 19; and hermits, 70–71; and Jabaliya Bedouins, 140, 168; land of, 6, 8; map of sacred places, **98**; modern developments of, **262**; monks' icons of,

131; as Mount Sinai, 3, 33, 46, 53, 68–69, 106–119, 168, 217; photographs of, **107**, **108**, **262**, **272**; physical properties of, 106–107; and pilgrims, 218–222; plants of, 17–18, 20; summit of, 123–126, 170–171, 271–277, **272**; and travelers, 252–253; visitors' routes, 96–102, 113; weather on, 10–12. *See also* Mount Sinai

Jebel Na'ja, 8, 26

Jebel Nimora, 61

Jebel Serbal, 26, 53, 68–69, 218

Jebel Sin Bisher, 52, 56

Jebel Tadra, 56

Jebel Umm Shumar, 26

Jebel Yeleq, 52

Jebel Zebir, 131

Jerome, Saint, 223

Jerusalem, 219

Jethro, 34–36, 115, 166

Jethro, Way of, 121

Jethro's Mountain. *See* Jebel Munayja

Jethro's Water, 172

Jews: and Mount Sinai, 33, 51; as pilgrims, 218; and Stairway of Repentance, 111–112. *See also* Israelis; Israelites

al-Jibaal, 142

al-Jindi, 141, 143

jinn, 203

John Klimakos, Saint (John of the Ladder), 61–62, 86, 94–95, 105, 236, 282

John the Baptist, Saint, 62, 68, 119, 282

John the Sabaite, 27

Joseph, 33

Josephus, Flavius, 51, 135

Joshua, 36, 39, 54

Judean Desert, 62

Justinian, 30, 68, 73–76, 124, 140–141, 154–155

Kafrawi, Hasibullah, 296

Kaiser, Alfred, 244

orchards. *See* gardens

Order of St. Katherine, 225

Orientalism, 242, 244, 246–247

Orlinsky, Harry, 56

Osborn, Dale, 28

Otto, Rudolph, 238

Paldor, Nathan, 55

Palgrave, William, 256

Palmer, Edward: and Bedouins, 156, 162, 171; and cleft in the rock, 126; description of Mount Sinai, 135; and Jabaliya Bedouins, 145–146, 157, 164–165; and Jebel Musa, 100; and miracles, 138; and monks, 256–257; and Mount Sinai, 53; and Muslim pilgrims, 219; and Plain of ar-Raaha, 97; and rain, 164–165; and Safsaafa, 122; and sanctity of Mount Sinai, 247; as traveler, 244; and Wadi al-Arba'iin, 127–128

Palmer, Henry: and Bedouins, 142; and Jabaliya Bedouins, 168; and leopard, 27; and monks, 136, 256; as traveler, 244; and tree conservation, 195

Parker, Alfred, 245

Pasha, Ibrahim 'Abbas, 115

pastoralism, 176–177, 207, 213

Path of Moses, 121

Paul, Saint, 118

Perdika, 130

Perevolotsky, Aviram, 71

Petrie, Flinders, 10, 53

Pharaohs, 34–36, 49

Philistines, 35

Phillip of Spain, 82

Phythian-Adams, W. J., 56

pilgrims: and animals, 21; Armenian, 221; Bedouin, 218; and biblical readings, 224; and black rock country, 8; and burning bush, 103, 105; and cable cars, 291–292; Christian, 218–219; clothing of, 227; compared with travelers, 241–242; and

costs of journey, 227; and Crusades, 225–226; depictions of Mount Sinai, 133–136; donations to Monastery of St. Katherine, 82–83; Dutch, 221; English, 221, 224–225; fantasy, 226; French, 224, 225, 271; German, **222**, 224, 271; Greek-Egyptian, 222; imposters disguised as, 245; Israeli, 218; and Jabaliya Bedouin escorts, 157; and manna, 48; mass-pilgrimages, 221; and monks and monasticism, 66–67, 126; motivations of, 223–226; and Mount Sinai, 3, 33, 53, 231–237; Muslim, 168, 218–219; numbers of, 217–218, 221; photograph of, **279**; pilgrimage feasts, 204–205; pilgrim certificates, 131–133, **132**; routes of, 96–102, 113–114, 116–121, 127, 227–231; Russian, **220**, 221–222; safety of, 227–279; and saints, 224; and South Galala Plateau, 71; as spies, 225; and Stairway of Repentance, 110–111; transformation of, 237–240; Tuscan, 8, 12, 77, 93, 102, 109, 130, 227–239, 254; types of, 218–222, 231; Western European, 221; women as, 222. *See also* tourism; tourists; travelers; *names of specific pilgrims*

pithon, 49

place names, origin of, 196–198

plague, 89, 221

Plain of ar-Raaha: animals of, 21, 24; and cable cars, 289; construction on, 1, 308–309; depictions of, 136; and Jebel Musa, 106; and Mount Sinai, 53–54; and pilgrims, 236; as Plain of Assemblage, 96–102; plants of, 21; structure prohibition on, 135, 145; and tourism, **263**, 284–286, 288; views of, **99**, **284**, **285**

Plain of Assemblage, 96–102

plants: annuals, 20; conservation of, 2,